HANDBOOK OF THE LONDON 2012 OLYMPIC AND PARALYMPIC GAMES

The *Handbook of the London 2012 Olympic and Paralympic Games* is an authoritative and comprehensive account of the world's greatest sporting and cultural event. It tells the complete story of the 2012 Games from inception, through the successful bidding process and the planning and preparation phase, to delivery, the post-Games period and legacy. Written by a world-class team of international Olympic scholars, the book offers analysis of the full social, cultural, political, historical, economic and sporting context of the Games. From the political, commercial and structural complexities of organising an event on such a scale, to the sporting action that holds the attention of the world, this book illuminates every aspect of the 2012 Games, helping us to better understand the vital role that sport and culture play in contemporary global society.

The book is divided into two volumes. *Volume One: Making the Games*, examines the build-up to London 2012, covering key topics such as:

- the bidding process;
- planning and decision making;
- financing the Games;
- developing the infrastructure;
- engaging national and international governing bodies of sport;
- engaging the UK public;
- engaging a global public;
- developing a legacy programme;
- the Cultural Olympiad.

Richly illustrated with the personal accounts of key stakeholders, from sports administrators and politicians to athletes and spectators, and including essential data and evocative visual material, this book is essential reading for anybody with a personal or professional interest in the Olympic and Paralympic Games, global culture or the development of sport.

Vassil Girginov is Reader in Sport Management/Development at Brunel University, UK. He is a founding board member of the Bulgarian Olympic Academy and has been researching, teaching and working for the Olympics for 25 years. His research interests and publications (including six books) are in the field of the Olympic Movement, sport development and comparative management and policy analysis.

HANDBOOK OF THE LONDON 2012 OLYMPIC AND PARALYMPIC GAMES

Volume One: Making the Games

Edited by Vassil Girginov

LONDON AND NEW YORK

First published 2013
by Routledge
2 Park Square, Milton Park, Abingdon, Oxon OX14 4RN

Simultaneously published in the USA and Canada
by Routledge
711 Third Avenue, New York, NY 10017

Routledge is an imprint of the Taylor & Francis Group, an informa business

British Library Cataloguing in Publication Data
A catalogue record for this book is available from the British Library

Library of Congress Cataloging in Publication Data
Handbook of the London 2012 Olympic and Paralympic games : volume one : making the games / edited by Vassil Girginov.
p. cm.
Includes bibliographical references and index.
1. Olympic Games (30th : 2012 : London, England) 2. Paralympics (30th : 2012 : London, England) I. Girginov, Vassil, 1956–
GV7222012 .H36 2012
796.48–dc23
2012007405

ISBN: 978-0-415-67194-1 (hbk)
ISBN: 978-0-203-13251-7 (ebk)

Typeset in Bembo
by Wearset Ltd, Boldon, Tyne and Wear

Printed and bound in Great Britain by
TJ International Ltd, Padstow, Cornwall

CONTENTS

ILLUSTRATIONS

Tables

Figures

CONTRIBUTORS

Dikaia Chatziefstathiou is Reader in Olympic Studies and the Social Analysis of Sport at Canterbury Christ Church University, UK. She is a sociologist of sport and an expert in Olympic Studies, focusing on the ideology of Olympism and its values. Chatziefstathiou is co-author of the book *Discourses of Olympism: From the Sorbonne 1894 to London 2012* (written with Ian Henry and published in 2012 by Palgrave).

Jon Coaffee is Professor of Spatial Planning and Urban Resilience in the Centre for Urban and Regional Studies at the University of Birmingham. His research focuses on the social and economic future of cities and the interplay of physical and socio-political aspects of urban resilience. Coaffee is author of a number of monographs on terrorism and urban risk, most notably *Sustaining and Securing the Olympic City: Reconfiguring London for 2012 and beyond* (Ashgate, 2011) and *Terrorism, Risk and the Global City – Towards urban resilience* (Ashgate, 2009).

Dave Collins is Professor and Director of the Institute of Coaching and Performance at the University of Central Lancashire. He is also Director of Grey Matters Performance Consultancy (www.gm4p.com). He researches in all aspects of performance, including the development of expertise in performers, coaches and support staff, and optimising systems for performance and talent development. As Performance Director for UK Athletics, he led the team for over three years, which covered the period of the Beijing Olympics. Dave has published widely, including an edited text *Performance Psychology: A Practitioner's Guide*, with Angela Button and Hugh Richards (Elsevier, 2011).

Mike Collins is Visiting Professor at the Faculty of Applied Science at the University of Gloucestershire. He specialises in sports development, sport and social capital and sport and religion. He edited *Examining Sport Development* (Routledge, 2010).

Andrew Cruickshank is a researcher at the University of Central Lancashire. He specialises in the field of culture change in elite sport performance teams. Andrew has been researching the critical success factors, mechanisms and challenges of this process as undertaken by Olympic sport performance directors and professional sports team managers. He is co-author of *Multidirectional Management: Exploring the challenges of performance in the World Class Programme environment* (Reflective Practice, 2012).

Gillian Evans is Lecturer in Social Anthropology at the University of Manchester. She specialises in the field of urban anthropology, particularly focusing on social class and the effects of post-industrial change in London. Gillian is author of *London's Olympic Legacy* (Macmillan Palgrave, forthcoming), which is a monograph based on three years' ethnographic research at the Olympic Park Legacy Company.

Pete Fussey is Senior Lecturer in Criminology at the University of Essex. He specialises in the areas of crime, security, counter-terrorism, surveillance and the city. Fussey is co-author of *Sustaining and Securing the Olympic City: Reconfiguring London for 2012 and beyond* (Ashgate, 2011) and co-editor of *Terrorism and the Olympics: Lessons for 2012 and beyond* (Routledge, 2010).

Beatriz Garcia is Head of Research at the Institute of Cultural Capital and director of Impacts 08 – European Capital of Culture Research Programme at the University of Liverpool. She has led research on the Olympic Games since 1999, undertaking data collection at eight Olympic Games editions so far (Barcelona, Sydney, Salt Lake City, Athens, Torino, Beijing, Vancouver and London) and has been involved as academic advisor on culture and education to the London 2012 team since the bid stage. She is the author of *The Olympic Games and Cultural Policy* and *The Olympics. The Basics*, both published by Routledge in 2012.

Vassil Girginov is Reader in Sport Management/Development at Brunel University. Vassil is an Executive Editor of Routledge Online Studies on the Olympic and Paralympic Games (http://www.routledgeonlinestudies.com/). His research interests, publications and industry experience are in the field of the Olympic Movement, sport development and comparative management and policy analysis. Vassil's most recent books as editor include *Sport Management Cultures* (Routledge, 2011), *The Olympics: A critical reader* (Routledge, 2010) and *Management of Sports Development* (Elsevier, 2008).

John R. Gold is Professor of Urban Historical Geography in the School of Social Sciences and Law at Oxford Brookes University, and is a member of the University's Institute for Historical and Cultural Research. A frequent radio and television broadcaster, he is the author or editor of 17 books, published and in press, on architectural and cultural subjects. The most recent are *Olympic Cities: City agendas, planning, and the world's games, 1896–2016* (edited with Margaret Gold, Routledge, 2011) and the four-volume set on *The Making of Olympic Cities* for Routledge's Major Works series (2012).

Margaret M. Gold is Senior Lecturer in Arts and Heritage Management at London Metropolitan Business School, London Metropolitan University. Her research interests cover festivals, museum and heritage management, and the relationship between large events and their host cities. Her most recent publication is *The Making of Olympic Cities*, a four-volume collection of readings in Routledge's Major Works series (2012).

John Horne is currently Professor of Sport and Sociology and Director of the International Research Institute for Sport Studies in the School of Sport, Tourism and the Outdoors at the University of Central Lancashire, Preston, UK. His research interests include sports mega-events, social movements and sport, and sport and globalisation. John Horne is the co-author of *Understanding the Olympics* (with G. Whannel, Routledge, 2012) and *Understanding Sport: A socio-cultural analysis* (with A. Tomlinson, G. Whannel and K. Woodward, Routledge, 2012).

Barrie Houlihan is Professor of Sport Policy at Loughborough University and Visiting Professor at the Norwegian School of Sport Sciences. His research is in the field of sport policy. His most recent publications include the *Routledge Handbook of Sport Development* (edited with Mick Green, 2011) and *British Sport Policy* (with Iain Lindsey, Routledge, 2012).

Mark James is Reader in Law at the University of Salford, Manchester, UK. He researches in the field of sport and the law, with particular specialisation on the Olympic Games and spectator regulation at football matches. Mark is the author of *Sports Law* (Palgrave, 2010) and co-editor of the *Entertainment and Sports Law Journal.*

Ian Jones is Associate Dean for Sport at Bournemouth University. He specialises in the areas of research methods and sport fandom. He is co-author of *Qualitative Research in Sport and Physical Activity* (Sage, 2012).

Iain MacRury is Professor and Associate Dean, School of Arts and Digital Industries at the University of East London and Director of the London East Research Institute. He has contributed to a number of Olympic legacy evaluation projects, for organisations including the Department of Communities and Local Government, OECD, the London Assembly and the IOC's LOCOG, as well as the ESRC-funded Olympic Games Impact Study (OGI) for 2012. He is co-editor of *Olympic Cities: 2012 and the remaking of London* (Ashgate, 2009).

Boria Majumdar is Senior Research Fellow at the University of Central Lancashire and Adjunct Professor at Monash University Melbourne. He specialises in the history of South Asian sport and has written extensively about the politics of sport in South Asia and the diaspora. Boria Majumdar is author of *Olympics: The India story* (with Nalin Mehta, second edition, HarperCollins, 2012).

Guy Masterman is Chair of the Academy of Sport and Physical Activity and Head of the Department of Sport at Sheffield Hallam University. He is also an International Professor at the Russian International Olympic University, Moscow/Sochi and the Universidade Nove de Julho (UNINOVE), São Paulo. His research interests are in the areas of sport event planning and legacies, sports marketing communications and in particular sport sponsorship. A third edition of his market-leading *Strategic Sports Event Management* is due for publication in March 2014.

Geoff Nichols is a Senior Lecturer in Sheffield University Management School. His area of expertise is volunteers in sport and he has published widely in peer-reviewed journals. Geoff is also Chair of the Sport Volunteer Research Network, with recent works including how and why Manchester Event Volunteers generated a volunteering legacy from the 2002 Commonwealth Games and a European Year of Volunteering project on developing good practice for sports clubs recruiting volunteers from outside their clubs.

Guy Osborn is Professor of Law at the University of Westminster, London, UK. He researches in the field of law and sport, with a particular specialisation in the Olympic Games and more generally the intersection between law and popular culture. He is co-author of *Film and the Law* (Hart, 2010), joint editor of the Routledge Research Monograph series, Studies in Law, Society and Popular Culture, and a founding editor of the *Entertainment and Sports Law Journal.*

Jae-Woo Park is Lecturer on Sport Policy and Sociology at Hanyang University and a member of the Sport for All Subcommittee of the Korea Sports Council. His research interest lies in sport policy and its socio-cultural analysis.

Andrew B. Powell has wide-ranging experience as a field archaeologist, having started his career in 1987 working for the Museum of London. In 1991 he joined Wessex Archaeology, where he is now a Senior Archaeologist specialising in post-excavation analysis and publication. He has had major roles in the excavation and publication of a number of large infrastructure projects, and is currently a principal author for the monograph on the London 2012 Olympic Park excavations.

Nick Rowe joined the Great Britain Sports Council research team in 1983. From 2009 until June 2012 he was Strategic Lead for Research and Evaluation at Sport England where he played a leading role in designing and delivering the Active People Survey. He was the lead author on the Sport England Strategy document 'The Framework for Sport in England'. He has been influential in international research initiating and for 5 years co-directing the COMPASS project and Chairing the Council of Europe Research Expert Group on Young People Sport and Ethics. He is now a freelance researcher in sport and public policy.

Charlie Tims is a freelance researcher and associate of the think tank Demos. He writes about learning, cultural policy and young people. Charlie's latest publications include *An Anatomy of Youth* (with Celia Hannon, 2010) and *The Biggest Learning Opportunity on Earth* (2007).

Mike Weed is Professor of Sport in Society and Director of the Centre for Sport, Physical Education and Activity Research (SPEAR) at Canterbury Christ Church University. He specialises in all aspects of the relationship between sport and tourism, but particularly in the implications of hosting the Olympic and Paralympic Games. He is author of *Olympic Tourism* (Elsevier, 2008) and Editor of the *Journal of Sport and Tourism* (Routledge).

Mayumi Ya-Ya Yamamoto worked for the World Anti-Doping Agency and now works for the Japan Anti-Doping Agency. She is also a visiting researcher at the Centre for Olympic Studies and Research at Loughborough University. Her research interests lie in the development of sport policy, elite sport and anti-doping in particular, and also in international relations and sport. She contributed to the *Routledge Handbook of Sport Development* and has published in the *International Journal of Sport Policy and Politics.*

ACKNOWLEDGEMENTS

Writing the *Handbook of the 2012 London Olympic and Paralympic Games* has been a long journey full of uplifting and frustrating experiences. I have no doubts that it was worth the effort as a great deal more has been learned as a result. I would like to record my appreciative thanks to a number of people I came across on this journey, without whom this project would not have been possible.

I am very grateful to Simon Whitmore from Routledge for his belief in this project, patience and great professionalism; to all contributors to this volume for their enthusiasm and insightful accounts and to several LOCOG officials for their helpful comments on earlier drafts of this collection.

Vassil Girginov
25 April 2012
London

Note on cover images

Cover images for both volumes of the *Handbook of the London 2012 Olympic and Paralympic Games* provided by Art at the Edge (sculptures by Tony Evans, represented by Turner Fine Arts, photographed by Jenny Scott). Art at the Edge CIC is a social enterprise raising funds through art projects to support disadvantaged and disabled young people. Their project 'Sculpture And Sport: A Celebration For 2012' involved over 50 artists whose work was exhibited during the the run-up to the Games in 2012 in a variety of venues such as corporate offices, museums, libraries, shopping malls, art galleries and public spaces (see www.artattheedge.org).

1

SOCIAL, POLITICAL, ECONOMIC AND OPERATIONAL CONTEXT OF THE 2012 LONDON OLYMPIC AND PARALYMPIC GAMES

An introduction

Vassil Girginov

On 27 July 2012 in front of a multimillion global television audience, as is customary for all Summer Games, the head of the British state Her Majesty the Queen will solemnly pronounce the words, "I declare open the Games of London 2012 celebrating the XXX Olympiad of the modern era" (IOC, 2007, p. 103). The declaration marks the start of the world's greatest sporting festival, the social, political and economic significance of which goes well beyond that of a mere competition in jumping higher, running faster and pushing stronger. This is because the main purpose of the Olympic and Paralympic Games is to celebrate human excellence irrespective of ethnicity, colour, ability, faith and gender. The Games also celebrates the end of an Olympiad, a four-year period, during which policy makers, sport officials, athletes, volunteers, scientists, educators and journalists around the world have been making efforts to improve the overall conditions that make excellence possible.

The modern Olympic Games was conceived in 1894 by Pierre de Coubertin as a developmental project, which uses sport for the betterment of the world. In particular, the Games was envisaged as a tool to draw the attention of the political class to the importance of young people's physical and moral development and to promote respect, mutual understanding and peace. The ontological limitations of Coubertin's philosophical ideal underpinning Olympism have been variously challenged and continue to generate debates today. This has led some commentators to refer to Coubertin as "a second rate thinker, but a first class marketer" (Seagrave, 2011). The growth of the Olympic Games and what it stands for seems to have proved this observation right. Yet, despite political and economic turmoil and controversy, the Olympic Games remains one of the very few cultural phenomena, if not the only one, that has been celebrated globally for over 116 years.

London 2012 differs from the 26 previous editions of the Games in three key aspects. First, it has set a historical precedent in that the host country's government has made a commitment to use the Olympic Games to affect social change on a mass scale and to deliver a range of legacies not just for London but for the whole of the UK (DCMS, 2007, 2008, 2009). The UK government has made its ambitions very clear: "Our mission for 2012 is to inspire people to get involved and to change the way they live their lives" (DCMS, 2007, p. 1). In particular, the Games was to be used as a catalyst for the regeneration of long-neglected East London, which is one of the most deprived areas in the UK. A second major departure for London compared to previous Games has been the government's specific plan to utilise the Paralympic Games to introduce a sea change in public attitudes towards disability. As the first of its kind policy document *London 2012: A Legacy for Disabled People. Setting New Standards, Changing Perceptions* declares, "Our aim is to influence the attitudes and perceptions of people to change the way they think about disabled people" (DCMS, 2009, p. 2). This policy is in sharp contrast with the reality during the 1908 London Games, when the UK government promoted a policy of segregation between able-bodied and disabled people both in general and in sport in particular (Stevens, 1995). A third major feature of London 2012 has been its efforts to rationalise the most intangible aspect of the Olympic idea – its inspirational power. To assist with this aim, a new non-commercial programme and an "Inspire" mark was created to promote grassroots projects across sustainability, education, volunteering, business, sport or culture that have been directly inspired by the Games (www.london2012.com/inspire-programme).

London 2012 is the most ambitious project in the history of the Olympic Games in terms of both its scope and level of change, as, in order to be implemented successfully, it has to address not only people's attitudes and behaviours but also deeply rooted social structures and relations. According to Seb Coe, Chair of the London Organising Committee of the Olympic Games and Paralympic Games (LOCOG), "the success of the Games will be measured in six Ss: (i) Sport must be vibrant and compelling, to inspire young people; (ii) Streets must be festive and buzzing, with a party atmosphere; (iii) Screens: large screens at Live Sites must be places where people can celebrate together; (iv) Stadia must be full of excited and passionate fans; (v) Service must be helpful with polite, friendly and well-informed volunteers; (vi) Sustainability must produce long-lasting social, economic, environmental and sporting benefits" (LOCOG, 2011, p. 8). Such visions of the Games greatly extend Coubertin's prophecies in terms of scope, level of detail and impact.

Staging the Games provides a rare opportunity to reflect and report on the extent to which the event's symbolic and material potential has been used to affect social change in the host city and country. The Games also provides a great learning opportunity as every aspect of its organisation – from venue and operations planning, to security and legacy – has been scrutinised by politicians, media, academics, various social movements, community groups and future organisers. Thus, the Games yields empirical insights and has the power to inform planning considerations and to shape future course of action.

The two-volume collection on the 2012 London Games is the first attempt to unpack a single edition of the Games, from inception to celebration and legacies, using a multiple-perspective approach. The original plan for this collection was to be endorsed by the Organising Committee of the Games as a licensed product, in order to allow a small group of researchers access to key officials and documentation, thus offering a greater breadth and depth of analysis. However, for a number of reasons this plan did not materialise and had to be reconsidered some three months before the publication of the first volume.

Naturally, the scale of the London Games, including a workforce of around 6,000 paid staff, up to 70,000 volunteers, around 100,000 paid contractors, 15,000 athletes and officials, 21,000 media personnel, 37 competition venues, 500,000 spectators per day, a public budget of £9.3 billion and an operational budget of £2 billion, represents a huge undertaking not only for LOCOG but for the whole country as well. Table 1.1 shows the main agencies involved in the making of the London 2012 Games and their responsibilities, while table 1.2 shows the public funding provided. Public sources of funding include Central Government – £6,248 billion (67 per cent), London – £875 million (10 per cent) and National Lottery – £2,175 billion (23 per cent).

The Olympic Games inevitably aspires to deliver social change on a mass scale, cutting across the interests of numerous stakeholders. Similar to any developmental project, London 2012 poses critical questions concerning what has been done in the name of the Games, for whom, at what cost and to what effect? These are complex and difficult issues that require equally complex investigations. Much of the complexity involved in staging the Games and delivering its promise stems from historically established structures and relations that shape current actions. Other issues arise from constantly changing economic and political environments. The speed of change has been such that some chapters in this volume had to be updated several times in the first couple of weeks after being written. It is the purpose of this introductory chapter, therefore, to offer an overview of the changing social, political and economic context of the 2012 Games,

Table 1.1 Main agencies and responsibilities in 2012 London Olympic and Paralympic Games

Agency	*Responsibilities*
Government Olympic Executive The GOE is a section within the Department for Culture, Media and Sport (DCMS).	Oversees the London 2012 project on behalf of the government, ensuring that it is delivered on time, within budget, represents value for public money and benefits the whole of the UK.
The Olympic Board An interim public / voluntary / private body, co-chaired by the Secretary of State for Culture, the Olympics, Media and Sport and the Mayor of London. Other members are the BOA Chairman and the Chair of LOCOG.	Coordinating the successful delivery of the Games and its legacy.
The London Organising Committee of the Olympic Games and Paralympic Games LOCOG is a private company.	Staging the London 2012 Games; reports to the International Olympic Committee (IOC) and the International Paralympic Committee (IPC).
Olympic Delivery Authority The ODA is a non-departmental public body.	Building the permanent venues and infrastructure needed for the Games.
The Mayor of London Elected public official / public body.	Leads on delivering the legacy of the London 2012 Games for London and ensuring that people across the capital benefit from London's role as the host city.
Olympic Park Legacy Company The OPLC is a not-for-profit company.	Long-term planning, development, management and maintenance of the Olympic Park and its facilities after the Games.
London Development Agency The LDA is a non-departmental public body.	Delivering and maximising the long-term sustainable benefits of the London 2012 Games for London's communities and economy.
British Olympic Association A voluntary organisation (The National Olympic Committee for Great Britain and Northern Ireland).	Selection, preparation and management of Team GB at every Games, including the London 2012 Olympics.
British Paralympic Association A registered charity (the National Paralympic Committee for Great Britain and Northern Ireland).	Selection, preparation and management of the British Paralympic team at each Paralympic Games and raising the money to meet the costs that this entails.

Source: (DCMS, 2011, p. 2).

as well as of its operational context, in order to set the scene for the rest of the chapters to follow in this and in the second volume. Moreover, after 1908 and 1948, this is the third time London will have hosted this event, which allows for some useful parallels.

London won the right to host the Games of the XXX Olympiad on 5 July 2005, just a couple of months after the general election which saw the Labour Party winning a historic third term in office. However, the election was won with a small majority of 66 seats, which was down from 160 seats in the previous parliament, and a popular vote of 35.2 per cent, the lowest of any majority government in British history. A critical issue for this election result, by the then Prime Minister's own admission, was the British invasion of Iraq in 2003, which had divided the country. As chapters 2 and 10 in this volume demonstrate, the three previous unsuccessful British Olympic bids, by Birmingham (1992) and Manchester (1996, 2000), never enjoyed wholehearted political support from the government, which made a hard and forthcoming political commitment to the 2012 bid. The two main concerns for the government backing of an Olympic bid were the public cost of the Games and guarantees for success. Eventually the UK government support and the personal involvement of the then prime minister Tony Blair proved critical for the success of the bid, but political reservations about this project have always existed.

The progress of the London 2012 project has taken place against a rapidly deteriorating economic climate. In 2005, when the bid was won, the UK budget deficit stood at £17,405 billion, or 36 per cent of the country's gross domestic product (GDP), which quickly rose to £20,469 billion at the start of the collapse of the housing market and the banking crisis in 2008. The Labour Party lost the 2010 general election and a Conservative–Liberal Democrat coalition government came into power. The new government inherited a massive net debt of £966.8 billion, or 62.6 per cent of GDP (*Guardian*, 2010). In December 2011 the unemployment rate had reached 8.3 per cent – the highest level since 1994 (ONS, 2011). Most worrying has been the fact that, of those people out of work, a record high of 1.027 million were young people aged 16–24, or the very people whose lives the London Olympics was set to transform. Interestingly, there are striking similarities in the government's ambitions and the economic conditions surrounding the 1908 and 2012 London Games.

In 1908–1909 Britain pioneered the launch of the modern welfare state by instituting workers' compensation, old-age pensions, health insurance and the world's first compulsory

Table 1.2 2012 London Olympic and Paralympic Games public sector funding package

Item	*£ million*
ODA	7,321
LOCOG Park Operations	67
Policing and wider security	475
Venue security	282
Paralympic Games	95
Funding available to LOCOG	63
City operations	22.5
Other operational provisions	63.5
Look of London	32
Elite and community sport	290
Contingency	587
Total	9,298

Source: (DCMS, 2011, p. 30).

system of unemployment insurance (Orloff and Skocpol, 1984). Yet in 1908 the UK was in recession, and although the Games was a modest operation with 23 participating nations, 2,035 athletes and a budget of £136,000, the event enjoyed virtually no public funding (Girginov and Hills, 2008). Similar to 2012, the unemployment among trades unionists reached 9.5 per cent in October 1908, with an annual level of 8.6 per cent, the highest on record for 23 years (Stewart, 1995). Both the 1908 Liberal and the 2012 coalition governments faced tough choices. In the injudicious words of the 1908 Chancellor of the Exchequer, David Lloyd George, "I have got to rob somebody's hen roost next year. I am on the look-out which will be the easiest to get and where I shall be least punished, and where I shall get the most eggs..." (cited in Offer, 1983, p. 120).

A central measure in the proposed solution to the recession in 1908 was an unprecedented increase of taxation, most of which was designed to fall upon the wealthy. In contrast, the 2012 "austerity budget" of Chancellor George Osborne envisages a much greater socialisation of the economic burden, but is similar to 1908 massive cuts in education, art and science. A total of £4.7 billion in 2009–10 alone was cut from the budgets of English local authorities, which are major sport and culture services providers; and although deprived areas received larger central grant sums, they – and those in Inner London in particular – were worst hit. As a TASC (2011, p. 4) report concluded, "overall, those on the lowest income were hardest hit by the measured budgetary changes". East London was at the heart of the notion of social change both in 1908 and 2012. It is worth mentioning that the Fifth Congress of the Russian Social Democratic Labour Party in 1907, attended by Lenin and Stalin, was held in Hoxton church in Hackney (Offer, 1983), one of the five host Olympic boroughs and still one of the most deprived areas of the UK.

Using the London 2012 Games to deliver government promises for social change presents significant political challenges and stretches the core message of Olympism beyond its original intention. Pierre de Coubertin (1936, p. 34) envisaged Olympism as a social reform or a foundation "*which will have no value or force unless it is firmly based on the principles of a completely new type of education*" (emphasis in original). Coubertin, therefore, sought to use sport to promote new values to drive social transformation by stressing the intrinsic benefits of sport or the joy found in physical exertion (i.e. "sport for sport's sake"), while current government policies have been very much about stressing sport's external benefits to society (i.e. "sport for good", DCMS, 2002, 2007, 2008).

Charging sport with a range of political, social and economic functions, and using it as a tool to address long-standing political issues, has not been unproblematic. This is partly because England is the second most unequal of the 23 world's richest societies, where inequality directly correlates with lower levels of sport provision and participation (Collins, 2010). The UNICEF Report Card, which provides a comprehensive assessment of the living standard and well-being of children and young people in 21 nations of the industrialised world, puts the UK at the bottom of the list. According to UNICEF, "*The true measure of a nation's standing is how well it attends to its children – their health and safety, their material security, their education and socialization, and their sense of being loved, valued, and included in the families and societies into which they are born*" (UNICEF, 2007, p. 1). Social exclusion of young people has been a major concern of a number of successive governments. In quantitative terms, 17 per cent of UK children were living in absolute poverty in 2009–10, but as an Institute for Fiscal Studies report predicts, by 2012–13 this will rise to 21.8 per cent (Jin, Joyce, Phillips and Sibieta, 2011).

Social inequalities have been particularly acute in East London. The five host boroughs (i.e. Greenwich, Hackney, Newham, Tower Hamlets and Waltham Forest) are home to 1.25 million people, approximately a sixth of London's total population. East London is also hugely culturally diverse with 42 per cent of the population being non-white. Young people in the five boroughs have suffered particularly from issues such as unemployment (35 per cent), violent crime, overcrowded conditions (between 18 per cent and 38 per cent of households), low educational attainment and obesity (one in four children, HBSU, 2009). The five boroughs' Strategic Regeneration Framework envisages the Games as an opportunity to reverse those negative trends so that within 20 years the communities hosting the 2012 Games will have the same social and economic chances as their neighbours across London (HBSU, 2009).

Economic and social inequalities adversely affect sport participation and engagement with the Games in general. The worsening economic conditions hit sport as well, with community and school sport bearing the brunt of spending cuts. In justifying the 30 per cent and 27 per cent cut to Sport England (the agency charged with promoting grassroots participation) and UK Sport (the agency in charge of elite sport development) budgets respectively, the sports Minister Hugh Robertson eloquently put it: "Let's be clear, the country's deficit is so large the daily interest payments are the same as Sport England's annual budget. This hasn't been an easy process but it's the best possible result for sport under the circumstances" (Slater, 2010). However, the Olympic budget was protected and no cuts were made to the public funding package of £9,234 billion agreed in 2007. On the contrary, public support has increased by an extra £282 million to meet the rising security cost and some £41million for the opening and closing ceremonies (DCMS, 2011).

Similar to other countries, there has been a tension between elite and mass sport in the UK (DCMS, 2002, Collins, 2008, Houlihan and Green, 2008). This tension is indicative of the Olympic aspiration, which seeks to use sporting excellence to promote mass participation. However, in the UK support for community sport is often contingent on the success of elite athletes. As experience from the Sydney 2000 and Athens 2004 Games demonstrates, sports that failed to deliver their target quota of medals had their public funding cut by millions of pounds (Green, 2007). Moreover, at the beginning of the Olympic year, the performance management system underpinning the work of national governing bodies (NGBs) has been further reinforced by putting in place a tougher regime of "payment by results" with regard to delivering mass participation targets (DCMS, 2012). England also invests less in sport per capita – just £36 in 2002, compared to the "peer-group" average for the seven advanced economies of £59, with Finland and France providing £84 and £110 per capita (Collins, 2010, p. 302).

For most of the twentieth century Britain has not been a major contender on the Olympic stage, and the home victories achieved during the 1908 and 1948 Games were marred with controversies over judging and other irregularities (Matthews, 1980, Baker, 1994). However, over the past 20 years the UK has established a comprehensive elite sport system modelled on the best practices from Eastern Europe and Australia, which also actively identifies and employs some of the world's best administrators and coaches. As a result, Team GB (a brand name of the British Olympic team) has significantly improved its Olympic performances and moved from tenth position in the overall medal table in Sydney and Athens to fourth place, with 47 medals, in Beijing 2008. Team GB's achievements at the Winter Olympic Games have been much more modest with only one medal from both Vancouver 2010 (nineteenth place) and Turin 2006 (twenty-first place), but there is an expectation that the success in Beijing ought to be repeated in London, not least because of the home advantage.

Whether the country would be able to capitalise on the inspirational effect of the Games is hard to predict given the huge disparities in community sport participation. Across the five host boroughs participation rates vary between 8.38 per cent and 14.13 per cent, which are amongst the lowest for the country. Of most concern is the fact that, despite promotional efforts and the inspirational effect since the awarding of the Games in 2005, there has been a decline or no change in sport participation among young people, in East London in particular (DCMS, 2012; Sport England, 2011).

The London 2012 Olympic Games is also very different from the two previous editions of the Games hosted by the city in 1908 and 1948. The White City site of the 1908 Games has long been transformed, and today perhaps its only link (sporting or otherwise) with the location of the 2012 Games, Stratford in East London, is that each is home to a branch of the modern shopping centre, Westfield. What seems to unite the 1948 and the 2012 Games is an expressed concern, albeit for very different reasons, with staging a sporting extravaganza amid times of austerity as well as a hope in the transformational potential of the Games. The post-Second World War Olympic Games in 1948 did not only go down in history as "the austerity Games", but it also helped ensure the continuity of Olympic ideals and the triumph of hope over devastation. In 2012 athletes will not have to bring their own food and sleep in barracks, as did their predecessors in 1948. They will be welcomed to a purpose-built Olympic Village, with restaurants serving free food 24 hours a day.

There have been remarkable similarities in the ways that the UK governments of 1948 and 2012 have characterised the Games as a beacon of hope and a counterpoint to the prevailing public concerns with the social and economic hardships of the day. The London 1948 Games were considered a catalyst for "as soon as possible resumption of temporarily shelved traditional sporting events as a matter of major importance" (cited in Baker, 1994, p. 58). Similarly, in his 2012 New Year's speech, Prime Minister David Cameron has pledged to use the global drama of the Games to help get Britain back on track: "The coming months will bring the global drama of the Olympics and the glory of the diamond jubilee. Cameras and TV channels around the planet will be recording these magnificent events. It gives us an extraordinary incentive to look outward, look onwards and to look our best: to feel pride in who we are and what – even in these testing times – we can achieve" (*Guardian*, 2012).

The relationship between the general public and the Olympic Games has also changed considerably. In 1948 the population of Britain was 47 million, of which less than a million (2 per cent) were from other countries. In 2012 the British population has reached 60 million, of which 4.02 million (6.6 per cent) are from from other countries (Eurostat, 2010). The rising number of immigrants has pushed the issue of multiculturalism high up the social and political agenda. The London bid document and subsequent strategies have been very explicit about the inclusive character of the Games, and the need to celebrate the multicultural character of a city that is home to 200 ethnic communities speaking over 300 different languages. One of the implications of multiculturalism is that it makes it difficult to communicate such universalising messages to diverse communities with equal success.

Another particularly relevant issue concerns the consumption of the Games by the general public. As only a few people will get the opportunity to spectate the Games in person, the majority will have to settle for mediated experiences: watching the event on television or the Internet and reading about it in the press. In 1948, a quarter of all British homes had no mains electricity, let alone computers or mobile phones. Television only became commercial in the UK in 1955. In 2012 virtually every household has a television set and 77 per cent had Internet access; there were 17.6 million mobile phone Internet users in 2011, representing 45 per cent of total Internet users (ONS, 2011). Advances in technology have changed the way people experience and consume the Games, presenting both an opportunity and a challenge to its mission to inspire people to be more physically active. There were real concerns about the degree of public interest in the 1948 Games, and eventually a last-minute marketing push by the organisers helped to sell most of the tickets and generate much needed revenue. Ticket sales reflected a non-business approach where, as mandated by the IOC, 50 per cent were to be distributed overseas and 50 per cent domestically. Interestingly, nearly 17 per cent of the domestic tickets were to be distributed by British NGBs of sport and only 33 per cent were available for applications by the general public (Baker, 1994). In contrast, LOCOG operates a computer-assisted ticketing software system, and some 15 months ahead of the Games, during a six-week window between 15 March and 26 April 2011, received applications from almost 2 million people for more than 22 million tickets. A further 116,000 people applied for 1.14 million Paralympic Games tickets between 9 September and 26 September 2011.

LOCOG needs to sell more than 10 million tickets to the Olympic and Paralympic Games, including 8 million to the British public. Of all the applications 95 per cent were from the UK, but the IOC rules stipulate that 12 per cent of the tickets should be allocated overseas. Some of the sports on the Olympic and Paralympic programme, such as handball, wrestling, volleyball and boccia, do not have any real tradition or media presence in the UK, which has created organisational and promotional challenges in finding qualified personnel to staff competitions and in selling those sports to the general public.

London 2012 has changed the relationship between the IOC and the cities and governments wishing to host the Olympic Games. It marks the first time the Olympic Games's explicit concern with social values has been backed by a concerted commitment by the host government to deliver a wider social agenda. The 2009 Olympic Congress expressed concerns over the commercialisation and spectacularisation of the Olympic Games and the need to uphold Olympic ideals (IOC, 2009). London has added its fair share to the commercialisation process by releasing over 500 different product lines in several categories, including memorabilia, homeware, jewellery and clothing (LOCOG, 2011). Thus, ensuring that the power of the Games is utilised not only for commercial gain but to affect positive personal and social transformations has been a major achievement for the Olympic Movement. The current collection of two volumes discusses to what extent those visions for social change have been implemented by interrogating what has been done in the Olympic name, for whom, at what cost and to what effect.

The operational context of the Games is equally important, not only for understanding the scale and complexity of this project but for shaping the relations between host countries' public authorities and Olympic organisers. From an operational point of view, the delivery of the Games presents massive challenges, mainly for the following three reasons.

First, once awarded the Games, the city of London has entered into a tripartite legally binding contract with the IOC, the UK government and the British Olympic Association (BOA). This contract creates LOCOG, which is a private company limited by guarantee and responsible for delivering all Games-time operations, including planning, funding, preparation and staging. LOCOG has no shareholders; it is underwritten by the government, and is accountable to its stakeholders, the Secretary of State for Culture, Olympics, Media, and Sport (DCMS), the Mayor of London and the BOA, under the terms of the host-city contract. LOCOG also enjoys a special financial status, as it is exempted from Corporation Tax (currently at 20 per cent) by virtue of section 65 (2) of the Finance Act 2006. It is, however, registered for and charges VAT on ticket and merchandise sales. In addition, LOCOG's operations have been subjected to an unprecedented level of public, civil activist, scholarly and media scrutiny, including regular parliamentary control, dedicated web platforms such as "more than the games" (www.morethanthegames.co.uk) and research and media reports. The heightened level of scrutiny coupled with the non-negotiable deadlines of the event (LOCOG has only one chance to get it right) requires very sophisticated and efficient planning and operational strategies and inevitably increases the risk of mistakes. As an organisation, LOCOG has a fixed lifespan from 2005 until early 2013 and has had to be created from scratch. The IOC knowledge transfer programme, designed to rescue OCOGs from having to reinvent the wheel every two years, supplied LOCOG with over 30 technical manuals on various aspects of the Games, as the newly created LOCOG had inherited limited know-how from 2008 Beijing and 2004 Athens organisers. However, general procedures described in technical manuals need to be adapted in the host country and LOCOG had to stay alert to discovering the best way of doing Olympic business in the UK. In addition, new people have replaced many members of the bid team to form the core of LOCOG, inevitably creating gaps in institutional memory and skill sets.

Second, LOCOG is an atypical organisation, not only because it exists for a limited period of about seven years but also because it gradually evolves in size and functions. Most business and not-for-profit organisations naturally strive for homeostasis or a state of stability, and this is central to their survival. LOCOG somehow defies this logic, growing in size at a rate of approximately 100 people per month in 2010 alone. In March 2011, some 15 months before the start of the Games, the organisation had 1,162 full-time staff compared to 510 in March 2010; but this number is set to increase to nearly 6,000 people during the Games, plus some 70,000 volunteers (LOCOG, 2011). LOCOG's life-cycle is set clearly and includes three distinct phases: planning, implementation and winding up. Its organisational structure and functions also change accordingly, and move from departmental to venue-based, functional orientations. These constant internal transformations, coupled with a very short period for staff induction and learning, create a challenging and dynamic operational environment, which places huge demands on performance, targets, efficiency, knowledge transfer, human resources and financial and risk management.

Third, to deliver the Games successfully, LOCOG has to rely on the partnership of a number of public, private and voluntary organisations, as well as more than 200 national Olympic committees (NOCs), 170 national Paralympic committees, 26 international sport federations and 20 international paralympic sport federations participating in London 2012, and to manage those relations effectively. Overall, the Organising Committee deals with some 150 different agencies within the UK. To that end, LOCOG has established a revenue target of around £2 billion to cover the operational cost of the Games. The operational budget is made up from contributions from the IOC, including $376 million from its worldwide sponsorship programme and a further $675 million from broadcasting rights. This contribution, however, comes with a number of requirements concerning the contractual and ethical commitments of global Olympic sponsors and broadcasters as well as IOC's own requirements to Games organisers. Furthermore, LOCOG needs to manage a procurement programme worth £1 billion, involving some 75,000 Games contracts across eight different sectors. In addition to that, the organisation has developed 44 domestic commercial partnerships, which have helped raise £700 million in sponsorship. The other two main sources of revenue include £500 million in ticket sales and £86 million in merchandise. In addition to working closely with the city of London and the Metropolitan Police, LOCOG depends heavily on the collaboration of a number of state departments, including, among others: the Department of Transport; the Department of Culture, Media and Sport; the Home Office; the Department of Health; and the NHS. Without the Organising Committee of the Olympic Games, it would be hard to think of any organisation – commercial or otherwise – which, without a track record in any field, appears on the public and business scene and is entrusted with managing massive public and private investments and the aspirations of millions of people.

Structure of the book

Since the two previous Games in 1908 and 1948, which were awarded to London without a bid, staging an Olympics has become a much more complex, competitive and expensive process in the last 40 years. In the case of London 2012 the process evolved over some 30 years and it was important for this collection to capture the key stages, actors and strategies involved in the making of the Games. The first volume of the *Handbook of the London 2012 Olympic and Paralympic Games – Making the Games* – is organised in six interrelated parts.

Part one engages with the bidding process and contains two contributions. First, John Horne interrogates the continuity and change in London Olympic narratives. London is the only city in the world that has hosted three Games (in 1908, 1948 and 2012), and Horne's account presents an understanding about how the city's interpretation of the Olympics has changed over time and why. Second, Guy Masterman offers an examination of the political, strategic and tactical issues and decisions involved in putting together and winning the London bid by drawing on first-hand accounts of the key figures involved.

Part two deals with the delivery of the Games as a complex process involving political negotiations, massive logistics and governance issues. In chapter 4, Gillian Evans provides a fascinating account of the deliberations and struggles that have led to choosing East London as a main site for the Games. She shows the importance of vision and introduces the dedicated people who have made the Olympic project for East London a reality, despite the odds. Chapter 5, by Andrew Powell, traces the physical and social transformations of the Olympic site over the centuries. It documents the role of archaeology in establishing the history of this part of East London. It is also a little-known fact that LOCOG and the ODA (Olympic Delivery Authority) have a contractual obligation to finance the excavation works and to document and publish the results of this work before construction of Olympic venues can start. In chapter 6, Mark James and Guy Osborn submit to scrutiny the dedicated Olympic legislation that has been passed by the British Parliament in 2006. The Olympic law of the host country is crucial for the success of the Games as it guarantees the lawful commercial exploitation of Olympic insignia, which is largely responsible for generating the operational revenue of the Games. However, as the authors demonstrate, the assumptions and application of law can also create tensions and controversies. Chapter 7 engages with the central pillar of the London Games – its proposed legacies. Mike Weed analyses the ambitions, promises and implementation plans that together represent the legacy strategies of two successive UK governments. He considers the extent to which the development of legacy strategy has been concerned with demonstrating what legacies have been achieved rather than with actually delivering them, and asks whether the British public will ever know whether the £9.3 billion Games budget has been a successful legacy investment. Chapter 8, by Jon Coaffee and Pete Fussey, engages with security, which has been an emerging issue concerning mega-events. The authors not only comment on the security planning for the Games but widen their analysis by considering issues of policing, surveillance, democratisation and governance. They propose that the emerging blueprint for would-be host cities of mega sporting events incorporates a strong element of both urban rejuvenation and securitisation, which are increasingly being combined into security designs and master plans. In chapter 9, Dave Collins and Andrew Cruickshank discuss the policy, strategic and tactical issues involved in preparing the host country Olympic team for the Games. The authors specifically consider the managerial challenge of setting, enhancing and maintaining the performance culture needed to ensure that the success achieved by Team GB at the 2008 Beijing Games is repeated in London. In chapter 10, Vassil Girginov examines the governance of the London Games as a central issue of modern politics surrounding mega-events. In particular, the author discusses the nature of the exchange between the British state and society in making the Games, the governance arrangements that have been put in place to ensure consensus amongst the stakeholders and the massive work to steer collective efforts towards the agreed goals, as well as the governance dilemmas faced by the UK government and LOCOG.

Part three focuses on the engagement of the UK public with the Games and demonstrates the scope of the efforts exerted and related issues in involving a range of diverse sectors, such as local communities, schools and universities, regional authorities, volunteers and sport governing bodies. Chapter 11, by Iain MacRury, charters community engagement in East London and explores how and where the debate agenda about what the Games can do for those communities has developed, as well as its long-term implications for them. Ian Jones, in chapter 12, looks at the involvement of different English regions with the Olympic and Paralympic Games by exploring the various strategies employed to capitalise on the opportunities presented by the Games and some of the specific issues that are being addressed in different regions. In chapter 13, Charlie Tims scrutinises the key features of the educational programme of the London Games, designed to reach out to every school and pupil. He considers whether the model of transaction at the heart of the programme – free tickets in exchange for Olympic engagement – could have reduced the value of the Games to schools. Chapter 14, by Dikaia Chatziefstathiou, takes a closer look at London 2012 visions and practices in relation to further and higher education as they have been developed in the run-up to the Games. In chapter 15, Beatriz Garcia considers a range of managerial, funding and promotional innovations in the context of the Cultural Olympiad that have created opportunities to maximise access to and engagement with Games-related activity throughout the country. She also draws attention to some important challenges in terms of synergy of vision, communications and Games association, as well as the opportunities that point at the ongoing struggle to position the Cultural Olympiad as a core dimension of the Olympic and Paralympic experience. Geoff Nichols, in chapter 16, examines the strategy for volunteers at the Games by analysing the key programmes that have been implemented by LOCOG and the implications for managing volunteers.

Part four specifically addresses the engagement of UK sports with London 2012. This is a very important yet under-investigated issue, which can yield valuable insights into the role of national governing bodies of sport (NGBs) in delivering Olympic visions. The Olympic Games presents unique opportunities for sport organisations in the host country to raise public awareness, showcase their work and build organisational capacities. In chapter 17, Vassil Girginov and Nick Rowe discuss the perceptions and involvement of a wide range of Olympic and non-Olympic UK NGBs with the London Games. The authors demonstrate that different NGBs have variously engaged with the Games. NGBs' involvement has been tactical rather than strategic, and has yielded limited organisational learning and capacity-building gains. Mike Collins, in chapter 18, looks at the role of local authorities, LOCOG and the Mayor of London programmes designed to ensure greater involvement with the Games and to deliver sport participation legacies. Collins raises a number of important points about the political vulnerability of sport participation legacies and challenges many assumptions about the positive correlation between the Games and participation in sport.

Part five makes an attempt to examine the world's engagement with the London Games. The Olympic Games presents a great opportunity, not only for promotion of the host country but for more than 200 participating nations around the world to assert their identities, to show their sporting and cultural prowess and perhaps, more importantly, to sustain their national sport systems. In chapter 19, Barrie Houlihan, Jae Woo Park and Mayumi Ya-Ya Yamamoto analyse the national elite sport policies of the UK, South Korea and Japan, and those countries' preparation for London. The authors provide a fascinating comparison of the elite sport policies in the three countries and outline a number of common trends, including an acceleration in the public funding of elite sport, a greater level of specialisation achieved by focusing on a limited number of sports with the potential to deliver medals and success, and the ever-rising cost of an Olympic medal. Chapter 20, by Boria Majumdar, scrutinises the relationship between Indian Olympic strategy, national prestige and London 2012. Majumdar argues that building upon the foundation created at the 2010 Commonwealth Games in Delhi and the Asian Games at Guangzhou, London 2012 is an opportunity for India's athletes to occupy centre-stage after years of administrative apathy and neglect. A success in London will give an unprecedented fillip to Indian Olympic sport. Conversely, a failure will result in more years of neglect and unfulfilled plans. In chapter 21, John Gold and Margaret Gold examine how hosting the Olympic Games has come to be widely regarded as the most significant prize on offer in the never-ending contest between the world's leading cities for prestige and investment. They interrogate three successive Olympic host cities – Beijing 2008, London 2012 and Rio de Janeiro 2016 – and reflect on the ever-changing nature of the competitive process and highlight the way that the local agendas have developed and been traded off against the stated preferences and implicit predilections of the Olympic Movement.

Part six provides the conclusions for volume one – *Making the London 2012 Games*. In chapter 22, Vassil Girginov summarises the main lessons from the previous five parts and outlines the overall context, political and organisational approaches and current and prospective legacies of the 2012 London Olympic and Paralympic Games. It is argued that London 2012 has made an unprecedented promise – to put to a comprehensive test the aspirations of Olympism in Britain through an equally unprecedented public contract. There has been conflicting evidence as to what portion of the Olympic aspiration has been achieved, but documenting the making of the Games has helped to reveal the complex tapestry of personal and organisational interests and political and economic arrangements involved in the Olympic and Paralympic Games.

References

Baker, N. (1994). Olympics or Tests: The Disposition of the British Sporting Public, 1948. *Sporting Traditions*, 11 (1), pp. 57–74.

HBSU. (2009). *Olympic and Paralympic Legacy: Strategic Regeneration Framework*. London: HBSU.

Collins, M. (ed.). (2010). *Examining Sports Development*. London: Routledge.

Collins, M. (2008). Public Policies on Sports Development: Can Mass and Elite Sport Hold Together? In V. Girginov (ed.). *Management of Sports Development*. Oxford: Elsevier, pp. 59–89.

de Coubertin, P. (1936). The Unfinished Symphony. *Olympic Review*, 99–100 (January–February 1976), pp. 32–34.

DCMS (Department of Culture, Media & Sport). (2012). *Creating a Sporting Habit for Life. A New Youth Sport Strategy*. London: DCMS.

DCMS. (2011). *Government Olympic Executive London 2012 Olympic and Paralympic Games Annual Report, February 2011*. London: DCMS.

DCMS. (2010). *London 2012 Olympic and Paralympic Games Annual Report, February 2010*. London: DCMS.

DCMS. (2009). *London 2012: A Legacy for Disabled People: Setting New Standards, Changing Perceptions*. London: DCMS.

DCMS. (2008). *Before, During and After: Making the Most of the London 2012 Games*. London: DCMS.

DCMS. (2007). *Our Promise for 2012: How the UK will Benefit from the Olympic and Paralympic Games*. London: DCMS.

DCMS. (2002). *Game Plan*. London: DCMS.

Eurostat. (2010). *Eurostat News Release 129/2010*, 7 September 2010. Brussels: Eurostat.

Girginov, V. and Hills, L. (2009). The Political Process of Constructing Sustainable London Olympics Sports Development Legacy. *International Journal of Sport Policy*, 1 (2), pp. 161–181.

Girginov, V. and Hills, L. (2008). A Sustainable Sports Legacy: Creating a Link between the London Olympics and Sports Participation. *The International Journal of the History of Sport*, 25 (14), pp. 2091–2117.

Green, M. (2007). Olympic Glory or Grassroots Development?: Sport Policy Priorities in Australia, Canada and the United Kingdom, 1960–2006. *International Journal of the History of Sport*, 24 (7), 921–953.

Guardian. (2012). David Cameron's New Year Message. Retrieved from www.guardian.co.uk/politics/2012/jan/02/david-cameron-new-year-message1, 20 January 2012.

Guardian. (2010). Deficit, National Debt and Government Borrowing – How has it Changed since 1946? Retrieved from www.guardian.co.uk/news/datablog/2010/oct/18/deficit-debt-government-borrowing-data, 20 January 2012.

HBSU. (2009). *Olympic and Paralympic Legacy: Strategic Regeneration Framework*. London: HBSU.

Horne, J. and Whannel, G. (2011). *Understanding the Olympics*. London: Routledge.

Houlihan, B. and Green, M. (eds). 2008. *Comparative Elite Sport Development: Systems, Structures and Public Policy*. Oxford: Butterworth-Heinemann.

IOC. (2009). *Twelfth Olympic Congress: The Olympic Movement in Society*. Lausanne: IOC.

IOC. (2007). *Olympic Charter*. Lausanne: IOC.

Jin, W., Joyce, R., Phillips, D. and Sibieta, L. (2011). Poverty and Inequality in the UK: 2011. London: IFS.

LOCOG. (2011). *One Year to Go. Annual Report 2010–2011*. London: LOCOG.

Matthews, G. (1980). The Controversial Olympic Games of 1908 as viewed by the *New York Times* and *The Times of London*. *Journal of Sport History*, 7 (2), pp. 40–53.

Offer, A. (1983). Empire and Social Reform: British Overseas Investment and Domestic Politics, 1908–1914. *The Historical Journal*, 26 (March), pp. 119–138.

ONS. (2011). *Internet Access – Households and Individuals*. London: ONS.

Orloff, A. and Skocpol, T. (1984). Why Not Equal Protection? Explaining the Politics of Public Social Spending in Britain, 1900–1911, and the United States, 1880s–1920. *American Sociological Review*, 49 (6), pp. 726–750.

Seagrave, J. (2011). Coubertin Aesthetic Ideal. Lecture presented at the Eighteenth International Seminar on Olympic Studies for Postgraduate Students. Olympia, Greece, 14 September 2011.

Slater, M. (2010). Community and School Sport Bears Brunt of Spending Cuts. *Guardian*, 20 October 2010. Retrieved from http://news.bbc.co.uk/sport1/hi/front_page/9111865.stm, 20 January 2012.

Sport England. (2011). *Active People Survey Results – 2011*. London: Sport England.

Stevens, A. (1995). Changing Attitudes to Disabled People in the Scout Association in Britain (1908–62): A Contribution to a History of Disability. *Disability & Society*, 10 (3), pp. 90–95.

Stewart, J. (1995). Children, Parents and the State: The Children Act. *Children and Society*, 9 (1), pp. 90–99.

TASC. (2011). *Winners and Losers Budget 2012*. London: TASC.

Tomlinson, A. (2004). *Olympic Survivals: The Olympic Games as a Global Phenomenon*. In Allison, L. (ed.). *Global Politics of Sport (Sport in the Global Society)*. London: Routledge, pp. 46–62.

UNICEF. (2007). Child Poverty in Perspective: An Overview of Child Well-Being in Rich Countries. A Comprehensive Assessment of the Lives and Well-Being of Children and Adolescents in the Economically Advanced Nations. Florence: UNICEF Innocenti Research Centre Report Card 7.

PART 1

Bidding for the Games

2

FROM 1908 TO 2012

Continuity and change in London Olympic narratives

John Horne

Introduction: London and the Olympic Games[1]

On 6 July 2005, on a humid night in Singapore, the IOC was about to announce the result of a two-year battle between candidate cities to stage the Olympic and Paralympic Games. It was 7.46 p.m., and just after midday in London. The envelope was opened, and IOC President Jacques Rogge announced the winner. In the final round of voting, London had beaten Paris by 54 votes to 50. For much of the long race Paris had been a strong favourite, with the bookmakers' odds favouring Paris right to the end, but the IOC had voted, and now London was to stage the 2012 Olympic and Paralympic Games. How this came to pass has been subject to much scrutiny since, but one insider, the director of communications for the London 2012 bid, Mike Lee, considered that a defining feature of Sebastian Coe's speech in Singapore was that its narrative was 'more about the Olympic movement than about London' (Lee, 2006, p. 183). By stressing both the importance of 'legacy', a discursively polysemic notion that emerged in IOC circles following the onslaught against its integrity in the 1990s about a set of (largely vague) benefits left behind after the sports mega-event has ended, and the potential role of London as a global media centre to help 'the IOC transmit the call for more young people to take up sport' (Lee, 2006, p. 183), the London bid team were able to win over the required number of delegates with a script in which 'London', 'Englishness / Britishness', 'sport', 'the world' and the future of 'Olympism' could be brought together.

In this chapter I want to consider in broad-brush fashion how these elements – London, Englishness, sport, the world and Olympism – have been constructed in narratives associated with the three London Olympic Games over time. The London Olympic narratives have been constructed over a period of some 100 years by both participant (e.g. government and Olympic officials) and non-participant (e.g. the media and historians) narrators, whose perspectives tell the story through the use of certain consistent features of communication. The focus of this chapter is neither to document the bid process in detail nor account for all the individuals or organisations involved in the building and organising of the Games (both of which are dealt with elsewhere in this collection), but to offer reflections on the framing and promotion of the *dominant narratives*, or stories, about the Games, and in passing to exemplify two themes in Roche (2000). First, he notes the ways in which international expositions and other mega-events reflect the development of capitalism, nationalism and imperialism. Second, he regards them as important focal points in the emergence of an international dimension in modern public culture. Clearly there is a potential contradiction here, indeed a contradiction manifest in the person of Baron Pierre de Coubertin, whose life project was the establishment of the modern Olympic Games. De Coubertin was a committed internationalist who inscribed internationalism into the founding documents, practices and rituals of the Olympic Games. He was also a patriot who was concerned about the poor physical state and indiscipline of French youth, and worried about the decline of his country and its eclipse by the rising power of Germany. The tension between nationalism and internationalism continues to be a significant feature of the Olympic Games.

Mega-events are rarely simply the realisation of a clear blueprint from a commanding designer; rather they are the outcome of competing intentions, interests, preoccupations and strategies. Hence different contemporary and historical narratives also reflect back on them. Where mega-events are concerned, a study of the relationships between national politicians, local politicians, sports administrators, builders, architects and town planners is often instructive. Another of the most striking features of mega-events – in the UK and I suspect elsewhere – is how rarely they utilise the sites of previous events, almost as if they wanted to avoid taking on the ideological detritus of a former conjuncture. In 1908 the London Olympic Games had close links with and shared a site with the Franco-British Exhibition (or Trade Fair) in Shepherds Bush, West London. The 1924 British Empire Exhibition shunned the option of the White City site from 1908, and established itself at Wembley Park, North-West London. In 1934 the Empire Games used the stadium and a newly constructed Empire Pool at Wembley, yet used White City for athletics. In 1948 the hastily arranged and financially pressed London Olympic Games did utilise the Wembley site originally constructed for the Empire Exhibition of 1924, but just three years later, in 1951, the Festival of Britain rejected both Wembley and White City and based its major attractions in Battersea Park and on the South Bank in Central London. The Millennium Dome, rejecting all other available options, was built on a derelict industrial site in North Greenwich. In many cases the sites subsequently suffered years of decline, neglect and decay. The White City stadium was demolished in 1985 and there is no easily visible memorial proclaiming its moment of glory as 'The Great Stadium' of the 1908 Olympic Games. The original Wembley Stadium has been demolished but rebuilt and reborn, and the Empire Pool survives, renamed Wembley Arena and recently renovated. The rest of the site has been crumbling for years, and is only now undergoing substantial redevelopment. Very few traces of the Festival of Britain remain. But, after the 2012 Games for which facilities are currently under construction around Stratford in East London, a vast privately owned shopping mall, alongside the Olympic Park, will also become the beneficiary of the massive public investment in infrastructure.

I focus in the next three sections on narratives about the three London Olympic Games of 1908, 1948 and 2012, but have also included mention of the 1924 British Empire Exhibition, the stadium of which was subsequently used for the 1948 Olympic Games.

The Olympic Games of 1908

The story of 1908 has been told extensively in several books, including the official record, overviews and books and articles published during the centenary in 2008 and since (Cook, 1909; Mallon and Buchanan, 2000; Baker, 2008; Jenkins, 2008; Kent, 2008; Llewellyn, 2011; Polley 2011). The basic outline is as follows. The 1908 Games were staged at short notice, in conjunction with a trade fair, and led to the construction of the first purpose-built Olympic stadium (intended to be a temporary structure, it lasted until 1985). The appointment of British officials and judges led to some contested moments over disqualifications and equipment used, but the British athletes won their greatest ever haul of gold medals and topped the medal 'table' for the first and only time.

The 1904 IOC session in London awarded the Games of 1908 to Rome. In 1906 the host designate withdrew. This was attributed to the impact of the Vesuvius eruption, but in fact the Italian prime minister was opposed to the project and prevented funding, which he wanted to spend on other projects like the Simplon Tunnel (Mallon and Buchanan, 2000). English Lord Desborough put forward London as the alternative and this was accepted. It was clear that no government funding would be available for building a main stadium, but the organisers of the Franco-British Exhibition, scheduled to run from April to October 1908, agreed to build the stadium complete with running and cycling tracks and a swimming pool, in return for 75 per cent of the gate receipts.

The Franco-British Exhibition had its roots in late nineteenth-century diplomacy. The decline of France after Napoleon, the end of the period of Franco-British wars, the French defeat by the Prussians in 1870 and the formation of Germany in 1871, with its growing power and ambition, meant that France had to forge alliances with Britain. The Entente Cordiale was signed in 1904, and the Franco-British Exhibition in 1908 was planned to celebrate it. The exhibition eventually attracted 8 million visitors, and only included the goods and produce of Britain, France and their respective colonies. The British Empire at this point still commanded one-quarter of the world's land, and one-quarter of the world's population. The British navy was twice the size of the next largest (Mallon and Buchanan, 2000). Founded on the imperatives of trade and diplomacy, the Franco-British Exhibition was structured around an imperial ideology of civilisation, brought to savage peoples, for their betterment. Like previous such events, it combined displays of technological mastery with educative, rational recreation and popular amusement.

The stadium was projected to cost £44,000 but some estimates suggest the real figure may have been a lot higher. The British Exhibition organisers also agreed to give £2,000 to the British Olympic Association, but this was later increased to £20,000 (Mallon and Buchanan, 2000, p. 4). It appears that the organisers were prepared to accept a loss on the stadium in return for the benefits of bringing extra visitors to the Exhibition, and of course they retained the use of the stadium after the Games. The BOA made £6,000 and the Franco-British Exhibition £18,000 from gate receipts (Mallon and Buchanan, 2000, p. 5). Although the Exhibition was prompted by diplomacy, its key organising figure was a showman and promoter, Imre Kiralfy (see Horne and Whannel, 2012, pp. 94–96).

The first initiative towards the Exhibition came from the French Chamber of Commerce and the Lord Mayor of London, the objective being for France and England to display their industrial achievements. Kiralfy was commissioned to create it. Initial costs were raised through donations and any profits were intended to go to 'some public purpose' (Knight, 1978, p. 1). The 140-acre site was eight times larger than that for the Great Exhibition of 1851, and '...it contained 20 superb palaces and 120 Exhibition buildings' (Knight, 1978, pp. 1–3). On the opening day there were 123,000 visitors, and the caterers, J. Lyons and Co., planned for feeding 100,000 people per day (Knight, 1978, p. 4).

The site featured elaborate white-walled palaces and waterways, and the central court had a lake and illuminated fountains. Orientalism was a dominant stylistic motif, with rickshaw drivers brought to London from Asia to work on the site. There was a distinct contrast between the elements of rational recreation and hedonism. At one pole was the London County Council exhibit of municipal works, and at the other the showmanship of Kiralfy. The latter is illustrated by the many attractions on the site, which by the time of the Japan Exhibition held two years later in 1910 still included: Brennan's Monorail, The Flip Flap, The Great Mountain Railway, the Wiggle Woggle (a form of slide), Witching Waves, The Motor Racing Track, The Submarine, Webb's Glassworks, Whirling Waters, the Canadian Toboggan, the Spiral Railway and the Hall of Laughter. In 1908 the so-called 'Great Stadium', the first purpose-built Olympic stadium, contained running and cycling tracks, an open-air swimming and diving pool, a pitch for football, hockey, rugby and lacrosse, and held at least 70,000 spectators. It is clear that, despite the large investment in the site, it must have been lucrative. The attractions alone generated much revenue, bringing in around £200,000 – close to £20 million in 2009 terms.

The site continued to be a viable exhibition venue for some years. In 1909, the Imperial International exhibited the imperial achievements of the Triple Entente powers: France, Russia and Britain. In 1910, the Japan-British Exhibition emphasised the suitability of Japan as a worthy ally of Britain. The 1911 Coronation Exhibition, the 1912 Latin-British exhibition and the 1914 Anglo-American exhibition followed these. During the First World War, the army used the site. From 1921 to 1929 it became the venue for the British Industries Fair, and in 1927 the Greyhound Racing Association (GRA) leased the stadium. The Amateur Athletic Association (AAA) Championships was first held there in 1932. The British Broadcasting Corporation (BBC) bought part of the site in 1949 and built the Television Centre, which opened in 1960. Athletics moved to Crystal Palace in 1971, the last greyhound racing took place in 1984 and the 'Great Stadium' was eventually demolished a year later (Mallon and Buchanan, 2000, p. 6). The stadium disappeared with no trace, and no proper commemoration of its historic role. The White City was not simply demolished but virtually obliterated from history, until 2005, when a memorial plaque was erected and an inscription marking the finishing line of the track of the 1908 Games was written in the paved concourse inside the BBC's media village (Polley, 2011, p. 125).

The idea of a great exhibition to celebrate empire trade was being discussed in 1913, when it was planned to stage it at White City. By the 1920s the British economy, damaged by the impact of the First World War, was already beginning to feel the impact of the rise to dominance of the USA, although the government provided the funding for the exhibition to go ahead. However, the site eventually chosen was Wembley Park in north-west London. Construction began in January 1922, with Wembley Stadium finished in time for the 1923 FA Cup Final. The project was framed by imperialism throughout, as is made explicit on the first page of the British Empire Exhibition Handbook:

> I welcome the opportunity that will be afforded by the British Empire Exhibition to increase the knowledge of the varied resources of my empire and to stimulate inter-imperial trade.
>
> *(HM the King, quoted in The British Empire Exhibition, 1924)*

After the Exhibition, the buildings were sold and many were demolished. The Stadium was saved. Before the Second World War some large engineering and luxury goods manufacturers took over the empty buildings of the Empire Exhibition. Unlike most previous expositions, which used temporary architecture, many of the buildings at Wembley were built as permanent structures with after-use in mind (Roche, 2000, p. 63). Despite this, there did not seem to be any significant after-use. Just as the Empire Exhibition had eschewed the White City site, so the Festival of Britain did not utilise Wembley. Newness and novelty constantly won out over economy and legacy.

The Empire Pool, now known as Wembley Arena, was built for the Empire Games of 1934. The building was built by private enterprise as a commercial project and is still owned by a private company. The swimming pool was closed at the outbreak of war (1939) and was subsequently only used as a pool for the 1948 Olympic Games. The Wembley Arena building was listed Grade II in 1976.

The 1948 Olympic Games

If the 1908 Olympic Games were held at a time when the empire was still just dominant, and the British Empire Exhibition in 1924 when it was under threat, the 1948 Olympic Games was staged by a country whose empire was being dismantled, with the USA now the dominant force. The old Empire Exhibition site at Wembley had already fallen into decline, and must have served as a poignant visual metaphor that Britain's economy was seriously weakened by the impact of the war. Post-war reconstruction was only just beginning to make an impact, with the relaunch of television enabling the first live broadcast of an Olympic Games (mostly to viewers in the London area, although one viewer 180 miles away in the Channel Island of Jersey was mentioned in the official Olympic report as being enthusiastic about the coverage).

After the Second World War, London once again took up the challenge of staging a Games at short notice, although this was marked by some ambivalence about the relevance to Britain of international sport and the Olympic Games (Baker, 1994; Llewellyn, 2011). In the context of war devastation, rationing of food, petrol and building supplies, and other general shortages, the 1948 Olympic Games was staged as economically as possible, and has subsequently been dubbed the 'austerity Olympics' (Hampton, 2008). There is a striking emphasis on economy in the official Olympic report, with the authors pointing out ways in which they attempted to control costs – no new facilities were built, for example. So the Games were not, unlike those of more recent years, to produce any architectural symbols of modernity, although they did utilise the rather hefty-looking halls of the Empire Exhibition constructed in the era of Art Deco.

A concern with how to mark Britishness drew on the past, tradition and heritage, with Games publicity posters referencing Big Ben and Kipling (Timmers, 2008). The Committee chose as a symbol the clock tower of the Houses of Parliament, with the hands of Big Ben pointing to 4.00 p.m., the hour at which the Games were to be declared open (BOA, 1951, p. 22). The art competition, in contrast, being restricted to works produced during the Olympiad, was predominately modernist in tone and style.

Financially, the Official Report on the 1948 Games laments that London was unable to benefit from public funds, in contrast with other nations:

> Many suggestions have been made for providing the large sum of money necessary to carry out adequately any celebration of the Olympic Games in modern times.... Different nations have naturally solved the problem in different ways; but in England we have hitherto been deprived of one form of assistance which is common, I believe, to the rest of the world; for we never have been able to count upon any Financial contribution from the public funds through the channels of Official Administration nor have we been able to avail ourselves of the patronage of the Government in raising money, by any officially-supported scheme, for these objects.
>
> *(BOA, 1951, p. 388)*

In fact, the Games engaged the British Labour government in a way that previous sports events had not (see Beck, 2008). Government ministers were persuaded that the Games might help to raise foreign currency reserves through tourist spending; hence government involvement came through support in kind rather than direct finance. As Dick Holt and Tony Mason have noted (Holt and Mason, 2000, p. 147), 'without Government aid the 1948 Olympics could not have been held'. Pragmatic concerns seem to have marked the organisation of the torch relay and the opening ceremony and these, as many other aspects of the 1948 Games, were run along military lines. Led by bastions of the establishment, the London Organising Committee – which had as its president the Rt Hon. Viscount Portal, DSO, MVO and as its chairman the Rt Hon. Lord Burghley, KCMG – was concerned to do things 'properly' and not to tamper unduly with tradition, and hence there was little innovation in the staging of the Games. There was, however, an excitement around the engagement with emergent technologies – particularly television, still only two years into its post-war relaunch. If post-war austerity made for a pragmatic approach, the Olympic Movement itself would seem ill equipped for both modernity and austerity. By the early 1980s, the IOC had become firmly wedded to commercialisation, but in 1948 the *Official Report* stated that because the IOC must ensure that the Games are promoted 'not so much as a commercial venture but in the best interests of sport' many means of raising money were not permissible, such as 'the inclusion of advertisements in the brochures and programmes' (BOA, 1951, p. 26).

In some ways this Olympic Games was on the cusp at the start of the transformation from a pre-media event to a global spectacle. The media management strategy has a fascinating quaintness about it, from today's perspective: 'The Press Officer decided to tackle every individual critic and follower on his own ground and persuade him by specialist treatment, of the rightness of the course. Those with influence on the sports side of the newspapers were encouraged and those hoping to intrude with political opinions avoided or completely ignored' (BOA, 1951, p. 105). The art competitions on which de Coubertin was so keen, first introduced in 1912, were staged for the last time in 1948 (Girginov and Parry, 2005, p. 206).

As far as legacy is concerned, £1,000 was to be allocated for the establishment of a permanent record of winners at the main stadium. There is a picture of two plaques on the external wall of the stadium, either side of the circular entrance gate between the two towers (Polley, 2011). Wembley was to establish itself as the home of international football in England, with the twin towers becoming mythicised, and the stadium was the venue for the 1966 World Cup Final. But the two Olympic Games staged in London have appeared to retreat from view. The lack of any real commemoration at either of the stadiums is striking, and the London 2012 bid in 2004 / 2005 chose not to make a lot of the previous Games. It was only in 2008, after the 2012 hosting decision had been made, that serious commemorations of both 1908 and 1948 took place.

The 2012 Legacy Games

The UK did not contemplate campaigning to stage the Games again until the late 1970s. An abortive London bid to stage the 1988 Games presaged a series of failed bids from Birmingham and Manchester, before eventual success in 2005. The London bid for 2012 has its roots in the 1990s. The failure of Birmingham and Manchester to attract significant support had forced the sports community to recognise that it was London or nothing. Bob Scott, the theatre entrepreneur who had set up the Manchester Olympic Bid Committee in 1985, noted:

> The international world thinks London when they think Great Britain. If you put up Manchester or any other city other than London, however sound the bid, you cannot get over the fact that you are not London. The world then comes to the conclusion that Britain has decided to send out its second XI and is not taking the competition seriously. I found myself between a rock and a hard place.
>
> *(Bob Scott, quoted in the* Daily Telegraph, *26 May 2003)*

The emergence of the 2012 bid, and its success, has to be seen in a much-changed economic, ideological and political context. Locally, the issue of a London-wide authority, development strategies for East London and the Thames Estuary region, and the development of the Channel Tunnel Rail Link were all relevant factors. If in 1908 and 1948 the key motifs underpinning host rationales for staging the Olympic Games included the maintenance of the amateur ideal, 'bread and circuses', economic benefits and its propaganda value, by the 1990s these had expanded to include urban regeneration and sustainable development, condensed into the phrase 'legacy'.

Although there were many individuals and groups of people who contributed to the formation of a bid (see chapter 4), from the outset the British media were heavily involved in attempts to shape public opinion around the bid process. It was the *Daily Telegraph*'s then sports editor David Welch who brought the British Olympic Association's decision to bid with London for the Games to wider public attention ('London Must Bid', *Daily Telegraph*, 18 July 2003), and he launched a sustained and partisan campaign through the *Daily Telegraph* to back the London bid. Welch and his sports team, including the former BBC sports editor Mihir Bose, were relentless in selling the merits of a London Games to a largely apathetic public, and lobbied politicians to get on side by backing the London proposal. Indeed, such was the link between the paper and the bid team, that as the process evolved the director of communications for the London 2012 bid, Mike Lee, recognised that steps needed to be taken to cultivate other newspapers, as the links with the *Telegraph* were leading to some disquiet among sections of the print media (Lee, 2006, p. 28). In contrast, another sports journalist, Oliver Holt – the award-winning sports writer of the *Daily Mirror* – had penned an extended essay about why London would lose the bid, by systematically identifying the misplaced political and economic myths that were surrounding the London bid in 2005.

The British government continued to worry about the vast scale of the project. A decision was delayed until after the Commonwealth Games in Manchester, where concerns about financing (particularly the huge drain on the public purse) and organisation had continued right up until the Opening Ceremony. Manchester was, however, seen as a success, both abroad and at home, and once again demonstrated the UK's ability to deliver major events. The resultant feel-good factor made an impact, and media interest in a London bid increased.

The *Daily Telegraph* continued to act as a committed lobbyist for a London bid. The attitude of the *Evening Standard* towards the Games has oscillated during the past decade. In 2002, an *Evening Standard* editorial commented that an Olympic bid would need 'wholehearted Government backing' and that the 'Government must not be penny-pinching if it genuinely intends to support a serious bid for the Olympics.' It declared that, 'A city of London's size and confidence should not shirk the challenge of attempting to host the biggest sporting event in the world' (*Evening Standard*, 2002).

Despite extensive lobbying from the BOA and the media, the government remained split on the subject, and unwilling to commit. Finally, on 15 May 2003, the then Secretary of State for Culture, Media and Sport, Tessa Jowell, announced that the government would back the London bid. An allocation of £2,375 billion was made to pay for the staging of the 2012 Games in London, with costs to be met by business, the London Development Agency (LDA) and the government. The then London Mayor Ken Livingstone agreed with Jowell that each London household would pay an average annual £20 Olympic tax from 2006–2007 for a maximum of ten years (Bose, 2003). The *Evening Standard* editorial proclaimed that this was 'a vote of confidence in London as a world city', whilst referring to 'reservations' amongst Londoners (*Guardian*, 2004). The eventual budget rose to nearly £10 billion and it has become clear that the initial calculations were underestimates, owing to the omission of certain elements such as the amount of value added tax (VAT) that would be due. There is always political pressure to scale down initial budgets in order to secure approval, and this would certainly appear to have occurred in the case of the London Olympic bid. The assurances for rigorous control over the Games' budget given by the Secretary of State in late 2005 were questioned by a House of Commons Select Committee, which noted that 'The Committee is disturbed that such statements have been disproved in such a relatively short space of time. It is particularly ironic that part of the extra costs (a fee of £400 million, explanation added) already identified will be incurred in paying a delivery partner to exercise cost control' (The Stationery Office, 2007, p. 21). The political context of the London bid made for potential tensions between political parties, between city and country, and between sport organisations and political organisations. These tensions were best embodied in the three figures of Lord Coe, Tessa Jowell and Ken Livingstone – an ex-Conservative MP, a Blair loyalist Labour MP and a figure on the Left. It speaks volumes about the enormous symbolic power of an Olympic bid that this arguably frail coalition was able to hold together.

A concerted campaign began to win public support, as any suggestion of an ambivalent or hostile public can damage the chances of success. The final bidding document was presented to the IOC on 15 November 2004; London 2012 Ltd, the London bid company, announced that 250,000 people had signed up to support the bid, and the Mayor used the subsequent New Year's Eve firework display to promote the bid. Although there were many individuals and small groups who were suspicious of, or hostile to, the London bid, especially in East London, they never succeeded in finding common cause, devising a united front or mounting a concerted and coherent campaign. The bid gathered significant momentum in the last six months, and by the time the Games were awarded to London in June 2005 it was of course too late for any practical opposition (for further details of this process, see Horne and Whannel, 2012, chapter 1).

The British media, often very critical of the planning of major projects, were, it appears, very well managed by the bidding team. Even the *Evening Standard* was now referring to 'massive public backing' and confidently asserting that 'the city will deliver on its promises' (*Guardian*, 2005). All Games organisers face this problem: they begin in the bright sunshine of great publicity when the bid is won, and then for the next six or so years have to face a blizzard of critical coverage. This is partly because of the old principle that bad news makes bigger headlines. For much of the build-up there are generally only two storylines: one that facilities will not be ready on time; and one that everything will cost too much. The first one has been proved wrong, but the second is almost always correct, as the House of Commons Select Committee has noted for London: 'The Committee is concerned about the distance between the figures submitted in the bid and the true costs, which will not become evident until after the Games' (The Stationery Office, 2007, p. 21) and Short has demonstrated for the past ten Summer Olympic Games (Short, 2008).

News coverage of the Games is a battleground between competing groups struggling for the power to define reality. Newspapers, of course, are not simply holding the ring, but – by their news selection, agenda setting, frames of reference, choice of language, order of priorities, use of photographs, perspectives and commentary – always impose a perspective, a positionality, on this struggle. News stories draw heavily on quotes from sources that are usually ranked in terms of power. Primary definers are granted a privileged ability precisely to define the issue, secondary definers are able to register competing definitions and other voices are marginalised (see Hall *et al.*, 1978). The structure of such stories, though, is dependent on various factors such as the political perspective of the newspaper, the configuration of public opinion and the fluctuating political fortunes of particular positions. The challenge for the Organising Committee is to organise and manage impressions, combating negative stories and promoting positive ones. Once the Games commence this becomes much easier, as there is a deluge of sport to report. In the build-up, however, media management presents a greater challenge. The situation is complicated by changes of government at both national and city levels. Boris Johnson became the Conservative Mayor of London in 2008, and his old fellow Bullingdon Club member David Cameron became prime minister at the head of a Conservative–Liberal Democrat coalition in 2010. While both will support the Olympic project, neither were involved in its genesis, and both will feel free to adopt a judicious critical distance on occasion.

The Olympic Delivery Authority (ODA), the organisation established to provide the infrastructure for the London Olympic Games, has had to grapple with a range of problems (details of the work and governance of the ODA can be found in chapters 5 and 10). Jack Lemley, the former ODA chair, left with a £388,000 pay-off 11 months into his job amid reports of clashes with staff. Decontaminating the land caused a 12-week delay to the timetable. Nine months was spent changing the design of the stadium and aquatics centre to bring the budget down, although at £303 million, the aquatics centre is still costing more than triple its original budget. Declining property values prompted a projected shortfall of £400 million in the value of the Olympic Village, which forced the ODA to reduce the number of apartments from the planned 4,200 to around 3,000, the minimum needed to give every athlete a bed. The decision to retain the Olympic Stadium in public hands in October 2011 (taken as this chapter was completed) creates another issue for the legacy agenda of London 2012. Despite these problems, the ODA can claim successful completion of all venues on time, and within the (revised) budget of £9.3 billion set in March 2007.

In conclusion

Olympic Games historical narratives tend to focus on capital cities, stadiums, elites, heroes and villains, and tend to overlook the local impacts on other communities of hosting the Olympic Games. Work by historians such as Polley (2009) tries to balance this Olympic story. Here I have tried to consider a few of the other elements that have underpinned narratives about London and the Olympic Games for the past 100 years.

At the Closing Ceremony of the 2008 Beijing Olympic Games, the Olympic Flag was passed from the Mayor of Beijing to the Mayor of London, Boris Johnson, and London moved fully into the spotlight. The world financial crisis began to unfold, and the impact of incalculable levels of toxic debt forced governments around the world to allocate unprecedented sums to prop up the banking system. Although the recession clearly created additional problems for the London Games, it also had some positive aspects in presentational terms. The recession presented a scapegoat. Any further cost overruns or cuts in the scope of plans could be blamed on the unforeseen financial crisis. In 2007 nearly £10 billion appeared to the public a huge sum, but once the governments of the world had found it necessary to commit hundreds of times as much to bail out the banks it seemed a relatively trivial sum by comparison. The major negative impact was associated with private sector involvement in the Games. The last remaining hope that Lend Lease would fund the costs of constructing the Olympic Village collapsed, as did the original optimism regarding viable tenants for the media centres after the Games. The Government had to intervene, allowing the contingency fund to be utilised.

The distribution of benefits compared with the bearing of the costs of hosting the Olympics remains an underlying issue that Games organisers have to contend with. Since 2008 though, the news has been largely good – the Olympic Park and its facilities have taken visible shape on time and to budget. The volunteer recruitment programme has been launched, the online ticketing system was criticised but has secured the interest of millions of people, and leaders have been found to direct the ceremonies. In 2010 the general election resulted in the defeat of the Labour Party and the establishment of a Conservative-led coalition with the Liberal Democratic Party. The coalition immediately implemented a programme of massive cuts in public expenditure, but of course it is largely too late for any significant sums to be saved by cutting the Olympic programme. The cuts to local authority expenditure and to sport budgets will inevitably have an impact on support for the legacy of the 2012 Games. However, if the economies of the world are emerging from recession, the London Olympic Games may be perfectly timed to contribute to a feel-good factor, possibly to the benefit of the current British government.

In keeping with global developments since 1908, and especially since 1948, British government involvement with sport, and in particular the staging of sports mega-events such as the Olympic Games, has grown. Specialist sport government departments, such as the Department for Culture, Media and Sport (DCMS) have become a part of virtually all political administrations. Political leaders regularly associate themselves with bids to host large-scale events, as Tony Blair did in Singapore in 2005, and join in popular sporting occasions and celebrations of triumphs. As Britain's empire disappeared and transformed into a more collegial 'Commonwealth', the imperial narrative associated with involvement in international sport has also mutated. Ahead of 2012 this has taken several forms, including the development of the International Inspiration programme (delivered through UK Sport and the British Olympic Association) aimed at spreading Olympic sports to young people in different parts of the developing world (www.london2012.com/get-involved/education/international-inspiration/, accessed 20 October 2011).

Commercially, however, Westfield, an Australian property development company, is a key beneficiary of the London 2012 Games as the main developer of homes, shops and accommodation for athletes on the Stratford site. It has established around 124 shopping centres in Australia, New Zealand, the UK and the USA, and with around £14.3 billion of assets can lay claim to being the – or at least one of the – world's largest retail property groups. The Stratford City mall development is one of the largest regeneration projects in Europe. In the media narration of the soaring cost of the 2012 Games, there was virtually no reference to Stratford City, although it looks likely to be one of the most tangible, long-lasting and not least profitable legacies of the Olympic and Paralympic Games.

The key economic dynamics of the Games today are associated with globalising processes, transnational corporations, urban renewal, consumption and new urbanism. Sports mega-events act as an enormous lever for moving public policy and uncorking infrastructural investment. However, the organisers of such 'grand projects' are required to provide justifications for their actions through much reference to sustainability and legacies, which can lead to opportunities for counter-narratives to be developed (see Sinclair, 2011, 2010, 2008). Arguably, 'legacy discourse' is today one way of publicly managing the contradictions of hosting a sports mega-event that would otherwise be unsustainable. Hence the 2012 Games combines talk about a broad decarbonisation agenda on the one hand, with corporate partnerships and individual mobility consumption-based lifestyles, linked to a massive infrastructural programme, on the other (Hayes and Horne, 2011).

Just as a major beneficiary of the 2012 Games will be the construction of Stratford City, a major development with a shopping mall at its heart, so the White City shopping mall opened in 2008, built on the site of and obliterating the last traces of the eight glass palaces that constituted the main entrance to the Franco-British Exhibition of 1908. The White City and Stratford City shopping malls have one other thing in common: they are both owned by Westfield, a company that was also associated for a while with Multiplex, who built the new Wembley

Stadium on the site of the 1948 Olympic Games. If in 1908 the focus was on trade and production, and in 1948 on raising foreign currency reserves through tourist spending, by 2012 the focus is very much on spectacle and consumption – courtesy of the shopping mall and the Olympic Park itself as a focus for leisure consumption. Hence the three London Games can be seen to chart the development of the Olympic and Paralympic Games as part of the development of the spectacle of modernity.

Note

1 I would like to acknowledge the research of Garry Whannel in providing background to some sections of this chapter, which draw upon chapters 1 and 4 of our book *Understanding the Olympics* (Horne and Whannel, 2012).

References

Baker, K. (2008) *The 1908 Olympics*. Cheltenham: SportsBooks.

Baker, N. (1994) 'Olympics or Tests: The Disposition of the British Sporting Public, 1948', in *Sporting Traditions* 11 (1), pp. 57–74.

Beck, P. (2008) 'The British Government and the Olympic Movement: The 1948 London Olympics', *International Journal of the History of Sport* 25 (5), pp. 615–647.

Bose, M. (2003) 'Livingstone Makes his Connections Count', *Daily Telegraph*, 9 October. Online: http://www.telegraph.co.uk/sport/olympics/2422940/Livingstone-makes-his-connections-count.html (accessed 20 August 2011).

British Empire Exhibition (1924) *British Empire Exhibition, Wembley, London, April–October: Handbook of General Information*. London: British Empire Exhibition.

British Olympic Association (1951) *The Official Report of the Organizing Committee for the XIV Olympiad*. London: British Olympic Association.

Cook, T. A. (1909) *The Fourth Olympiad: Being The Official Report. The Olympic Games 1908 Celebrated in London*. London: British Olympic Association.

Evening Standard (2002) Editorial. Online: http://www.standard.co.uk/news/bidding-for-the-olympics-6326798.html (accessed 20 August 2011).

Girginov, V. and Parry, J. (2005) *The Olympic Games Explained*. London: Routledge.

Guardian (2005) 'It Would be a Golden Moment. The IOC's Visit to London is a Chance to Sell the City to the World', *Guardian*, 17 February. Online: http://www.guardian.co.uk/uk/2005/feb/17/olympics2012.society (accessed 20 August 2011).

Guardian (2004) 'A Vote of Confidence in London', *Guardian*, 17 May. Online: http://www.guardian.co.uk/sport/2003/may/17/theeditorpressreview (accessed 20 August 2011).

Hall, S., Critcher, C., Jefferson, T., Clarke, J. and Roberts, B. (1978) *Policing the Crisis: Mugging, the State and Law and Order*. London: Macmillan.

Hampton, J. (2008) *The Austerity Olympics. When the Games Came to London in 1948*. London: Aurum.

Hayes, G. and Horne, J. (2011) 'Sustainable Development, Shock and Awe? London 2012 and Civil Society', *Sociology* 45 (5), pp. 749–764.

Holt, R. and Mason, A. (2000) *Sport in Britain, 1945–2000*. Oxford: Blackwell.

Horne, J. and Whannel, G. (2012) *Understanding the Olympics*. London: Routledge.

Jenkins, R. (2008) *The First London Olympics 1908*. London: Piatkus.

Kent, G. (2008) *Olympic Follies. The Madness and Mayhem of the 1908 London Games*. London: JR Books.

Knight, D. (1978) *The Exhibitions: Great White City 70th Anniversary*. London: Barnard & Westwood.

Lee, M. (2006) *The Race for the 2012 Olympics: The Inside Story of How London Won the Bid*. London: Virgin.

Llewellyn, M. (2011) 'Rule Britannia', special issue of *International Journal of the History of Sport* 28 (5), pp. 639–841.

Mallon, B. and Buchanan, I. (2000) *The 1908 Olympic Games: Results of All Competitions in All Events, with Commentary*. Jefferson, NC: McFarland.

Phillips, B. (2007) *The 1948 Olympics. How London Rescued the Games*. Cheltenham: SportsBooks.

Polley, M. (2011) *The British Olympics. Britain's Olympic Heritage 1612–2012*. Swindon: English Heritage/Played in Britain.

Polley, M. (2009) 'From Windsor Castle to White City: The 1908 Olympic Marathon Route', *The London Journal* 34 (2), pp. 163–178.
Roche, M. (2000) *Mega-Events and Modernity: Olympics and Expos in the Growth of Global Culture*. London: Routledge.
Rogan, M. and Rogan, M. (2011) *Britain and the Olympic Games. Past, Present, Legacy*. Leicester: Matador.
Short, J. (2008) 'Globalization, Cities and the Summer Olympics', *City* 12 (3), pp. 321–334.
Sinclair, I. (2011) *Ghost Milk. Calling Time on the Grand Project*. London: Hamish Hamilton.
Sinclair, I. (2010) *Hackney, That Rose-Red Empire, A Confidential Report*. London: Penguin.
Sinclair, I. (2008) 'The Olympics Scam', *London Review of Books*, 30 (12), 19 June, pp. 17–23.
The Stationery Office (2007) *House of Commons Culture, Media and Sport Committee London 2012 Olympic Games and Paralympic Games: funding and legacy Second Report of Session 2006–07*, Volume I. London: The Stationery Office.
Timmers, M. (2008) *A Century of Olympic Posters*. London: V & A Publishing.
Welch, D. (2003) 'London Must Bid', *Daily Telegraph*, 18 July.

3
PREPARING AND WINNING THE LONDON BID

Guy Masterman

Winning the bid in Raffles Hotel, Singapore

Introduction

This chapter is concerned with how London won its bid for the 2012 Olympic Games and Paralympic Games. The analysis draws on various documentation, texts and three interviews: Sir Craig Reedie, Chair of the British Olympic Association (BOA) and an International Olympic Committee (IOC) Executive Board member; Mike Lee, the Director of Communications and Public Affairs for the London bid; and Richard Caborn, the UK Government's Sport Minister at the time of the bid.

There is a mystique that surrounds the bid, in particular around the final presentation in Singapore to the IOC members when London was declared host. With London seemingly going into those final days in third place, certainly with the media extolling Paris as the favourite, the question arises as to how influential that presentation was. This chapter will look at that question but is more focused on an analysis of the extensive planning prior to that event, which enabled that presentation to be effective.

How the bid developed

It is important to consider where the London 2012 bid came from. Why and how London was selected and how previous bidding contributed are important questions, not only for the selection of London for the 2012 Olympic Games and Paralympic Games, but also for the development and shape of the bid.

Previous bidding

London hosted its first Summer Olympic Games in 1908, having stepped in after the winning bidding city, Rome, had pulled out. London therefore did not bid for these Games. London then unsuccessfully bid for the eventually cancelled 1940 Games and successfully for the 1944 event; however, these latter Games were also then cancelled due to the ongoing Second World War. As a consequence, the first post-war Games, in 1948, were awarded to and hosted by London.

London and the Greater London Council, led by Horace Cutler, did undergo a feasibility study into a west London-based and Wembley Stadium-focused 1988 Games, but this was not supported by the Government (Barker, 2003). More recently the city unsuccessfully rivalled Manchester and Birmingham for Britain's 1992 bid. The winner, Birmingham, bid for the 1992 Games and in so doing was only the second British city to bid to host the Games. The selection of Birmingham was made by the BOA (Great Britain's National Olympic Committee) following a Britain-wide process; at the time this selection was somewhat controversial in that London, the capital city, was not put forward.

In retrospect we can see that the BOA, with the Government in support, was keen on hosting a Summer Games. Despite Birmingham's fifth-place ranking, it was decided that a further bid should be made and thus Manchester was given the immediate opportunity for the following Olympiad. This bid also failed (fourth place), but again this failure was put aside and Manchester went again for the 2000 Games. It fared better, ranking third, but what the BOA was left with was a series of failed bids. There are two important points to make here in relation to what has since followed. First, London had clearly not been favoured in any way as a potential bid city – its campaigns to be the BOA's nomination had been weak in comparison and it had lacked support from the Government (Reedie, 2011). Second, despite three attempts, provincial bids from England's second and third largest cities had not been capable of winning.

1997 feasibility study

These failed bids were key factors when the BOA first started sowing the seeds for a future London bid. Despite their size and prominence, an Olympic Games in any one city starts as only an early notion of an idea; in London's case this started as early as 1993. Manchester's second losing bid in 1993 was a significant factor in how the BOA would press forward. For Craig Reedie, the relatively new Chairman of the BOA, this was a key point at which to determine which direction the BOA should take. Reedie became an IOC member the following year and was then able to gauge critical opinion. What became apparent was that only London would be capable of winning any future bid:

> It became quite clear that if we were ever going to bid successfully again, it had to be with London, they [the IOC] simply wouldn't do it with a provincial city, no matter how worthy.
>
> *(Reedie, 2011)*

It also became clear to Reedie that a bid led by the National Olympic Committee (NOC) was critical – the BOA was Britain's NOC. A BOA-led bid would not only be more warmly received by the IOC, it would also provide a more solid base for a future set of stakeholders to be involved in the bid, history having shown that this is not the case where there are disjointed relations (Reedie, 2011).

The idea remained small at this point and there were still important questions about how London could be a host, and indeed which Olympiad would be the best one to go for. A research-underpinned feasibility exercise was required and BOA Chief Executive Simon Clegg gave that task to the goalkeeping hockey player from Britain's 1996 Olympic hockey team, David Luckes (Lee, 2006). In 1997, Luckes set about the task of producing a report that was focused on ensuring that a winning bid could be produced, something that ultimately would not become clear until 6 July 2005.

East London focus

There were different options available, and an Olympic Games based in west London was on the planning table. However, it became clear that the Football Association would not support that with a new Wembley Stadium that was for anything but football, and so the most feasible option was an east London bid with a regeneration angle. A long stretch of available and mainly derelict land had been identified along the Lea Valley, but what was critical was that it would not remain available for long (Lee, 2006). In 1997, British sport wasn't hugely successful and relationships in sport were also complicated and the Government was not that engaged; consequently, there was no point in submitting a bid that year and going for the 2004 Games. Athens would be too tough a competitor in any case. Similarly, the thought of taking on Beijing and bidding in 2001 for the 2008 Games appeared futile. Indeed, a 2001 bid would only have served as a trial run at best and that was considered to be a route too expensive to take (Reedie, 2011). In retrospect it is clear that when Paris bid against Beijing in 2001 they 'got rather badly bruised by the process' (Reedie, 2011). The BOA did not feel that it had either the time or the funding to compete or trial for these Olympiads and so it became clear that if London was to bid for an Olympiad and also take advantage of the favoured option identified in the feasibility study it would have to be for 2012.

Early impacting factors

There were two events that had contradictory impacts on the development of preparation towards a decision on whether to bid or not. In July 2001, London, having won and accepted its bid to stage the 2005 World Athletics Championships, withdrew on the order of Tessa Jowell, Secretary of State for Culture, Media and Sport following late financial assessments. While avoiding a financially disastrous event was to be admired, unfortunately London instantly gained a reputation as a city that could not deliver an international sports event (Masterman, 2009). At best this would be a mantle that would need to be addressed by a bid, and at worst would be a factor standing against going ahead with a bid at all.

However, another event may have provided a counterbalance. The 2002 Commonwealth Games were hosted in Manchester and in many ways were hailed a great success. Jacques Rogge, the President of the IOC, saw that event firsthand and witnessed the fact that Britain could indeed deliver an international sports event.

The Cassani period

The bid team began from very humble beginnings and with an American businesswoman in charge. Barbara Cassani, formerly with the British Airlines budget airline, Go, was the first appointment and took up her role as Chair of the Bid in August 2003. She was responsible for building the team from scratch and was critically acclaimed in providing the solid base that was required to work towards the first target, completion of the IOC applicant city questionnaire, due to the IOC by 15 January 2004.

Cassani came in on the back of a number of months of wrangling over costs. In late 2002 expenditure had been estimated at £1.8 billion in an Arup-produced study (Arup, 2002). This was received somewhat sceptically by a number of Government cabinet members and an internally derived estimation from civil servants came up with a substantially higher figure of £2.4 billion. It is difficult to know whether this was contrived by ministers who were clearly against hosting an Olympic Games, but in any case the estimate was a formidable barrier to overcome. This new cost was seen as too prohibitive and a new financial model was required if progress was to be achieved. This came from key player Tessa Jowell, working with her Sports Minister Richard Caborn and supported by a deal made with the City of London. London Mayor Ken Livingstone, while not an expert on sport, was aware of what a Games might do for London and so agreed to a deal that provided the difference in costs via a model that saw £0.9 billion coming from the London Development Agency (LDA) and an increase in Londoners' taxes. The remaining £1.5 billion was to come from Lottery funding supported by a whole new programme of ticket sales.

There was a nagging doubt at this time and, in particular, Prime Minister Tony Blair wanted to know if London could win a bid. This was far from being only an internal concern as the media had picked up on the significance of Tessa Jowell going to Lausanne to meet IOC President Jacques Rogge in January 2003 (*Sports Illustrated*, 2003). Although she returned with positive news that London had as good a chance as any other applicant city, it still took until 15 May 2003 for Blair's Cabinet to finally declare that it would bid for the 2012 Games (Parliament, 2003).

The decision to bid

Cassani was appointed relatively quickly in June 2003, taking up her role two months later. Next came Keith Mills as Chief Executive and Mike Lee as Director of Communications and Public affairs, with further team building having to run alongside a BOA official declaration to the IOC that London was an applicant city. This was done by 15 July 2003 and the required fee of US$150,000 was paid the following month. This allowed London to use a 'mark' in the public domain that denoted its status as a 2012 bidding city. By this time the decision to bid had taken six years to develop. The focus now was on the preparation of answers to the IOC questionnaire.

The Applicant Questionnaire

The questionnaire is relatively short and a response is submitted in report form, which is then evaluated by an IOC team consisting of technical experts to assess each applicant city. Generally applicants are assessed on: (1) the city's and host country's potential in hosting the Games; and (2) a demonstrated compliance to the Olympic Charter, ethical and anti-doping codes as set by the IOC.

The questionnaire is designed to provide the IOC evaluation team with an overview, rather than detail, of an intended event concept. In this case each of the applicants – Havana, Istanbul, Leipzig, London, Madrid, Moscow, New York, Paris and Rio de Janeiro – had to cover seven themes, with each answer required in both French and English. At 25 pages per language, the challenge was to ensure there was sufficient detail to convince the evaluation team to select a city to go through to the next round as a Candidate City. The themes were as follows:

1 Motivation, concept and public opinion. This section covers measures of public support, indication of intended legacies and how the venues would look from a geographical perspective. For London this was a section that needed to show how there was widespread support for an Olympic Games in the city, bearing in mind London had not been the preferred choice for the 1992, 1996 or 2000 bids from the BOA.
2 Political support. For this section London had to clearly demonstrate a serious intent for hosting the Games. Therefore the withdrawn hosting for the 2005 World Athletic Championships could have been perceived as a limiting factor, while the successful 2002 Commonwealth Games were an asset. Letters from the Government, the City and the BOA, and declarations of key personnel involved from both a political and management perspective were required in order to demonstrate just how serious the city was.
3 Finance. This section required each city to give a breakdown of how it would fund both a hosting of the Games and also the upcoming candidacy phase. London submitted the financial model it had agreed the previous year.
4 Venues. This section was where London showed how it would reclaim and build a new zone in east London with a sports focus consisting of new venues. It also had to relate its Olympic Park to other venues at a distance from its main delivery centre, showing that this was a benefit for those areas rather than a geographical or transportation problem.
5 Accommodation. Hotel provision was confidently presented by London as it showed how it could cater for event visitors, including the media, adequately without any new investment.
6 Transport infrastructure. For many cities this is a section that requires considerable consideration; transportation was certainly an area of concern for London. It had to try and demonstrate how it would move large numbers of event-related people by air, road, rail, underground and light rail in a capital city already suffering congestion issues. Little had been prepared or negotiated in the five months the team had to prepare for this questionnaire, so this was an area of vulnerability.
7 General conditions, logistics and experience. This section required information on city population expectations at the time of the event, meteorology conditions, environmental approach and security provision. It also required a 10-year history of expertise in hosting major international sports events. Clearly this was another section to be wary of, considering the 2005 World Athletics Championships issue, but a great opportunity to play up the 2002 Commonwealth Games success.

What was important for the BOA was that the Applicant Questionnaire was produced so that it was clearly coming from Britain's NOC (the BOA) and from a sport perspective, 'rather than from the city or anybody else so that the whole campaign was based on sport and from sport' (Reedie, 2011). The overall highlight for London was that its concept was based on a very compact plan and that there would therefore be a Games predominantly based in a new Olympic Park. It was also felt that there would be a substantial legacy, particularly because the new venues would be located in a new park setting that would bring about much-needed regeneration to this part of east London (Reedie, 2011).

Candidacy

To coincide with its submission of the Applicant Questionnaire response on 15 January 2004 the London team provided a launch event at the Royal Opera House in order to promote public and media support. It had achieved the first task – registering the bid – but would have to wait until 18 May 2004 to find out if London was indeed to be taken seriously.

Only five cities went through to the next phase, with London joining Madrid, Moscow, New York and Paris as a Candidate City. However, this success came with a fair degree of negative feedback and a clear indication that it would have to improve its bid if it was going to win. Indeed, London was a good way behind Paris (8.5 points) and Madrid (8.3 points), with only 7.6 points; New York was almost level pegging at 7.5 points. Moscow appeared a long way behind with 6.5 points (*Daily Mail*, 2004; Lee, 2006). Worryingly, London only came top in one of the seven themes, accommodation, and even that was a joint-first placing. The feedback London gained indicated that security, low public support (62 per cent) and a lack of event management expertise and experience were all areas of concern. The loss of the 2005 World Athletics Championships in particular appeared to be counting against London (Caborn, 2011). However, the most critical area of concern was transportation. This was certainly not the start the Government had wished for as many ministers remained unconvinced that London could win (Caborn, 2011). The production of a Bid Book (Candidature File) was the next task; this was due on 15 November 2004, so the London team only had six months to progress from third to first place.

The clear message from the IOC was that London would have a problem with its 'obsolete transport infrastructure' (Reedie, 2011). This meant the task was to produce a Bid Book that would provide sufficient technical detail on what the venues would be, where they would be and how London would organise a great sporting event. A critical part of this was to address a whole programme of work with a new diverse set of stakeholders in order to get London's transportation systems up to the necessary standard. What transpired was a lot of work pulling together the right parties to achieve upgrades on the Underground, extensions on the Docklands Light Railway, implementation of construction of a new railway system, and also the establishment of a link to the Games using the Channel Tunnel rail system. The bid team therefore entered a high learning curve whereby it had to effect change in order to eradicate the IOC's damning evaluation.

Other key Bid Book considerations were Government support and guarantees and also a strong effort to make the Games sustainable and environmentally friendly. A firm budget is also required in a Bid Book, which was complicated by the fact that it had to be bid in US dollars based on 2004 prices. This planning was further complicated by the numbers of stakeholders involved, each with their own budgets and development agendas. Ostensibly the bid team had to function as a catalyst. For example, the issue of transportation was the city's concern and indeed their cost, but if London was to win a Games there had to be considerable collaborative effort in producing a solution. What transpired was a plan to build an improved infrastructure as part of a development programme focused on the Olympic site, 'so that 75% of the total enhanced cost was effectively infrastructure and 25% was the sports facility' (Reedie, 2011). Innovation was also applied with a declaration that spectator tickets were to be sold at a price that included travel on the London Underground on the day of the event (LOCOG, 2004).

From a communications perspective the post-questionnaire position was seen more positively. While a lot of new and original work was now required, there was a confidence in the London bid team that this could be achieved. The Applicant Questionnaire allows only so much detail and bid teams at this stage of the process are small and generally without specific expertise to hand. Getting through that stage and then having the chance to build that expertise and detail was a relatively positive place to be (Lee, 2011).

The competition

While London would, of course, focus on its own bid, there is always the need to keep an eye on the competition. Each of the other four cities had their own differential, but there was a public perception that Paris and Madrid were clearly in the lead following the scoring of the Applicant Questionnaires.

Paris

Having bid for one recent Games (1992) and the immediate previous Games (2008), Paris was considered by many to be the 2012 favourite. They also appeared to have 'an air' of being the favourite too (Lee, 2011). A key factor was that the city is considered a major tourist destination and therefore would make a good Host City for IOC members, athletes and tourists alike (Reedie, 2011). The city also had a strong technical base in an already established focal point in its main stadium, the multi-use Stade de France (Lee, 2011). In addition, Paris looked to have a reasonable, centrally located village concept. This amounted to a better set of existing facilities than London had, and utilisation of those venues was perceived to be in a 'safe set of hands' from an event-management perspective (Caborn, 2011). Overall, and because this was their third bid in recent times, there was a feeling within the London bid team that Paris had a key factor of 'it's our turn' (Caborn, 2011). Ironically, this was considered by some to lead to the city's downfall, their communications strategy appearing conservative throughout their campaign as if not wanting to upset a 'winning game' (Lee, 2011).

Madrid

Madrid was generally seen to have built its concept well. It had a large indoor convention centre at its disposal and was also a capital city that had not hosted before. Barcelona is generally considered to have put on a successful Games and indeed developed its legacy since, and as it is the only city in Spain to have hosted a Games there was a fear that if it was not Paris, then it was Madrid's turn. There was also the 'Samaranch factor' (Lee, 2011). Former IOC President Juan Antonio Samaranch and his son, Juan Antonio Samaranch Jr, the leading executive for the Madrid bid, were visibly well connected to the IOC. There was a fear that Madrid could even be a more formidable opponent than Paris if it came down to a two-horse race (Caborn, 2011).

New York

New York was not considered to be offering strong competition, despite a strong, charismatic leader in Dan Doctoroff. There also appeared to be strains in the relationship between the US Olympic Committee and the IOC (Lee, 2011). While New York has an aura that extends worldwide, the London team were not convinced it offered a strong Games concept and saw early that there would be issues surrounding security and its proposed main stadium (Reedie, 2011). This did indeed prove to be New York's downfall in the latter stages as its intended Manhattan-based site fell through.

Moscow

The London team saw Moscow as being last in the race. The venues that were the base of Moscow's plan were already built and while for some this could be considered an asset, these were the facilities that had been used when the city hosted the 1980 Games. These were generally seen as tired and in need of upgrading (Reedie, 2011).

Highlights from the Candidature File

The Candidature File that London eventually put together and submitted on 15 November 2004 was clearly a successful Bid Book. It had taken the previous Applicant Questionnaire feedback and used that to produce a winning position. It is therefore important to consider how this was done.

There was a sense that 'British sport was beginning to come together in a way that it didn't always do', this being a helpful position to promote as well as use to achieve a coherent bid (Reedie, 2011). There was also growth in public support via bid communications and supporter sign-up mechanisms, and while the British media can be sceptical, even cynical on occasions, when London became a Candidate City the bid seemed to pick up momentum. A key moment was the visit of the evaluation commission in February 2005. This needed to be a success of course, but London also used this to promote the notion that it had a chance of winning. In order to get this event right, the team ran its own trial event with Craig Reedie chairing a mock-up event. He was able to bring expertise to that role, having previously been on two evaluation committees. Alongside a team of other experts, Reedie presided over five days of rehearsal and as a result this process revealed a number of issues that the team were then equipped to address and thus receive the evaluation commission with confidence. The outcome was a very satisfactory report (Reedie, 2011).

The London bid: key success factors

The Bid Book cannot stand alone. Its content needs to be believed and for that there needs to be considerable activity in the public domain throughout the six months prior to submission and then up to the decision day itself. This is how and when a bid is won; a team has to work hard to create and promote its own success factors. In analysis, London had a number of key success factors that combined to help them get the job done. These are discussed below.

The bid team

The outcome of any project is entirely dependent on the quality of the people and the decisions they make. For an event project there is an overarching target and an immovable deadline, and so whatever decisions are made the event has a date on which it must take place. This makes for an intense environment. Management teams are composed with that one target in mind, and event planning periods have little time to waste. It is important, then, that talented individuals are selected. However, what is also critical is the composition of the event-management team as a cohesive unit whereby individuals are moulded into a team for optimum performance.

The London bid team did this very well. What is clear to see is that there remains great loyalty, respect and admiration between members of the bid team, and yet at the outset this team was made up of a disparate set of individuals. There was a pride in the job that was done and the comradeship among members demonstrates just how close this team became. The combination of the three major stakeholders (BOA, the Government and the City of London) working together was a significant advantage and no mean feat to achieve (Caborn, 2011).

Barbara Cassani was a critical first appointment as Chair of the London Bid. She built the team from scratch, putting all the initial blocks in place in order to assemble what was ultimately a winning team. She receives a great deal of praise for this and yet there was a certain amount of controversy created by the media both at the time of her appointment and at the time of her resignation (Caborn, 2011; Lee, 2011; Reedie, 2011). In particular, there was some surprise at an American being appointed to such a role, and indeed this may have been a factor in the reason she left the post in May 2004 (Reedie, 2011). The media made quite a big deal out of her resignation as it came at a time when London had won through to be declared a Candidate City (*Telegraph*, 2004). This looked to be bad timing for a bid that had just come through the first stage but was sitting in third place. However, in retrospect it appears to be both critical that Cassani was appointed to successfully kick things off and equally important that she left the post when she did. She was pivotal in bringing people together to achieve the mission of getting the bid through the first stage and onto the shortlist (Caborn, 2011). However, she herself perhaps recognised that she could not take the lead role beyond this point and take the bid to an IOC membership she did not understand (Caborn, 2011). While the media questioned whether she was moved aside, the reality is that she had resigned several days before the IOC decision and that a new Chair had been found very quickly but expertly kept under wraps until after the decision (Caborn, 2011; Lee, 2011).

For some commentators, Sebastian Coe was also a controversial choice to take over from Cassani. Indeed, it was an interesting issue for the Government's Labour Cabinet to endorse the appointment of a former Tory Member of Parliament (Caborn, 2011). However, Coe has been seen since to have taken on the role and dispelled any thoughts that he was not the right choice. The role he played is seen as critical in winning the bid and is discussed below, but an important point to make here is that events are projects that require clear leadership and hierarchy structures (Masterman, 2009). The decision-making processes from planning to implementation require clear lines of communication within those structures and that is what Cassani started and what Coe was then able to develop.

Keith Mills is seen to have played a significant role. Mills was appointed Chief Executive for the London Bid, but was already a very successful businessman and sports enthusiast. He appeared to take on the role for the love of it, and in so doing brought both a great amount of deal-making skill to the team as well as dedication (Caborn, 2011; Reedie, 2011).

Craig Reedie's role as BOA Chairman and the initiating of the bid is clear to see in the discussion above, but Reedie continued to play an important role, in particular alongside Coe and Mills after the submitting of the Candidature File. His position as an IOC member allowed him access to other members, providing invaluable insight into where the bid needed to focus.

There were several figures from politics who played key roles. Tessa Jowell, as Secretary of State for Culture, Media and Sport, was important at the outset. She and her Sports Minister Richard Caborn, having decided that they wanted to back the bid around late December 2002, became very supportive of the BOA. She, more than any other Cabinet member, was influential in persuading her colleagues that the bid was worthy of support, clearly understanding that a successful bid would need to be led by sport but underpinned by the Government, rather than the other way around (Lee, 2011). At the outset there were no offices, funding or committee, just a number of enthusiasts and a report from Arup indicating that an event could be hosted in the East End of London with support from Mayor Ken Livingstone. Jowell provided the funds and stood back to let the BOA develop the project (Reedie, 2011). Livingstone was a key political figure with an agenda for the redevelopment of the city but, along with his counterparts, he approached his role by ensuring that no-one or their individual agenda was more important than the team effort required to win (Lee, 2011).

A number of team executives stood out. Mike Lee was one of the first employees appointed by Cassani, and as Director of Communications and Public Affairs he proved to be a skilful operator and shrewd in identifying issues early. An example of one of the trickiest issues was the BBC *Panorama* broadcast dealing with bribery (see below), but this was ably dealt with by Lee and his team (Caborn, 2011). David Magliano worked very closely with Mike Lee in his role as Marketing Director and played a key role in the whole communications plan.

Consultants were also used. Of particular importance was the hiring of Jim Sloman and his MI Associates consultancy to help move on from the Applicant Questionnaire and through to the more detailed Candidature File. Sloman was one of the key operating officers at the 2000 Olympic Games hosted by Sydney, an appointment that in itself was a good story to tell at that stage in the process (Lee, 2011). Sir Howard Bernstein, Chief Executive of Manchester City Council, brought important advice, having been instrumental in a successful delivery of Manchester's 2002 Commonwealth Games. Bernstein also introduced Alison Nimmo, who put together the original plans for the Olympic Park and then went on to establish the Olympic Delivery Authority (ODA), which is now responsible for delivering the infrastructure for London 2012.

Communications

There were a number of successful aspects to the communications that were undertaken by the London team during the bid period. The 'Back the Bid' campaign generated three million signed-up supporters to show that London wanted the Games. London was presented as one of the world's great cities using its landmarks alongside sport in its campaign (London.net, 2005). High-profile supporters such as politicians and Olympians were well utilised. For example, Daley Thompson was cleverly used to show how a global sports star could emerge from the East End of London (Lee, 2011).

Successful plans need to be able to respond to issues because they can often be usurped by surprises. The key is to react quickly with planned response systems. There was one particular threat that required all of these elements. In August 2004, the BBC's *Panorama* programme unearthed a bribery issue with a claim that IOC votes for bidding cities could be bought. There were no allegations that London was going about this prohibited practice, but it was perceived as a BBC attack on the IOC and consequently became the most potentially damaging crisis London had to contend with (Lee, 2006). When the issue was raised at an IOC Session in Athens at the 2004 Games, the key response by the team was to ensure the IOC members got to see the programme, but in a private airing as had previously been agreed by Craig Reedie and Jacques Rogge. Members of the team, including Sebastian Coe, Craig Reedie and Mike Lee, were waiting outside, and after the screening spent their time quashing the rumour that the bid team had been involved. They ostensibly distanced the London bid from the broadcast. The suspicion may still have remained, but the quick and personal response from key team members was critical in dampening this touch paper. Fortuitously this was also helped by another incident in which two sprinters failed drug tests, pulling media attention away from London.

The key theme throughout all communications was the need for distinguishing London from four other great cities, and this was captured in the vision (Lee, 2011).

The vision

The focus on using a London Games to inspire young people to take up sport was a key vision. As part of this approach, a critical decision was also made to ignore the temptation to focus on highlighting comparisons with the other cities and to concentrate on how the Olympic Movement could be developed for the future. Michael Payne, a former IOC Marketing Director, served as an advisor and he was used to identify how London might transform the IOC and the Movement. The team agreed that the decision to take the previous 2008 Games to China was a momentous, historic point for the IOC and that a similar impact might be required for 2012. The concept that this should be a bid that was focused on inspiring the young was further enhanced by talking with sponsors as well as IOC members, and, interestingly, broadcasters. In the United States, for example, there were concerns that Olympic television audiences were getting older and so consequently broadcasters might be keen to hear of a focus on getting the young more engaged (Lee, 2006, 2011). It was a bold decision, but London decided to focus on an inspiration of young people from around the world to get them into sport, a focus that would hopefully be welcomed by many stakeholders because of their concerns over future audiences and markets.

Lobbying

A successful skill and tactic adopted by the team was in the lobbying of all the different people that needed to be swayed and brought on board throughout the different stages of the bid. At the outset it was a nationally focused job to get politicians and the Government's Cabinet on side. This worked and it led to the Diplomatic Service, Foreign Office, UK Trade and Investment and British Council all working towards this common goal. Caborn himself travelled many miles to ensure the British Council got behind it in the 30+ countries they were active in with sport-led projects (Caborn, 2011). At the outset the City of London was also an important stakeholder to win over.

The latter stages became highly focused on one target area – IOC members' votes – and while the London team had a strategy, it was not one to be found in any document. Effectively this was something that evolved between three key players: Coe, Mills and Reedie. Unlike Coe or Mills, Reedie was able to legitimately access IOC members at many more events because he was a fellow IOC member. Together they worked out where they could and should be, and how they should contact people. This was supported by a comprehensive approach to intelligence gathering, and so the team of three was underpinned by a whole host of other executives who were knowledgeable about IOC members' opinions and feelings in different parts of the world. An international relations department was set up for this process and they provided analysis whereby the three leads could operate effectively. However, the real success of this approach was the communication they had between themselves, despite being miles apart most of the time, they were in constant contact with each other and always evolving the strategy. Essentially, the strategy was in their heads. The outcome was an ongoing analysis of the likely intentions of IOC members who would and would not be sympathetic towards London, who would be in favour of the other cities and a complex set of scenarios consisting of who might second-pick London once cities were eliminated in the voting (Reedie, 2011).

Another successful aspect in support of this approach was the development of a good presentation system. When the team was allowed to go and make presentations to NOCs, for example, they would frequently be accompanied by distinctive athletes, so it was made clear that the London bid was derived out of sport rather than politics and that it was for the development of sport. The fact that Reedie led, demonstrating his IOC and BOA affiliations, followed by Coe, an Olympic athlete, with politicians only coming later, was key in this approach. This was in contrast with the Paris approach, for example, in which presentations were led by politicians who came in, made their presentation, and then left directly afterwards (Reedie, 2011).

The London team made another critical decision – to go to Singapore early. The IOC decision day was 6 July 2005 and the other teams came into town just prior to that. The London team was there a week early, in another hotel. Here they rehearsed their presentation many times and so were ready when IOC members came to town around 4 July. By that time they were comfortably established in the hotel and had a clear plan about how they would organise the approaches they needed to make. The main thrust of this was the use of a Prime Minster and personal audiences with IOC members. They planned it so that some members would see Tony Blair, Cherie Blair, Richard Caborn and/or Ken Livingstone. Craig Reedie's wife, Rosemary, was also able to introduce Cherie Blair to IOC members' spouses. The time spent with IOC members in this way was seen as a critical advantage compared with the other teams' approaches (Reedie, 2011).

The presentation

A lot has been made of the effect the presentation in Singapore had, so it is important to put this into perspective. It was of course a presentation that was given on behalf of what turned out to be the winning bid, and because of the widespread feeling that Paris went into that day as the favourites, for many what transpired was a presentation that won the day. However, a successful final day presentation such as this can only portray what is already prepared and the success of this presentation was that it portrayed the depth of a bid that was already very well conceived and built (Caborn, 2011). Reedie (2011) put it succinctly: 'You could never win the Games by a presentation but you could lose one with a bad presentation.' The key to the presentation and its success was that it was able to draw on the vision of inspiring young people to take up sport, a plan that took two years to create (Lee, 2011).

The decision to focus on this vision and devote the presentation in this way was brave, especially as the norm had always been for cities to focus on key aspects of a city and country and what they could offer, more or less from a visitor's perspective. The bid team had thought long and hard about whether to pursue the new, risky route as it was unprecedented. However, the decision was made to go into it wholeheartedly, and if they were going to take 30 children into the presentation hall then they needed to do so bravely, out front and with that as the whole focus. The prospect of competing at an event against four of the greatest cities in the world also inspired the team to go with this approach because it gave them the differential it believed it would need. The films that were used were inexpensive but were able to support this integrated focus by focusing on children, in particular a young runner, young cyclist, young gymnast and young swimmer. Including David Beckham was also carefully thought through in that his presence was based on him not being there as one of the most famous sports persons in the world, but as an East End lad wanting to host the Games (Caborn, 2011; Lee, 2006). They did gamble on the other cities going with the usual approach, and in particular London needed Paris to go this way. The other cities did take a tourist-focused approach, with Paris using a very expensive technical video that focused on the city, its buildings and lifestyle.

In further testament to the whole approach taken by the London team, the team had a strong feeling they were going to Singapore with a bid that could win (Reedie, 2011). Interestingly, the scoring from round to round in Singapore shows that preparation and presentation were a good match, as London came out of the first round ahead and was only ever behind in the second round (see Table 3.1).

Tony Blair

Tony and Cherie Blair committed time to go out to Singapore. Not only that, they worked very hard to ensure their presence and support were felt. This alone is perceived by some to have been critical (Caborn, 2011; Lee, 2006). Once he was convinced the bid could win, Tony Blair wanted to give it full support; his decision to work the two days in Singapore and meet the IOC members was critically important. He is said to have thrown himself enthusiastically into this task, conducting back-to-back meetings over an intense few days (Lee, 2011). Whilst he was unable to stay for the final day, this appears not to have been significant, as his reason was to attend the internationally significant G8 Conference in Scotland. On the other hand, Jacques Chirac, the French President, did attend that day but his decision to only come to town the night before and also leave early (to go to the G8) was perceived to be a comparatively poor one (Caborn, 2011; Lee, 2006).

Sebastian Coe

When Sebastian Coe took over as Chair for the London bid in May 2004 he came with a strong set of credentials: Olympic double gold medallist, national hero, political and business experience. He had also been one of three vice-chairs for the bid and so he had prior experience. He was able to work with and inspire various stakeholders, in particular Tony Blair and Ken Livingstone – two Labour politicians often opposed to each other – were brought together to work in harmony for the good of the bid. Coe brought thoroughness and presentability and demonstrated this particularly by leading from the front. His thorough rehearsal of the Singapore presentation and its polished delivery, capped by his own role in that event, is an example of that style. Generally, the 'Coe factor' has been seen by many to have made a difference in winning the bid (BBC, 2005; Lee, 2011).

Summary and conclusions

It can be seen above that while the presentation in Singapore was strongly delivered, it was the culmination of many years of work and strong decision making that won this bid. Of critical

Table 3.1 Election of the 2012 Host City by the IOC Session, Singapore, 6 July 2005

	First round	*Second round*	*Third round*	*Fourth round*
London	22	27	39	54
Paris	21	25	33	50
Madrid	20	32	31	Eliminated
New York	19	16	Eliminated	
Moscow	15	Eliminated		

Source: Gamesbids.com, 2011.

importance was the boldness of the decision to go with the vision, whereby sport was at the heart of the London bid. This decision led to a bid that had significant competitive differential. London also produced a bid that was successfully aimed at Olympic ideals and therefore had great appeal to IOC voters. This had to be built and promoted well and so a strong and cohesive team was required, with communications and a very personal approach to lobbying coming to the fore. The bid was supported well by the Government, including key political players such as Tony Blair being able to provide an impact on the IOC when Paris, in particular, did not. The cohesion that can be seen in the delivery of these factors was also inspired by Sebastian Coe, but what is clear is that it is the combination of all of the above and not any one factor that led to London winning its chance to host the 2012 Games.

References

Arup (2002) *London Olympics 2012 Costs and Benefits: Summary*. In association with Insignia Richard Ellis, 21 May. Available: www.olympics.org.uk/library/boa (accessed 11 November 2002).

Barker, P. (2003) 'Wembley Stadium: an Olympic chronology 1923–2003', *Journal of Olympic History* 11 (2): 14–18.

BBC (2005) 'The Coe factor'. Available: http://bbc.co.uk/sport/hi/other_sports/olympics_2012/4618507.stm (accessed 17 May 2011).

Caborn, R. (2011) Interview, Sheffield, 15 September 2011.

Daily Mail (2004) 'London blasted by Olympic chiefs'. Available: www.dailymail.co.uk/sport/othersports/article-303354/London-blasted-Olympic (accessed 6 October 2011).

Gamesbids.com (2011) '2012 bid city profiles and documents'. Available: www.gamesbids.com/eng/bid_archives.html (accessed 17 May 2011).

Lee, M. (2006) *The Race for the 2012 Olympics: The Inside Story of How London Won the Bid*, London: Virgin.

Lee, M. (2011) Telephone interview, 14 September 2011.

LOCOG (2004) 2012 Olympics and Paralympics Candidature File, Transport, Volume 14.

London.net (2005) 'The London 2012 Olympic bid'. Available: www.london.net/olympics-bid (accessed 6 October 2011).

Masterman, G. (2009) *Strategic Sports Event Management: Olympic Edition* (2nd edn), Oxford: Elsevier.

Parliament (2003) *Hansard, 15 May 2003*. Available: www.publications.parliament.uk.pa.Id200203.Idhansrd/vo030515/text/30515–14 (accessed 10 October 2011).

Reedie, C. (2011) Telephone interview, 13 September 2011.

Sports Illustrated (2003) 'Prevarication will not affect London bid'. Available: http://sportsillustrated.cnn.com/olympics/news/2003/02/17/london_bid (accessed 10 October 2011).

Telegraph (2004) 'This is a wake up call not a death knell'. Available: www.telegraph.co.uk/sport/olympics/2379272 (accessed 6 October 2011).

PART 2

Delivering the Games

4

MATERIALIZING THE VISION OF A 2012 LONDON OLYMPIC GAMES

Gillian Evans

This chapter tells of the early stages of planning for an Olympic Games and its legacy in London. It emphasizes the long lead-in time – a period of almost two decades – in the evolution of London's bid for the 2012 Games, and draws attention to the dedication and leadership of visionary figures whose early involvement was somewhat eclipsed by the triumph of the final bid team in 2005. The chapter explains the importance of early bid-related documents, which acted as technologies of persuasion,[1] materializing sets of ideas, accruing prestige to key advocates, substantiating social relationships between interest groups, recruiting allies to the cause and thereby increasing the project's scale and chances of success. Highlighted in the chapter are important historical moments relative to the London, UK and global contexts of the 2012 Olympic Games bidding process, including: the internal competition between cities, in this case with Manchester; the associated development of a discourse of urban sporting regeneration and legacy; international aspiration to demonstrate world city status and the national politics of the late 1980s and 1990s, which left London lacking and having to reinvent a strategic sense of itself as a capital city.

In the late 1980s, Richard Sumray arrived late at a meeting of the London Council for Sport and Recreation (LCSR) of which he was Vice-Chair. The topic of conversation was how to get young people in London more involved in sport. As Richard sat down, he said, hurriedly, off the top of his head: 'Why not bid for the Olympic Games?'[2] It had never occurred to him before, but Richard's remark got him thinking: why not bid for a London Games?

At the time Richard was a local councillor in the Labour-led North London area of Camden; he had been Chair of Leisure and was Chair of the Social Services Committee. He was committed to promoting the positive benefits of sporting activity and was one of a cadre of civic-minded London politicians with a finger in such a multitude of pies that their dedication to the health and social welfare of London's population might itself be described as Olympian (Evans Forthcoming).[3] Richard explains[4] that the topic of conversation at the LCSR meeting was still relatively unusual: it was a new thing, from the mid-1980s, to speak of sporting participation. Up until that point the focus of grassroots sports thinking had been about sporting infrastructure – sports centres and buildings, making sure that facilities were in place. The new challenge was how to encourage people, and especially young people, to access the sporting opportunities that were available to them in London. Richard chaired a strategy group, which then published a sports strategy for London (LCSR 1987).

Bidding for the Games was not a topic that anyone had been talking about in the late 1980s, because the Greater London Council (GLC) had recently disappeared. Remembering the political challenges of the time, Richard emphasizes that

> there was no London-wide entity which was able to give a broader strategic view of London. Literally, strategy disappeared from London for a while.

The Local Government Act abolished the GLC in 1985. Its demise was the result of conflict between Margaret Thatcher's national Conservative government, which implemented drastic cuts to local authority spending, and the Labour-dominated GLC led by socialist Ken Livingstone, who was a thorn in the government's side because he refused to lie down and quietly take the Conservative assault on public spending. It was not until the year 2000 – 14 years later – that a London-wide strategic political entity was re-established (again led by Ken Livingstone) under Tony Blair's Labour government.

In the intervening period, from 1986 until 2000, London-wide organizational groups and associations took up the mantle of specific, citywide strategy – for example, relating to sporting issues. Hence, the original thinking for a proposal to bid for a London Olympic Games came from a sports council and not from a political entity pursuing a broader set of London-related interests. The lack of strategic authority in the city also meant that the emergence of tactical initiatives was often due to the leadership of inspired individuals, which was remarkable, but collective energies were, therefore, dissipated. For example, by the beginning of the 1990s, three separate bids for a 2000 London Olympic Games were mooted. One was the proposal being put together by Richard Sumray and the LCSR, focusing on East London sites; one was a more tentative proposal from a private construction company, Tarmac; and the third was a high-profile bid being assembled by Sebastian Coe, supported by Peter Lawson of the national sporting alliance, the Central Council of Physical Recreation (CCPR), and centring on West London's iconic venues such as the Royal Albert Hall and Wembley Stadium.

Sebastian Coe had only recently retired from a stellar career in athletics: he had won Olympic gold in both 1980 and 1984 for the 1,500 m and silver medals in the same years for the 800 m. In total he had broken 13 world records. Among many other sporting roles, Sebastian became, in the late 1980s, Vice-Chair of the Sports Council of Great Britain; he also started his own business in fitness clubs and began a career in politics, sitting, in 1992, as Conservative MP for Falmouth and Camborne. Clearly a competitor on and off the track, Sebastian Coe was ready to give Richard Sumray a run for his money. The rivalry between the two bids upped the ante and made each team more determined in what might have seemed a healthy competition to raise London's sporting profile. What Richard Sumray lacked in sporting prestige he compensated in strategic London savvy and where Sebastian Coe fell short in terms of tactical advantage relative to the capital city's political scene, he won out in charismatic determination to turn personal sporting prestige to diplomatic gain.

The regeneration Games

In contrast to the GLC, the once notoriously left-wing Manchester City Council decided, in the late 1980s, not to fight the Tories in Central Government but instead to play the governance game aggressively and take a decisive 'entrepreneurial turn' (Peck and Ward 2002: 13). This meant that the council had to learn how to work with the government and develop new partnerships with local businesses. In practice this amounted to a 'new modus operandi' (*ibid.*) for local politics, with influence distributed out of council committees and into a new power-sharing elite, which included a whole range of city movers and shakers. The decisions to bid for the 1996 and 2000 Olympic Games were key moments in the restructuring of Manchester governance (Cochrane *et al.* 2002) and in the reordering of the city's sense of itself. These were desperate times and Manchester came out fighting, setting the agenda and influencing other UK cities, including London. Long-term strategic thinking in Manchester led to a new discourse of urban 'regeneration', which included bidding for sporting mega-events in order to be able to attract investment towards the redevelopment of the run-down post-industrial eastern part of the city.

In Barcelona too, preparation for the 1992 Olympic Games was seen to be about more than the staging of a sporting spectacle. The event was being used as a catalyst, to realize, in a short amount of time, plans for the spatial reshaping of the city that would otherwise have taken decades to achieve (Coaffee 2008; Brunet 2009). The regeneration of the built environment of the city was clearly an achievable outcome of and justification for the public investment required for the organization of large-scale sporting events. For Richard Sumray, in London, this meant that bidding for the Olympic Games became about much more than citywide sporting participation. This made him more determined than ever to propose that the best location for a London games would be the post-industrial East End, where large areas of derelict brownfield land were already the focus of government attention. In 1981 the government had created the controversial London Docklands Development Corporation (LDDC) and awarded it unprecedented planning and enterprise powers with the aim of kickstarting investment (Fainstein 1994). This led to the birth of a new financial district for the City of London and associated infrastructure, such as transport initiatives, which caused London to begin to look eastwards. Most of the early development was in the western Docklands and vast areas of largely derelict land remained in the eastern parts; it was on these sites that Richard began to focus his attention.

Appreciating the broader potential for regeneration in the East End of London, Richard managed to persuade a group of colleagues to dedicate the necessary time and energy, without pay, to formulate a serious proposal to bid for the 2000 Olympic Games. The team was assisted by Coopers and Lybrand (later to become Price Waterhouse Coopers (PWC)), who also worked for free, and whose job it was to begin to translate the ideas behind the proposal into the framework of what an Olympic bid should look like. At the same time, Sebastian Coe, assisted by David Teasdale (a senior civil servant and Director of the Sports Council of Great Britain), was also working on a rival bid for West London. The difference between the two teams was that for Sebastian Coe the Games were all about a festival of sport using existing facilities and for Richard Sumray they had become about an opportunity for urban renewal, which made new facilities essential (Hill 1996).

Eventually, the British Olympic Association (BOA), already irritated by the fact that Sebastian Coe's intention to prepare a London bid had been announced to the media without official consultation, intervened in the squabble and issued an ultimatum: either the rival bid teams overcome their differences and put together a single cohesive proposal for a London Games or the UK bid would automatically come from Manchester. Bob Scott, Manchester's charismatic and entrepreneurial advocate, had already made clear his intention to try again after losing the 1996 Games to Atlanta, and Manchester was the widely favoured bid candidate.

In response to the BOA's intervention in London, the third party – the construction company, Tarmac – withdrew its proposal and played instead a mediating role, bringing the capital city's rival teams together. Only on the day of the BOA deadline, in February 1991, were tensions finally resolved between the two groups and agreement about a single proposal was reached. A London Olympic 2000 Campaign Board was formed, with Sebastian Coe taking political precedence as President.[5] His sporting profile lent prestige to the campaign and anticipated the schmoozing of the International Olympic Committee (IOC) that would be inevitable in the lead-up to a bid for the Games. A few weeks later, however, in terms of the proposal's content, Richard Sumray's group appeared to have won the day. The shape of the Games was based mostly on East London sites close to the River Thames,[6] with a new athletics stadium at Silvertown in Docklands and Wembley Stadium included only as the venue for football in the west of the city. In answer to the question, 'What can the Games do for London?' the proposal reflected the lessons of Manchester and Barcelona, answering:

> A great advantage of a bid oriented to East London is the contribution it would make to urban regeneration. East London has been suffering from decline of its port and manufacturing industries, and is part of the capital most in need of new development and investment. In Docklands and East Thameside, it offers extensive 'brownfield' opportunities for new activities providing urban renewal.
>
> *(Olympic Proposal of 1991: 57)*

Produced in a remarkably short period of time, the proposal document symbolized the men's passionate determination to work together to bring the Games to London. As a clear statement of intent, it spoke of the Board's self-belief, sang the city's praises and emphasized that this was a campaign 'inspired by sport and led by sport'. Board members paid out of their own money for the production of a 73-page document, entitled *London Olympic 2000.* As a materialization of the Board's ideas, the proposal worked on a number of levels. First, it substantiated a set of social relationships between the bid's creators; this was important because it resolved conflict between interest groups and brought together men whose differences had previously seemed insurmountable. Second, the document functioned to attempt to bring into being a new set of relations: these were connections with the particular kinds of people – officials from the BOA, for example – whom the Olympic Board hoped to influence. Third, in order to appear influential the document adopted a certain style: it took the form of a proposition statement, which described a future reality for London as if the bid for the Games had already been won. This created the impression of absolute surety, which it was hoped would inspire confidence and, therefore, recruit allies to the project and also investors to a cause with an estimated Games budget of almost £3 billion. Ultimately, however, the document did not achieve enough: it lacked substance and detail, photographs and vision statements outweighed in-depth analysis, and in April 1991, after the presentation of proposals to the BOA, it was no surprise when official UK bidder status was awarded to Manchester. Soon after this, London's hastily formed Olympic Board disintegrated and Sebastian Coe went his own way, focusing on his political career, while Richard Sumray continued to work on developing his vision for a London Olympic bid.[7]

London as a world city

Manchester lost the bid for the 2000 Olympic Games to Sydney and Bob Scott later reluctantly admitted in an interview with the *Telegraph* newspaper that after having lost out twice in a row he had to come to terms with the fact that a regional city in Britain was never going to win a bid to host the Games:

> I was aware that I was not leading the first XI ... The international world thinks London when they think Great Britain. If you put up Manchester or any other city other than London, however sound the bid, you cannot get over the fact that you are

> not London. The world then comes to the conclusion that Britain has decided to send out its second XI and is not taking the competition seriously. I found myself between a rock and a hard place.[8]

Learning from Manchester's experience, the London bid team realized that over a significant period of time, the northern city had built the necessary capacity and competence to submit credible bids. It also became clear that Manchester had benefited from the bidding process alone. Unlike London, Manchester's entrepreneurs had the backing of a single, strategically minded and business-oriented council, which had given the city a greater sense of purpose and won it many allies nationally. This was a turning point for London. It was the only UK city to be taken seriously on the international stage, and yet the city lacked a clear and confident sense of itself, and without a strategic authority to support it the bid for the 2000 Games lacked powerful allies. Other avenues had been sought to underwrite the bid, but even the wealthiest authority in the capital – the Corporation of London – had refused to lend its backing (Hill 1996: 106).

Then, in the early 1990s, a discourse emerged which made all the difference: Coopers & Lybrand Deloitte organized a conference to launch a report (Kennedy 1991) of research, partly sponsored by the London Planning Advisory Committee, on the theme of what makes a global city. The report anticipated the coming of the new millennium; it compared Tokyo, New York, Paris and London and argued that what distinguished these cities was all the different elements – economically, politically, culturally and infrastructurally – that make up a world city.[9] Richard Sumray remembers this as a pivotal moment: by this time, he had become obsessed about the Olympic bid and could not let the idea go. The discourse about London as a world city provided him with the strategic inspiration he needed for learning how to promote London on a global stage:

> until then I hadn't really thought about London and its place in the international sphere. For me it had been about London as an internalized city, as a city that needed to work for its own people. The Games suddenly opened things out and said something more about what London was as a city of the world. It also said that these sorts of mega-events can be catalysts and they can be catalysts for significant change.[10]

Richard describes how he and colleagues then put all their strategic energies into preparing London to compete internationally with other cities to host sporting events of all kinds. The idea was to gain valuable experience, build capacity and understand what constituted meaningful and successful bids in an emerging complex inter-city global marketplace for mega-events. Attracted by the prospect of a 2002 Commonwealth Games expanded to include more team sports, Richard put together a team, which worked for six weeks with Brian Wolfson – the Chair of Wembley – to produce a bid based on existing West London venues including Twickenham. Once again, London competed against and lost to Manchester.

Richard explains that within two weeks of defeat he was pleased, and not demoralized that London had yet again not been successful. This was because the Commonwealth Federation had decided, after all, not to enlarge the Games and the event at a smaller scale would have got lost in London. In Manchester, however, the Commonwealth Games made complete sense. Despite a lack of data collection to aid systematic evaluation, the 2002 Commonwealth Games have been widely hailed as a success (Gratton and Preuss 2008). Discourses around 'regeneration', which had originated in Manchester Olympic bids formulated in the 1980s, were translated in the late 1990s into a broader concept of 'legacy', which now involved aspirations to a whole range of event and post-event benefits including community engagement, sporting participation, provision and upgrading of sporting facilities and transformation of the city's built environment. The Manchester Commonwealth Games are famous, for example, for delivering a stadium with a sustained legacy use (Manchester City Football Club) and the 2002 event is held up as the model of what a sporting mega-event can do for a host city and nation. Just after the event, Jacque Rogge, President of the International Olympic Committee, said that the overall success of the Commonwealth Games in Manchester had restored faith internationally that the UK could host major sporting events and that it had impressed with its legacy planning.[11] Indeed, without the triumph and determination of Manchester it is questionable whether London would ever have won its bid to host the 2012 Olympic Games, or whether London's bid would have become what it is renowned for, which is the proposal for a 'Legacy Games'.

The building blocks of an Olympic bid

After London's failed bid for the Commonwealth Games, Richard, with the help of Andy Sutch of Sport England, formed a pan-London, cross-sector organization called London International Sport (LIS). In 1993, after establishing and consolidating LIS, Richard decided it was time to approach the BOA again about his determination to try for a London Games; he felt sure that the building blocks were now in place and that if he could persuade the BOA to work with London then a credible bid could be crafted. BOA Chair Craig Reedie said he would play a leading role, but only if Richard could persuade him that he had the backing of key London organizations and authorities. Encouraged, Richard then set about assembling a collective of key London players, including: the Chair of London First; Lord Shepherd, the Chief Executive of Wembley; Trevor Philips, Chair of the Arts Council; Toby Harris, Chair of the Association of London Government; the Head of the Government Office for London; Robin Young, Permanent Secretary of the Department of Culture, Media and Sport; the Chair of the London Tourist Board – in short, the sorts of people who were key to the overall London context and who had to be persuaded that London could and should bid for the Olympic Games. A collective narrative emerged from this grouping, which Craig Reedie then sold to the BOA, whose support was won on the understanding that the Games to work towards was 2008, and not 2004, which was felt to be too soon.

However, when Athens won the bid for the 2004 Games, it was clear that London had to set its sights on 2012 because no two European cities could host consecutive Olympic Games. Richard Sumray then worked closely with David Luckes who had been appointed in 1997 to work with LIS on a London bid. David played a pivotal role: he was a logistics expert and took on the task of synthesizing the knowledge emerging from four working groups convened by Richard. The groups' four themes were: transport; the Olympic Village; sporting venues; and the environment, which was a relatively new consideration arising from Sydney's preparations for a 2000 'Green Games'. In London all the cards were back on the table, with the West and East London locations open for consideration again. The process of preparing the bid itself brought together and gave a strategic focus to the huge number of different groups focusing on what London had to offer. For example, all the transport stakeholders came together in one working group to evaluate the transport capacities and needs of the city. The work in the various themes was systematic and comprehensive: for example, the London Planning Advisory Committee took charge of the Olympic Village focus group, exploring the potential of more than 50 different sites across London.

The year 1997 was also an important one because a new national government was elected, under the Labour leadership of Tony Blair. This proved to be critical, in the medium to long term, to the development of London's bid – first, because a citywide strategic political entity was re-established in 2000, with a directly elected Mayor; and second, because Tony Blair's support for the bid later proved to be critical. In the short term, however, between 1997 and 2000, the bid team struggled on without significant political oversight or support.

Turn-of-the-century mega-events

From the beginning, the Olympic stadium was a sticking point and source of controversy.[12] In 1996 Wembley Stadium had been selected by the English Sports Council as the preferred site for a new national stadium able to host a crowd of 90,000 and capable of hosting three major international sports – football, rugby and athletics. The existing stadium was to be demolished in the year 2000 and replaced by a new design by 2002. Even in the very early stages, however, financing of the project became uncertain, which caused delays. Funding schemes shifted to and fro from the promise of public funds for the stadium build to the negotiation of private monies and back again to the idea of lottery funding. The suitability of the stadium design for athletics use also came under question: in 1998 Richard Sumray expressed concerns that in athletics mode Wembley could only accommodate an audience of about 60,000, which was not sufficient to Olympic Games capacity. The BOA then took this up with Sport England and the Department of Culture, Media and Sport (DCMS), and Chris Smith, Secretary of State at the DCMS, commissioned a group of architects to look into the issue further. In 1999, after Lord Foster's triumphant arch design had been unveiled, Chris Smith rather hastily and without proper consultation announced that Wembley would be developed as a football-only venue.

Controversies over funding continued and demolition did not begin on the site until 2002. Further scandal about management of Wembley and construction problems hampered the project and in 2006 the FA Cup Final had to be relocated and played in Cardiff in Wales instead of in London. Not until 2007, and way over budget, did the project reach completion, and the shambles for which it became infamous along the way did little to lend national and international weight to the argument being proposed by leaders in London sports, like Richard Sumray, that the capital city could be relied on and was capable of hosting international sporting competitions.

The argument for London's world-class sporting profile was not helped either by the debacle over the 2005 World Athletics Championships, which was supposed to have taken place in Wembley Stadium. With the loss of athletics use in the stadium an alternative venue for the Championships quickly had to found. The recommended venue was Picketts Lock in north-east London, in the Lea Valley. A purpose-built stadium with a capacity of 43,000 was proposed, and Chris Smith, whose political reputation was by now on the line, promised £83 million of funding. However, in 2001 Tessa Jowell succeeded Chris Smith as Secretary of State at the DCMS. She called for a review of the costs of the Picketts Lock project, and in the face of spiralling costs she decided to withdraw government support for the venture. This caused a scandal in the world of UK athletics; Britain's international reputation was seriously undermined and another host for the Championships had to be found quickly. Helsinki stepped into the breach and Richard Sumray remembers being incensed: all his years of work to convince the world that London was ready to host major international sporting competitions appeared to be in vain. It seemed at this point that all the political odds were stacked against the Olympic bid team: not only were they struggling with the lack of a strategic London authority, but battling too against the fumbling of national government. None of these challenges were conducive to the development of a successful Olympic bid. The Labour leadership had ambitions to present the UK to the world as a confident, ambitious, youthful nation, but this was undermined repeatedly by controversy over its turn-of-the-century attempts to stage mega-events, including, of course, the infamous Millennium Dome project (Kirchner 2004).

An East London Games

It had always been argued that, to create the right atmosphere, the Olympic and Paralympic Village for a London Games should be relatively near the stadium, which meant that so long as Wembley had been proposed as the site for a potential Olympic Stadium the draft bid had begun to centre again around a West London location, or at least around a proposal for two main sites. However, when questions arose about the suitability of Wembley for athletics use, Richard Sumray continued to focus on developing the work around the East London sites, initiating conversations and winning the support of key East London figures, including senior officers and leaders of relevant boroughs. He anticipated correctly that the support of local government was going to be key to persuading London and national government that there was sufficient political buy-in to the project of sporting-led regeneration in the east of the city.

The site proposed for the stadium in the 2000 draft BOA document was 'the railway lands at Stratford', which did not mean necessarily that those working on the bid had ruled out West London sites. The new bid document mentioned the possibility of a stadium at Northolt, and in fact the scoping work continued to contain the whole range of viable choices of location for sporting venues and the Olympic Village. The aim was to work towards a document that could systematically demonstrate both the range of options London could explore and the progress that had been made in terms of the sophistication of consideration required in order to meet International Olympic Committee (IOC) requirements. Encapsulating years of work and responding in depth, in 24 chapters, to issues and themes that the IOC requires potential host cities to consider, David Luckes completed, in December 2000, a weighty 385-page document entitled 'London Olympic Bid', with detailed cost–benefit analyses of other Olympic cities' Games and a positive case study focusing on Barcelona, but without a commitment to costs in London.

Key themes in the section that justifies London as the location for the Games included 'London as a Global City' and 'Regeneration possibilities', where a concept of legacy more sophisticated than reference to transformation of the built environment is introduced for the first time:

> The principal reason for holding the Olympic Games is based upon the ability to deliver the necessary sporting infrastructure and services for athletes, officials and spectators. However, it is important to provide a fitting legacy for the local community and the Games can be seen as a means of adding regeneration in the areas around the competition and village locations, through the creation of suitable supporting infrastructure. With London having 13 out of the top 20 most severely deprived districts in England there is considerable scope for tying in with regeneration projects.

By now it had become clear that although the LDDC's Canary Wharf project in Docklands was deemed to be an economic success at the level of the city, it was plagued by local outcry about disregard for working-class residents of surrounding social housing estates who were shut out of the development. This raised critical doubts about the distribution of social and economic effects associated with post-industrial regeneration and the ongoing competition for world city status. Serious deprivation characterized the Labour-led boroughs surrounding Docklands' new finance district, and residents living proximate to the towering skyscrapers experienced little or no trickle-down development. Richard Sumray discerned that a bid for an Olympic Games in the East End of London would have to go one step further than the current trend for regeneration of the built environment and also prioritize, as Manchester had done for the Commonwealth

Games, engagement of 'local communities' who could, for the first time in any Olympic Games, be put centre stage.

The new bid document emphasized that in the same year of the draft's production a new strategic entity, the Greater London Authority, had come into existence, with the appointment of an elected Mayor, answerable to a cross-party London Assembly. This was correctly considered to be pivotal to the political conditions conducive to the production of a successful bid for an Olympic Games. Without citywide political backing, no Olympic bid, no matter how well thought through or how passionately defended, could get past the first post. As luck would have it, the debacle over the Picketts Lock stadium also worked in Richard's favour, because the Olympic project had to become the vehicle through which a national stadium for athletics would be delivered and this lent legitimacy to the proposal for a stadium in East London.

In the beginning, the GLA was preoccupied with establishing and strengthening its purpose and making its presence felt on the London political scene. With challenges of transport and policing to deal with, the last thing on people's minds within the GLA was a sporting spectacle, but finally, two years after the scoping document had been completed, Richard managed to persuade Neale Coleman – one of the Mayor's key advisors, to take an interest and persuade the Mayor, Ken Livingstone, that he should hear a presentation from the BOA about the Olympic bid. Richard describes how Simon Clegg, who was then Chief Executive of the BOA, began the presentation and within 30 seconds Ken interrupted to say, 'I don't need to hear anymore, I fully support it as long as it is in East London.' Richard was by now the only member of the original 'Olympic Six' (comprising the first Olympic Board for London in 1991) who had managed to go the distance, seeing his vision through to this critical juncture. The result was that London government was now on side and the BOA-centred bid team was jubilant. Richard was particularly thrilled that his strategic vision for urban renewal in the east of the city happened now to tally exactly with what the Mayor had in mind in terms of planning for London's future. Richard became one of the Mayor's representatives on the Olympic Stakeholders' Group 2012, and now faced the harder task of winning national government over to the campaign.

More than three times as substantial as its 1991 predecessor, the BOA's draft bid document had evolved, over a significant period of time, into a serious consideration – first, of what kind of an Olympic Games London could host; and second, of how this would compare and contrast to the Games that had preceded it. The document properly anticipated the possibility of a future interface with the IOC, which required bid documents to take a particular form, and it materialized a new alliance with the BOA, which lent the proposal to bid for the Games the legitimacy and institutional support it had lacked in the first iteration. The four working groups and the pan-London organizational support cultivated by Richard increased the number of allies rallying to the bid's cause, and with the triumph of mayoral support it was safe to say that the document had functioned efficiently, not only to increase the number of powerful allies backing the project but to expand the scale of the project to such a level that it was now impossible to ignore.[13]

Once bitten twice shy

The government had already been stung by unanticipated costs associated with the Commonwealth Games, Wembley and the Dome, and the disgrace of the World Athletics Championships hung in the air. It was unsurprising, therefore, that the DCMS refused to back the London bid for the Olympic Games without a proper cost–benefit analysis. Tessa Jowell, Secretary of State at the DCMS and Member of Parliament for Dulwich, enjoyed a highly successful and meteoric rise up the Labour ranks and had everything to lose. She could not lightly afford to stake her political career on an Olympic Games in London. Before lending her support to the Olympic bid project, Tessa asked Richard to chair a steering group overseeing a cost–benefit analysis of a London Games that it commissioned from Arup.

The report of the Culture, Media and Sport Committee, published in January 2003,[14] showed a high level of enthusiasm for the bid, but scepticism and trepidation about costs (House of Commons Culture, Media and Sport Committee, 2003). The Arup findings, produced publicly in May 2002 as a 12-page summary[15] of a much longer report of 250 pages, estimated project costs in the region of £2 billion, but the figures were deemed to be too vague to be properly informative for the purposes of public accountability and, with intentions to bid due at the IOC before July 2003, time was of the essence (Arup/Insignia Ellis 2002). The committee clearly felt pressured about the proper course of action and had promised a decision by 30 January:

> hosting the Olympics, the most 'mega' of mega-events, is a challenge and involves a substantial commitment of funding, attention and energy over an extended period and, crucially, the whole-hearted backing and financial under-writing of it all by the Government. The bulk of these resources, and of course the overall guarantee, will be in the form of taxpayers' money for which the Government is accountable to Parliament and this Committee. Nine and a half years out we could not, and do not, expect the bill to be calculable down to the last penny with delivery of each facility signoff, but the government must assure itself, before deciding to support a bid, that it understands what it is committing itself, London and the country as a whole, to spend and deliver.

It is telling, given contemporary controversies over the Olympic Stadium in London, that even at this very early stage, in 2003, particular concern was expressed about 'legacy' issues:

> An East London bid needs an 80,000 seat athletics stadium but East London itself does not. The government gave us evidence of the difficulties faced by a number of former hosts of the Games in relation to their legacy stadia. We were concerned about the role of a new Wembley national stadium whose capability of hosting athletics including the Olympics was one very controversial strand in a web of dispute and contention during that project's development. The evolution of both projects, Wembley and an Olympic bid, is set out in supplementary memoranda … from these it is clear that there was to say the least of it some shortfall in strategic thinking across the two projects. London might well end up with a stadium at Wembley specifically built with the capability to host the Olympics without legacy issue and another in East London actually built to host the Games with an uncertain future. If this duplication were in fact to occur much of the responsibility would lie with the sporting bodies and agencies whose discussions with each other and with government have led to this confusion.

On 30 January 2003, Tessa Jowell presented details of the Olympic bid proposal to the government's Cabinet Committee. The timing was not great: the potential excitement of the project was completely overshadowed by international events and the announcement by the USA of its intention to go to war against Iraq. Hesitation from Gordon Brown as Chancellor about the potential costs of the Games led to further delays, and it was not until May that Tony Blair finally threw his weight behind the bid and Tessa was able to announce on 15 May that London was going to bid to host the 2012 Olympic Games. The government promised a £3 billion public funding package for the Games and East London regeneration, but it was made clear that this was only on the understanding that were London to win the bid costs would be reviewed.[16]

In June 2003 a brand new bid team was announced, with Sebastian Coe as Vice-Chair and sporting counter party to go-getting American businesswoman Barbara Cassani as London's entrepreneurial lead. London finally had the strategic government it required to take an Olympic bid forward, and against all the odds it had won the support of national government and the necessary funding. The draft bid document had successfully recruited its final allies and, as a consequence, the project had increased exponentially in scale and become translated in financial terms into millions and then billions of pounds worth of money for further development. Richard's years of work and dedication to realize an Olympic dream for London had paid off. Ironically, however, the existence of the proper strategic authority in London meant that the key strategic role that Richard had been playing – leading on the bid for London – had to be handed over to the relevant lead in the GLA. This was Neale Coleman, Ken Livingstone's Senior Policy Officer, who took the baton from Richard Sumray and ran with it.

Sporting and Olympic politics of previous years may have played a part in his marginalization, but within weeks of Cassani taking charge, Richard, who now had no direct locus of control, with great regret and disappointment, was coming to terms with the fact that he was not going to be called to take a leading role on the new bid team. Nevertheless, when London won the Games in 2005, Richard continued to play various leading roles in the 2012 project, focusing especially on the regeneration and community angles he had so passionately pursued in the build-up to the bid, and which remained central to it. Richard took a place on the Legacy Board, which was the earliest forum for thinking about planning Games legacies; he became Chair of the 2012 Forum for Community Engagement and led on the Changing Places project for community-led transformations in local environment. In 2006 Richard Sumray and David Luckes were awarded MBEs in recognition of the part they played in London's successful Olympic bid. Craig Reedie of the BOA was knighted and Sebastian Coe added a knighthood to his life peerage of 2000.[17]

The legacy Games

When I asked Richard, in 2011, to reflect on what has been achieved so far in terms of Games planning and delivery and whether, in hindsight, he would have done anything differently, he said that he had only one regret. He emphasized that the Olympic Delivery Authority (ODA), which was tasked with constructing the Olympic Park and sporting venues, had done a phenomenal job, completing 'the build' almost a year early, which is unprecedented for any Olympic city. He also stressed that, notwithstanding transport and security issues, the London Organising Committee of the Olympic and Paralympic Games (LOCOG), which had the responsibility of finding £2 billion in private funding, selling tickets and then staging the Games in 2012, is also on track – preparing to deliver a successful sporting spectacle to a worldwide audience. London has also, Richard explained, done what no Olympic city has ever done before, which is to establish a dedicated organization – The Olympic Park Legacy Company (OPLC) – with the responsibility for planning an Olympic legacy even before the Games has taken place. Although he was clearly proud of the separate achievements of London's Olympic bodies, Richard worried about the 'silo' effect, which meant that the promised communities'[18] legacy had too easily become separated from the remit to build an Olympic Park and stage the Games.

In retrospect, Richard saw that what he cared most about – the engagement of local communities and the transformation of the lives of Londoners through sport – was at risk of being thought of as the 'soft option', a priority sidelined in the race to meet 2012 delivery deadlines. He wondered whether it would have been possible to instead have one organization working to a single regeneration remit. This entity would have been tasked with planning and delivering the Games with local socio-economic legacy and community engagement more systematically included as a necessary part of the outcome of every phase of design and development from 'the build', to the staging of events in 2012 and preparation for the Park's future. Whilst he felt optimistic about OPLC, Richard felt that the creation of the company, in 2009, was too late in the day compared to ODA and LOCOG, which were established in 2005, and he worried that OPLC had been left with too much to do in too short a space of time.

On 24 November 2011, OPLC organized a public debate in association with the Real Estate Club of the London Business School as part of OPLC's Legacy Lecture Series. The debate was entitled '246 Days to Go: What Legacy for London?'[19] Geraldine Blake, Chief Executive of Community Links, was one of the speakers. Community Links is in Newham, one of the Olympic host boroughs, and is one of the country's largest voluntary sector organizations, delivering front-line services to people living in some of the most challenging socio-economic circumstances in the East End. Geraldine argued strongly that the challenge of marrying physical transformation in the Park with change in the lives of people living locally had largely failed. Whilst the completion of the build and the likelihood of a successful Games is very good news for London and 'brand UK', none of this yet appears, Geraldine insisted, to have made much difference to young people living on local housing estates who form part of the generation that were promised to be 'inspired' by the Games. So far, she said, she could see very little evidence of how what is being built in the Park and what is supposed to take place there in 2012 is being brought into relationship with those young people in the East End whose youthful energy and cultural diversity brought the bid for the Games to life, but who now worry that the promises that were made to them by the bid team and the government are proving to be empty.

Geraldine explained that the Olympic Park Legacy Company is showing all the signs of being open for dialogue and wanting to do things differently. For example, the Community Engagement Team supports a schools programme for informing children, teachers and parents in the eleven wards closest to the Park about future plans, post-Olympic Games. It also hosts a Legacy Youth Panel, which comprises a group of local youth who have been involved in long-term consultation about the spatial Master Plan for the Park – the Legacies Communities Scheme (LCS) – which is a planning application that sets out a vision for what kind of place the Olympic Park could become over the next two decades of sporting, residential, parkland and business development. The Legacy Youth Panel sets a hopeful precedent for developing new ways of working that include 'local' young people, leading to a genuinely transformative and collaborative planning process, but Geraldine expressed concern that initiatives like this are a drop in the ocean.

Overall, it appears that outside of statutory consultation processes, even where, in the case of OPLC, best practice is being far exceeded, an opportunity has been lost, since the Games were won in 2005, to think through and develop an appropriate and systematic mechanism for bringing local residents (even in the eleven closest electoral wards) into relationship with the Olympic Park and what is to happen there, either in 2012 or in the future. Long-term, properly funded, project-based programmes (rather than tick-box, information-giving programmes), delivered in association with the Olympic host boroughs at the level of the housing estate and including some kind of scheme for preferential Games-time ticket allocation, appear to be a trick that has been missed. There is a risk, therefore, that OPLC inherits a negative legacy of community engagement from other Olympic bodies, and, as Geraldine explained, time is running out to minimize what she and other community groups in the East End perceive to be the damage done by failed promises and poorly managed expectations.

Also speaking at the Legacy Lecture Series debate was the Olympic Park Legacy Company's new Executive Director of Regeneration and Community Partnerships, Paul Brickell. Paul was one of the original local politicians that Richard Sumray went to see in the mid-1990s, when he was testing local reaction to the idea of an Olympic Games in East London. From the beginning, Paul saw the possibility of an Olympic Games as an opportunity to accelerate the pace of post-industrial regeneration that he and other local changemakers[20] had been struggling for so long to realize. Paul explained at the debate why regeneration means more than the transformation of the built environment and how it involves a much more complicated challenge, to do with creating places that work better by building relationships of mutual benefit to people living inside and outside of new developments. This means harnessing the energies and potential of surrounding, long-standing, less well-off local communities, and making this the basis for building connections with new amenities and residents in new housing and employment schemes. From his long-standing experience of regeneration in the East End, Paul gave examples of community-led regeneration, such as the development of the Langdon Park Docklands Light Railway (DLR) station (Evans forthcoming), and he emphasized the challenge facing OPLC in attempting to deliver regeneration on a more massive scale over the next 20 to 30 years. He outlined the achievements of OPLC in the planning and delivery of legacy so far and celebrated some of the milestones that have been reached since OPLC was created in 2009:

- the deal over the ownership of the parkland agreed with government in 2010;
- securing funding for OPLC during the coalition government's Comprehensive Spending Review, at a time when all other quangos were abolished;
- the submission of a planning application for the land in 2011;
- the procurement, in 2011, of estates and facilities management contracts for the Park with an imperative for collaboration with / inclusion of small and medium local enterprises;
- the announcement, in 2011, of the call for development partners for the first phase of residential development – Chobham Manor – adjacent to the Olympic Village, with a commitment to include a Communities Land Trust in the Olympic Park;
- the opening, in 2011, to expressions of interest of the employment hub in what during the Games will be the Press and Broadcast Centre;
- the completion, in 2011, of the iconic visitor destination, the steel sculpture and viewing platform, the Orbit, designed by Anish Kapoor;
- the beginning of the struggle to secure a tenant for the Olympic stadium, which remains, at time of writing, unresolved, but which is nevertheless further ahead in legacy planning than any other Olympic city at this point in time before the Games;
- the development, with the Five Host Boroughs Unit, of the Strategic Regeneration Framework (SRF), leading to agreement with London and national government on the 'convergence agenda', which aims to use the catalyst of Olympic-related development as the means, in the next 20 years, to create the conditions in the East End of London for people to expect the same living standards that residents of West London boroughs enjoy.

The host boroughs

What is remarkable about London's Olympic Games is the extent of political alignment that Games-related governance requires.[21] The task of holding this tense knot of interest groups together is in itself phenomenal, and with each change in the political cycle – at both London and national level – the stakes of the political game change. The DCMS, the GLA, OPLC, ODA and LOCOG all have to work together, and they must do so in collaboration with the host boroughs, of which there are six, and among whom there is no obvious or necessary agreement about what is in their best interests.[22] Greenwich is London's fifth host borough, and

Barking and Dagenham became the sixth in 2011. The other four host boroughs – Newham, Tower Hamlets, Hackney and Waltham Forest – have political territories that border the Olympic Park and were the subject of compulsory purchase orders for the assembling of the Olympic land. These are the areas that contain the neighbourhoods and 'communities' comprising the East End of London, and that were placed at the heart of London's bid for the Games. One of the government's five Olympic promises[23] was that the Games should 'transform the heart of East London' because the area, as Richard Sumray observed so early on, was the part of the capital city that contained some of the most 'deprived' wards in the country.

The 'host boroughs' are, then, key political stakeholders of the 2012 project, and alignment between what the bid documents promised and what the Games are delivering remains a point of discussion at every stage of preparation for the Olympic Games and in the planning and delivery of London's legacy. Inevitably, tensions between the host boroughs, London and national government centre around Olympic legacy promises, and the question of whose responsibility it is to deliver – for example, on the convergence agenda – will remain a contested topic for years to come, long after the Games are over.[24]

Conclusion

This chapter has traced the evolution of London's Olympic Games from vision to materialization through early bid documents; the formal bid in 2004; the set of strategic social alliances between stakeholders and local, London and national government, which led to the promise and actuality of billions of pounds of funding in 2005; the purchase of land, construction of venues, a sporting spectacle and the beginnings of a realization of a dream of legacy in 2012. Critical to this process of development, two decades long, was the unwavering determination of passionate idealists, project leaders – change-makers – like Richard Sumray. This proves a more general point about the way that humans have ideas and go about bringing new realities into being: the materials, like documents, for making things happen do not do their own work. They function as technologies of persuasion, but they need to be directed, led and driven, relentlessly, like vehicles[25] of change, or lines of force, until they take on enough passengers – i.e. recruit sufficient allies – that they become scaling devices, reaching a critical mass, morphing into more massive versions of themselves. Then they might just generate sufficient momentum to push into and create the space of change, determining the shape of the future.[26] And there is always a politics to this because what existed before either gets moved, forcibly, out of the way or is recruited too, to the vision of the way things will be from now on. The point is that without proper leadership reality cannot and will not hold, and there is always a risk, therefore, that things will fall apart.

Notes

1 As an anthropologist I am interested in documents as highly specific kinds of ethnographic objects. I take inspiration from Riles (2006), whose edited collection asks what kinds of tools documents are in modern life. The collection features the work of seven anthropologists who explore the contemporary significance of documents among a diverse range of peoples around the world.

2 The assumed correlation between the hosting of the Olympic Games and an increase in sporting participation has been challenged by research, which suggests that demonstration of elite sporting activity might inspire those who are already active in sport to become more active, but has no effect on those who currently have no engagement in sports (Weed *et al.* 2009). This suggests that a legacy of increased sporting participation requires strategic attention to the question of how to use the Games proactively as leverage to get the inactive motivated enough to engage with sporting activity.

3 Richard was also, at this time, Chair of the Association of London Authorities Arts and Recreation and Social Services Committees, Deputy Chairman of Greater London Arts 1986–1990, member of the Camden and Islington Family Health Services Authority and a magistrate in the London Juvenile Court.
4 Richard Sumray kindly agreed to a series of interviews in 2011 and parts of the text that follow present his interpretation of the events.
5 Other 2000 Olympic Board members were Fred Smallbone, Chair of the LCSR; David Teasdale; John Lelliott of Lelliott Construction; and Ron Emes, Chair of CCPR. The most vociferous naysayer to Richard Sumray's proposals was Peter Lawson of the CCPR who withdrew his support for the London 2000 campaign immediately prior to the 2000 Board being formed, which arguably made it possible for a last-minute compromise to be reached between the two proposals. Lawson was later sacked by his former supporter, the Duke of Edinburgh, and imprisoned for fraud.
6 East London locations of sporting venues included: the London Arena; the Brunswick Centre near the Blackwall Tunnel; the London Dome, Silvertown; The Royals, Royal Albert Dock, Newham. There would be an Olympic Village at Greenwich Peninsula with a second option for the Village in Barking.
7 Richard worked alongside Fred Smallbone and John Lelliot and then, later, Andy Sutch, who was Director of the London Region for Sport England.
8 www.telegraph.co.uk/sport/olympics/2404821/Olympics-Capital-way-to-win-votes.html (accessed 7 July 2011).
9 Urban sociologists also picked up on this transitional moment, but marked it out critically in terms of the relationship between new forms of globalization and growing urban inequalities (Sassen 1991). Following up on this theme Massey (2007) has recently criticized, as a product of the Thatcher era, the 'neoliberal settlement', which freed the finance sector in London from government regulations, opened it out to global market forces and made it a dominant force for unprecedented wealth creation and elite formation in London.
10 The idealistic enthusiasm of Olympic visionaries and Games planners is contradicted by critics, who argue that the investment in hosting Olympic Games will not necessarily pay off in economic terms even if a successful Games might deliver host-city and national 'feel-good' benefits. See, for example, the critique of Professor of Sporting Economics Stefan Zymanski (Zymanski 2009). More recently, journalist Michael Pascoe, writing about Australia, has likened the staging of sporting mega-events to cargo cults, whose rationale is that a city seeking inward investment only has to 'stage a major sporting event and the money will come' (Pascoe 2011).
11 http://news.bbc.co.uk/sport3/commonwealthgames2002/hi/features/newsid_2170000/2170208.stm (accessed 17 July 2011).
12 This continues to be the case. At time of writing, October 2011, the deal for legacy use of the 2012 stadium negotiated between Newham Council, West Ham Football Club and the Olympic Park Legacy Company has been suspended. This is because of controversy over legal fees arising from challenges by Tottenham Hotspur and Leyton Orient over the process through which West Ham was chosen as the preferred bidder.
13 My analysis of Olympic bid documents lends itself well to recent literature on urban assemblages (Farias and Bender 2010). This work uses the concepts of actor network theory from science and technology studies to rethink urban studies. The point is to trace the history of transformations brought about by complex relational objects such as planning documents, which recruit human and non-human allies as they evolve from plan to reality.
14 www.publications.parliament.uk/pa/cm200203/cmselect/cmcumeds/268/268.pdf (accessed 15 July 2011).
15 www.arup.com/_assets/_download/download368.pdf (accessed 15 July 2011).
16 Monies were to come from the National Lottery and an additional £20 per year charge on Council Tax for Londoners in order not to place an unacceptable drain on the Treasury. Government and the London Mayor jointly committed over £10 million to cover the cost of producing an official bid, which had to be produced within eight months for submission in January 2004.
17 Anthropologists might interpret the narrative of the development of London's successful Olympic bid, in part, as an example of how the prestige of 'big-men' (Strathern 1979) is produced through what they are able to materialize in the world. This self-making, through Olympic planning, is just one small aspect of the Olympic legacy and part of what documents, as technologies of persuasion, can make possible as dreams are materialized and become reality. I am grateful to Dr Mark Jamieson and students at the University of East London for insights on this chapter gained during the departmental anthropology seminar in November 2011.

18 There is an assumption that outside of the Olympic Park, in the East End, there are 'communities', but exactly what this means is rarely made clear. There are certainly housing estates and various kinds of community organizations in the East End, but whether people living on these estates understand themselves to be simply residents, living individually and as families, or as collectively organizing communities is another matter, and this varies from one location to another.
19 To listen to this debate and access materials from it, go to: www.londonlegacy.co.uk/community/get-involved/annual-lecture-series/.
20 See, for example, the work of local regeneration companies Leaside Regeneration, Renaisi, Hackney Wick Partnership and Bromley by Bow Centre, and the development projects of the University of East London, among others, which make it clear that the Olympic Games is not the only game in town, and is, in fact, a latecomer to the scene. This puts the story of change in the East End in perspective, but does not in any way undermine the significance of the Olympic Games as the catalyst of rapid change – making possible in five years spatial transformations that might otherwise have taken 20 or 30 years to achieve.
21 This question was at the heart of the second in the series of OPLC Legacy Lecture debates in 2011. To listen to this debate and access materials from it, go to: www.londonlegacy.co.uk/community/get-involved/annual-lecture-series/.
22 This is why a Host Boroughs Unit was set up in 2008 with the aim of creating alignment between the host boroughs and leading on the production of a mutually agreed Strategic Regeneration Framework (SRF).
23 The five Olympic promises were: to make the UK a world leading sporting nation; to transform the heart of East London; to inspire a generation of young people; to make the Olympic Park a blueprint for sustainable living; and to demonstrate the UK as a creative, inclusive and welcoming place in which to live, visit and do business.
24 See, for example, controversy in January 2010, when the Economic Development, Culture, Tourism and Sport Committee of the London Assembly tried to hold the Host Boroughs Unit to account for publishing the SRF after the majority of the ODA's budget was spent.
25 Indeed, before it became the Olympic Park Legacy Company, OPLC was known in government circles as a special purpose vehicle (SPV).
26 The fact that failure is the more usual outcome of attempts to realize new ideas (Latour 1996) makes the story of success a more phenomenal tale.

References

Arup/Insignia Ellis. 2002. London Olympics 2012: costs and benefits, 21 May.

Brunet, F. 2009. The Economy of the Barcelona Olympic Games. In Poynter, G. and MacRury, I. (eds) *Olympic Cities: 2012 and the Remaking of London*. Surrey: Ashgate.

Coaffee, J. 2008. Urban Regeneration and Renewal. In Gold, J.R. and Gold, M.M. (eds) *Olympic Cities: city agendas, planning and the world's games, 1896–2016*. Surrey: Ashgate.

Cochrane, A., Peck, J. and Tindell, A. 2002. Olympic Dreams: visions of partnership. In Peck, J. and Ward, K. (eds) *City of Revolution: restructuring Manchester*. Manchester: Manchester University Press.

Evans, G. forthcoming. *London's Olympic Legacy*. Basingstoke, Hampshire: Macmillan Palgrave.

Fainstein, S. 1994. *The City Builders*. Oxford: Blackwell.

Farias, I. and Bender, T. (eds) 2010. *Urban Assemblages: how actor–network theory changes urban studies*. London: Routledge.

Gratton, C. and Preuss, H. 2008. Maximising Olympic Impacts by Building Up Legacies. *The International Journal of the History of Sport*, 25 (14), Special issue: Olympic Legacies: Intended and Unintended – political, cultural, economic, educational, pp. 1922–1938.

Hill, C. 1996. *Olympic Politics*. Manchester: Manchester University Press.

House of Commons Culture, Media and Sport Committee. (2003). A London Olympic Bid for 2012. Third Report of Session, 2002–2003, HC268. London: The Stationery Office.

Kennedy, R. 1991. *London: world city moving into the 21st Century*. London: HMSO Publications Centre.

Kirchner, M. 2004. *Cool Millenium Projects for Old Britannia? A Challenge for New Labour*. Germany: GRIN Verlag.

Latour, B. 1996. *Aramis: or the love of technology*. Massachusetts: Harvard University Press.

London Council for Sport and Recreation. 1987. A Capital Prospect: a strategy for London sport.

Massey, D. 2007. *World City*. Cambridge: Polity Press.

Pascoe, M. 2011. The Fairytale of Olympic Gains for Cities. Online: www.smh.com.au/business/the-fairy-tale-of-olympic-gains-for-cities-20111117–1nk5a.html (accessed 29 November 2011).

Peck, J. and Ward, K. 2002. *City of Revolution: restructuring Manchester*. Manchester: Manchester University Press.

Preuss, H. 2004. The Economics of Staging the Olympics. A Comparison of the Games 1972–2008. Cheltenham: Edward Elgar.

Riles, A. (ed.) 2006. *Documents: artefacts of modern knowledge*. Michigan: Michigan University Press.

Sassen, S. 1991. *The Global City: New York, London, Tokyo*. Princeton: Princeton University Press.

Strathern, A. 1979. *Ongka: a self-account of a New Guinea Big Man*. London: Duckworth.

Weed, M., Coren, E. and Fiore, J. 2009. *A Systematic Review of the Evidence Base for Developing a Physical Activity and Health Legacy from the London 2012 Olympic and Paralympic Games*. London: Department of Health.

Zymanski, S. 2009. Five Myths About Hosting the Olympics. *Washington Post*, 4 October. Online: www.washingtonpost.com/wp-dyn/content/article/2009/10/01/AR2009100103891.html (accessed 15 November 2011).

5

FROM A PREHISTORIC VILLAGE TO AN OLYMPIC PARK SITE

Transforming East London

Andrew B. Powell

The creation of the Olympic Park, as the venue for the 2012 Olympic and Paralympic Games, has completely transformed the character of a large area of the East London landscape. However, the multidisciplinary investigations into the site's cultural heritage, undertaken as part of that transformation process, have shown that such a dramatic change is nothing new for this area of London. The Lower Lea Valley has a long and varied history, and the legacy that future generations will inherit from 2012 has its roots firmly in the past.

What had once been a wild landscape, flanking the lower reaches of the untamed River Lea as it flowed towards the Thames, became an enclosed and farmed landscape, settled first by prehistoric communities exploiting the rich natural resources the valley had to offer, not least the river itself. Then, from the establishment first of Roman *Londinium*, then Saxon *Lundenwic*, and finally the city of London itself, life and work in the valley became bound irreversibly to the growth of the nation's capital – through trade and commerce, politics and power.

While, in many respects, the land long retained its character as a rural hinterland, crossed by people going elsewhere and goods passing through, the gravitational pull that London has exerted – on communities and their skills, and on the products of agriculture and industry – has, throughout history, offered economic opportunities to local people (and caused many problems too). This relationship created, in the end, a wholly industrial landscape, only recently declined – but now transformed into the Olympic Park.

The background to the cultural heritage investigations

The Olympic, Paralympic and Legacy Transformation planning applications were submitted to the Olympic Delivery Authority (ODA) Planning Committee (which has representatives from the London Boroughs of Hackney, Newham, Tower Hamlets and Waltham Forest), and were supported by an Environmental Statement that included a chapter on Archaeology and Cultural Heritage (Olympic Delivery Authority 2007). This contained generic method statements for conducting the fieldwork, all of which was undertaken according to project designs approved by the Greater London Archaeology Advisory Service (GLAAS) and following the standards and codes of practice laid down by the Institute for Archaeologists (IfA).

The ODA took a multi-stage and multi-stranded approach to the investigation of the Olympic Park's cultural heritage, in order both to minimise the impact of the site's development on its archaeological and historic resource, and to enable the examination of many aspects of the area's past.

Thus five key phases of archaeological work were defined (these are summarised in Table 5.1), culminating in the publication of the results in a monograph entitled *By River, Fields and Factories: The Making of the Lower Lea Valley – archaeological and cultural heritage investigations on the site of the London 2012 Olympic Games and Paralympic Games*, as well as in a popular publication, and on the Learning Legacy website (http://learninglegacy.london2012.com).

The nature of the investigations

Historical, documentary and cartographic research contributed to the DDBAs (detailed desk-based assessments), which sought to predict, or at least flag up, areas in each of the PDZs (planning delivery zones) where there was the potential for significant archaeological remains. Further historical research was undertaken during the initial assessments of the fieldwork results, and as part of the analysis, in order to elucidate the background to many of the historical features recorded.

Geoarchaeological research, combining data from thousands of geotechnical boreholes and from the archaeological trenches, has resulted in the creation of a new 'deposit model' that maps both the valley's original topography and the sequence of sediments and deposits resulting from combinations of natural forces and human actions, which over the centuries have blanketed the valley floor, in places to great depth (Wessex Archaeology 2011). This, accompanied by the palaeoenvironmental examination of soil samples taken during the archaeological excavations and a comprehensive programme of radiocarbon dating, has enabled detailed reconstructions of the past environments that have evolved in the valley, and the ways local communities have interacted with them.

The depth of the valley sediments, often buried below many metres of modern made ground, provided severe challenges for the archaeologists. Across the site 122 evaluation trenches were excavated, some targeted on areas identified as having high archaeological potential, others positioned to provide as full a coverage of the landscape as possible (Figure 5.1). However, in order to expose even small areas of the earliest archaeological horizons it was often necessary to excavate much larger trenches, their sides stepping down to provide safe working conditions at their bases. Chemical contamination from the valley's former industries, and frequent flooding caused both by heavy rain and the hydrostatic pressure of the groundwater, created the most difficult conditions for the careful exposure, and precise recording, of the archaeological remains.

Nonetheless, archaeological remains spanning some 10,000 years were found: a wide range of objects and materials, from pieces of flint and pottery to an abandoned boat. The findings from eight of the trenches led to these sites being extended and subjected to full-scale excavation.

Table 5.1 Summary of cultural heritage investigations within the Olympic Park

Phase	*Works undertaken*
1	Detailed desk-based assessments (DDBAs) for each planning delivery zone (PDZ); formulation of written schemes of investigation (WSIs)
2	Field evaluation (122 trenches excavated)
3	Mitigation excavations (8 trenches); geoarchaeology sampling, assessment and analysis
4	Site-wide integrated assessment and formulation of updated project design
5	Post-excavation analysis and dissemination of results (ongoing at the time of writing)

They ranged from a site of Early–Middle Neolithic (*c.* 4000–2850 BC) riverside activity (Trench 118), near the southern end of the Olympic Park, south-east of Stratford High Street, to a Victorian industrial estate complete with workers' cottages (Trench 75), towards the north end of the Park, at Temple Mills.

The latest feature excavated at the Temple Mills site, a well-preserved cobbled street buried nine metres below the modern ground surface, brought the archaeological investigations into

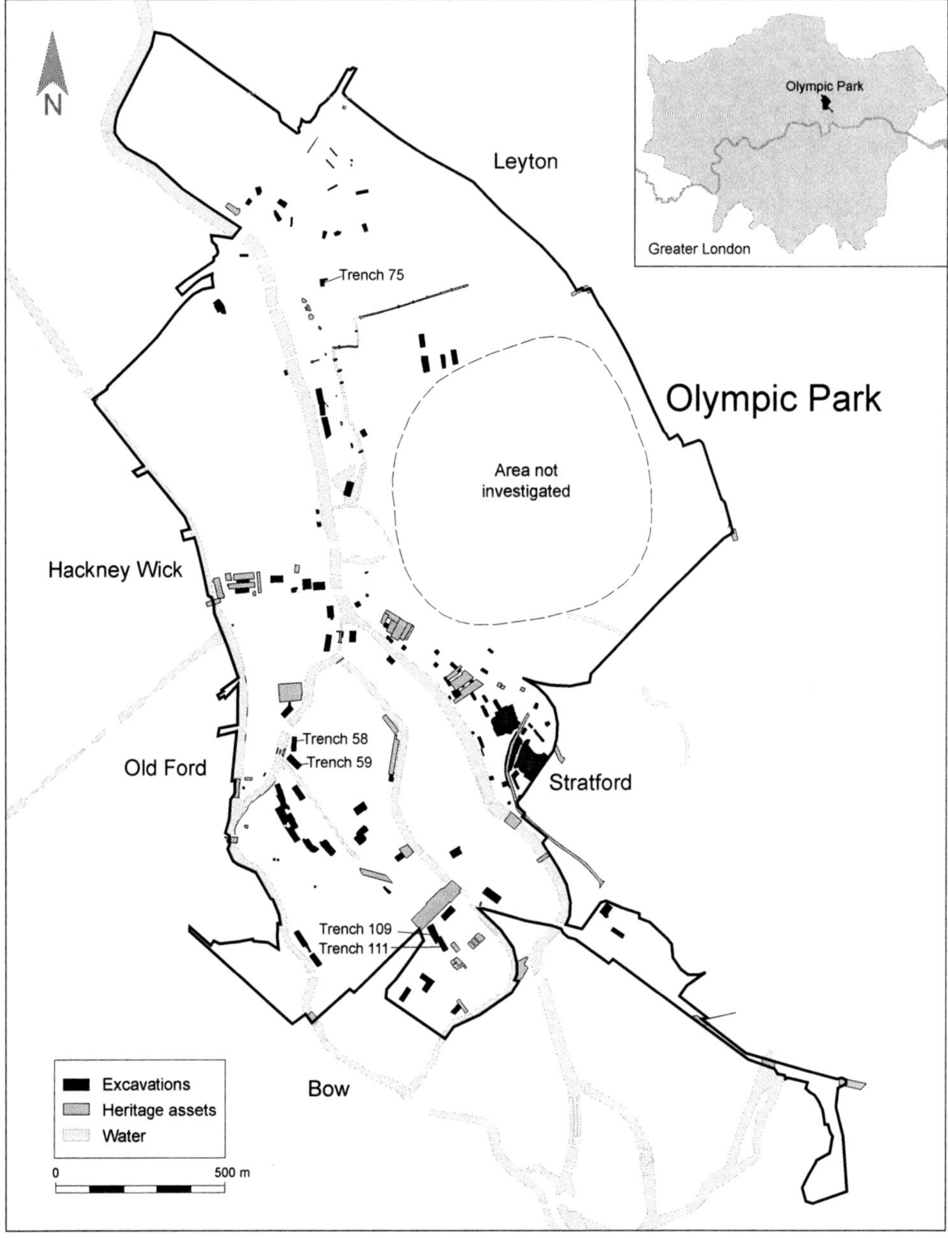

Figure 5.1 A plan of the excavations and the built heritage assets within the Olympic Park, and selected trenches mentioned in the text.

the twentieth century. However, other features of historic interest, many relating to East London's rich industrial heritage, had survived as standing structures, mostly at ground level, and these were subject to a wide-ranging programme of building recording. Some of these 'built heritage assets' were industrial buildings; others were infrastructure features associated with the railways, water and sewage works, the waterways and World War II defences.

Many of these built features form part of the lived experiences of the members of the present community – such as the World War II heavy anti-aircraft gun emplacement and radar station complex recorded south-east of Temple Mills, an echo of life during the London Blitz, or the Yardley of London soap, powder and perfume factory on Carpenters Road or the Clarnico sweet factory at King's Yard, where local residents were perhaps employed. It was to tap this potentially rich source of community history that the investigations included documentary workshops and an oral history project, involving people who have lived and worked in the area of the Olympic Park site.

A number of different organisations were involved in the Olympic Park investigations – AOC Archaeology Group, Eastside Community Heritage of Museum of London Archaeology, Pre-Construct Archaeology, RPS Planning and Development and Wessex Archaeology – bringing a wide range of specialist expertise.

Aspects of the past

For many centuries textile industries played an important part in the life of the Lower Lea Valley – with fulling mills, dyers, calico printers, lace makers, flock makers and silk weavers – and the many strands of evidence from the Olympic Park can be woven together to build up our understanding of the past. They cannot provide a complete picture – by the nature of the evidence this will always be work in progress building on previous research (for example, Museum of London 2000, 2003) and awaiting new opportunities for study – but each new thread adds detail to the fabric of history and, occasionally, brings into focus some unanticipated aspects of a lost way of life.

The past can be examined from many angles – in relation to the evolving landscape, the changing patterns of domestic life and working life, the nature of agriculture, industry and trade, and with respect to the wider social, political and economic forces that have shaped society over time. It can be presented, therefore, as more than just a chronological narrative. As far as the Olympic Park is concerned that is just as well since, despite concerted efforts, there remain large time gaps in what the investigations have been able to tell us about its past. This is not due to bad luck (at least not wholly). Given how deeply the valley's sediments were buried, the small total area of the Park that was excavated, and how little of its industrial heritage had survived decades of demolition and decay, it was no mean achievement for the investigations to have accumulated such a large body of data for analysis.

Moreover, the very location of the site, on the valley floor, has played a significant part in determining what was likely (and unlikely) to be found. In the early, prehistoric phase of human settlement, the Lower Lea Valley consisted of a mosaic of different dry-land and watery environments, offering a variety of resources to its inhabitants – areas of agricultural (possibly cultivable) land, riverside gravel terraces well suited for settlement, remnants of woodland and areas of marsh, as well as stretches of flowing river. It is perhaps no surprise, therefore, that evidence was found for the long-term and extensive use of the valley landscape for prehistoric settlement.

However, even by the end of the prehistoric period, increased flooding of this low-lying landscape was forcing permanent settlement onto the higher, drier ground along the valley sides, leaving the wet and marshy ground of the valley floor (and hence the site of the Olympic Park), which was suitable as summer pasture, and later for the siting of watermills, but for little else. So it remained, not significantly changed, until the nineteenth century, when, first, infrastructure developments – reservoirs, railways and sewers – were imposed on the landscape, and then industry spread rapidly out from the mill sites to cover much of the valley floor. For that reason, the prehistoric and modern periods are well represented in the archaeological record (the latter also in the built heritage record), but the Roman, Saxon, medieval and post-medieval periods are much more sparsely represented.

Nonetheless, evidence from across the Olympic Park has thrown unexpected light on different aspects of the past. The findings from a selection of the sites investigated are presented below, illustrating some of the interim issues raised by their excavation and the different themes that have emerged during the analysis stage.

The evolution of a river channel (Trench 118)

Interpreting the findings from the evaluation and subsequent mitigation excavation of Trench 118 proved to be one of the major challenges of the analysis stage. The trench, 830 m² at the top, was stepped down around all four sides to just 55 m² at the base, 7 m below ground level – the base requiring constant pumping to remove ground water. Even a cursory inspection of the deposits exposed in the sides of the trench revealed a complex sequence of deposition and erosion events, with interleaving layers of gravel, sand, peat, silt and clay (and combinations of these), cut through by the channels of an ancient waterway whose course, shifting over time, had eroded and redeposited earlier sediments, mixing the environmental and archaeological materials contained within them.

What made this trench of particular interest, however, was the recovery of a few small scraps of pottery, flint and animal bone, found near its base. The pottery consisted of three rim sherds from Early Neolithic (4,000–3,350 BC) bowls. The flints (11 pieces) were of potentially similar date but were less closely datable. Some of the bone – of cattle and red deer – could also be Neolithic, while other pieces – such as those from horses, a species not found in Britain at that date – indicate some mixing of material at this level. These finds appeared to derive from a layer overlying an early river channel, into the fills of which, furthermore, had been driven a number of timber stakes, some in a square arrangement. Together, these finds were potentially very significant – in fact the three sherds proved to be the only Neolithic pottery recovered from the whole of the Olympic Park.

Consequently, the trench was selected for further excavation. It was not possible to expand the area of excavation significantly, but the lowest deposits from among which this material had been recovered were subjected to much closer examination, with large soil samples being sieved on site in an attempt to recover further artefacts. This process was rewarded by the recovery of a complete flint axe, in near-perfect condition. The thin-butted axe, flaked on both sides but not ground or polished, is of a type with a date range of Early to Middle Neolithic (that is, fourth millennium BC), and it is therefore almost certainly contemporary with the pottery.

Objects such as this axe are unlikely to have been dropped accidentally, and reports of similar axes having been found along the River Lea, such as at Temple Mills just upriver (MoLAS 2000: 7 – NH1), as well as along the Thames (and more widely) (for example, Adkins and Jackson 1978), raises the possibility that this axe represents some form of deliberate, possibly votive offering with symbolic or religious significance. Establishing its precise location and context, and its relationship to the earlier finds, was therefore of particular importance.

However, despite an anecdotal account of the axe having been 'found deliberately buried on its side', the only excavation record of it referred to it coming from one of the soil samples sieved on site. It was because of the difficulties in recovering artefacts from the very wet site conditions that this sieving had been carried out, and the recovery of the axe certainly proved the effectiveness of the strategy; but it left open the question of the exact place, for instance in relation to any river channel and the other artefacts, from which the object had come.

Establishing the sequence of layers within the trench was made all the more important by the additional recovery (albeit in small quantities) of pottery of Late Bronze Age/Early Iron Age (1100–400 BC), Late Iron Age/early Roman (100 BC–AD 120/130), medieval (AD 1066–1500) and post-medieval (AD 1500–1800) date, as well as further timber stakes of possible prehistoric and historic date. Furthermore, a series of nine radiocarbon dates obtained from the deposits covered the Neolithic and the Bronze Age, and the Roman, Saxon and medieval periods. Trench 118 clearly had a long and complex story to tell.

The analysis of Trench 118 continues as this chapter is being written. Early interpretations of the stratigraphic sequence have been substantially revised in the light of detailed geoarchaeological, palaeoenvironmental, artefactual analysis and further radiocarbon dating. What emerges is the story of an evolving river channel, the earliest dating from the Late Glacial period (12000–9500 BC), and the latest from the medieval period, but which was exploited on many occasions in between.

It is perhaps fitting that the earliest (Neolithic) evidence of human activity associated with the river channel draws attention to aspects of community life that resonate through the valley's subsequent history. It combines what might be classed as domestic or settlement waste (pottery, flint-knapping debris and animal bone), a timber structure suggesting the exploitation of flowing water, and the deposition of an artefact (the flint axe), which would have had not only practical value, such as for woodland clearance, but also a symbolic significance.

Interestingly, this channel appears to become a 'lost' channel from early in the medieval period. Its location in the valley suggests that it could once have been the southward continuation of what is now Waterworks River, cut off by the river's westward diversion when the Bow to Stratford causeway was built across the valley in the early twelfth century. The channel would eventually have been infilled, and sealed (and hence concealed) below later sediments.

Prehistoric settlement and land use (Trench 9)

The value of the river's edge during the later phases of the prehistoric period was clearly demonstrated by the excavation of Trench 9 on the eastern side of Waterworks River. The evaluation trench revealed a dense array of ditches and pits, and curving gullies indicating the presence of roundhouses. Fortunately, the alluvial and made ground deposits sealing these features were relatively shallow, permitting a large area (4,800 m^2) to be opened up and subjected to full excavation. This revealed the nearly continuous use of this location over a period of up to 1,500 years.

In the Middle Bronze Age (1600–1100 BC) an extensive rectilinear field system was laid out on the east side of a former river channel. The field system was of a type widely established across the landscape in many parts of the country over a relatively short time at the start of this period, including elsewhere along the River Lea (Yates 2007, 30–1). Finds of pottery, flint, animal bone (cattle and sheep/goat) and charred cereal grains, indicating nearby settlement, were recovered from the ditches as well as from a number of pits. Although no settlement structures were found in Trench 9, the gully of a Middle Bronze Age roundhouse was uncovered in another trench, 130 m to the south.

The field system, perhaps laid out as much for social and political reasons – enclosing and laying claim to land – as for agricultural reasons, appears to have gone out of use by the Late Bronze Age (1100–700 BC), although continued activity on the site is indicated by a large number of pits, often clustered in groups. What these pits, which contained varying amounts of settlement debris, were used for is unclear, and no Late Bronze Age houses were uncovered, but the presence of two burials of cremated human remains, radiocarbon dated to around 1130–890 BC, suggests a wider range of activities close by.

While radiocarbon dating is able to provide relatively precise dates for organic materials (such as bone, charcoal and wood), much of the chronology is based on the typologies of finds, particularly pottery. A number of sherds of pottery from Trench 9 were sufficiently distinct in their forms and fabrics to allow them to be assigned either to the Middle Bronze Age, the Late Bronze Age, the Early Iron Age (700–400 BC) or the Middle Iron Age (400–100 BC). Much of the pottery from this and other trenches, however, consisted of small undiagnostic body sherds made from clay containing crushed flint (a pottery fabric used over a long period). This material could potentially date anywhere from the Late Bronze Age through the Middle Iron Age, and while it was possible, by careful stratigraphic analysis, to assign much of it with some confidence to a particular period, many of the small features on the site could still only be described as 'late prehistoric'.

It is hard to say, therefore, to what extent the late prehistoric activity on this site was continuous, or whether there were significant breaks – although the span of radiocarbon dates suggests that any breaks in activity were short-lived. What is clear, however, is that by the Middle Iron Age a small nucleated settlement had been established. Evidence for up to seven roundhouses was found, although not all were contemporary. The settlement was originally unenclosed, but a square ditched enclosure (approximately 30 m^2) was subsequently constructed, either around some of the houses or in place of them. The enclosure, possibly used eventually for the control of livestock grazing the valley floor, also went through a number of phases of modification.

Periods of flooding, indicated by spreads of alluvium over the house gullies and pits, may have led to a gradual shift of settlement eastwards onto drier ground, and certainly by the Late Iron Age (100 BC–AD 43) there was no evidence of settlement activity nearby. That the exploitation of the valley floor continued into the Roman period, however, is indicated by an early Roman (AD 43–120/130) ditch which wound its way around the edge of the silted-up (but evidently still visible) Iron Age enclosure.

The only other feature of known Late Iron Age/early Roman date was the burial of a woman aged around 35–40 years. In the absence of any datable grave goods, a sample of bone was submitted for radiocarbon dating, which produced a date (when calibrated) of 110 BC–AD 60 (SUERC-33678, 2020±30 BP). There were three other inhumation graves on this site, also without grave goods. Although samples of bone from each were also submitted for radiocarbon dating, these failed to produce results. To get one date was therefore fortunate, but it cannot be assumed that all the graves were even broadly contemporary, given the long duration of activity on this site.

The question of the Roman road

The assessment of potential for cultural heritage remains can be an imprecise undertaking. Only occasionally is it possible to predict with some degree of certainty where an archaeological feature is likely to be found. An illustration of this process is to be seen in relation to the investigation of the Roman road.

The Olympic Park lies just 5 km north-east of *Londinium*, the long-term capital of the Roman province of *Britannia*, and it spans the line of the Roman road to *Londinium* from the fort and former capital at *Camulodunum* (Colchester) to the east. Because the line of the road on the west side of the River Lea had been precisely established from a series of excavations, but less confidently located on the east side (Brown 2008), a number of evaluation trenches (Figure 5.1) were excavated across the full span of the road's various projected lines, in the hope of determining its exact course across the valley, and discovering where and by what means it crossed the river channels.

Despite these concerted efforts, however, no traces of the road, nor of any features likely to have been associated with it, such as the road-side ditches typical of Roman road construction, were identified within the Olympic Park.

The original topography of the valley, as revealed in the geoarchaeological deposit model, would have strongly influenced the river's course during prehistory. By the Roman period, however, the increased deposition of sediments, resulting from woodland clearance and cultivation within the river's catchment, would have started to lift the river out of its confining channels, enabling it, when in flood, to carve new, meandering and shifting courses across the floodplain.

While the Roman road may have crossed some of these channels via fords, perhaps reinforced by stones and gravel laid on the channel bed, the valley's increasingly marshy conditions could have made this type of crossing ill-suited to the heavy, military traffic that such a strategic road was originally designed to carry. It seems more likely that the road's crossing of the valley included lengths of causeway, as well as bridges and possibly raised timber walkways. Although Roman roads are renowned for being straight, showing little regard for the shape of the landscape they crossed, it is possible that the road negotiated a more irregular route across the valley, possibly linking areas of drier land; the route may even have changed over time as ground conditions varied.

It is also possible that the road has simply not survived to the present day, having been erased from the landscape by later activity (at least at the trench locations). The road at Old Ford does not appear to have been maintained after *c.* AD 400, although it was still used in the Saxon period, and in the medieval period the main river crossing was moved south to a causeway on the line of the present High Street, linking Bow and Stratford. Like many other stretches of abandoned Roman road across the country, the old Roman road across the Lea Valley may have simply been eroded away during the many centuries of post-Roman agricultural use, or obliterated by later industrial developments.

Whatever the case, the concerted, but in the end unsuccessful, attempt to solve a very specific (and what had probably been considered a relatively easily answered) archaeological question, is an object lesson in the unpredictability of archaeological investigation.

Mills and water management along Pudding Mill River

While the channels of the River Lea may have presented an obstacle for Roman road builders, they became vital to the local economy in the post-Roman period. The eight mills listed in the manor of West Ham in the *Domesday Book* (1086) had their origins in the Saxon period; there had been nine in 1066. These were tidal mills, powered by water that had flowed upriver on the incoming tide and was penned in the channels behind the mills, then released when the tide had ebbed sufficiently to create a head of water to power the undershot millwheels.

None of the watermill sites within the Olympic Park was subject to archaeological investigation, but features associated with the management of the water supply on which they relied for power were recorded in a number of trenches, as were features associated with another method of milling – with windmills. This is well illustrated by trenches along Pudding Mill River. This was the mill stream for 'two mills under one roof' at its southern end – at various times called Fotes Mill, St Thomas's Mill, Hart's Mill and Pudding Mills.

In addition to the watermills, there is documentary and cartographic evidence for four windmills along Pudding Mill River. These were post mills – for which there is evidence in Britain from the late twelfth century – in which the body of the mill containing all its machinery was mounted on a large vertical post. The windmill could be rotated to face into the wind, by pushing a tiller beam extending from its back. The post would be supported on two horizontal timber crosstrees, braced by angled quarter bars, either laid directly on or buried in the ground, or, to prevent rotting, on brick piers. Windmills were often owned by the watermills; unlike the watermills, which could only operate for short periods twice every day when the tide was ebbing, windmills could operate for much longer periods – so long as the wind was blowing.

A number of evaluation trenches were positioned close to the sites of the windmills on Pudding Mill River, but missed the structures themselves by just metres. In the case of one of the St Thomas's windmills, located on the east bank of the river just upstream from the watermills, features associated with the raised circular platform on which the windmill was constructed (as shown on early maps) were revealed in two adjacent trenches (Trenches 109 and 111), but the windmill site itself lay just between them.

At the north end of the river, also, the site of a windmill lay just between two other trenches (Trenches 58 and 59). Documentary evidence indicates that this windmill had originally been located on City Mill River, but was dismantled and re-erected at this site in 1807 (Farries 1981: 34). The windmill was associated with a cluster of mill buildings to its immediate south, labelled 'Nobshill Mill (Corn)' on the First Edition Ordnance Survey map of 1867–1868.

Nobshill Mill was located at the north end of a narrow strip of land, between the river to the west and a nineteenth-century drainage ditch that ran parallel to the river to the east. Although missing the windmill site, the excavation of Trench 58 revealed that this ditch followed the line of a much more substantial earlier channel, whose banks (almost as wide as the river itself) were defined, during one phase of use in the post-medieval period, by wattle revetments. The function of this earlier channel is unclear, but it may have had some early role in feeding the watermills at the southern end of Pudding Mill River.

The excavation of the adjacent trench (Trench 59) revealed a substantial timber revetment, and possible wharf, on the east bank of Pudding Mill River immediately adjacent to the Nobshill Mill buildings. Lying against this wharf was one of the most spectacular finds from the investigations, an abandoned clinker-built boat, possibly originally a ship's tender, later converted as a small pleasure craft and finally used as a gun punt for wildfowling on the sheltered waters of the lower River Lea and the Thames.

Temple Mills: an industrial community (Trench 75)

The boat at Nobshill Mill had been well preserved in the silts that accumulated in Pudding Mill River at a time that the watermills were going out of use. The mills were succeeded by new types of industry using new forms of power, whose rapid spread in the second half of the nineteenth century resulted in the large-scale industrialisation of the Lower Lea Valley, transforming the working and home lives of the local population. Part of this process can be seen in microcosm at Temple Mills, where a nine-metre deep excavation site, surrounded by a sheet-piled cofferdam, revealed domestic and industrial activity on the margins of a medieval/post-medieval mill site (Figure 5.2).

Figure 5.2 Excavations under way at Temple Mills (Trench 75); note the cobbled road.

Once owned by the Knights Templar (hence the mills' name) there had long been two mills ('under one roof') spanning the Shire Stream (later known as Waterworks River), as well as a windmill and other mills. In addition to grinding corn, Temple Mills had a long history of milling and manufacturing other products, such as oil and smalt (a pigment used to colour blue starch for washing linen). There had been a leather mill, a gunpowder mill (which blew up), a mill boring gun barrels (made of an alloy, Prince's metal, invented by Prince Rupert, grandson of James I), a cutter's mill (making pins), a logwood mill (boring logs for water pipes) and manufacturers of sheet lead, brass kettles and tin and latten plates, as well as calico printers and flock makers (Fairclough 1991; Victoria County History 1973).

As a result, a small industrial estate eventually developed on the land south of the original mills, which was investigated in Trench 75. A number of industrial features were recorded, including a brick building with an oven or furnace, and a timber-lined water channel, probably for turning an undershot mill wheel powering some form of machinery, or possibly bellows, within the building. Clay tobacco pipes from the channel point to this mill's operation in the early eighteenth century, but the mill appears to have been demolished later in the century to make way for further industrial buildings that operated during the nineteenth century.

This site was also home to some of the workers' families, who lived in a short terrace of six cottages, known as Temple Mill Cottages (later called White Hart Cottages after the local public house). The cottages, only the fronts of which were excavated, may have been built in the late eighteenth century, although they are first shown clearly on maps of the mid-nineteenth century. Finds from the cottages, recovered mainly from their drains, provide insight into the standards and way of life of the Victorian working population, with evidence for their diet, kitchen and table wares, and cottage-industry crafts, such as button making.

These cottages had been built in a largely rural setting, the character of which had been established many centuries earlier. However, over the course of their occupation, their inhabitants would have witnessed the transformation of that landscape and the rapid encroachment up the valley of dirty and dangerous industries. The cottages lasted through the nineteenth century, although by the turn of the century some of the adjacent workshops had been demolished when a new road, surfaced with granite cobblestones, was laid down through the site. This road provided access to a series of new businesses further to the south, such as artificial manure works and a piggery. An aerial photograph taken at the end of World War II appears to show the cottages as derelict, their walls still standing but their roofs gone.

An Olympic and Paralympic legacy

The investigations within the Olympic Park have uncovered a story of repeated transformation of the landscape since the end of the last Ice Age approximately 12,000 years ago. Evidence for early prehistoric activity is fairly sparse but a glimpse of life during the Neolithic period has been uncovered, establishing a pattern of human interaction with the landscape that has continued up to the present.

By the Middle Bronze Age we find evidence for relatively small-scale settlements that exploited the varied resources of the valley bottom. These settlements changed and adapted to the increased flooding from the later Bronze Age onwards.

The Roman invasion of Britain in AD 43 had a major impact and brought innovations in almost every aspect of life (for example, technology, governance, food, dress, burial customs and religion). Despite the impact of the Romans in *Londinium*, and around the Olympic Park (for example, such settlements as Old Ford), surprisingly little evidence was found during the excavations.

Although historical records tell us about the role of the Olympic Park site in the political changes of the Saxon period, in the economic life of the medieval church and in the development of post-medieval industry, the centuries following the end of the Roman occupation in AD 410 also provided limited archaeological evidence for these periods. It was only in the nineteenth century that substantial changes were again being made to the landscape with the development of infrastructure (railways, roads and waterways) and the valley's rapid industrialisation. Part of this process was revealed by the excavation of a small industrial complex at Temple Mills. Here archaeology and documentary research revealed evidence for everyday life in the late eighteenth to early twentieth centuries.

Compared to many areas of the Olympic Park at the start of the twentieth century, there remained around Temple Mills islands of open and accessible space, such as allotment gardens to the east, and football grounds, belonging to a local public house, to the north. These areas, as well as Hackney Marsh to the north, acquired by London County Council as an open space in 1893, would have provided recreational facilities for the local community and offered some respite from the routines of industrial life.

In the early 1930s the football grounds became the Eton Manor Sports Ground, with football, rugby and cricket pitches; tennis, squash and netball courts; and a bowling green. There was also a running track, which was eventually relaid (under the supervision of gaffers Dicky and Dodger) with material from the athletics track at the stadium at Wembley used during the 1948 London Games (Lewis 2010, 8–10). The sports ground became derelict in 2001, but new sporting facilities have been built at Eton Manor for the London 2012 Olympic and Paralympic Games. These facilities, which will be the venue for the Wheelchair Tennis tournament, will become part of the legacy of the Olympic Park's rich heritage.

Acknowledgements

The Olympic Delivery Authority funded the excavations and post-excavation analysis. Dermot Doherty (ODA), Russell Pottrill and Janet Miller (Atkins) are thanked for their support and advice during the project. Julie Gardiner (Wessex Archaeology), Simon Knowles (ODA) and Vassil Girginov provided helpful comments on an earlier draft of this article. The illustration in Figure 5.1 was drawn by Ken Lymer (Wessex Archaeology).

References

Adkins, R. and Jackson, R. (1978) *Neolithic Stone and Flint Axes from the River Thames*, London: British Museum Occasional Paper.

Brown, G. (2008) 'Archaeological evidence for the Roman London to Colchester road between Aldgate and Harold Hill', in J. Clark, J. Cotton, J. Hall, R. Sherris and H. Swain, *Londonium and Beyond: essays on Roman London and its hinterland for Harvey Sheldon*, York: Council for British Archaeology Research Report 156, 82–89.

Fairclough, K. R. (1991) 'Temple Mills as an industrial site in the seventeenth century', *Essex Archaeology and History* 22: 115–21.

Farries, K. (1981) *Essex Windmills, Millers and Millwrights, Volume 4: a review of parishes, F–R*, London: Charles Skilton.

Lewis, J. (2010) *From Eton Manor to the Olympics: more Lea Valley secrets revealed*, Farringdon: Libri Publishing.

Museum of London Archaeology Service (2003) *A Research Framework for London* (2000) *The Archaeology of Greater London: an assessment of archaeological evidence for human presence in the area now covered by Greater London*, London: MoLAS.

Museum of London Archaeology Service (2003) *A Research Framework for London Archaeology 2002*, London: MoLAS.

Olympic Delivery Authority (2007) *Olympic, Paralympic and Legacy Transformation Planning Applications: environmental statement for the Olympic Park in Hackney, Newham, Tower Hamlets and Waltham Forest*, London: ODA.

Victoria County History (1973) 'Leyton: economic history, marshes and forests', in W. R. Powell (ed.) *A History of the County of Essex: volume 6*, 197–205. Online: www.british-history.ac.uk/report.aspx?compid=42769 (accessed 7 September 2011).

Wessex Archaeology (2011) 'Olympic Park phase 3b: geoarchaeological assessment and analysis report', Salisbury: unpublished Wessex Archaeology report.

Yates, D. T. (2007) *Land Power and Prestige: Bronze Age field systems in southern Britain*, Oxford: Oxbow.

6

THE OLYMPIC LAWS AND THE CONTRADICTIONS OF PROMOTING AND PRESERVING THE OLYMPIC IDEAL

Mark James and Guy Osborn

Introduction

Since the Sydney 2000 Games, each edition of the Olympics has produced a raft of legislative measures that have impacted upon the event, and on the Olympic experience, in a number of ways. This creation of new law is unsurprising, being an unavoidable aspect of winning the right to host the Olympic Games, although its extent and applicability has often proved to be contentious (James and Osborn, 2011b; Scassa, 2010). It is a requirement of the Host City Contract that legislation is introduced to provide specific protection for the commercial rights associated with the Olympic Movement (Department of Culture, Media and Sport, 2011d: 2), and in the UK this legislation, the London Olympic and Paralympic Games Act 2006 (LOPGA, 2006), has been the means by which the body responsible for developing the necessary sporting, transport and security infrastructure, the Olympic Delivery Authority (ODA), was created and its powers defined. Despite the necessity of such legislative provisions, and their often controversial nature, these Olympic laws remain a field of Olympic studies that, with some notable exceptions, has rarely been subjected to academic analysis (James and Osborn, 2010, 2011b; Maestre, 2010).

In this chapter, the Acts of the UK Parliament that deal specifically with Olympic issues will be examined. In conducting this analysis, the focus will be on the London Olympic Games and Paralympic Games (Advertising and Trading) (England) Regulations 2011 (the Regulations), their impact on businesses in the vicinity of London 2012's Olympic venues and upon the public in general, and the consistency of these laws with the fundamental principles of Olympism, and, more broadly, the Olympic values (see, for example, Tavares, 2006). The analysis will demonstrate that the UK's Olympic laws go beyond what is necessary for the protection of the Olympic brand and the smooth running of the Games and will have a disproportionate and negative impact on anyone who is not considered to be a member of the Olympic family.

The legislative context

There are two Acts of Parliament that constitute the UK's statutory contribution to the ever-expanding body of what can be termed Olympic laws: the aforementioned LOPGA 2006 and the earlier Olympic Symbols etc. (Protection) Act 1995 (OSPA, 1995). Of these, the former is by far the more important as it provides the legal framework within which the London 2012

Games will take place, and because it is this Act that is supplemented by the Regulations that constitute the focus of this chapter. The latter, however, is clear evidence of the contested nature of Olympic laws. In contrast to the World Intellectual Property Organisation's Nairobi Treaty on the Protection of the Olympic Symbol 1981, OSPA 1995 creates the Olympic Association Right, which grants exclusive use of the Olympic symbols in the UK to the British Olympic Association, as opposed to the International Olympic Committee (IOC) as per the Treaty. Further, there are only 49 contracting parties to the Nairobi Treaty out of the 205 national members of the Olympic Movement. Thus, it is not universally accepted that the additional protections sought by the IOC are either necessary or desirable.

In order to facilitate the building of the necessary infrastructure and to provide further and more explicit protections for the commercial rights associated with staging the Games, LOPGA 2006 was passed by the UK Parliament and came into force on 30 March 2006. In its preliminary assessment of the legislation, published five years after the Act came into force, the Department for Culture, Media and Sport (DCMS) stated that the main measures of the Act were, *inter alia*, to provide for:

> The establishment of the ODA, its powers, duties and functions;
> The delivery of transport needs for the Games, including the necessary preparations in the lead up to 2012;
> Controls of marketing in connection with the Olympic and Paralympic Games, including the protection of intellectual property, restrictions on commercial association with the Games, the regulation of outdoor trading and advertising in the vicinity of Games venues and the prohibition of ticket touting in connection with Games events.
>
> *(Department of Culture, Media and Sport, 2011b: 1–2)*

The majority of the Act is devoted to the first of these issues. The ODA was created as a statutory company whose aims are to coordinate the building of the necessary venues and accommodation, upgrade the transport network and ensure the security of the attending athletes, officials, spectators and media representatives. It has been involved at every stage of the process, from purchasing the necessary land and applying for associated planning permissions to building and testing the venues prior to delivery. Alongside this, the ODA has prepared the Olympic Transport and Security Plans, to ensure that London's transport network can cope with the influx of people into the city and move them around London safely and efficiently. Most of the ODA's powers in respect of the development of the infrastructure of the London 2012 Games can be seen as a necessary, if not always uncontroversial, element of hosting a global mega-event. These have included dealing with the compulsory purchase of land for the Olympic Park and other event venues and the disposal of the Olympic Stadium post-Games, in conjunction with the Olympic Park Legacy Company, both of which have proved problematic and contentious (see Chapter 2).

In addition to these powers, the ODA is also involved with the regulation of street trading and the enforcement of new event-specific anti-ambush marketing laws in the vicinity of Olympic venues. It is these laws and their associated powers of enforcement that will have the greatest impact on local businesses operating near Olympic venues and on members of the public who are not directly associated with the Olympic family (this concept embracing athletes, international sports federations and Olympic organising committees, as well as, more tenuously, broadcasters and sponsors), and that are likely to produce the most visible applications of the Olympic legislation.

The Host City Contract incorporates the guarantees that must be provided to the IOC in order to host the Games (see Stuart and Scassa, 2011). In the 2012 Candidature Questionnaire, these guarantees include a requirement that the word mark '[City] 2012' (i.e. London 2012) is protected in the host territory and that all necessary measures be taken to protect the Olympic properties. These are defined in the Olympic Charter and include the Olympic symbol (R.8), the Olympic flag (R.9), the Olympic motto (R.10), the Olympic emblems (R.11), the Olympic Anthem (R.12) and the Olympic flame and torches (R.13). The Charter specifies in R.7.1.2 that:

> The Olympic Games are the exclusive property of the IOC which owns all rights and data relating thereto, in particular, and without limitation, all rights relating to their organisation, exploitation, broadcasting, recording, representation, reproduction, access and dissemination in any form and by any means or mechanism whatsoever, whether now existing or developed in the future.
>
> *(International Olympic Committee, 2011: 20)*

Thus, legislation must be introduced by a host city to reduce the possibility of ambush marketing (on ambush marketing: Hoek and Glendall, 2000; Michalos, 2006; Cran and Griffiths, 2010) and to sanction those who engage in advertising campaigns that undermine the position of the official partners. In particular, this includes controlling advertising and air space around Olympic venues and designated transport hubs during the Olympic and Paralympic Games periods (James and Osborn, 2011b) and the regulation of street trading in the vicinity of Olympic venues.

These various obligations are discharged by sections 19 to 29 of LOPGA 2006. Sections 19 and 25 of the Act require the Secretary of State for Culture, Media and Sport to produce Regulations restricting advertising and street trading around Olympic venues respectively and make their breach a criminal offence punishable by a fine under sections 21 and 27. These Regulations provide the detail missing from the Act and will define the activities that constitute unlawful ambush marketing and trading. The first draft of these Regulations went out to consultation in March 2011 (Department for Culture, Media and Sport, 2011a) with DCMS reporting back on the submissions in October 2011 (Department of Culture, Media and Sport, 2011c). The Regulations were published conterminously and became law once they received the approval of both Houses of Parliament, a procedure that is a procedural formality rather than an opportunity to renegotiate the content.

An analysis of these Regulations provides the opportunity to examine the relationship between these Olympic laws and the fundamental principles of Olympism. In framing this analysis it is important to understand the underlying issues and context within which these Regulations, and indeed all the Olympic laws, operate. Essentially, there is a tension at the heart of these provisions between protecting the commercial rights vested in the Olympic Games to an extent that enables LOCOG to raise sufficient funds to stage London 2012, and the impact that these protections will have on society as a whole and local businesses in particular (James and Osborn, 2011a, 2011b). The balance is often a difficult one. The first iteration of the proposed Regulations (Department for Culture, Media and Sport, 2011a) appeared to tip the balance too far in favour of the official sponsors and failed to take into account the nature and extent of the symbiotic relationship that has to exist between LOCOG and local businesses if a successful Games is to be staged. The final version was altered as a result of some of the submissions to the Consultation, with DCMS noting that 'The responses have been extremely helpful and have informed the shape of the regulations ... DCMS has made some changes to the regulations as a result of these comments' (Department for Culture, Media and Sport, 2011c: 4). Whether the Regulations have adequately ameliorated the problems identified will be analysed below.

The legislation in practice: a case study of the London Olympic Games and Paralympic Games (Advertising and Trading) (England) Regulations 2011

In October 2011, following consideration of the responses to the Consultation on the original draft Regulations, the plans for regulating advertising and trading in open spaces at the London 2012 Olympic Games were published. The Regulations will take precedence over any existing provisions concerning advertising and street trading in the restricted event zones (Department for Culture, Media and Sport, 2011a) and have as their underlying justifications the need to ensure a consistent celebratory look, prevent ambush marketing and to ensure that people have easy and unencumbered access to Olympic venues (Department for Culture, Media and Sport, 2011a: 4).

To ensure that the Olympic venues are free from advertising and to prevent ambush marketing campaigns from undermining the value of the official sponsors' investments, the Regulations prevent all unauthorised advertising activities in designated event zones. All event zones are defined on maps alongside their times of operation in order to ensure the minimum amount of disruption for the minimum amount of time. All forms of advertising are covered by Regulation 5, which ensures that any display of an advert or logo, or the distribution of any promotional material by any means, is a criminal offence unless authorised. A very limited number of activities are exempted from this absolute prohibition.

Regulation 7 allows demonstrations in support of a cause or belief, so a campaign against a rival to one of the official sponsors accusing them of using sweatshops or acting in an environmentally unsustainable way would be lawful. Regulation 8 exempts individuals who are using personal property in the normal manner. This means that wearing branded clothing or viewing adverts on a mobile communication device is not now unlawful unless it is part of a concerted or organised ambush marketing campaign; spectators can all turn up in the same top unless it has been provided by the advertiser or worn as part of an orchestrated ambush. Advertising on taxis and buses is also exempt, despite the massive potential for ambush by buying up space on these iconic London vehicles; preventing this kind of advertising was considered by DCMS to be unreasonable, despite the acknowledged risk, because it would be too difficult to enforce.

Where street trading is concerned, all existing licences will be suspended and permission to trade in event zones during the restricted periods must be sought from the ODA. A criminal offence is committed by anyone trading without the relevant licence. The exemptions to this offence are even more limited and include the sale of newspapers, deliveries of groceries and fast food and allowing shops, restaurants, bars and pubs to trade outside their premises without fear of prosecution.

Whereas there is a clear reason for, if not a convincing justification of, the need for restrictions on advertising in the Regulations, the reasons for regulating street traders is much less clear in the absence of specific and identifiable health and safety issues. The lack of explanation for why this part of the Regulations has been introduced, apart from coercion by the IOC, could lead to difficulties in enforcement due to challenges from existing licensed traders who claim a legitimate expectation that they will be able to ply their trade during the Olympic and Paralympic Games.

During discussions relating to minor technical amendments to the 2006 Act, concerns were raised regarding the impact of the Olympic legislation as a whole. In response to the concerns of Mark Field, MP for the Cities of London and Westminster, that there was a danger of the Olympic Park becoming 'a state within a state' and in answer to the suggestion that the draconian measures were effectively a sop to the commercial interests involved in delivering the Games, Hugh Robertson, Minister for Sport and the Olympics, argued that the Regulations were no more draconian than those that had been in place at previous Games, and that he was personally very comfortable with them. By promising legislation of this scope, more than £700 million had been raised through commercial sponsors and he noted further that he considered the regulatory framework to be fairly standard:

> Such regulations are not a particularly Olympic phenomenon. Exactly the same things happen at almost every other major sports event, including a host of events that we are trying to attract to this country. They happen at cricket world cups, and I am pretty sure that they happen even at highly commercial events such as the Indian premier league. Exactly the same regulations apply at football World cups. They are standard, and they are in place to protect the vast amounts of sponsorship income for such events.
>
> *(House of Commons, 2011: 4)*

Not only is this a moot point, but the fact that such restrictions are commonplace does not make them appropriate. Further, in the Committee Stage Report several members made clear their concerns about the scope of the Regulations by stating that they would need to be applied sensibly and proportionally and that there should be 'light touch' enforcement (House of Commons, 2011). The efficacy of the enforcement regime will be key to the impact of the Regulations but cannot, of course, be tested until implemented at the Games themselves.

The breadth of the Regulations is justified on the three grounds noted previously: to protect the corporate look and feel of the cities dressed for the Games; to prevent ambush marketing of official sponsors (by others); and to provide clear and unencumbered access to the Olympic venues. However, the Regulations themselves are a blunt instrument with the potential to prevent any suggestion of an association with the Games that has not been officially sanctioned by LOCOG, whether or not the three justifications are engaged by the offending conduct. This, in turn, gives rise to a number of specific problems.

Who is caught by the Regulations?

Anyone who is anywhere within one of the event zones during an event period is covered by the Regulations and must abide by the restrictions on advertising and trading. Despite their very wide-ranging application, the need for, and scope of, these restrictions is not clearly articulated anywhere. The restrictions on advertising are to ensure clean, advertisement-free stadia and to prevent ambush marketing of the official sponsors. They are supplemented by the conditions included on all Olympic tickets that prevent spectators from bringing food, drink and other items into the venues, as this could be a way to orchestrate ambush marketing campaigns (London 2012, 2011: 19.2.3). There is, however, no legitimate justification for why the state, as opposed to LOCOG, the IOC or their partners, should carry the financial and investigatory burden of protecting these valuable commercial rights, beyond it being a specific requirement of the Host City Contract. It is highly unlikely that the same protections would be granted if any other body – for example, a pharmaceutical company – had demanded it for its products or intellectual property rights.

Further, the focus of these Regulations appears to be as much on individual members of the public and small businesses as on concerted ambush marketing campaigns run by major multinational corporations. In the first draft, the Regulations even caught those members of the public wearing branded goods in an event zone, however, it appears that DCMS took heed of these potential problems:

> We accept that there is a risk of individuals unintentionally breaching the regulations by simply going about their normal daily activities; such as viewing the internet on a Smartphone or carrying personal items with visible branding. This clearly is not the policy intent of the regulations. It is helpful to have these specific examples raised and we have amended the regulations to ensure these activities are permitted. We will also make additional changes to prohibit advertising on the human body.
>
> *(Department for Culture, Media and Sport, 2011c: para.18)*

As a result, visitors to the event zones can now wear and carry branded goods and view advertisements on mobile communications devices provided that they are not part of a deliberate ambush marketing campaign, as reinforced by the terms and conditions of Olympic tickets (London 2012, 2011: 19.2.3). Thus, unless a company provides an individual with branded items to wear or otherwise display their logos, as was the case with the 'Bavaria Girls' at the 2010 FIFA World Cup (James and Osborn, 2011b: 425), no offence will be committed.

In respect of the restrictions on trading in open spaces, as opposed to shops, the aims of the Regulations could just as easily, and much more effectively, be achieved by placing temporary conditions on existing licences rather than creating what might be seen as a 'super law' to regulate this. Further, there is no explanation of how or why street traders would act in a manner that offends the three justifications put forward for the creation of these Regulations.

The exempted categories of traders are both understandable and reasonable, and in line with the advance notice (Olympic Delivery Authority, 2009: 21); this should allow many businesses to continue to trade as normal. Regulation 14 exempts all sales and deliveries to premises adjoining the road, extending the original proposal from milk deliveries to, for example, all grocery and fast food deliveries. The sale of newspapers on the street, the provision of public toilets and telephone kiosks and the use of land by restaurants, bars and pubs to serve clients are also exempted under Regulation 14. This should ensure that as many local businesses as possible are able to trade as normal without being caught by the Regulations. The exemptions do not cover existing licensed street traders, only permanent businesses, deliveries and newspaper vendors. All other traders will have their licences suspended for the relevant event periods and will have to reapply in order to operate during these times.

A further, more esoteric, example can be provided by the impact on fishing in Weymouth and Portland bays, the event zone for both the Olympic and Paralympic sailing events. It is unclear from the Regulations whether the prohibition on the use of the sea for trading includes preventing fishing in the bays during the event periods. As the bays have one of the longest restriction periods – from 28 July to 12 August for the Olympic sailing competitions and 31 August to 7 September for the Paralympic events – it appears that all use of this part of the sea will be restricted during event times, which would prevent fishing boats from operating off Weymouth and Portland. At present, there is no mechanism for compensation in such circumstances, despite the potentially substantial impact on specific local businesses if such a ban is imposed. Finally, the Response noted that a number of changes to the event zones had taken place during the Consultation:

> Generally, map changes have been made to help ensure spectators have a positive experience during the Games. We have extended some zones to capture coach drop off points and provide clear walking routes from public transport hubs as well as taking into account high rises where there is a risk of ambush marketing.
>
> *(Department for Culture, Media and Sport, 2011c: 12)*

The impact of this change, and the extent of this specific event zone can be seen in Figure 6.1.

It is clear that the event zone has expanded during the consultation process to deal with possible infractions. As can be seen, the area covered is large, and many areas that would have afforded a free view of the event are covered. If we see this in terms of the 'positive experience' of the Olympic Games, in this case it appears to relate to the enjoyment of the 'look and feel' of the Olympic event zones, and it can be argued that this has gone too far. In general, the event zones have been extended in some cases to ensure that users of public transport will not be ambushed at stations and interchanges and that high-rise buildings just outside a zone will not be draped in advertisements for official sponsors' rivals. At Weymouth for example, the event zone has been extended to the top of the ridge on the sea front at Fortuneswell to ensure that potential ambushers do not utilise the high ground above the shoreline for their campaigns (see Figure 6.1).

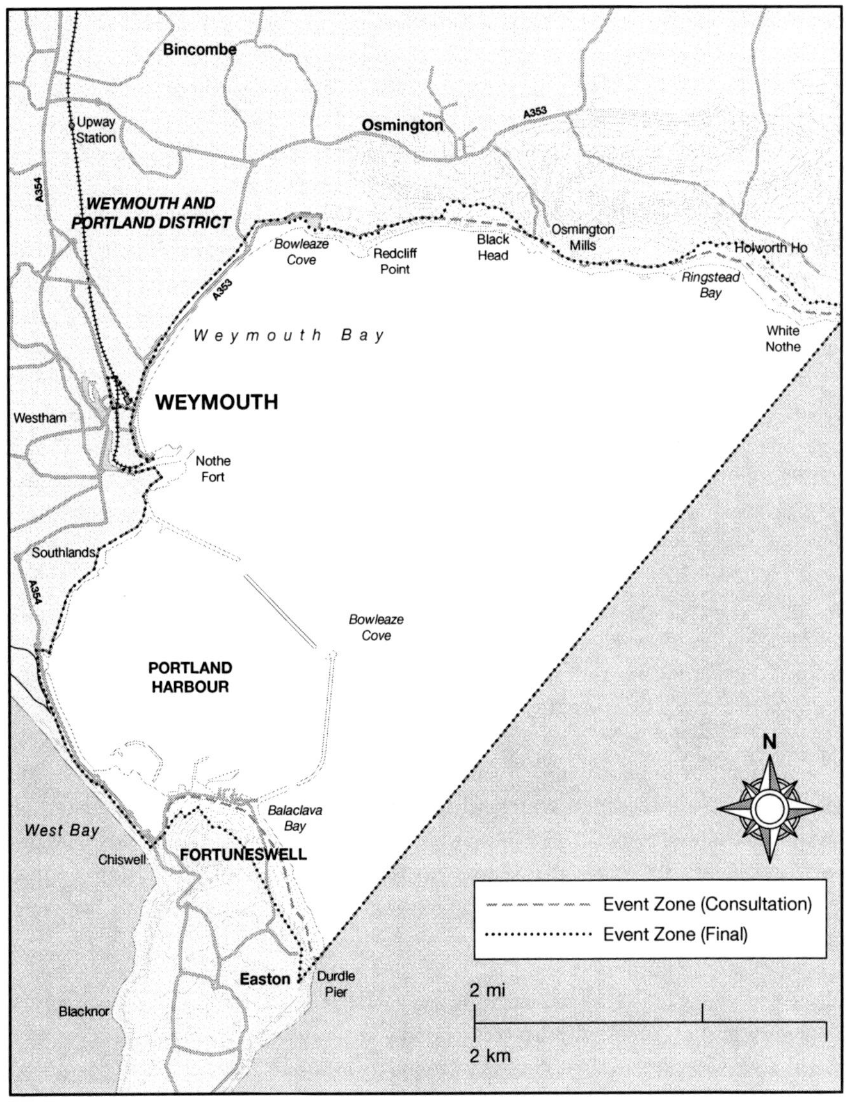

Figure 6.1 Weymouth and Portland map.

Do existing licence holders and traders have a legitimate expectation that their businesses will be allowed to operate as usual?

The impact on the earning potential of traders covered by the Regulations could be substantial. This is likely to be the busiest period of their working lives, yet traders are being restricted, if not prohibited, from exploiting their prospective good fortune. Their legitimate expectation is that they will be allowed to trade and any restriction that cannot be justified objectively on a sound evidential basis runs the risk of being struck down as being unreasonable and disproportionate. Further, any Regulations that cannot be proved to be necessary and capable of achieving their aims will also run the risk of being struck down. In their current form, it is difficult to see how these Regulations will bring about the desired ends, as there is no apparent link between the stated justifications for their introduction and their application to these categories of trader. In reality, the only justification for these restrictions is that the IOC demands them. As Parliament has been left to determine the appropriate means of discharging its obligation to the IOC, then a less restrictive alternative, such as a temporary variation of the licence conditions, could be seen as a legally preferable response.

Will the Regulations ensure that traders engage with the 'look and feel' of the city?

The impact of the Regulations on local businesses is potentially severe and their extent is still not fully justified. For example, it is unclear why such extensive restrictions, accompanied by criminal sanctions for failure to comply, are necessary to facilitate the aim of *dressing* the Olympic and Paralympic event zones. The rationale behind the Regulations appears to be based on a reaction to what occurred at Atlanta 1996, where many official street vendors operated in breach of the terms of their licences, acting in a manner that was said to have ruined the Olympic experience for visitors to the Games:

> [Atlanta] was characterized as a trade fair, flea market, product exhibition center, shopping mall, temple of consumerism, streets full of junk, state fair, tacky, cheap, a superstore, supermarket, oriental bazaar, with pushy vendors and naked hucksterism. Such an atmosphere of profiteering was said to be an 'attack on the Olympic spirit' and the 'rape' of the Games.
>
> *(Rivenburgh, 2008: 479)*

Despite this precedent, neither the IOC nor the British government has provided any evidence to suggest that existing licensed traders operating in the vicinity of London 2012 venues will act in a similar manner, or will otherwise act in breach of their licences by trading unlawfully, as opposed to embracing the festivities. The imposition of temporary conditions on existing licences requiring adherence to the 'look and feel' scheme, and a ban on all new licences, would achieve the same aim in a much less intrusive way whilst maintaining traders' legitimate expectation that they will be able to share in the social and commercial benefits of London 2012.

There is a further and very different argument against this coercive approach to controlling the 'celebratory look' of the areas around Olympic and Paralympic venues. Discussing Vancouver during the 2010 Winter Games, Boykoff (2011: 41) noted that the area around the venues 'felt like entering some sort of immaculate repression zone'. When dressing the cities, care must be taken to ensure that the character of the areas in which events take place is not lost completely in creating a homogenised corporate look and feel. If there is genuine concern over the engagement of local businesses in the 'Look and Feel' programme, then encouraging participation, perhaps on the grounds that it will improve business, rather than threatening non-participation with criminal sanctions may be a more constructive and less restrictive approach.

Are the Regulations capable of restricting campaigns of ambush marketing?

Ambush marketing has become a growing problem for commercial rights holders since exclusive sponsorship arrangements have become the norm at major sporting events and brands that are not associated with the official partnership programme seek to gain some advertising capital in increasingly innovative ways. Ambush marketing is generally defined as the creation of a brand owner's unauthorised association with an event in order to exploit for commercial advantage the goodwill associated with it. In most discussions of the technique, it is taken to be one major company deliberately attempting to subvert the exclusive sponsorship arrangements of a commercial rival with the event organiser (Hoek and Glendall, 2000; Johnson, 2008; Lawrence, Taylor and Weingarten, 2008).

In Regulation 5, however, an ambush marketing campaign is defined so broadly as to include one act, or a series of acts, intended specifically to advertise a good or service and/or a person or company that provides a good or service in an event zone during an event period. A local pub, bar, restaurant or hotel trying to attract passing trade by advertising Games-related offers will be considered to be acting just as unlawfully as an official sponsor's commercial rival deliberately engaging in an ambush marketing campaign. This all-encompassing definition, which does not require the advertiser to claim an unauthorised association with the Games but simply to advertise without permission, has become the accepted standard of protection around Olympic and Paralympic venues (VANOC, 2006).

Where London 2012 is concerned, it is at present unclear against which category of 'ambusher' these Regulations will be enforced. The published guidance is of a similar nature to that issued by previous mega-event organisers and focuses on the use of protected words, phrases and symbols by local businesses rather than acting as a briefing note aimed at multinational companies (London Organising Committee of the Olympic and Paralympic Games, 2010). In respect of deliberate and premeditated campaigns to undermine the official sponsorship programme, the Regulations ensure that LOCOG will be able to protect the goodwill associated with London 2012 in particular and the Olympic Movement in general. However, concerns remain about how these Regulations will be enforced on the ground against local businesses during the Games period.

It is important that LOCOG and the ODA engage with local businesses to ensure that an appropriate balance is reached, protecting the commercial interests of the Games and its sponsors on the one hand, but enabling local businesses to share in the benefits of hosting the Olympic and Paralympic Games on the other. London 2012 is not a gift from LOCOG to local businesses that can be withdrawn on a whim. There is an inadequately recognised symbiotic relationship between these traders and the success of the Games that should be fostered appropriately. If the definition is intended to be so wide and is enforced in a manner that prevents local businesses from encouraging passersby to use their facilities, then the good will of local traders and the experience of visitors to London 2012 could be seriously affected.

Local businesses and street traders may well be attempting to exploit their good fortune at being able to operate in close proximity to the venues, but they are not engaging in ambush marketing as it is commonly understood. As is it highly unlikely that street traders will, individually or collectively, advertise a brand rivalling one of the official sponsors, it appears that the Regulations are indeed aimed at restricting the ability of these businesses to encourage visitors to buy their goods or use their services (London Organising Committee of the Olympic and Paralympic Games, 2010: 32–33). Further, the criminalisation of such promotional activity sits uncomfortably with the exception granted to advertising on taxis and buses during the Games period, despite the acknowledged risk of such an ambush occurring in this way (Department for Culture, Media and Sport, 2011c: para.19). Whereas street traders and local businesses will be acting criminally by advertising their own deals, a genuine ambush marketing campaign can be run lawfully by a competitor of one of the members of the Olympic Partnership programme simply by buying up space on London buses and taxis.

In attempting to restrict instances of ambush marketing, the underlying aim of the Regulations is entirely legitimate; however, given their potential for targeting local businesses and street traders, they appear to be disproportionately restrictive and lacking any proven need. Although local businesses will undoubtedly be attempting to maximise their profits during the Games period, it is difficult to see how their promotional activities are ambush marketing of the kind that impacts negatively on the goodwill of the Olympic Movement or the value of its exclusive sponsorship agreements. Likewise, street traders are extremely unlikely to engage in ambush marketing of any kind that could impact on the official sponsors, as opposed to acting in breach of their licensing conditions or failing to adhere to the look and feel of event zones.

Are the Regulations capable of improving the safety of visitors to London 2012?

The final justification for the restrictions on street trading is to ensure visitors have easy and unencumbered access to Olympic and Paralympic venues. Again, the reasoning underpinning this justification is weak and less restrictive alternatives would be at least as effective as the removal of licences from existing traders and criminalising their attempts to operate as normal.

The proposed restrictions will apply to existing stadia that will be hosting the events in the same way that they apply to those newly constructed for London 2012. One implication of this is that spectators at Olympic and Paralympic events are in need of greater protection than cricket fans attending Lords, or tennis fans going to Wimbledon, as they will be incapable of running the gauntlet of local street traders. Another implication is that there is something wrong with the existing licensing regime, and that it allows an unsafe number of street traders to operate in the vicinity of these venues when sporting events currently take place at them. Whichever viewpoint is taken, it seems that the cancellation of all existing licences and the requirement that anyone seeking to trade during the event period apply for a separate licence is a disproportionate means of guaranteeing safe entry to and exit from these venues; there is neither proof that existing traders are causing access problems at the moment, nor that they will change their behaviour leading to such danger during the Games period.

Where the new venues are concerned no licences to operate in the Olympic Park have yet been created; therefore, the regime proposed could be seen as appropriate for these short-term licences. For converted venues, such as Horse Guards Parade, or for the events using public highways, including the road cycling, marathon and triathlon, where there may be genuine bottlenecks or where congestion may occur on specific event days, the temporary suspension of all existing licences or the use of trading exclusion zones is more justifiable. But generally, as with the previous justifications, it appears that the claim that the new licensing regime will promote the health and safety of visitors to the venues appears to be at best lacking a proper evidential basis or appropriate risk analysis and at worst a means of raising revenue by making existing traders reapply for the right to do something they are already licensed for.

Conclusion

The London Olympic Games and Paralympic Games Act 2006 and the accompanying London Olympic Games and Paralympic Games (Advertising and Trading) (England) Regulations 2011 produce what is likely to become the minimum requirement for the state protection of commercial rights vested in future Olympic Games. Together, they discharge the obligations imposed on the UK government and LOCOG by the IOC as defined in the Host City Contract. They provide the framework within which ambush marketing can be prevented, restrict street traders from disrupting the corporate look and feel of Olympic event zones and promote safe and unencumbered access to competition sites and venues. Taken in their entirety, the UK's Olympic legislation has enabled LOCOG to secure the investment necessary to host London 2012.

Despite discharging the obligations owed to the IOC, the unquestioning acceptance of both the need for and form of the legislation on street trading and ambush marketing has resulted in the potential failure of the UK's Olympic Laws to achieve their stated aims and raises questions concerning the evidential bases on which their application is justified. This in turn could lead to accusations that the sole aim of the Regulations is the protection of the commercial rights associated with the Games rather than the otherwise legitimate concerns that they claim to be addressing: ensuring a consistent celebratory look, preventing ambush marketing and ensuring visitors' safe access to Olympic venues. Whilst it is essential that organising committees are able to exploit these valuable commercial rights in order to raise sufficient revenue to host the Games, justifying these new laws on the grounds of protecting the look and feel of the city, and on health and safety, obfuscates the anti-ambush marketing regime and its application against genuine rivals of the official sponsors.

As the Regulations have not been amended to address concerns about their necessity and proportionality, the focus will now switch to their interpretation and enforcement during their operative period. Although a key aim of the Regulations is the restriction of opportunities for ambush marketing, there appears to be a belief that is evidenced by the prospective targets of these offences that any business attempting to 'freeload' on the back of the Games should be punished for doing so, even if it is supplying an essential service to visitors to the Games. This concern is reinforced by the way in which similar legislation has been applied at previous sporting mega-events, and suggests that the grander and more audacious the infringement the less likely it is that it will be punished, whilst minor infringements are vigorously pursued against local businesses and street traders (James and Osborn, 2011b: 422–426).

The Regulations fail to acknowledge the value of the contribution of local businesses to the provision of the Olympic experience. Such an experience is not just about attending the events and purchasing merchandise from official stalls; it is also about enjoying the local colour and texture provided by pubs, bars, restaurants, hotels and stallholders. Without the cooperation of these businesses, the Games cannot be said to be truly inclusive and the enjoyment of those attending is likely to be affected negatively. The revenue generated indirectly by the Games is not a gift to local traders; their input to visitors' experience is integral to the overall package. If that good will is lost through the over-zealous application of these Regulations, the organisers will feel the impact, as well as the businesses. At the Vancouver 2010 Games, VANOC produced a detailed guide for those most likely to be affected by the Canadian legislation, and concentrated its application to 'real' ambushers in order to maintain the good will of local businesses (Vancouver Organizing Committee for the 2010 Olympic and Paralympic Winter Games, 2006).

In contrast, the powers granted to the ODA, its enforcement officers and the police are extensive, and the guidance produced by LOCOG in 2010 suggests that there will be a zero-tolerance approach to anyone breaching these Regulations (London Organising Committee of the Olympic and Paralympic Games, 2010) and the ODA is also clear that the enforcement will be just as rigorous for the Paralympic as for the Olympic Games.[1] Where this is justifiable against multinational corporations intentionally ambushing the official sponsors, it is impossible to justify such enforcement against local businesses attempting to operate in event zones. If LOCOG hopes to rely on the good will of local businesses to provide the necessary support infrastructure for visitors to the Games, they need to work with the ODA to devise a reasonable, proportionate and transparent enforcement strategy, consult with those likely to be affected by it and operate it sympathetically.

The success of the UK's Olympic laws will be measured not just by the number of convictions secured but by the impact of their enforcement. If they prevent ambush marketing by major multinational brands or punish appropriately those who deliberately infringe the Regulations, then they will be seen to be an effective mechanism for deterring similar campaigns in the future and will become a template for legislation at Sochi and Rio. However, if the laws are used only against local traders who have technically infringed the legislation but cannot be considered to be ambush marketing in the sense in which it is usually understood, then they will be considered to be a disproportionate and unnecessary attack on ordinary people trying to earn a living. In this last respect, the potential impact of these Regulations contrasts starkly and unfavourably with the London Olympic Games and Paralympic Games Tax Regulations 2011, which define the taxation regime for the Olympic family during 2012. Whilst ordinary traders risk being restricted or prohibited from maximising their earnings during the Olympic Games, some of the world's highest-paid sports stars, administrators, officials and media commentators will be able to live and work in the UK tax-free in the run-up to London 2012. This is unlikely to be the kind of sharing in the Games that the public has in mind in respect of what constitutes social benefit.

We have argued previously that the terms of the Host City Contract could be better used to reinforce values more in keeping with the fundamental principles of Olympism rather than simply protecting the commercial rights associated with the Games (James and Osborn, 2011b). The need to raise sufficient revenue to host an edition of the Olympic Games means that it is essential to protect and exploit the commercial rights vested in the Olympic Movement. However, what may be the most efficient and effective way of doing this may not be the most appropriate one, in the light of the guiding principles of the IOC. The Regulations are open to the criticism that they subjugate the fundamental principles of Olympism to commercial imperatives and the demands of sponsors. If the Games are to be truly inclusive and 'for the people', respecting universal ethical principles and the preservation of human dignity (such as the right to earn a living), as required by the Olympic Charter, then the IOC may need to revisit the guarantees that it seeks from future candidates for host city status.

Note

1 This was made clear in an interview granted to the authors by the ODA in London, 15 September 2011.

References

Boykoff, J. (2011) 'The Anti-Olympics', *New Left Review*, 67: 41–59.

Cran, D. and Grifffiths, S. (2010) 'Ambush Marketing: unsporting behaviour or fair play', *Entertainment Law Review*, 21 (8): 293–297.

Department for Culture, Media and Sport (2011a) *Regulations on Advertising Activity and Trading around London 2012. A Consultation.* Online: www.culture.gov.uk/consultations/7759.aspx (accessed 25 October 2011).

Department for Culture, Media and Sport (2011b) *Post Legislative Assessment of the London Olympic Games and Paralympic Games Act 2006*, Memorandum to the Culture, Media and Sport Select Committee, CM 8112.

Department for Culture, Media and Sport (2011c) *The Government Response to Advertising and Trading Regulations London 2012.* Online: www.culture.gov.uk/images/publications/GovtResponse_advertising_trade_london2012.pdf (accessed 25 October 2011).

Department for Culture, Media and Sport (2011d) *Explanatory Memorandum to the London Olympic Games and Paralympic Games (Advertising and Trading) (England) Regulations 2011.* Online: www.legislation.gov.uk/ukdsi/2011/9780111515969/memorandum/contents (accessed 25 October 2011).

Greenfield, S., James, M. and Osborn, G. (2012) 'The Olympics, the Law and the Contradictions of Olympism', in Lenskyj, H. and Wagg, S. (eds) *Handbook of Olympic Studies*, Basingstoke: Palgrave Macmillan.

Hoek, J. and Glendall, P. (2000) 'Ambush Marketing: more than just a commercial irritant', *Entertainment Law*, 1 (2): 72–91.

House of Commons (2011) 'London Olympic Games and Paralympic Games (Amendment) Bill: Committee Stage Report', Research Paper 11/61, Bill 165 of 2010–12, 22 August 2011.

International Olympic Committee (2011) *Olympic Charter*, Lausanne: IOC.

James, M. (2010) *Sports Law*, Basingstoke: Palgrave Macmillan.

James, M. and Osborn, G. (2011a) 'Response to Regulations on Advertising Activity and Trading around London 2012: a consultation', unpublished submission to DCMS, May 2011.

James, M. and Osborn, G. (2011b) 'London 2012 and the Impact of the UK's Olympic and Paralympic Legislation: protecting commerce or preserving culture?', *Modern Law Review*, 74 (3): 410–429.

James, M. and Osborn, G. (2010) 'Consuming the Olympics: the fan, the rights holder and the law', *Sport and Society: The Summer Olympics through the lens of social science*, British Library: London. Online: www.bl.uk/sportandsociety (accessed 23 May 2011).

Johnson, P. (2008) 'Look Out! It's an ambush!', *International Sports Law Review*, 2/3: 24–29.

Lawrence, C., Taylor, J. and Weingarten, O. (2008) 'Proprietary Rights in Sports Events', in Lewis, A. and Taylor, J. (eds) *Sport: law and practice*, Haywards Heath: Tottel Publishing Ltd.

London 2012 (2011) 'Terms and Conditions of Ticket Purchase'. Online: www.tickets.london2012.com/purchaseterms.html (accessed 17 November 2011).

London Organising Committee of the Olympic and Paralympic Games (2010) *London 2012's UK Statutory Marketing Rights: brand protection.* Online: www.london2012.com/documents/brand-guidelines/statutory-marketing-rights.pdf (accessed 25 October 2011).

Maestre, A. (2010) *Law and the Olympics*, Cambridge: Cambridge University Press.

Magnay, J. (2011) 'London 2012 Olympics Diary: government clamps down on ambush advertising at Games', *Telegraph*, 14 October. Online: //blogs.telegraph.co.uk/sport/author/jmagnay1/ (accessed 24 October 2011).

Michalos, C. (2006) 'Five Golden Rings: development of the protection of the Olympic insignia', *International Sports Law Review*, 3: 64–76.

Olympic Delivery Authority (2009) 'London 2012. Advertising and street trading regulations, advance notice'. Online: www.london2012.com/documents/imported/advertising-and-street-trading-regs-strategy.pdf (accessed 25 October 2011).

Rivenburgh, N. (2008) 'For the Cinderella of the New South, the Shoe Just Didn't Fit: the "most exceptional" Games of 1996', *International Journal of Sport Communications*, 1 December: 465–486.

Scassa, T. (2010) 'Faster, Higher, Stronger. The Protection of Olympic and Paralympic Marks Leading Up to Vancouver 2010', in Girginov, V. (ed.) *The Olympics. A Critical Reader*, London: Routledge.

Stuart, S. and Scassa, T. (2011) 'Legal Guarantees for Olympic Legacy', *Entertainment and Sports Law Journal*, 9 (1). Online: www2.warwick.ac.uk/fac/soc/law/elj/eslj/issues/volume9/number1/stuart/ (accessed 30 October 2011).

Tavares, O. (2006) 'Olympic Values in the Twenty-First Century: between continuity and change', in Crowther, N., Barney, R. and Heine, M. (eds) *Cultural Imperialism in Action. Critiques in the Global Olympic Trust*, London, Canada: University of Western Ontario. Online: www.la84foundation.org/SportsLibrary/ISOR/ISOR2006t.pdf (accessed 26 October 2011).

Vancouver Organizing Committee for the 2010 Olympic and Paralympic Winter Games (2006) *REAL 2010: protecting the brand*, Vancouver: VANOC.

7
LONDON 2012 LEGACY STRATEGY
Ambitions, promises and implementation plans

Mike Weed

Ambitions – the genesis of London's legacy strategy

As a result of a recommendation from the IOC Olympic Games Study Commission, in November 2002 the IOC Olympic Charter was amended to emphasise the importance of 'promoting a positive legacy from the Olympic Games to the host city and host country' (IOC, 2002). The bidding process for the 2012 Olympic and Paralympic Games, which concluded in July 2005, was the first Summer Games bidding process conducted under this amended charter. Consequently, although previous host cities had included a consideration of legacy as part of an internal justification for public sector investment, London, together with Paris, Moscow, Madrid and New York, were the first candidate cities for the Summer Games explicitly invited to address the issue of legacy as part of their bids for the 2012 Games. It was an invitation to which London enthusiastically responded.

The notion that there might be rationales and outcomes beyond the simple organisation of a sport competition for hosting the Olympic and Paralympic Games is not new. In the last 20 years, hosts have articulated various rationales for wishing to stage the Games. For example: the 1992 Games in Barcelona were used as a mechanism to accelerate the delivery of an extensive programme of urban regeneration; a key aim for the Sydney Games of 2000 was to position Australia as a centre for business in emerging Asian markets; and the Beijing Games of 2008 were used to help China interact with the global economy, promoting the country as a welcoming place in which to live and visit, and with which to do business (Xu, 2006). But these were largely rationales that were used by the hosts to justify the public sector investment in the Games. For London, though, the notion of 'legacy', or the imprint left by the Games before, during and after the event, was articulated from the outset as the *raison d'être* of the bid. No previous host had been so ambitious or explicit about using the Olympic and Paralympic Games as a catalyst for economic and social good, not only in the host city but across the country as a whole (Weed, 2010).

London's candidacy for the 2012 Games sought to differentiate itself from both previous editions of the Games, and from its bid competitors, by explicitly and extensively referencing the legacy that a London Games would seek for the host city and the host country, but also for the Olympic Movement and for the youth of the world. For the IOC, with its firmly held belief that sport and the Olympic values and ideals can be a global force for good, this was a powerful and attractive message.

The bidding process for the 2012 Games was concluded at the one-hundred-and-seventeenth IOC session in Singapore in July 2005. London's bid presentation included contributions from the British Prime Minister, the Secretary of State for Sport and the Olympics, the Mayor of London, the Chair of the British Olympic Association, and Sebastian Coe, the Chair of the London bid. Each of these contributors explicitly highlighted the legacies that London and Britain would seek from hosting the Games for sport participation, sport facilities, future sport events, community regeneration and the environment. Furthermore, a much wider legacy 'vision' was presented to the IOC session:

> In the past, London and the Olympic Movement have come together when there were serious challenges to be faced ... In 1948, our predecessors re-united a devastated world through sport ... Today, London is ready to join you in facing a new challenge. And to provide another sporting legacy ... London's vision is to reach young people around the world. To connect them with the inspirational power of the Games. So they are inspired to choose sport.
>
> *(Coe, 2005)*

This was London's primary legacy ambition – to inspire the youth of the world to choose sport. It was an ambition to which the IOC members responded positively, awarding the Games of the thirtieth Olympiad to London. However, London now faced the challenge of translating the ambitions of the bid presentation into a meaningful legacy strategy for London and the UK.

Promises: formulating London's legacy strategy

The first question facing the London Games was who would be responsible for delivering a legacy. LOCOG, the London Organising Committee for the Olympic and Paralympic Games, was the body that had outlined legacy ambitions at the IOC Session in Singapore, but LOCOG's responsibility is to organise the Games. Government had given commitments to provide the stadium, venues, athletes' village and other infrastructure, and announced in 2007 that the required budget for these elements of the Games would be £9.3 billion (up from the £4.1 billion budget estimated at the time of the bid). But this £9.3 billion did not include any allocation for developing and delivering a legacy strategy.

In June 2007, the government's Department for Culture, Media and Sport published *Our Promise for 2012* (DCMS, 2007), which outlined five promises to 'set the scale of our ambition', with a further promise that a more detailed 'legacy action plan' would be published the following year. In setting out the UK-wide scale of the promises, the involvement of the devolved administrations in Scotland, Wales and Northern Ireland and the nine English regions in providing 'the building blocks of this document' (DCMS, 2007: p. 4) was noted. However, while this publication answered the question of who would take responsibility for legacy strategy, there were no details on where the funding for legacy development and delivery would come from.

The legacy action plan, *Before, During and After: Making the Most of the London 2012 Games* (DCMS, 2008) was published in June 2008. It was a glossy 80-page document that added details and some targets to the five legacy promises outlined in *Our Promise for 2012* (DCMS, 2007). In introducing the legacy action plan, the Minister for the Olympics, Tessa Jowell, claimed:

> This is an action plan that explains in detail how we intend to keep our promises and provides a check on our progress. It sets out concrete objectives for tourism, jobs and skills, education and sustainability. It explains how we plan to use the Games to boost

> sport and physical activity, and to make the UK the place to do business. And it shows how the regeneration brought about by the Games will have a lasting impact in terms of housing, jobs, transport and infrastructure for East London.
>
> *(Jowell, in DCMS, 2008: p. 2)*

Jowell was thus claiming that the legacy action plan not only provided detail about the five legacy promises, but that it included targets and objectives that could be measured and used as a 'check on our progress'. These details included the five promises themselves, but also fourteen headline ambitions sitting under the promises, each of which had a related target or targets (see Table 7.1). The plan also outlined some of the reasons 'why the London 2012 Games are different', the first of which was because the Games would aim for UK-wide benefits, whereas 'previous Games have often focused on the host city and its surrounding region' (DCMS, 2008: p. 9). In seeking to deliver a UK-wide legacy, the legacy action plan outlined the establishment of a Nations and Regions Group responsible for maximising engagement and benefit across the UK, comprising representatives of Scotland, Wales, Northern Ireland and the nine English regions, each of which had developed their own legacy plans focusing on 'sport and physical activity, culture, volunteering, sustainability, skills, business and tourism' (DCMS, 2008: p. 13). Although the legacy action plan claimed that 'the long-term economic benefits will be felt beyond East London' (DCMS, 2008: p. 4), a previous analysis by Blake (2005) had suggested that there would be a macro-economic flow from the rest of the UK into London of around £4 billion as a result of the Games. Perhaps the nations and regions recognised this, as most of their individual legacy plans focused on the social, cultural and sporting elements of legacy, rather than planning for any significant economic benefits.

The legacy action plan claimed that 'measurable headline ambitions' (DCMS, 2008: p. 5) had been detailed to underscore the five legacy promises. However, although some of these targets were clear and measurable (e.g. a 50 per cent reduction in carbon emissions from the built environment of the Olympic Park by 2013), others were nebulous and virtually impossible to measure (e.g. encouraging people to live more sustainably as a result of London 2012). More interesting, though, were those that had the veneer of measurability, but that left room for considerable interpretation. For example, the headline ambition for new cultural activities under the promise to inspire a generation of young people had a target of 'tens of thousands of young people participating in cultural activities as a result of the 2012 Games' (DCMS, 2008: p. 43). First, 'tens of thousands' could presumably range from 20,000 to 90,000 young people. But, second, how would 'as a result of the 2012 Games' be measured? If 20,000 new young people took part in cultural activities in the years following the award of the 2012 Games to London in 2005, would this be presented as the achievement of this legacy ambition? If so, it would be a sleight of hand, because there would be no way of knowing how many (if any) of these hypothetical 20,000 young people were participating 'as a result of the 2012 Games'. Some may have participated anyway, others may engage with cultural activities as a result of other initiatives not related to London 2012 and others may be drawn into cultural participation through ongoing initiatives rebranded as London 2012 legacy programmes. The key question is which, if any, of the young people engaged in these ways might be truly regarded as contributing to the 'tens of thousands' legacy target?

These issues of assessing legacy have been long discussed in relation to economic impact studies of major events. The work of, *inter alia*, Crompton (2006), Kasimati (2003) and Preuss (2007) has highlighted common sources of error in measuring economic impacts, some of which are due to methodological incompetence, but many of which are deliberate acts of obfuscation (Weed *et al.*, 2009) intended to magnify the perceived impacts of such events to justify

Table 7.1 The five legacy promises

Promise	*Headline ambitions*	*Targets*
To make the UK a world-leading sporting nation	'Inspiring young people through sport'	To offer all 5–16-year-olds in England five hours of high-quality sport a week, and all 16–19-year-olds three hours by 2012.
	'Getting people more active'	To make at least two million more people in England more active by 2012.
	'Elite achievement'	To put the UK at fourth position in the Olympic medal table and at least second in the Paralympic medal table in 2012.
To transform the heart of East London	'Transforming place'	To build over 9,000 new homes, a 'large proportion' of which should be affordable.
	'Transforming communities'	To help 20,000 workless Londoners from the five host boroughs into permanent employment by 2012; to create 12,000 job opportunities in the area of the Park post-Games
To inspire a generation of young people	'Giving time and expanding horizons'	'Tens of thousands' more young people giving time to their local communities as a result of London 2012.
	'New cultural activities'	For 'tens of thousands' of young people to participate in cultural activities as a result of the 2012 Games.
	'Engaging and learning'	For 'thousands' of schools, colleges, universities and other learning providers to inspire young people through the Olympic and Paralympic values.
	'Going Global'	To allow three million young people overseas to access quality physical education and sport, with at least 1 million participating in these regularly by 2010.
Make the Olympic park a blueprint for sustainable living	'A model of sustainable development'	To achieve a 50 per cent reduction in carbon emissions from the built environment of the Olympic Park by 2013.
	'Inspiring sustainable living'	To encourage people to live more sustainably as a result of London 2012, 'such as' reducing their carbon footprint, being energy efficient, or recycling on a greater scale.

public sector investment. As Weed and colleagues (2009) showed in a systematic review of evidence for potential legacies, many of these sources of error are relevant beyond economic impact studies. For example, Preuss (2007) notes that one source of error in economic impact assessment is to count all expenditure as being induced by an event, including the expenditure of people who would have visited the host city anyway, regardless of the event. For cultural engagement, the related error would be to count those who would have participated in cultural activities in any case as being new participants 'as a result of the 2012 Games'. The key to measuring legacy accurately, as noted by Weed (2010), is to focus on the additionality of activities attributable to the 2012 Games, through a comparison of Games-related initiatives with the opportunity cost of the impacts that might have been secured from investments in alternative programmes had the 2012 Games not been awarded to London. However, the detail of funding for legacy initiatives outlined in the legacy action plan suggested that the DCMS had something slightly different in mind.

The earlier publication *Our Promise for 2012* (DCMS, 2007) had not detailed how the delivery of legacy promises would be funded, but the legacy action plan was clear about what resources would be available:

> Many of the benefits will come from enhancing existing programmes, and within existing Departmental budgets. There is therefore no addition to the total Games funding package of £9.3 billion. But we have jointly created a new, London 2012-inspired charity called Legacy Trust UK. The Trust's mission is to use sporting and cultural activities to ensure communities from across the UK have a chance to take part in London 2012, and to leave a sustainable legacy after the Games. Using money from existing sources, including the Lottery and the Arts Council, it is endowed with £40 million of expendable funds.
>
> *(DCMS, 2008: p. 8)*

As 'many of the benefits will come from enhancing existing programmes, and within existing Departmental budgets', the question of assessing the additionality and attributability (Weed, 2010) of legacy programmes and initiatives becomes paramount. Without any additional funding, how will existing programmes be enhanced? And how will we know how far they are attributable to the 2012 Games? The main answer appeared to be the establishment of a 'new community recognition mark available to not-for-profit and governmental organisations that have developed activities inspired by the hosting of the Games' (DCMS, 2008: p. 4). This was called the Inspire mark:

> The Inspire Programme harnesses the London 2012 brand. The Inspire Programme will recognise non-commercial projects and events genuinely inspired by the London 2012 Games through the award of the Inspire Mark. The Inspire Mark will begin to appear on a limited number of high quality, high impact projects and events following the Beijing 2008 Games – working across sports, culture, education, environment and volunteering business skills.
>
> *(DCMS, 2008: p. 15)*

The institution of the Inspire Mark appeared to be a response to criticisms (of both London 2012 and previous Games) that access to the Olympic and Paralympic brand was only available to commercial sponsors, and that community organisations seeking social good rather than profit from an association with the Games had, in the past, had their activities restricted in the name of protecting the profits of multinational sponsors. However, as of December 2011, the 'limited number of high quality, high impact projects' numbered almost 2,000,[1] and there might be some question about how far these 2,000 projects collectively represent attributable legacy impacts 'genuinely inspired by the London 2012 Games' that are additional to activities that would have taken place if the Games had not been awarded to London. A cynic might suggest that as much as 'enhancing existing programmes', the Inspire Mark is about claiming legacy outcomes, irrespective of whether they are attributable to the Games and additional to the opportunity cost. At the very least, any outcomes secured through Inspire marked programmes should be offset against the opportunity cost of the investments that 'existing sources, including the Lottery and the Arts Council' would have made had £40 million of their funding not been endowed to Legacy Trust UK. And Legacy Trust UK is but one example of the reallocation of 'existing Departmental budgets' to the five legacy promises, for which there will also be opportunity costs.

The key issue here is the difference between seeking to deliver a legacy and seeking to demonstrate a legacy. If the imperative were the former, then strategies would be established in the belief that they would deliver genuine attributable and additional legacy outcomes. If the imperative were the latter, then strategies would be established to ensure that the outcomes and impacts of as many programmes as possible could be claimed as demonstrating that legacies have been secured from the 2012 Games. Delivering legacies requires an understanding of what legacies are possible, how and for whom. Demonstrating legacies requires an understanding of methodological smoke and mirrors and political sleight of hand.

However, the legacy action plan did represent a more detailed set of promises and ambitions than had been set out by any previous Games, and it did recognise that the lessons from previous Games, later supported by evidence analysed in two major systematic reviews of the deliverability of legacy outcomes (McCartney *et al.*, 2010; Weed *et al.*, 2009), was that:

> Too often in the past, governments have expected major events to bring automatic windfall benefits. But we know now that nothing is guaranteed without careful planning and initiative from the outset. This [legacy action plan] explains what needs to be done between now and 2012, how we will monitor progress and how we will measure success or failure.
>
> *(Jowell, in DCMS, 2008: p. 2)*

Given that the legacy action plan was published in mid-2008, still several months ahead of London and Britain's four-year Olympiad as Olympic and Paralympic hosts, it did appear that the advanced planning and long-term legacy goals that McCartney and colleagues (2010) suggest are required to secure legacy benefits were in place for London 2012, but with one rather glaring exception.

The five legacy promises, the headline ambitions, and the targets detailed in Table 7.1 make no mention of legacies for the disabled population. Given that the IOC and IPC give equal billing to the Olympic and Paralympic Games, this omission attracted considerable criticism (e.g. Weed and Dowse, 2009). Eventually, almost two years after the legacy action plan had been published in June 2008, the DCMS and the government Office for Disability Issues published *London 2012: A legacy for disabled people* (DCMS and ODI, 2010) in March 2010. This added a belated sixth legacy promise with three headline ambitions relating to disabled people:

- Influence the attitudes and perceptions of people to change the way they think about disabled people.
- Increase the participation of disabled people in sport and physical activity.

- Promote and drive improvements in business, transport and employment opportunities for disabled people.

However, in March 2010 the Olympic and Paralympic Games were less than two-and-a-half years away, and the possibility for advance legacy planning was quickly receding, making the Disability Legacy Plan feel like an afterthought. Furthermore, there was an impending threat to the full spectrum of long-term legacy goals, as a General Election was looming in Britain in May 2010, and the Labour Party, which had been in power since 1997, seemed highly unlikely to be re-elected. The issue that dominated the May 2010 general election was how to deal with the economy and secure an economic recovery. Both more austere economic times and the desire of a new administration to put its stamp on legacy strategy would disrupt advance legacy planning and modify long-term legacy goals as implementation plans were developed in the final two years before the Games.

Implementation plans: rationalising London's legacy strategy

No party secured an overall majority in Britain's May 2010 general election, and so a coalition government was formed comprising Members of Parliament from the Conservative and Liberal Democrat Parties (who had secured 47 per cent and 9 per cent of the available seats in Parliament respectively). With the exception of an immediate statement from the newly appointed Secretary of State for Culture, the Olympics, Media and Sport that 'The Olympics is our number one priority and what we need to do is to grasp the opportunity',[2] and two relevant bullet points in the swiftly written post-election document, *The Coalition: Our Programme for Government* (Cabinet Office, 2010), the issue of Olympic and Paralympic legacy largely disappeared from the government's agenda for the next six months, leaving the previous government's legacy plans (DCMS, 2008; DCMS and ODI, 2010) as the lame-duck default position in an effective legacy strategy vacuum until December 2010.

In this policy vacuum, one of the coalition government's early policy announcements created problems for the delivery of legacy across the UK, albeit unintentionally. In June 2010, the Secretary of State for Communities and Local Government announced that the nine regional development agencies that served the nine English regions were to be abolished.[3] This was part of a wider 'localism' agenda in which decisions about local people are intended to be devolved to more local bodies. In effect, this meant the abolition of the nine English regions, which significantly undermined the ability of the Nations and Regions Group, having lost three-quarters of its members, to fulfil its role to deliver UK-wide Olympic and Paralympic legacies.

The two legacy-relevant bullet points in the Coalition Programme for Government published in May 2010 suggested that changes to legacy strategy would be forthcoming, but whether these would be real changes or repackaging of existing strategy remained open to question:

- We will work with the Mayor of London to ensure a safe and successful Olympic and Paralympic Games in London in 2012, and urgently form plans to deliver a genuine and lasting legacy.
- We will support the creation of an annual Olympic-style school sports event to encourage competitive sport in schools, and we will seek to protect school playing fields.

(Cabinet Office, 2010: p. 14)

The first of these bullet points suggests either that the coalition did not feel that the previous government's legacy plans (DCMS, 2008; DCMS and ODI, 2010) were likely to 'deliver a genuine and lasting legacy' or that the Coalition wished 'urgently [to] form plans' that would allow them to claim that their legacy strategies and policies were responsible for any legacies that could be demonstrated as resulting from the 2012 Games. This adds a further complication to the difference between seeking to deliver and seeking to demonstrate legacy: namely, the need to demonstrate that any legacies that are delivered or claimed are the result of the new policies and strategies of the coalition government, rather than the former policies and strategies of the previous Labour government.

The second bullet point in the coalition programme foreshadows an attempt to create something – an 'Olympic-style school sports event to encourage competitive sport in schools' – that already existed. The previous government's legacy outline, *Our Promise for 2012* (DCMS, 2007: p. 7) noted that: 'staging a UK School Games will galvanise competitive school sport in this country'. In 2010, when the post-election coalition programme was published, the UK School Games was in its fourth year!

Although the coalition government had stated that it would 'urgently form plans to deliver a genuine and lasting legacy', as the clock ticked past the two-years-to-go landmark in August 2010 there were no politically legitimate legacy plans in place. This hardly represented the sustained advanced planning and long-term legacy goals that McCartney and colleagues (2010) suggest are required to secure legacy benefits. However, in December 2010, with less than 600 days to go to the start of the 2012 Games, the coalition published its *Plans for the Legacy from the 2012 Olympic and Paralympic Games* (DCMS, 2010).

One of the ways in which the coalition government had sought to differentiate itself from the previous Labour administration was to move away from what it condemned as a target-setting culture, which the coalition claimed detracted from the delivery of real policy outcomes. Hence the coalition's legacy implementation plans were short on targets, and focused more on a smaller number of specific programmes. The document itself, an austere, 14-page, 6,000-word, text-only document, represented a considerable rationalisation of the previous government's legacy action plan, although the four headline areas could, without any great need for imagination, be mapped onto four of the original five promises in the Legacy Action Plan (DCMS, 2008). Falling by the wayside was the sustainability promise, although 'Growth in the Green Economy' (DCMS, 2010: p. 7) was mentioned as part of the delivery of economic growth, whilst the possibility of a legacy for disabled people is dealt with in a short paragraph of less than 100 words. The four major legacy areas detailed were:

- harnessing the United Kingdom's passion for sport to increase grassroots participation, particularly by young people – and to encourage the whole population to be more physically active;
- exploiting to the full the opportunities for economic growth offered by hosting the Games;
- promoting community engagement and achieving participation across all groups in society through the Games; and
- ensuring that the Olympic Park can be developed after the Games as one of the principal drivers of regeneration in East London.

(DCMS, 2010: p. 1)

There is little mention of targets or measurability in the document, although there is a recognition that 'it is important that we are able in the future to assess the benefits of the games and their legacy', noting that a meta-evaluation of Games legacy and benefits is being carried out 'which brings together evidence relating to the benefits of individual legacy initiatives into a coherent whole' (DCMS, 2010: p. 14). Setting aside the flawed assumption that legacies are benefits (legacies can also be negative), the existence of a meta-evaluation says nothing about what legacy return would be an acceptable or, indeed, successful return on the £9.3 billion public investment in hosting the Games. Without an explicit statement about what legacy outcomes government would see as representing value for money, a meta-evaluation is all but useless in evaluating the success of legacy strategy and policy.

In place of specifying legacy outcomes, *Plans for the Legacy from the 2012 Olympic and Paralympic Games* (DCMS, 2010) specifies programmes in each of the four legacy areas, but they are programmes for which targets are largely absent. While the previous government's legacy action plan (DCMS, 2008) had set out mostly malleable targets, with less than 600 days to go the coalition's implementation plans included barely any targets at all. This could represent an attempt to focus on delivering 'genuine and lasting legacy' (Cabinet Office, 2010) rather than focusing on targets, or it could be a slightly different approach to seeking to demonstrate that government policies and strategy are responsible for anything that might be claimed as legacy. In concluding this chapter, these issues are discussed in relation to sport participation legacies.

First among equals? London's legacy strategy for sport participation

From the ambitions of the Singapore bid presentation, through the promises of the Legacy Action Plan (DCMS, 2008), to the rationalised *Plans for the Legacy from the 2012 Olympic and Paralympic Games* (DCMS, 2010), sporting, social, cultural and economic development legacies have all been referenced. The previous government's legacy action plan and the new coalition government's plans for legacy each appear to give equal billing to legacies in different areas. However, undoubtedly the sport participation legacy is 'first among equals' in the minds of the IOC, LOCOG, the government and the UK media.

Sport participation legacy ambitions were integrated throughout the Singapore bid presentation, whilst the legacy action plan (DCMS, 2008) allocated almost twice as many pages to the sport promise than to any other legacy area. Unfortunately for the new coalition government, with its aversion to targets, the previous government set a very clear and very public legacy target for sport participation – that a million more adults in England would be inspired to play sport at least three times a week by 2012/2013 – a target that is easy for the media to understand, and that is derived from the most robust rolling survey of sport participation habits ever carried out in England, the Active People survey.[4] While the coalition government has tried to distance itself from this target, as yet (Decemer 2011) it has been unable to come up with an alternative.

Following the election in May 2010, the coalition had 'quietly dropped' a related target to get a further million people more active through more general informal activity, such as gardening or walking to work, and in March 2011 the Secretary of State for Culture, the Olympics, Media and Sport, Jeremy Hunt, signalled that the sport participation target would also be dropped:

> In an interview with the *Guardian*, Hunt confirmed the [physical activity] target had been quietly dropped shortly after the coalition government came to power. The [sport participation] target, towards which the sports have made only glacial progress, nominally remains in place for now but it is understood that it too will shortly be dropped in favour of a 'more meaningful' national measure.
>
> *(Gibson, 2011)*

Nine months after trailing the establishment of a 'more meaningful national measure', and with less than 250 days to go to the start of the Olympic Games, a 'more meaningful' measure has yet to be announced. Meanwhile, progress towards the 1 million target, which 'nominally remains in place for now' is such that this most prominent and most resonant of legacy goals is likely to be reached sometime around 2035.[5] It is unsurprising, then, that something 'more meaningful' is being sought, but with less than 250 days to go to the start of the Games it is difficult to see how establishing 'a more meaningful national measure' will contribute to the delivery of a sport participation legacy. Undoubtedly, though, changing the success indicator at this late stage could contribute significantly to the government's ability to demonstrate that a legacy has been achieved.

While a legacy target provides a success indicator, it does not represent a sport participation legacy strategy, and in this respect the coalition government does have some plans in place. *Places People Play*,[6] the government's 'mass participation legacy plan' was launched in November 2010, and is funded by £135 million diverted from the National Lottery. However, the overwhelming majority of this £135 million investment is in supply: £90 million for facilities and fields, £2 million for leaders and £4 million for provision capacity. Even the sum of £32 million to be invested in 'Sportivate', a programme of opportunities for 14–25-year-olds, is for the supply of opportunities. As such, the government's mass participation legacy plans contain no strategies to harness the London 2012 Olympic and Paralympic Games to stimulate demand. This appears to be because the government believes that there is an inherent inspiration to play sport deriving from hosting the Games in the UK, and that the only requirements of a legacy plan are to provide the supply to satisfy the increase in demand that will inevitably come, something that the Sport Minister, Hugh Robertson, implied at the launch of the plan:

> With more Lottery money being invested in facilities, volunteering and protecting and improving playing fields, there will be opportunities for everyone to get involved. When people talk about the legacy of the Games, we want them to talk about Places People Play – and then we want them to get out there and join in.
>
> *(Robertson, 2010)*

The only mention of demand here is that 'we want them to get out there and join in'. However, 'wanting' something does not represent a strategy or a delivery plan, and as such the wholly supply-led mass participation legacy plan appears to be based on the assumption that if new facilities are built, people will come to use them. In this assumption, Robertson and his coalition colleagues are likely to be correct. New facilities and fields carrying the London 2012 Inspire Mark are likely to be well used, but they are most likely to be used by people who are already participating in sport, to play a little more often in better surroundings, and people playing more often is not the same as more people playing. However, counting the extent of new provision (numbers of new facilities and fields) and counting the numbers of people utilising such provision will provide some statistics that can be used to demonstrate that a sporting legacy is being achieved. But this will not change the fact that the latest results from the Active People survey[7] show that the number of adults participating in sport three times a week in England has only increased by an average of 38,000 a year in the last three years. This suggests that no matter how 'more meaningful' the coalition government may wish it to be, counting the number of people, many of whom may be existing participants, that make use of improved provision carrying a London 2012 Inspire Mark does not represent the delivery of a mass participation legacy for sport. The places may be inspired by London 2012, but the people are not.

This chapter has sought to outline and analyse the ambitions, promises and implementation plans that together represent the legacy strategies of successive UK governments. It has shown that, following initial enthusiasm and a subsequent detailed legacy action plan, legacy strategy has more recently been rationalised, as might be expected in tough economic times. However, while legacy strategies for the 2012 Games have been rationalised, the £9.3 billion Games delivery budget has not. Consequently, the British public has every right to expect a return from the £150-per-head investment being made in the Games by the Treasury on its behalf (Weed, 2010).

The analysis of legacy strategy for sport participation reflects similar policy changes and manoeuvres taking place across the other legacy areas, with both legacy initiatives and success indicators being changed, dropped or rebranded in the final two years before the Games. This would appear to suggest a greater concern with demonstrating that legacies have been achieved than with actually delivering them. In fact, as there remains no politically endorsed 'meaningful national measure' (Gibson, 2011) for the sport participation legacy, it is possible that in this and other legacy areas we will never know whether the £9.3 billion Games budget has been a successful legacy investment.

Notes

1 www.london2012.com/inspire-programme (accessed 8 December 2011).
2 www.guardian.co.uk/media/2010/may/12/jeremy-hunt-new-culture-minister (accessed 8 December 2011).
3 www.bis.gov.uk/policies/economic-development/englands-regional-development-agencies (accessed 8 December 2011).
4 www.sportengland.org/research/active_people_survey.aspx (accessed 8 December 2011).
5 Based on the most recently available sport participation figures released from the Active People Survey in December 2011 – www.sportengland.org/research/active_people_survey/aps5.aspx (accessed 8 December 2011).
6 www.sportengland.org/about_us/places_people_play_%E2%80%93_deliverin.aspx (accessed 8 December 2011).
7 www.sportengland.org/research/active_people_survey/aps5.aspx (accessed 8 December 2011).

References

Blake, A. (2005). *The Economic Impact of the London 2012 Olympics*. Nottingham: Christel DeHaan Tourism and Travel Research Institute.

Cabinet Office. (2010). *The Coalition: Our programme for government*. London: Cabinet Office.

Coe, S. (2005). London 2012: Candidate City to Host the 2012 Olympic and Paralympic Games. *Presentation to the One-Hundred-and-Seventeenth IOC Session*, Singapore, 6 July.

Crompton, J. (2006). Economic Impact Studies: Instruments for political shenanigans? *Journal of Travel Research*, 45 (1), 67–82.

DCMS (Department for Culture, Media and Sport). (2010). *Plans for the Legacy from the 2012 Olympic and Paralympic Games*. London: DCMS.

DCMS (Department for Culture, Media and Sport) & Office for Disability Issues. (2010). *London 2012: A legacy for disabled people. Setting New Standards, Changing Perceptions*. London: DCMS/ODI.

DCMS (Department for Culture, Media and Sport). (2008). *Before, During and After: Making the most of the London 2012 Games*. London: DCMS.

DCMS (Department for Culture, Media and Sport). (2007). *Our Promise for 2012: How the UK will benefit from the Olympic Games and Paralympic Games*. London: DCMS.

Gibson, O. (2011). Jeremy Hunt Admits London 2012 Legacy Targets will be Scrapped. *Guardian*, 29 March.

IOC (International Olympic Committee). (2002). *Olympic Charter: In force as from November 2002*. Lausanne: IOC.

Kasmati, E. (2003). Economic Aspects and the Summer Olympics: A review of related research. *International Journal of Tourism Research*, 5 (6), 433–444.

McCartney, G., Thomas, S., Thomson, H., Scott, J., Hamilton, V., Hanlon, P., Morrison, D.S. and Bond, L. (2010). The Health and Socioeconomic Impacts of Major Multi-Sport Events: A systematic review. *British Medical Journal*, 340: c2369.

Preuss, H. (2007). The Conceptualisation and Measurement of Mega Sport Event Legacies. *Journal of Sport & Tourism*, 12 (3–4), 207–227.

Robertson, H. (2010). London 2012 Mass Participation Sports Legacy Launched. DCMS press release, www.culture.gov.uk/news/news_stories/7565.aspx (accessed 1 December 2011).

Weed, M. (2010). How Will We Know if the Olympics and Paralympics Benefit Health? *British Medical Journal*, 340, c2202.

Weed, M., Coren, E., Fiore, J., Mansfield, L., Wellard, I., Chatziefstathiou, D. and Dowse, S. (2009). A Systematic Review of the Evidence Base for Developing a Physical Activity and Health Legacy from the London 2012 Olympic and Paralympic Games. London: Department of Health.

Weed, M. and Dowse, S. (2009). A Missed Opportunity Waiting to Happen? The Social Legacy Potential of the 2012 Paralympic Games. *Journal of Policy Research in Tourism, Leisure and Events*, 1 (2), 170–174.

Xu, X. (2006). Modernizing China in the Olympic Spotlight: China's national identity and the 2008 Beijing Olympiad. *The Sociological Review*, 54 (s2), 90–107.

8
SECURING THE GAMES

Jon Coaffee and Pete Fussey

Since the 1970s, safety and security, and the management of incivility, have become key issues for Games organisers (Fussey and Coaffee, 2011; Bennett and Haggerty, 2011), spreading beyond event-based venues to the wider urban realm. Concerns for security, resulting from the fear of international terrorist attacks at international mega-events, such as the Olympic Games, and against the associated crowded places and critical infrastructure of the host city, has also meant that security is increasingly designed into the regenerating built environment and embedded within the behaviours and practices of those responsible for construction and securing of the Olympic venues and sites (Coaffee and Fussey, 2010). Nowhere in Olympic history is this more obvious than in the preparation for the 2012 Summer Games in London.

Towards the redesign and securitisation of Olympic cities

Since Munich 1972, and particularly since 9/11, Olympic security has grown in scale and complexity. One corollary of this development has been the permeation of Olympic-related regeneration projects with wider concerns for safety and security. The response of urban authorities to embedding such concerns into Olympic-led regeneration projects encompasses physical design and surveillance initiatives and strategic spatial planning intervention, as well as a restructuring of governance and management functions in response to an array of potentially disruptive challenges and policing requirements. Amid such processes, especially those associated with countering the terrorist threats that often foreshadow mega-events, military security perspectives are commonly bound up with neoliberal agendas connected directly to the redevelopment of the city (Atkinson and Helms, 2007; Eick, 2011). Here, the search for urban security exists within a climate of regional, national and global competition between cities for footloose capital, company relocation, cultural assets and visitors (Coaffee and Murakami Wood, 2006), and builds upon existing processes that define the competitive entrepreneurial city (Harvey, 1989). Moreover, at the local level within the planning system, built-environment professionals are increasingly being made responsible for safety in public spaces through design intervention intended for crime prevention and the control of human behaviour (Raco, 2007: 50). This has led to accusations that the newly generated urban spaces, such as those connected to mega-event-led construction, are not 'open' to all (Coaffee and Johnston, 2007) and that the aim of urban authorities is often to 'spatially purify' such spaces for selective user demographics (Sibley, 1995).

Often in Olympic history this search for safety has resulted in large-scale and punitive policing methods being deployed, and the eviction or removal of 'offending' groups or unwanted activities that do not fit with the planned – or contrived – vision for the Olympic city (*inter alia* Fussey *et al.*, 2011). For example, commentators have noted how, before the 2000 Sydney Games, permitted activities in public spaces became heavily restricted and systematic 'street sweeping' occurred across the host city, made possible by special legislation that gave the police 'exceptional' powers to 'move on' those who were causing 'inconvenience' (Saul, 2000: 35, cited in Fussey *et al.*, 2011). It has been argued that these practices have been repeated in subsequent host cities. Variations on such initiatives range from the concealment of 'undesirable' areas from the gaze of visitors (evinced in Atlanta in 1996, London in 2012 and also at the 2010 FIFA World Cup in South Africa) to, in more extreme cases, reports of at least 300,000 evictions in Beijing during the run-up to the 2008 Games (Cook, 2007). It has also been reported that over a million people suffered forced evictions in relation to the urban redevelopment preceding the 1988 Seoul Olympic Games. Here it has been alleged that the Korean government ordered the demolition of slum housing visible from main roads and major hotels (Lenskyj, 2004).

This chapter identifies and examines key issues relating to the provision and application of security at the London 2012 Games. In doing so, it is organised over three broad areas of discussion. First, some of the key recurring security approaches and techniques are identified alongside a temporal framework relating to their application. The second area of discussion considers the application of these techniques and temporalities with specific relation to the forthcoming 2012 London Olympic and Paralympic Games. In doing so, particular emphasis is placed on security planning in the run-up to the games. The chapter will then conclude with a discussion of legacy and security knowledge transfer issues as they apply both to London and to future host cities.

Techniques and temporalities of security design

Linked to the above discussion, in recent years concepts and practices of security have been increasingly utilised by planners and other built-environment professionals in attempts to create safer places. It has been argued that security has become a core concern in professional planning and design practice as attempts have been made to make the built environment increasingly resistant to external risk from natural hazards, crime or from new security challenges orientated around the perceived threat of terrorism (Coaffee and O'Hare, 2008). Such processes have served to draw neo-liberal planning agendas and their attendant security-focused ambitions towards the heart of new regeneration schemes. The ongoing regeneration of central urban areas in many cities in the last decade and renewal schemes associated with mega-event-led upgrading have given many opportunities to apply such practices to the design and construction of new buildings and public spaces, facilitated by changes in building regulations and codes, and the planning system more broadly. However, such events, the newly beautified spaces of associated developments and their new congregations of visitors are also subject to the competing trend of being an increasingly attractive target for an array of local, national and international terrorist groups (Richards *et al.*, 2010).

Since the 1970s, and after the terrorist attacks at the Munich 1972 Games, security-planning considerations have become an integral and requisite part of bidding documents, processes, preparation and delivery of mega-sporting events. The cost and sophistication of undertaking such planning has advanced steeply in the last decade (Coaffee and Johnston, 2007). Particularly prominent urban security measures typically relate to technological, territorial, design and governance interventions. We can categorise five such interventions. *First*, the growth of electronic surveillance within public and semi-public urban spaces, in particular automated software-driven systems that can track people and vehicles across the urban terrain (Fussey, 2010). *Second*, the increased emphasis on physical or symbolic notions of the boundary and territorial closure, which serve a defensive purpose, often through the erection of reinforced security barriers and bollards around 'at risk' sites (Benton-Short, 2007). *Third*, the increasing sophistication and cost of security and contingency planning undertaken by and between organisations and different levels of government, intended to decrease their vulnerability to attack and increase preparedness in the event of an attack (Coaffee, 2006), in addition to providing a number of reassuring and symbolic functions (Boyle and Haggerty, 2009). *Fourth*, the way that security has been embedded within the urban context through carefully crafted urban design interventions, which focus upon the construction, remodelling and management of public spaces, taking into account issues such as public access, socio-cultural preferences, the structural robustness of building materials and heritage concerns (Németh, and Schmidt, 2007). *Fifth*, following processes inaugurated at the 1994 Lillehammer Winter Games, the creation of new policing coalitions that deliver an expanded and intensified mandate. It is important to note, however, that whilst many of these processes are *internationalised*, and are traceable across large temporal and geographical frames, they are not simply and uncritically applied to the hosts. Instead, the delivery of mega-event security is also shaped by a range of regional and local processes, including extant infrastructural capacities and the identity of local security cultures (Fussey *et al.*, 2011).

Although the types of interventions mentioned above have obvious spatial and institutional imprints, where mega-events differ from other forms of security, or 'target' risk, is in the different temporalities that make up the 'event'. In the case of Olympic security planning we can usefully distinguish between three interlinked stages where different activities occur and which serve to shape the built environment and its management in a myriad of connected ways. Initially we can discern the *pre-event or pre-planning* stage. This involves technically scrutinising and designing out weaknesses and vulnerabilities well in advance of the event. This is increasingly taking the form of permanent design alterations to the built fabric of the city. As the event draws ever nearer, the intensity of such security preparations becomes more pronounced. Here the pre-existing security regime in the host city will mediate what is deemed necessary. *During the event* particular types of largely temporary security measures and policing tactics are deployed, which commonly attempt to utilise what the police and security services refer to as 'island security' to physically 'lock down' key venues through barrier methods of physical security, and the use of advanced surveillance equipment to screen spectators and collect data from across the full spectrum of the venue environment. After the event, there is also an increasing trend emerging regarding the *post-event* retention of security features, be they CCTV networks, security-conscious building design or cultures of policing and emergency response (Fussey *et al.*, 2011). This threefold phasing of security planning will be discussed in the next section in relation to the forthcoming London 2012 Olympic Games.

Securing London for 2012

Although London's bid to host the 2012 Summer Games was strongly promoted as being about urban transformation, security concerns were also a central part of the application. Here, particular reference was made to London's prior experience of policing and mitigating a range of urban threats. In this sense, specific Olympic security preparation would mesh with – and become grafted over – pre-existing expertise at dealing with the threat of urban terrorism (Fussey and Coaffee, 2011). For London 2012, the 7 July 2005 bombings, the day after the IOC's decision to award the 2012 Games to London, was a reminder of the threat the Games would face from terrorist violence, and subsequently led to a massive increase in security budget and prompted Olympic organisers to draw up ever more detailed contingency plans (Coaffee and Johnston, 2007).

Early pre-event planning

In the *pre-event* phase of the London 2012 Games a number of well-documented design interventions have been observed, which have embedded concepts of security into the regeneration of the wider urban area. These interventions are of differing sizes and hold differing geographical effects, ranging from designing protective security into individual venues to pan-London emergency planning, thus reflecting the physical and organisational features of resilience outlined above. A specialist coalition of agencies overseen by the Home Office – the Olympic Security Directorate – has developed detailed security plans based on actuarial and risk-based approaches in order to plan out prospective vulnerabilities as well as enhance the ability of

Figure 8.1 The initial perimeter security surrounding the Olympic park site in 2008.

emergency responders to cope in the event of a disruptive event, notably a terrorist attack. Key Olympic sites have been temporarily and then permanently 'sealed', with public access heavily restricted (see Figures 8.1 and 8.2).

The venues themselves, and their immediate surroundings, have been 'protected' with an array of security features that have been seamlessly designed into the regenerating urban landscape. This is not only for the purposes of Games-time protection but is linked to the desire for the security/safety legacy that will follow.[1] Here the entire Olympic Park area – the site containing the majority of the venues and Olympic and Paralympic Village – is to be afforded 'Secured by Design' (SBD)[2] status in the post-Games period. As the Association of Chief Police Officers noted on awarding the Olympic Park SBD status:

> The award centres on the adoption of design and physical security measures that have been shown to reduce day-to-day crime, vandalism and antisocial behaviour. Whilst the Olympic venues will have significant but discreet security for the period of the Olympics, the application of the SBD project ensures that the general public, residents and retailers will enjoy the benefit of a prestigious and safe environment long after the Games have concluded.[3]

Counter-terrorism measures will be applied to more prosaic offences in the post-event period. Over recent years numerous access and control zones have also been established in and around key venues, most visibly at the northern Hackney Wick, southern Stratford and eastern Angel Lane (Leyton) entrances to the site. London's pre-existing Automated Number Plate Recognition CCTV systems have also been adapted and expanded to meet the need of Olympic security

Figure 8.2 Upgrade perimeter security surrounding the Olympic park site in 2010

organisers (Coaffee *et al.*, 2011). Moreover, and in relation to attempts to 'purify' Olympic spaces in advance of such overt securitisation, the area surrounding the Olympic Park was subject to the compulsory purchase and then eviction of a number of social housing blocks and local businesses, 'clearing them away in the first stage of a longer regeneration process' (Raco and Tunney, 2010: 14).

Olympic security and its links to the urban transformation taking place in London has, however, been a fluid and uneven process but is becoming more intense as the 2012 Games draw near. At the time of writing (March 2012), with less than a year until the opening ceremony, the majority of the security preparations (such as those noted above) have been undertaken or at least put in train. These plans are undergoing final refinements, however, with new security fears and counter-responses being factored into last-minute preparations. This temporal period is explored in more detail in the next section.

The immediate pre-event phase

The immediate security-planning phase has begun in earnest in London, with security work seen by many as the top priority in the Games preparation. In March 2011 an updated *Olympic and Paralympic Safety and Security Strategy* was published, which set out the key aims and objectives for the police and government. The strategy's overarching aim was 'to deliver a safe and secure Games, in keeping with the Olympic culture and spirit' (Home Office, 2011a: 7).

This strategy drew from the latest revised UK National Security Strategy: *A Strong Britain in an Age of Uncertainty: The National Security Strategy*, published in October 2010, and was to be operationalised in line with the third iteration of the UK's overarching counter-terrorism strategy, CONTEST (HM Government, 2011). The CONTEST strategy itself specifically focused on the 2012 Games, noting that the UK has guaranteed to the IOC that it will to 'take all financial, planning and operational measures necessary to guarantee the safety and the peaceful celebration of the Games' (HM Government, 2011: 105).[4] Specifically, the *Olympic and Paralympic Safety and Security Strategy* highlighted a set of issues related to the threat of and response to possible terrorist attack:

> Terrorism poses the greatest security threat to the Games. Experience from previous Games and elsewhere indicates that global sporting events provide an attractive and high-profile target for terrorist groups, particularly given the potential for malicious activity to receive enormous international publicity. London 2012 will take place in an unprecedentedly high threat environment. Threat levels can change rapidly but by planning against a threat level of Severe we have maximised our flexibility to respond to a range of threats.
>
> *(Home Office, 2011a: 106)*

Responses to these challenges are being developed through five workstreams, set out below, and contained within the '2012 section' of CONTEST. The collective aim is to enhance the resilience of the Games through planning and design guidance (Protect) and related issue of governance, contingency planning and intelligence gathering:

- *protect* Olympic and Paralympic venues, events and supporting transport infrastructure, and those attending and using them;
- *prepare* for events that may significantly disrupt the safety and security of the Games and ensure capabilities are in place to mitigate their impact;

- *identify and disrupt* threats to the safety and security of the Games;
- *command, control, plan and resource* the safety and security operation; and
- *engage* with international and domestic partners and communities, to enhance our security and ensure the success of our strategy.

(*Ibid.*: 107)

Local, regional and national policing strategies are also seen as key vehicles for the delivery of this strategy.

Given the high profile of the security operation, it was no surprise, therefore, that much international press coverage to celebrate the one-year countdown to the London Games was replete with stories highlighting the security infrastructure put, or being put, in place by Olympic managers and security experts. In a media story entitled 'Security a top challenge in London in year before Olympics', the Associated Press (2011b) highlighted both the regeneration and security legacies expected from the Games. Whist noting that 'the Olympic park area was changing the face of a previously run down area of east London' and mentioning the iconic sporting venues being constructed, it also asserted that 'underpinning the sports festival will be one of the biggest security operations ever mounted', with security blanketing the English capital (*ibid.*).

Although much current security planning has focused upon enhancing the resilience of the Olympic venues, non-competition sites are also being closely monitored as the Games draw near. This concern connects to ongoing streams of government work in the fields of security and urban planning around the protection of 'crowded places' deemed at risk from terrorist groups using innovative and novel methods. These targets of choice – crowded areas – have certain features in common, most notably their easy accessibility that cannot be altered without radically changing citizens' experience of such generally public places (Coaffee, 2010a). As Chris Allison, Deputy Commissioner of the Metropolitan Police, noted when talking about the 'soft targets' that terrorists' might seek out in 2012: 'If you secure the venues so the opposition [terrorist] can't get in, they will look for a soft target like parallel events linked to the Olympics but with less security' (BBC, 2011b).

As one newspaper noted in October 2011, 'senior sources believe that rather than targeting Olympic venues, where security will be extremely high, terrorists will be tempted to attack areas where crowds are likely to congregate such as train stations and public events' (*Daily Telegraph*, 2011). Indeed, one such Olympic-related yet non-official site constituted Eric Rudolph's choice of location for his bomb during the 1996 Atlanta Olympic Games. Moreover, for London 2012, these associated spaces are subject to different governance arrangements, falling under the remit of (currently financially constrained) local municipalities, rather than the more centralised and better-funded Olympic authorities. Subsequently this has led to a wave of pre-emptive counter-terrorism interventions being rolled out across London in an attempt to make such spaces more resilient (Coaffee, 2009a). Such mitigation measures, which planners, architects and other built environment professionals have been encouraged to integrate within new and existing buildings and public spaces, range from enhancing the robustness of materials used in construction or in the retrofitting of buildings, restricted parking and the enhancement of electronic surveillance capabilities to constraints on access to public spaces, particularly those surrounding high-profile locations, through the use of crash-rated bollards.

However, the very migratory and innovative nature of urban terrorism means that methods of attack change and migrate across international boundaries (Croft and Moore, 2010). Notably, recent commando-style attacks against non-Western cities – in Mumbai and Lahore in late 2008 and early 2009, respectively – and against soft, unprotected targets internationally, has led to a reassessment of Western urban security strategies and a fear that such terrorist *modus operandi* will migrate to Western cities (Coaffee, 2009b). Indeed, a Mumbai-style attack will be one of the scenarios utilised in the security exercises being carried out by the Olympic security teams in the run-up to the 2012 Games (Gardham, 2011; see also below). Such fears were confirmed by events in Norway in July 2011, when over 70 people were killed by a lone gunman.[5] In an interview with the Associated Press, Jacques Rogge, the IOC President, reflected on the Norwegian events and noted that police intelligence, combined with the physical and managerial measures already in place, will be crucial to providing a safe and secure Games for London:

> It's not just a fence and a wall and the armed patrol ... It's much more than that. It's intelligence.... It's not just the physical security of the athlete in the Olympic village ... It's not just sweeping a bus with mirrors under the floor. There's also the surveillance on the Internet, and the collaboration between different agencies of different countries. There is a lot of intelligence going on.
>
> *(Associated Press, 2011a)*

Hugh Robertson, the British Olympics Minister, was cited in the same article, noting that Olympic security was already making contingency for so-called 'lone wolves' but would re-examine its plans: 'Clearly where there are lessons to be learned from Norway we will learn them.' Moreover, he noted that: 'I am sure as you can possibly be one year out from the games that we have done everything that we need to deliver a safe and secure games' (Associated Press, 2011a).

Security planning in the immediate pre-Games period therefore evolved to cope with both known threats and those security planners can only envision, but were role-played to enhance preparedness (*LA Times*, 2011). With one year to go before the Games, the UK Home Office[6] released a statement on its website arguing that 'we are confident that the right plans are in place to deliver a safe 2012 Games' and that 'a programme of security exercises are taking place to test government, police and other agencies'. These exercises are focused upon a range of possible disruptive scenarios but are being continuously tested to 'make sure that they are going to operate in the way we anticipate so that when it comes to Games time we're ready and know what to expect' (Home Office, 2011b).[7]

Learning from such contingency planning attains greater importance in the wake of government cuts in police funding which some felt might affect Games-time operations which will see over 12,000 officers needed at peak times. The Home Secretary noted, however, that 'I am confident we have the planning in place to deliver a safe and secure Olympics' (cited in the *Daily Mirror*, 2011). In July 2011 there were also fears that security preparation would be thrown into chaos by the resignation of Metropolitan Police Commissioner and Head of Olympic Security for 2012 Sir Paul Stephenson, whose professional integrity was questioned in relation to the News International phone hacking scandal (*London Evening Standard*, 2011). Olympics Minister Hugh Robertson, however, argued that since the strategic nature of the security plan was already in place, drawing on an emerging international standardisation practice for mega sporting events (Coaffee and Fussey, 2010), any potential organisational upheaval will not affect overall security preparations.

Panic on the streets of London?

In early August 2011 there were further fears expressed about London's policing capacity to cope with the wide-ranging security demands of hosting the 2012 Games. Following a spate of urban riots and civil disobedience in a number of London boroughs – including the Olympic boroughs of Hackney and Waltham Forest – and the subsequent forced cancellation, on police advice, of high-profile sporting fixtures, those in charge of security planning for 2012 were forced to reflect upon how they would cope in the event of multiple security breaches and how far this would stretch the police manpower on the streets. One leading local government expert was quoted as saying:

> You can imagine how stretched the police would be if this were to occur during the Olympics ... so I think this will create a worry within City Hall and the Home Office.
>
> (Globe and Mail, *2011)*

The urban rioting that engulfed London (and other areas of the UK) coincided with an IOC Coordination Commission visit to check on progress ahead of the 2012 Games and a series of 'test events' in some Olympic venues. In response, the IOC noted that it was confident that the Games would be secure and that this was the responsibility of London authorities:

> Security at the Olympic Games is a top priority for the IOC. It is however directly handled by the local authorities, as they know best what is appropriate and proportionate. We are confident that they will do a good job in this domain.
>
> *(cited in* Daily Telegraph, *2011)*

Such sentiments demonstrate the international and domestic forces that impact on the staging of the Olympic Games. Nevertheless, the international community was less optimistic. The Chinese government highlighted its concerns about safety and security ahead of 2012, noting in the wake of the riots: 'The image of London has been severely damaged, leaving people sceptical and worried about the public security situation during the London Olympics' (*ibid.*). London officials argued in response that such disorder would not impinge upon 2012 security and that such disturbances had already been factored into their contingency planning:

> public disorder is one of those risks which we have already been planning against ... obviously in light of the appalling events in London over recent days, we will review our planning to ensure that any lessons are identified.
>
> *(cited in the* Guardian, *2011a)*

As the Games drew near, increased importance is also being placed upon balancing the needs of safety with the requirement of ensuring that such securitisation does not get in the way of the sporting spectacle or 'spirit' of the Games. The Associated Press (2011b) noted a renewed emphasis by organisers on ensuring security is not overwhelming, citing the example of the Royal Wedding in London on 29 April 2011 as an example of where a million people lined the procession route without any overly obtrusive security presence. As the Organising Committee leader, double Olympic gold medallist Sebastian Coe noted, 'We're very good at policing in a discrete way ... the real challenge is to maintain security to protect athletes, protect people, protect assets, but at the same time having people leaving your city feeling they haven't been pushed from pillar to post' (*ibid.*). Yet at the same time, it can be argued that hosting a Royal Wedding and an Olympic Games, although both constituting significant events, hold different policing and security demands. Most obvious here are the temporal differences between the events. In addition, despite aspirations (or public claims) for unobtrusive policing during Olympic and other mega sporting events, intensive and visible zero-tolerance-style policing strategies have been a common reality. Not only are relationships between the police and the capital's youth particularly strained in the run-up to the 2012 Games (which are hosted in neighbourhoods with some of the highest proportions of young people in the country), but such tensions also exist against a background of recession and austerity, factors long recognised as incendiary catalysts for urban disorder.

The ultimate aim is for 'customer-sensitive' security to prevail, which will provide the highest possible levels of security without the need to 'lock down' the entire city, as at other Games where sterile environments have been created to facilitate enhanced security (Coaffee *et al.*, 2011). The *LA Times* (2011), for example, noted security measures in Beijing that 'discouraged public gathering and involved a force of more than 100,000 creating an oppressive atmosphere'. By contrast, the ambition for London 2012 is to build on 'the United Kingdom's practice of discrete and effective security, while remaining in keeping with the sprit and culture of the Games' (*ibid.*).

The price of security?

Costs of Olympic security programmes are often articulated and nearly as frequently used also as a barometer of the intensity of the overall operation. Thus we have estimates of securing the 2004 Athens Games at US$1.5 billion (Samatas, 2007) and those of securing the 2002 Salt Lake City Winter Games at $500 million (Toohey and Veal, 2007). Yet it is perhaps prudent to retain a degree of scepticism about such claims and their prospects for comparability.

In the first instance, the variance between different estimates of the same event is simply too wide to take the figures seriously without understanding their methods of calculation. For example, Giulianotti and Klauser (2009) put the security costs at Atlanta 1996 at $108.2 million, and Sydney 2000 at $179.6 million. Sanan (1996), by contrast, places the Atlanta figure at $342 million, whilst Decker and colleagues (2005) estimate Sydney's security project at $310 million. It is possible that they are all correct, but that they are measuring different things and have varying conceptions of what is included and excluded in the notion of Olympic security. Thus variations over whether these figures include or exclude wider (non-event) policing costs, whether they refer to the embedding of physical securing of the venues during construction or simply the expenditure on human and technological assets and definition of where the geographical boundaries of Olympic security end are all unclear. The same accounting and auditing processes are also highly unlikely to be applied across different host cities, making longitudinal comparisons highly unreliable. Such statistics are rarely, if ever, adjusted for inflation, a particularly important consideration when seeking to compare expenditure over extended periods. For example, the quoted $100 million security costs at Montreal 1976 (Clarke, 1976), would today be equivalent to somewhere in the region of $380 million, higher than Decker and colleagues' (2005) estimate of those at Sydney 2000. Costs are also never adjusted to reflect different human resourcing overheads (such as the considerable differences in personnel costs between 1980s Russia and London in 2012). In other respects, calculations for security expenditure are simply incorrect. For example, Hinds and Vlachou's (2007) much-quoted review of Olympic security expenditure almost certainly contains errors in key places. Here, an overall figure for Olympic security is divided by the number of athletes at a particular Games, to arrive at a figure for the overall security expenditure per competitor. The same process is repeated for each spectator. Thus the same overall figure is counted twice and, on closer inspection, occasionally appears to be arbitrarily 'adjusted' by several hundreds of thousands of dollars, depending on the calculation. In short, at best, estimates of Olympic security costs are an extremely crude measure and afford little detail.

It is with great caution, therefore, that the security costs for the London 2012 Games are now discussed. Here, common to other Olympic security projects, many of the above accounting caveats also apply. For London 2012, one of the most quoted statistics is that of the £600 million security cost, yet this figure is also subject to considerable debate. In the first instance, an additional £238 million contingency fund also exists that may be included or excluded in such calculations, depending on political expediency and the availability of clear post-Games accounting. At the same time, the Treasury has requested (but not prescribed) that the Home Office deliver this project for £475 million. Perhaps more importantly, this '£600 million' figure only represents a partial element of the overall Olympic security project. In particular, it relates to the wider policing and security of the Games and is thus additional to the cost of embedding security features into the venues and Olympic Park. Remarkably, this £600 million budget was omitted from the initial bid for the London Games and became a particularly controversial feature of the 2007 revised Olympic budget (see Public Accounts Committee, 2008). The 2010 UK government spending review estimated the cost of securing Olympic venues at £282 million (National Audit Office, 2011). Finally, at the time of writing (March 2012), the review of Olympic security following the August 2011 urban disorders has identified a need for substantially increased numbers of private security guards. Despite difficulties in reaching the original target of 7,000 (see Fussey *et al.*, 2011), ambitions for over 20,000 guards were articulated (*Guardian*, 2011b). Such late emphases on highly aspirational targets are likely to further and significantly raise the costs of securing the 2012 Games and generate questions over whether this requirement can be met. In December 2011 the National Audit Office estimated that the 2010 spending review figure has now almost doubled to an estimated £553 million, representing a £271 million increase (NAO, 2011). This sum has yet to be finalised and has 'increased the strain on the Public Sector Funding Package' (*ibid.*: 7) with some fearing that taxpayers might be asked to contribute more. Further clarity was also provided in December 2011 by the Ministry of Defence, which highlighted what its own involvement in the 2012 security operation would be. This amounts to over 13,500 military personnel being used: 5,000 troops to support the police; 7,500 to provide venue security; and 1,000 for 'logistical support'. In addition, it was announced that a 1,000-strong unarmed contingency force would be set up and deployed in an 'Olympics-related civil emergency' (MOD, 2011). It was also noted that a vast amount of military hardware would be utilised to secure the Games. As the Defence Minister noted, 'Military hardware will be used, we'll be deploying helicopters, we'll be deploying Typhoon fighters to defend London's airspace, we'll be deploying ground-to-air missile systems' (cited in BBC News, 2011c).

Planned legacy and policy transfer

The designing of security features into Olympic venues and other public spaces in the city requires knowledge of how built-environment professionals, alongside security specialists, can actively contribute to the longer-term regeneration vision for the area. In the case of London, organisers have produced the most comprehensive plans seen for urban regeneration *and* security in modern Olympic history. The merging of these agendas in a host of *permanent* design and architectural features, and within systems for managing emergencies, has been widespread. In previous host Olympic cities such features have been largely *temporary* (Coaffee and Fussey, 2010).

In its development of secure regeneration spaces, London's built-environment community is creating a security 'blueprint' for knowledge transfer across the globe for when mega-events come to town. Such legacies are conceptual as well as physical. The intended 'permanence' of security infrastructure is readily being transferred to other 'host' cities, indicating a degree of policy learning and transfer. The aforementioned revised UK CONTEST strategy (HM Government, 2011) highlights explicitly how lessons from the 2012 security operation will be fed back into security planning for the 2014 Glasgow Commonwealth Games. Moreover, the UK's Association of Chief Police Officers has also highlighted how safety and security principles are being embedded within the ongoing regeneration and build standards underway in Glasgow:

> For the overall success of the Games it is vital that security measures can be embedded throughout the entire process from design, through build, to delivery of the event itself and onto the legacy. Early awareness and consideration of security issues and requirements will also contribute to the long term success and sustainability of the new communities created.
>
> *(ACPO, 2011)*

Rio's successful candidacy to host the 2016 Olympic and Paralympic Games also draws on these continuities of mega-event security, yet colours them with local idiosyncrasies. Although security practices are likely to be prioritised towards localised criminality rather than international terrorism (Rio2016, 2007), security is likely to be a major concern for Rio's Organising Committee (Coaffee and Fussey, 2010). These concerns can be more specifically related to the city's murder rate (that annually stands at triple that of the entire UK), and fears of theft against tourists. Such issues are likely to elevate the attention afforded to security. To mitigate these risks a familiar plan is being formulated, similar to that being developed in London and building on the principles of perimeter security, technological surveillance, crime prevention through environmental design (CPTED) principles and intensified policing strategies (Rio2016, 2007).

Such 'solutions' couple required Olympic security standards with Rio's tradition of delineating 'high-value' spaces from their urban context though crime-prevention measures, and reinforce the risk of further splintering of Rio's divided landscape, providing a significant challenge to its regenerative aspirations. Indeed, recent visits to Brazil by the UK Foreign and Commonwealth Office, intended to allow the UK security industry 'to pursue commercial opportunities and become the partner of choice for sport security' have resulted in reports that

> Brazil sees a step change in the security situation in Rio as a legacy of the Olympic Games in 2016 in particular and is making progress on sustainable 'pacification' of favelas.
>
> *(FCO, 2011)*

Overall, the emerging blueprint for would-be host cities of mega sporting events incorporates a strong element of both urban rejuvenation and securitisation, which are increasingly being combined into security designs and master plans. Without a commitment to such strategies individual cities and nations are unlikely to be given the opportunity to host such events in the future. The legacy of the coupling of regeneration and security concerns within cities that have hosted or are about to host such events is evident both as material and design changes within the built environment alongside greater surveillance and emergency response capabilities. This is a trend that has been steadily growing, since the terrorist attacks in Munich in 1972, through international networks which have been evolving a standardised approach to security, albeit one that is shaped locally to a great extent. This approach is likely to reach its zenith through the security planning put in place for London 2012, where security features are being made permanent and embedded seamlessly with urban regeneration plans.

Notes

1 As Sinclair (2011) notes in his psycho-geographic reflection on East London, these security features, particularly the electrified fence that encircles the Olympic site, are conspicuously absent in the various computer-generated marketing images produced by London's Olympic authorities.
2 Secured by Design (SBD) began in the late 1980s as an award scheme, managed by the Association of Chief Police Officers (ACPO) and supported by the Home Office, that aims to encourage developers to design space so as to minimise crime opportunities.
3 See www.securedbydesign.com/news/viewstory.aspx?id=1449&url=www.securedbydesign.com/editable_pages/SBD_1296560660316.html.
4 Prime Minister's Guarantee to the International Olympic Committee, November 2004.
5 This attack was combined with a vehicle bomb that exploded in the capital, Oslo, killing a number of people and causing widespread damage to the cityscape.
6 The Home Office is the lead UK government department for policies on counter-terrorism, immigration, policing, drugs and crime.
7 The Home Office had previously announced that it would run at least ten simulation exercises in order to test security preparations and inter-agency working practices at selected venues (BBC News, 2011a). This follows on from extensive preparatory work since London was awarded the right to host the Games (in 2005) undertaken by the London Resilience Forum, which was commissioned to scope the extent of Olympic resilience preparedness across agencies in London and to coordinate pan-London resilience activity for the Games (Coaffee, 2009a).

References

Associated Press (2011a) IOC Confident in 2012 Security after Norway Attack. Online: www.google.com/hostednews/ap/article/ALeqM5jEAvW8oNQteUILtu9u35CRBfOz0A?docId=9f35f78940ec4cab8e7fef18cf7c05dc (accessed 25 July 2011).

Associated Press (2011b) Security a Top Challenge in London in Year before Olympics. Online: www.tsn.ca/olympics/story/?id=372250 (accessed 22 July 2011).

Association of Chief Police Officers (2011) Secured by Design Accredits the Commonwealth Games Village for 2014. Online: www.securedbydesign.com/news/viewstory.aspx?id=1445&url=www.securedbydesign.com/editable_pages/SBD_1290529722870.html (accessed 22 July 2011).

Atkinson, R. and Helms, G. (eds) (2007) *Securing and Urban Renaissance – Crime Community and British Urban Policy*, Bristol: Policy Press.

BBC News (2011a) London 2012: How ready is the capital? Online: www.bbc.co.uk/news/uk-england-london-14251906 (accessed 26 July 2011).

BBC News (2011b) Olympic Security Preparedness Tests Launched. Online: www.bbc.co.uk/news/uk-14020722 (accessed 5 July 2011).

BBC News (2011c) London 2012: 13,500 troops to provide Olympic security. Online: www.bbc.co.uk/news/uk-16195861 (accessed 15 December 2011).

BBC News (2003) Blair backs Olympic bid. *BBC News*. Online. Available HTTP: http://news.bbc.co.uk/sport1/hi/other_sports/3029851.stm (accessed 5 May 2011).

Bennett C. and Haggerty, K. (eds) (2011) *The Security Games: Surveillance and control at mega events*, London: Routledge.

Benton-Short, L. (2007) Bollards, Bunkers, and Barriers: Securing the National Mall in Washington, DC, *Environment and Planning D: Society and Space*, 25 (3), 424–446.

Boyle, P. and Haggerty, K. (2009) Spectacular Security: Mega-Events and the Security Complex, *International Political Sociology*, 3, 257–274.

Candidate file 2012 (2004) London: London 2012.

Clarke, G. (1976) Olympic Security: A $100m task, *New York Times Magazine*, 6 June, 8.

Coaffee, J. (2010a) Protecting Vulnerable Cities: The UK resilience response to defending everyday urban infrastructure, *International Affairs*, 86 (4), 939–954.

Coaffee, J. (2010b) Urban Regeneration and Renewal at the Olympics, in Gold, J. R and Gold, M. (eds) *Olympic Cities: urban planning, city agendas and the world's games, 1896 to the present*, London: Routledge (second edn), 180–193.

Coaffee, J. (2009a) *Terrorism, Risk and the Global City – Towards Urban Resilience*, Farnham: Ashgate.

Coaffee, J. (2009b) Protecting the Urban: The dangers of planning for terrorism, *Theory, Culture & Society*, 26 (7–8), 343–355.

Coaffee, J. (2006) From Counter-Terrorism to Resilience, *European Legacy – Journal of the International Society for the Study of European Ideas* (ISSEI), 11 (4), 389–403.

Coaffee, J. (2003) *Terrorism, Risk and the City*, Aldershot: Ashgate.

Coaffee, J. and Fussey, P. (2010) Security and the Threat of Terrorism, in Gold, J. R. and Gold, M. (eds) *Olympic Cities: city agendas, planning and the world's games, 1896 to 2012* (second edn), London: Routledge, 167–179.

Coaffee, J., Fussey, P. and Moore, C. (2011) Laminating Security for London 2012: Enhancing security infrastructures to defend mega sporting events, *Urban Studies*, 48 (15), 3311–3327.

Coaffee, J. and Johnston, L. (2007) Accommodating the Spectacle, in Gold, J. R. and Gold, M. (eds) *Olympic Cities: Urban planning, city agendas and the world's games, 1896 to the present*, London: Routledge, 138–149.

Coaffee, J. and Murakami Wood, D. (2006) Security is Coming Home – Rethinking Scale and Constructing Resilience in the Global Urban Response to Terrorist Risk, *International Relations*, 20 (4), 503–517.

Coaffee, J., Murakami Wood, D. and Rogers, P. (2008) *The Everyday Resilience of the City: How cities respond to terrorism and disaster*, Basingstoke: Palgrave-MacMillan.

Coaffee, J. and O'Hare, P. (2008) Urban Resilience and National Security: The role for planners, *Proceeding of the Institute of Civil Engineers: Urban Design and Planning*, 161, DP4, 171–182.

Cook, I. (2007) Beijing, 2008, in Gold, J. R. and Gold, M. (eds) *Olympic Cities: City agendas, planning, and the world's games, 1896 to 2012*, London: Routledge, 286–297.

Croft, S. and Moore, C. (2010) The Evolution of Threat Narratives in the Age of Terror: Understanding terrorist threats in Britain, *International Affairs*, 86 (4), 821–835.

Daily Mirror (2011) London 2012: Theresa May says Olympics are safe from terrorists despite police cuts, *Daily Mirror*. Online. Available HTTP: www.mirror.co.uk/news/top-stories/2011/07/06/london-2012-theresa-may-says-olympics-are-safe-from-terrorists-despite-police-cuts-115875–23250442/ (accessed 6 July 2011).

Daily Telegraph (2011) 'Robertson rejects Chinese criticism of 2012 security', (Sport) 10/8/2011, p. 4.

Daily Telegraph (2001) 200 Suicide Bombers Planning Attacks in UK. Online: www.telegraph.co.uk/news/uknews/terrorism-in-the-uk/8815574/200-suicide-bombers-planning-attacks-in-UK.html (accessed 8 October 2011).

Decker, S., Greene, J., Webb, V., Rojeck, J., McDevitt, J., Bynum, T., Varano, S. and Manning, P. (2005) Safety and Security at Special Events: The case of the Salt Lake City Olympic games, *Security Journal*, 18 (4), 65–75.

Eick, V. (2011) Secure our Profits!: The FIFA in Germany 2006, in Haggerty, K. and Bennett, C. (eds) *The Security Games*, London: Routledge.

Essex, S. and Chalkley, B. (1998) Olympic Games: Catalyst of urban change, *Leisure Studies*, 17, 187–206.

Foreign and Commonwealth Office (2011) Brazil: Rio 2016 Olympics: Sport Security, Rio de Janeiro: British Consulate General, March.

Fussey, P. (2010) The Role of Surveillance in Securing Major Events, in Richards, A., Fussey, P. and Silke, A. (eds) *Terrorism and the Olympics: Lessons for 2012 and beyond*, London: Routledge.

Fussey, P. (2007) Observing Potentiality in the Global City: Surveillance and counterterrorism in London, *International Criminal Justice Review*, 17 (3), 171–192.

Fussey, P. and Coaffee, J. (2011) Olympic Rings of Steel: Constructing security for 2012 and beyond, in Bennett, C. and Haggerty, K. (eds) *The Security Games: Surveillance and control at mega events*, London: Routledge, 36–54.

Fussey, P., Coaffee, J., Armstrong, G. and Hobbs, R. (2011) *Sustaining and Securing the Olympic City: Reconfiguring London for 2012 and beyond*, Farnham: Ashgate.

Gardham, D. (2011) Olympics 2012: Police to take part in terror exercises ahead of games, *Daily Telegraph*. Online: www.telegraph.co.uk/sport/olympics/news/8617312/Olympics-2012-police-to-take-part-in-terror-exercises-ahead-of-games.html (accessed 5 July 2011).

Giulianotti, R. and Klauser, F. (2009) Security Governance and Sport Mega-Events: Toward an interdisciplinary research agenda, *Journal of Sport and Social Issues*, 34 (1), 49–61.

Globe and Mail (2011) Rioting in London Raises Olympic Games Security Questions. Online. Available

HTTP: www.theglobeandmail.com/sports/more-sports/rioting-in-london-raises-olympic-games-security-questions/article2123305/ (accessed 8 August 2011).

Gold, J. R. and Gold, M. (eds) *Olympic Cities: City agendas, planning and the world's games, 1896 to 2012* (second edn), London: Routledge.

Guardian (2011a) 'Rioting threatens Premier League's opening weekend', (Sport) p. 1 10/8/2011.

Guardian (2011b) 'US officials worried about security at London 2012 Olympics', page 1. 14/11/2011.

Harvey, D. (1989) *The Condition of Postmodernity*, Oxford: Blackwell.

Hinds, A. and Vlachou, E. (2007) Fortress Olympics: Counting the cost of major event security, *Jane's Intelligence Review*, 19 (5), 20–26.

HM Government (2011) *CONTEST: The United Kingdom strategy for countering terrorism*, London: Stationery Office.

HM Government (2010) A Strong Britain in an Age of Uncertainty: The national security strategy.

Home Office (2011a) London 2012: Olympic and Paralympic safety and security strategy.

Home Office (2011b) One Year To Go. Online: www.homeoffice.gov.uk/media-centre/news/olympics-one-year (accessed 26 July 2011).

Home Office (2009) Working Together to Protect Crowded Places: A consultation document, London: Home Office.

London Evening Standard (2011) Dangerous Void at Top of Met Threatens Olympic Security. Online: www.thisislondon.co.uk/standard/article-23970862-dangerous-void-at-top-of-met-threatens-olympic-security.do (accessed 18 July 2011).

LA Times (2011) Security Strategy Evolves One Year Ahead of London. Online: http://articles.latimes.com/2011/jul/26/sports/la-sp-olympics-security-20110727 (accessed 26 July 2011).

Ministry of Defence (MOD) (2011) Military Support to 2012 Olympic Games Announced. Online: www.mod.uk/DefenceInternet/DefenceNews/MilitaryOperations/MilitarySupportTo2012OlympicGamesAnnounced.htm (accessed 15 December 2011).

National Audit Office (2011) Preparations for the London 2012 Olympic and Paralympic Games: Progress report, December 2011 (summary), London: HMSO.

Németh, J. and Schmidt, S. (2007) Toward a Methodology for Measuring the Security of Publicly Accessible Spaces, *Journal of the American Planning Association*, 73(3), 283–297.

Observer (2009) Biometric tests for Olympic site workers. Online. Available HTTP: www.guardian.co.uk/uk/2009/oct/11/biometric-tests-for-olympic-site (accessed 11 October 2011).

Poynter, G. (2009) The 2012 Olympic Games and the Reshaping of East London, in Imrie, R., Lees, L. and Raco, M. (eds) *Regenerating London: Governance, sustainability and community in a global city*, London: Routledge, 131–150.

Public Accounts Committee (PAC) (2008) The Budget for the London 2012 Olympic and Paralympic Games: Fourteenth report of session 2007–08, London: HMSO.

Raco, M. (2007) Securing Sustainable Communities Citizenship, Safety and Sustainability in the New Urban Planning, *European Urban and Regional Studies*, 14 (4), 305–320.

Raco, M. and Tunney, E. (2010) Visibilities and Invisibilities in Urban Development: Small Business Communities and the London Olympics 2012, *Urban Studies*, 47(10), 2069–2091.

Richards, A., Fussey, P. and Silke, A. (2010) *Terrorism and the Olympics: Major event security and lessons for the future*, London: Routledge.

Rio2016 (2007) *Rio de Janeiro Applicant File – Theme 13: Security*, Rio de Janeiro: Brazil.

Samatas, M. (2007) Security and Surveillance in the Athens 2004 Olympics: Some lessons from a troubled story, *International Criminal Justice Review*, 173, 220–238.

Sanan, G. (1996) Olympic Security Operations 1972-–94, in Thompson, A. (ed.) *Terrorism and the 2000 Olympics*, Sydney: Australian Defence Force Academy.

Saul, B. (2000) Olympic Street Sweeping: Moving on people and the erosion of public space, *Polemic*, 11 (1): 34–37.

Sibley, D. (1995) *Geographies of Exclusion*, London: Routledge.

Sinclair, I. (2011) *Ghost Milk: Calling time on the grand project*, London: Hamish Hamilton.

Toohey, K. and and Veal, A. 2007 *The Olympic Games: A Social Science Perspective*, Wallingford: Cabi.

9

PREPARING TEAM GB FOR LONDON 2012

Dave Collins and Andrew Cruickshank

Introduction

As the euphoria following the success in Singapore abated, administrators, performance directors and head coaches across the UK started to wrestle with the additional challenges represented by a home Games. Preparing a team across an Olympic cycle is a multifaceted problem in itself. The award of the Games to London brought great benefit, as we mention later (this is covered in other chapters), but also some additional pitfalls that needed to be addressed. Developing a structure that exploited these benefits, across both the long and short term, whilst countering the pitfalls was the issue from a performance perspective, however, and this is the thrust of this chapter.

Accordingly, the chapter is built around consideration of the macro/longer-term to micro/short-term challenges of preparing a team for the London Games. Particularly at the micro level, these challenges clearly varied from team to team: sailing and swimming presented different issues despite the hydro-similarities! In a similar fashion, the issues also varied across teams on other factors, including: previous records of success (e.g. track cycling versus handball); 'status' of the sport in the public perception (e.g. athletics versus air pistol); and the consequent issues of media pressure. The number of journalists 'assigned' to the sport also impacts on this pressure. For example, the existence of the British Athletics Writers' Association ensures a constant background of copy and attention (not always a positive feature), whilst football will always get coverage (e.g. Hassan, 2011). Other sports, by contrast, only seem to experience the media spotlight once a quadrennial, or when particularly good or bad news occurs: it is interesting to note the apparent preference for the latter, at least amongst some sections of the media (as instanced by the media storm around the RFU and World Cup performance, which was raging as this chapter was finalized). This highlights some of the macro issues around preparation, which means that this chapter will stray into political factors even though these are certainly covered more ably and in more depth elsewhere (see Chapter 22, for example). Accordingly, we start and conclude with the macro political picture and how this has impacted on team preparation. In between, we consider the tactics and strategy of team preparation, exploring how this has been modified to meet the particular challenge of London 2012. In all cases the perceptions are our own, although these are informed by personal experience as a performance director (PD), ongoing contact with elite Olympic sport as support practitioners and our work on the pressures and methodology of culture change, which has been informed by interviews with current and recently retired PDs. We start by reviewing the political climate and how it impacted on the preparation challenge.

Before and after Singapore – how the goalposts moved

The world before

The major development in UK sport before the award of the Games was the initiation of the World Class Performance Plans (WCPPs) and the associated structure of institutes started by British Prime Minister John Major as a response to the UK's poor performance in international sport. Kicked off in the mid-1990s (Department of National Heritage, 1995), the resulting revolution of cash, resources and a tight focus on performance generated an immediate – even worryingly[1] – positive outcome at the 2000 Sydney Olympic Games. The extent to which this thrust was overly Antipodean (with a strong slant towards the Australian Institute of Sport as *the* model) is a matter for debate (see Collins and Bailey, 2012). However, there is no doubt that the changes and their interactions made an indelible impact on the Olympic sports that were the main thrust of the initiative. The impact was, however, undoubtedly differential. Some sports took the money and unashamedly used it to support the status quo, with (we would suggest) insufficient recognition of the need for evolution of accepting such a 'with strings' award. Others, starting perhaps from a lower/less-developed base and, interestingly, with inherent advantages due to structural centralisation, can trace a new genesis to the inception of WCPP funding. Notably, cycling, sailing and rowing initiated a rapid growth process from the kick provided *and* their willingness to think in new ways with a more focused and (some at the time would say) cutthroat approach has generated obvious benefit in terms of results, status and probable longevity.

There is one other, slower-burning change that is worthy of consideration as a formative influence on the pre-Singapore environment. The work of the British Olympic Association (BOA), particularly that of Technical Director Kevin Hickey (previously a national coach in boxing), set a new standard in professionalism of approach, application of sport science and medicine, and the use of now-staple features such as holding camps. With a variety of partners and contacts, the BOA designed and deployed steering groups (SGs) of discipline-specific professionals who, in turn, developed training and structures for practitioners gathered in advisory groups (AGs – for example, the Psychology or Coaches Advisory Group – PAG and CAG respectively). So effective were these structures that the early days of the UK Sports Institute (which involved for 'some reason or other' the usurping of the AGs and SGs) were accurately seen by many as a retrograde step! This short-term hiccup notwithstanding, the environment had already been changed forever through these systems and the training days and camps that served to spread the new philosophy. As a result, the award of the Games to London was made to an already well-developed world-class system.

Inevitably perhaps, the juxtaposition of these two developments also laid the basis for an altogether more negative but still pervasive influence on British performance sport, namely the clash between the BOA, which had established itself as *the* source of knowledge on matters of performance, and what eventually became UK Sport, the government-based, 'funding and more' agency with the allocated responsibility for the establishment, evolution and driving of the new order. We return to this ongoing tension later in the chapter. For the moment, consider the problems that accrue when one organization is considered by another to be a usurper, especially when the early days of the new kid on the block are particularly unclear in terms of direction and approach.

All these initiatives were history by the time of Singapore. The waves were still impactful, however, resulting in a well-established government agency with a burgeoning staff with the stated desire to be 'more than just a bank', against a largely self-funding Olympic Association who wanted to be seen as more than just a 'quadrennial travel agency'.

The world after

With the announcement of the Games to London, several predictable and a few less predictable cycles swung into action. On the 'easy to see coming' side, the public interest cycle followed the same pattern as first identified by the International Olympic Committee's (IOC's) own consultants in Sydney: namely, high euphoria and enthusiasm, followed by cynicism and critical comment, swinging back to a wave of interest and excitement as the time approached. This had little direct influence on PD preparations, although the way the pattern was reflected in the media was at least a distraction and sometimes – when the low coincided with some poor performances, for example – led to more 'noise' than usual for a number of sports.

Less predictable and altogether more impactful (unless the sport system was very careful) was the influx into the UK sporting scene of numerous 'specialists' and their ideas. This is not to say that the new blood wasn't bringing something useful; in many cases (some of which were unfortunately ignored) the messages were overwhelmingly correct. It was just that the timing and implementation of the consequent change could have been better managed to accentuate the positives (more on this crucial factor of change management later in the chapter). For several sports, this influx involved new coaches (often at significant expense), new PDs and management teams and, most notably in the case of the BOA, a completely new technical director (Sir Clive Woodward) and management structure, from Chair and CEO downwards. All these changes created tensions, some positive but many less so. There is little doubt, however, that the implications of these changes, facilitated, enabled, driven by or, at the very least, announced on the back of London 2012, had significant impact upon the sporting landscape against which preparation took place.

Having set the scene and context against which preparation took place, this chapter will now consider the finer detail of what was done. To facilitate the contrast, we start by offering an overview of how it is 'usually' done, focused on the preparation for, and run in to, the Games.

The preparation process

Generics – getting a team ready for world-class competition

Clearly, a full exposition on the training and preparation of elite athletes across all the Olympic sports is somewhat beyond the scope and space of this chapter. Accordingly, we will focus on the generic elements that all PDs, coaches and administrators must consider. Far and away the biggest consideration is the need, or lack thereof, for adjustment to the venue – specifically the climate, time difference, venue characteristics and any special issues such as local diet and crowds.

The usual way to counter these issues starts with the establishment of a holding camp, a venue far enough from the competition site to enable access to training facilities and, where necessary, practice opponents, whilst close enough to offer sufficient similarities in climate and time zone. For example, Team GB used the Gold Coast (Sydney), Cyprus (Athens) and Macau (Beijing) as the holding camp venue across the last three Summer Olympiads. In each case, the holding camp needed to be as climatically 'extreme', or maybe even more so, as the competition venue, to enable acclimatization. Thus, heat and humidity were if anything slightly higher than in the host city. Some aspects were deliberately avoided, however. For example, Beijing and to a lesser extent Athens were both seen as carrying a pollution-related challenge. Scientific calls that no acclimatization to this aspect was possible then resulted in a 'minimal exposure' strategy, whereby athletes flew into the host city normally three days before their event. The ease of this transition was another issue in holding camp selection. Avoiding a tiring day's travel two days before your event is a key factor. Accordingly, camp site selection looked at direct communication lines (single flights wherever possible), together with a raft of tactics to minimize the travel lag further. Water at regular intervals, baggage being brought early and handled by others, mealtimes catered for and, wherever possible, direct entry and exits with little or no queuing. The latter is facilitated by the modern trend to have Olympic lanes and special entry facilities at host city airports.

Table 9.1 provides an example of the levels of detail needed, showing a plan for a track and field athlete preparing for the World Championships in Beijing in 2006. Two things to note here: first, the additional notes, which personalize the generic plan to the athlete's needs; second, the fact that the eventual Beijing Olympic planner was about twice as long, as new details were layered into the plan. The point is that holding camps are rarely used just once pre-Olympic Games. Good sense demands that procedures are trialled and tested several times; in this case, World Juniors in 2006, Worlds in 2007 and the Olympic Games in 2008.

At the holding camp itself, time and climatic adjustment are the key benefits. Accordingly, PDs spend some time thinking through how the first few days will take place, and Table 9.1 shows steps to ensure that time change goes in the right direction (sleep late, curtain closed) and heat/humidity acclimatization is carefully accomplished. Training is sparing – final polish rather than repair – and PDs must be aware of the need to hold athletes back from doing too much. As the plan in Table 9.1 shows, countering boredom (and its close bedfellow, anxiety) is also key. As detailed above, leaving the holding camp and travelling constitute another potential pitfall, being almost invisible if done well, but disastrous and highly damaging if one gets it wrong. The potential impacts of the holding camp have been well seen in the last two Olympic Games, with the Cyprus camp seen as 'a challenge' whilst the excellent work of Bernie Cotton in Macau drew almost universal praise and an MBE into the bargain!

Finally, arrival into the competition venue, how the last few days are spent and ensuring that all necessary details are covered are big concerns in this last phase. Not much, if anything, can be done here to make things better but a lot can go wrong, which can wreck the chances of even the hottest favourite! Access and moving around the venue is always a big concern at Olympic Games, where accreditation rules and security are even tighter than normal. Checking where one can go, how quickly and with what accreditation level is an important part of the parallel games played by PDs, coaches and administrators. Knowing where everything is and how quickly support can reach a performer are essential parts of the support staff armoury.

Two other major considerations merit attention. First, the venue-specific challenges that characterize certain sports and how these may (or may not) be overcome. The ecological challenges for sailing are obvious, for example, requiring a vast amount of extra intelligence and background information, which, in turn, informs a research and development phase to address these venue-specific issues. Thus, since Beijing was on calmer than usual water, with lower than usual winds predicted, a whole raft of procedures were developed, practised and deployed in the years leading up to the Games. These sorts of challenges impact a wide variety of factors including: the physical size and shape of the athletes; selection criteria and methods; team assembly; and the amount of time one can spend at the venue in the years before and the year of the Games (often necessitating a specialist holding camp at the venue itself).

Table 9.1 Anonymized performance logistics plan for a World Junior Championships team

Travel and Acclimatization

Phase 1: UK Departure Saturday 5 August London Heathrow Term. 1 BA 31 21:15 (12 hours flight time, GMT + 7 hours).
Arrival HKG Sunday 6 August Hong Kong International 16:05 (transfer to Macau by TurboJet).
HKG–Macau Departure Sunday 6 August HKG–Macau 18:00 18:50 or 22:00 22:50.
Macau–team hotel Westin Resort 20 mins.
Evening meal or supper in hotel before bed.
www.westin-macau.com 1918 Estrada de Hac Sa, Coloane, Macau.

WEBSITES OF INTEREST

www.westin-macau.com
www.macautourism.gov.mo
www.huaduhotel.com.cn

	PHYSIOLOGICAL	*MENTAL/ORGANIZATIONAL*	*TECHNICAL/TACTICAL*	*PHYSICAL/MEDICAL*
Depart UK to Macau preparation camp	**Hydration strategy:** Which drink? How much? Bottled water. *XX to decide what drink/how much.*	**What to pack:** Baggage allowance (20 kg) GB kit check Essential items for main bag and hand luggage? What can be left behind? **Passport/Visa.**	**Technical Plan:** How much training? What aim? **Medallist in both events.** *Coaches to liaise.*	**Training:** Training loads before departure. Training schedule for Macau. Timing of sessions.
	Nutrition strategy: Food and drink for flight. What and when to eat. *XX to take responsibility for flight food and drink.*	**Mental preparation plan:** Distraction techniques (e.g. good book, DVD, cards). *XX giving this some thought – doesn't play golf but caddies well!*	**Qualifying and final requirements? (see phase 4)** IAAF rules, esp. for qualifying.	**Medical plan in UK:** Complete UK: medical form. TUE/Anti-doping. History of childhood breathing problems. *XX to complete.*

Acclimatization: How long will it take? Is there anything I can adapt in the UK? Heat/humidity adaptation. *3 days before – 1hr early to bed/1hr early up advances difference 3 days.*	**Plan Bs:** *XX to give this some thought.*	**Training load:** Danger of overtraining. Check schedules. *Good experience now and has worked with Lead Coach before.*	**Vaccinations summary:** Hepatitis A (last 10 yrs). Typhoid (last 3 yrs). Tetanus (last 10yrs). *XX to arrange NOW!*
Recovery from travel: Tips for travelling. Sleep on flight. Sleep on arrival. Sleep disruption. *LEG ROOM ESSENTIAL FOR FLIGHT.*	**Getting 'away from home' mentally:** No problems here.	**Sessions with Coach?** ***Or someone else?*** Team Coach contact details. *Sessions with Lead Coach to be planned.*	**Medical plan for Far East:** Physiotherapy. **Massage.** *Performance Manager to check Masseur and confer.*
Confirm flight details here: FLIGHTS AS SHOWN AT THE TOP OF THIS SHEET.	**Sharing a room with a team mate (unavoidable!):** Simple rules of sharing. Healthy living. *Will share with YY (1st choice) or ZZ. Bed length needs to be considered.*	**Come the competition phase, do I want to discuss tactics and opposition with Team Coach?** *Yes. Coaches to confer.*	**Recovery:** Ice baths. *Ice baths used. PM to check availability in Macau and Beijing. Portable IB to be considered please.* As stated in above notes.

continued

Table 19.1 Continued

Phase 2: Macau preparation camp (From Tuesday 8 August – Saturday 12 August).
Suggested Stadium training times 08:00–11:30 and 17:30–20:30 (see PM re. endurance options).
Meal timings 06:30–09:00 12:00–14:00 19:30–21:30 (will be some flexibility providing request is made in advance).

		PHYSIOLOGICAL		*MENTAL/ORGANIZATIONAL*	*TECHNICAL/TACTICAL*	*PHYSICAL/MEDICAL*
DAY 4 (Tues. 8) TO DAY 8 (Sat. 12)	Macau (Westin Hotel)	**Hydration strategy:** As above. Practice hydration strategy that will be implemented at competition venue. Hot/humid. Living with air-conditioning.	XX	**Refinement of mental preparation:** Plan Bs. Boredom.	**Technical plan:** Preparing for IAAF competition rules. One early and at least two later sessions – reflecting comp. schedule.	**Medical plan:** Physiotherapy. Massage. *Massage required.*
		Nutrition strategy: Maintaining or adapting normal diet to meet Far East conditions. Danger of overeating? Confirming nutritional pack for competition day? *Essential behaviour:* *Drink bottled fluid.* *Caution with uncooked/cold food.*	XX	**Distraction plans to be employed:** Recreational and leisure activities (www.macautourism.gov.mo). Group and individual mentality. Trips to town.	**Tapering strategy:** See training plan below. *Lead and personal coaches to confer.* *Availability of grass for strides?*	Pee test. Check daily weight at same time. Sleep. Mood.
				Team meetings: Sun. 6th – 20:00 team briefing. Mon. 7th – 10:00 team and coaches. Sat. 12th – 13:00 team meeting – pre-Beijing departure. *Press conference arranged in advance.*	**Tests:** Formal or informal (establish a taper test). *Establish the session and stick to it!*	**Medical – general health:** Insect repellent/cream. Wear appropriate clothes at dusk! Gastroenteritis – take sensible precautions – wash hands regularly!

	Recovery/cooling strategy: At training site. *Access to ice bath needed.*		**Communication plan for significant others!** Keeping in touch with Personal Coach. Keeping in touch with family in the UK.	XX	**Squad sessions:** Relay squad sessions (to add). *Relay coach to plan.*		**Training plan:** Tapering. 'Competing' at pre-set comp. time. *Practising day of…?*
	Environmental (see preparation CD): Sunburn. Humidity/pollution. Exhaustion.		**Preparing for Beijing:** Washing kit. Packing bags for departure. Competition kit check.		**Review:** Of prep. camp with Personal or Team Coach.		**Warm-up:** Confirm and/or adapt its timing and content. *Modify warm-up in the conditions.*

Phase 3: Departure for Beijing Sunday 13 August Macau–Beijing NX 2 12:00–15:10 (flight time 3hrs 10 mins, GMT + 8 hours) 08:30 departure from team hotel.

	PHYSIOLOGICAL		*MENTAL/ORGANIZATIONAL*		*TECHNICAL/TACTICAL*		*PHYSICAL/MEDICAL*
Depart preparation camp	Hydration strategy. Nutrition strategy.	*XX to take respon.*	Distraction plan for flight. Essential items to hand baggage.	*XX to take respon.*	Training on departure day?	*NO.*	Individual medical support plan.

continued

Table 19.1 Continued

Phase 4: Arrival in Beijing Sunday 13 August 15:10–16:45 (travel time to team hotel 30 mins).
Hua Du Hotel, No. 8 Xinyuan Nanlu, Chaoyang District, Beijing 100027; www.huaduhotel.com.cn; hdfd@huaduhotel.com.cn.

	PHYSIOLOGICAL	*MENTAL/ORGANIZATIONAL*	*TECHNICAL/TACTICAL*	*PHYSICAL/MEDICAL*
? Add per individual Days to event.	Hydration strategy for competition day. Nutrition strategy for competition day. *XX to take responsibility and sort out.* **Recovery/cooling strategy:** At trackside AND in team hotel. **Ice bath.**	Hotel familiarization. Major championship atmosphere. Visit stadium (Monday). *What should I look for?* Team meeting time. **Final pre-comp. team meeting.** **Preparing for day(s) of competition (bringing it all together on a repeated basis).**	*Coaches* **Add current heat and final time for athlete.** Rd 1, 15 August 1140/SF; 16 August 1900/F; 17 August 1925. 4×4 19/20 August 2035/2050. *Qualifying/team times/tactics?* **Travel/timing arrangements to venue:** *Call room times?*	**Physio/massage?** *As normal?* *What is normal?* **Assisted stretch/mobilization prior to running please!** **Warm up:** Timing and content. *Coach to provide details.*
	Environmental: Pollution. Sunburn.	**When to rehearse?** Schedule/timing. *When to relax?*	**ANY practice?** *What will be allowed within stadium?* *How intense?*	**Massage warm up/down?** As normal? **Ice bath and rubdown after running (incl. finals!).**

Phase 5: Departure from Beijing Monday 21 August Beijing–LHR 1 BA 38 11:25–15:10.

NOTES FROM MEETING BETWEEN Performance Manager/XX/Personal Coach Thursday 8 June.

- Dentist appointment to be added to the list (month before departure).
- Kit issued where? *XX issued kit last year senior – same kit. Anything missing will need to be sorted. Distributed at U23/U20 Trials.*
- Masseur with team to be confirmed and to collaborate with XX's masseur at L'boro.
- Portable ice bath to be taken – just in case. *No. Baths are available at the competition site, plus ice machines, therefore guaranteed. No problem.*
- Grass running in Macau to be confirmed. *The Westin Resort (website above – click on link to 'country club') Golf course available good grass.*
- Personal coach accreditation for TWO coaches. *Team Leader is aware of the requirements for N and M – to be sorted on location.*
- PCs in same hotel – arrange best package deal and who with – please advise. *I will let you know of available tours ASAP.*
- Which stadium is it in Beijing? Is there a website for familiarization purposes? *BEIJING CHAOYANG SPORTS FITNESS AND LEISURE PARK.*
- Meeting to be arranged for XX with N/M in Beijing sometime on 14 August. *No problem with the meeting but access to track for team only; therefore, will have to rely on feedback through Lead Coach*

Second, and emerging from similar sport-specific challenges, it may be the best option for sports to remain in their own familiar environments for the maximum time (obviously the best idea in principle). Thus, for Beijing, the track cycling team stayed put at the Manchester Velodrome, flying business class direct to Beijing and into the Village a few days before kick-off. Obviously, this option is only available for certain sports with certain venues; the air-conditioned indoor track offers cyclists this possibility. However, given the home venue for 2012, this option is worth considering as a model for more sports. We turn to this possibility in the next section.

For the moment, how the final few weeks are structured has been acknowledged as a key part of the performers' preparation and, accordingly, receives an increasing amount of attention by cross-sport agencies. This brief overview should hopefully provide a context for the specific challenges that London posed and which Team GB had to meet.

Specifics – getting ready for London

From a purely practical point of view, the intended size for Team GB in London was an early issue. Estimates of 550–600 athletes, yielding a team size of over 1,000 when the formula-permitted support and administrative staff were added, compared alarmingly with previous team sizes (311 athletes in Beijing, for example). However, such pragmatics are both easily seen and (comparatively) easily overcome against the more subtle and complex challenges inherent within a home games.

As in other aspects of life, the glass half-empty/half-full differential manifests itself clearly in opinions on the pros and cons of London for Team GB. Much of the argument swings around the home advantage versus home 'choke' phenomena, both of which are well documented and investigated in psychological literature. For example, the home advantage is well established in football (in the English Premiership, a home team can be expected to score 37.29 per cent more goals than the away team), with this effect seen as contributing to the World Cup success of England (1966), Germany (1974), Argentina (1978) and France (1998). More pertinently for 2012, however, are the ways in which this home advantage may come about. Is it largely due to referee bias (see Boyko, Boyko and Boyko, 2007) or crowd effects (Wolfson, Wakelin and Lewis, 2005)? If so, in either case the home advantage at an Olympic Games may be far less tangible. By contrast, the literature also discusses the disadvantages of competing at home (Baumeister, 1984, 1995; Baumeister *et al.*, 1984, 1985), the so-called home 'choke'. In either case, some intellectual consideration of the pros and cons (see Pollard, 2008) of home advantage seems merited, even though the balance of the literature is currently for the home advantage (De Bosscher *et al.*, 2006). These academic considerations notwithstanding, the vast majority of athletes, supporters, commentators and hoi polloi have held such a significant expectation of advantage pre-London that the well-known power of expectancy effects seem likely to ensure that it applies. This sort of 'positivity' exerts a subtle but inexorable pressure for athletes to perform well (see Rosenthal, 2002). However, it does need to be carefully monitored as it can quickly become negative.

Given that almost everyone expects an advantage, and consequently expects improved performance over the remarkable team achievements in Beijing, how have sports people and 'powers that be' acted to (try to) ensure the realization of this advantage? We now consider the steps taken, comparing and contrasting them with the 'normal procedures' characterized in the previous section.

Following their well-established form from previous cycles, the BOA were in the game early, exploring possibilities for a holding camp well before the London Games. Early negotiation with three leading possibilities changed quickly to the emergence of Aldershot as a new front-runner. The military presence in this historical garrison town ensured well-secured, private accommodation, with a range of facilities and the promise of 'upgrading and more', as required. Although this centralization was seen as undesirable by many sports people, there seemed to be a strong groundswell of opinion in support, reflecting perhaps the well-organized and successful Macau experience.

At that time, another issue emerged which was a previously unconsidered feature of London 2012. As part of their responsibility, the London Organizing Committee of the Olympic Games (LOCOG) had to develop and distribute a 'brochure' of training facilities across the UK, which could be used as holding camps by other national Olympic committee (NOC) teams. As usual, the bigger teams were well in advance of this process, with enquiries to one noted UK sports university reportedly occurring the week after the Singapore announcement! The issue that arose was related to this list. Building on the benefits of WCPP finance, British sports had established specific training venues and/or networks of training centres at which their own athletes were busily preparing. Now, faced with the possibility of prestigious foreign teams (and hard cash), many councils were enthusiastically advertising the very facilities (such as the cycling track that had been used before Beijing) that should now form the basis of the home advantage. In track and field, for example, potential medallists in 2011 were drawn from nine different training venues. To the best of our knowledge, seven venues were committed to foreign teams up to seven weeks before the Games, removing the opportunity for many British athletes of a reassuringly normal and consistent preparation in their home venue. This problem was exacerbated for Paralympic athletes, who faced a potential loss of training venues twelve weeks before their event. So far as we know, at the time of writing these issues remain unaddressed.

Of course, another big feature of home advantage is local knowledge and experience: not such an issue for swimming or track and field (although note our comments later), but absolutely basic to sports such as sailing, slalom canoeing or mountain biking. It would be fair to suggest that equal access to competition venues has *not* been a feature of the GB experience at previous Olympic Games, neither Summer nor Winter. Indeed, restricting access has been publicly stated by some nations as a benefit of holding the Games: it is certainly a commonly acknowledged issue, and one that remains unaddressed by the IOC! It is unclear what restrictions were or were not in place for visiting teams wishing to get early experience of the competition venues around London. Our own perceptions suggest, however, that access has been a good deal more equable than in previous Olympiads. Whether this is positive or negative, we leave the reader to decide.

With regard to the establishment of a holding camp, the managerial changes at the BOA brought about a parallel set of modifications elsewhere. The final venue for this, Loughborough University, was clearly a home training venue for a minority of athletes. The degree of disturbance they will experience, given the venue's function as a holding camp, remains unclear. Certainly it is our understanding that all selected athletes are expected to pass through the camp some time before entering the Village (also note that the team is selected and run by the BOA on the basis of recommendations from each sport). Given that several sports arranged holding camps abroad, there was a significant potential for this requirement to be a pain at best, and at worst to provide a burst of media scrutiny, rendering pointless many of the reasons for teams training abroad (and out of the public eye).

Another issue, the simple accessibility of Team GB athletes to their friends and family, also needs consideration. Increasing use of social media has made the world a smaller place. However, that often ignored technical feature, the 'off' switch, does mean that athletes away from home can control levels of communication and fully exploit the 'in a bubble' environment which preparation camps endeavour to engender. How much should athletes be allowed to go home in the run-up to an event that makes them the centre of social attention wherever they go? Members of the rowing team were discussing taking one Sunday per month as a day of rest in the run-up to the Games. Interestingly, their recent World Championships in the UK may have given rowing one of the best test runs of any sport; so was their decision to stay in the bubble a good one? Or, since these athletes are over the age of consent, should they merely be prepped and inoculated against the endless questions and left to their own devices? The answer is, of course, both complex and individual, but, for you the reader, the 20:20 hindsight of reading this evaluation after the Games could offer an answer. As a general rule, however, it is worth assaying how 'different' the levels of attention will be for different athletes. For tennis or football the levels are almost nothing new, whilst for shooting or handball the experience is altogether more novel. There will be a good deal of 'learning after the event' for all but the most informed and best-prepared sports.

Finally, let us return to team size issues; specifically in this case the challenge for sports that through lack of performance have been comparatively absent from recent British teams. Of course, the home games format offers 'automatic qualification' to these sports, most notably for team sports. Very early in the quadrennial, before Beijing in fact, the BOA (with whom the final selection decision rests) stated that 'no reasonably credible performance' from a British athlete should be rejected; a statement which fuelled further speculation about team size! As another consequence, and building on seed-corn investment from UK Sport, these new kids on the block embarked on a variety of ingenious 'get good quick' schemes in an attempt to reach a level strong enough to get a place on the London team. Handball, for example, selected a team through the use of UK Sport and English Institute of Sport talent-transfer initiatives, then moved the whole lot to Denmark (a handball hotbed) for intensive development. Women's volleyball pursued a similar option, which, until their funding was cut in 2010, seemed to be yielding success. It is to the credit of all concerned that the team have continued to develop, working hard at various fundraising schemes to keep going and achieving their most successful season ever in 2011! Clearly, development of the complex skill sets required in team games represents the hardest challenge for talent transfer athletes. Despite a plethora of publicity (almost propaganda), it will need a post-Games forensic examination to see how effective such initiatives have actually been (see MacNamara and Collins, 2011).

'Noises off' – distractions from the task at hand

From Singapore onwards, high-level interactions in sport entered a new set of challenges with the large-scale BOA changes alluded to earlier. Certainly the 'trough' phase of the public perception cycle (see above) was characterized by a continuation of 'discussions' that had started pre-Beijing. Relating to a broad range of topics, including finance (e.g. how much the BOA should get from LOCOG), coach education/athlete support (Sir Clive's suggestions versus the extant systems) and sport liaison/representation (both the BOA and UK Sport now have a staff dedicated for this), these were at best distractions or, in the damage done to key functional relationships and the almost knee-jerk changes of personnel and responsibility, rather destructive. In our opinion, the impact of these various events has been mediated by the structural and systemic bubbles established by the PDs of the various sports. As with any team, the cracks will only really appear when the pressure mounts.

Accordingly, in evaluating the 2012 experience, it is worth considering the principles underlying this culture building and how these ideas may have been differentially applied across the political and Olympic-related phases preceding and following London.

Coping with the challenge – setting and maintaining the culture

Although a vast number of factors are implicated in Olympic performance, from individual performer refinement (e.g. of physical/technical efficiencies) to optimizing team processes (e.g. effective communication) to the organizational functioning of the BOA (e.g. holding camp planning), the unique culture of each sport is, as outlined above, one of the most significant leading into and during any Games. Indeed, reflecting culture's agency in shaping day-to-day, moment-to-moment thinking, emotion, behaviour and (most significantly) performance (Cruickshank and Collins, 2011; Krane and Baird, 2005), the merits of PDs' meticulous attention to this feature are clear – especially when rushing headlong into the high-pressure environment of a home Games. Of course, the wider culture of Team GB is always important, but even the BOA's '15 minimum standards' for London, focused on generic, pan-sport expectations in areas such as hygiene, good manners and clothing, were defined by Woodward as enabling a 'baseline culture' rather than anything more comprehensive (Gibson, 2011). Furthermore, and akin to our discussion of home advantage/home choke, the 'one shot at glory/last chance saloon' element of Olympic competition will always unexpectedly propel some pre-event 'also-rans' into the stratosphere of jubilation and plunge some odds-on favorites to the depths of despair. However, barring extreme outliers, the shared cultural values, beliefs, standards and practices instilled by each sport can do much to ensure that, on the whole, opportunities are maximized (e.g. home advantage) and potential losses minimized (e.g. external 'noise') when it comes to preparing to perform on the day.

In terms of creating and regulating high-performing cultures, the optimization of coherent and integrated coaching, sports science and sports medicine systems is primarily and logically central to success. Specifically, without a concerted effort to enhance performers' physical, technical, mental and tactical attributes alongside their avoidance/recovery from injury or illness, the production of medal-winning athletes would not be possible. Beyond this fundamental feature, a number of mechanisms focused on optimizing the social milieu are also required to ensure that all members of the environment (incorporating performers, support staff, team management and PDs themselves) consequently remain focused on the task at hand, make decisions that continually support the actualization of peak performance and, most importantly, self-govern the maintenance of performance-optimizing processes. For these purposes, PDs have had to act both internally (within the organization/sport) and externally (with outside stakeholder/partner agencies) in the run-up to 2012. Regarding the former, harnessing the social power of key staff members and performers to drive the desired culture from within was one valuable approach (Railo, 1986), and this was clearly utilized by cycling, for example. Regarding the latter, PDs also worked hard to facilitate positive perceptions in wider socio-political contexts (e.g. with the BOA, UK Sport and the general public), to reinforce the desired culture and protect staff and performers from 'noise'. A read through pre-Games interviews provides evidence of this.

Certainly, although not explicitly described in the job description, a crucial role of the PD involves preventing distractions from top-level governance reaching and disrupting the performance environment. Importantly, however, while PDs must fight their corner to ensure that any anxiety/conflict-inducing reverberation is minimal, this is juxtaposed, rather problematically, with the need to ensure political sensitivity and avoid situations in which their actions could be construed as contradictory or defamatory. In the case of 2012, for example, as funding from UK Sport was vital for success, PDs needed to be extremely wary of failing to establish, optimize and protect a strong relationship with this organization, particularly if pre-Games results failed to meet expectations and/or negative media agendas were in operation. In fact, recognizing the sensationalist reporting now synonymous with high-profile sporting events/

individuals (Carter, 2007) – playing the 'media game', even if things are going well – is a necessity; once again, a critical read through media interviews offers a demonstration of how well, or how badly, this has been done.

How were these prominent culture-building principles (i.e. coherent/integrated support systems, group-governed perceptions and practices, managing above, managing the media) tailored to exploit the benefits and counter the pitfalls of the WCPP and post-Singapore contexts? And how will they evolve beyond London and into the next Olympic quadrennial?

Taking the WCPP first, the increased funding that arrived from its induction opened many previously locked doors for PDs and their efforts to deliver sustained success. Reflecting the scale of restructuring, a key role of the PD was therefore to ensure that the optimism generated from this new focus on performance was harnessed to a pragmatic and scrupulous planning process aimed at deciphering when, where and how newly available resources should be introduced and packaged for maximal and lasting impact. Indeed, it is no surprise that some of the most successful sports leading into 2012 (e.g. cycling, sailing and rowing) did not only ride the initial funding-revolution wave but also engaged in a level of forethought that would see them catch the next one. Additionally, although liberated from previous financial shackles, a new emphasis on maintaining positive perceptions in those above (i.e. UK Sport) was born to ensure that funding was sustained, with a major focus on facilitating realistic medal targets and educating the funders about the processes, not the outcomes, of performance.

Having undoubtedly felt the benefit of the WCPP, the need for Team GB to take another purposeful step forward in their medal-winning capabilities after Athens was invigorated by the award of the 2012 Games. However, while this unique tipping point (Kim and Mauborgne, 2003) provided PDs with an opportunity to aid their staff and performers' rapid acceptance and uptake of new/adjusted systems, processes and procedures aimed at facilitating success in 2008 and forming robust foundations for 2012, this was tempered by the task of ensuring that their environments remained entirely focused on performance in Beijing (which had now taken on a whole new level of significance in terms of its impact on the funding and approach for London).

As noted earlier, a large part of this challenge lay in managing the influx of 'specialists' who, along with performers, incumbent staff and top-level governance, sought a stake in potential London glory. With the pressure of success in Beijing raised to a level only a looming home Games could elicit, so, therefore, did the PDs need to deploy a range of mechanisms to quell the likelihood of serious and distracting introspection by members of their environment – a challenge not made any easier by the major reconstruction of the BOA and then, for some, drastic financial cuts in UK Sport's 2012 funding programme (the £600 million originally pledged across all sports in 2006 being cut to £550 million as a result of the global financial crisis). For example, even though table tennis had delivered its agreed targets, its support was reduced by 50 per cent the year after Beijing (Gilmour, 2011). Furthermore, the cycle of public opinion also meant that PDs (more so in historically higher-profile sports) had to ensure that the cultures constructed and regulated within their respective environments were robust enough to handle the ensuing media scrutiny demanded by a home audience in the years, months, weeks, days and hours preceding competition (whether coverage was unrealistically expectant or unjustly critical). Accordingly, with PDs' decision making now widely open to contest from above (by national governing bodies/BOA/UK Sport), below (performers/staff) and the side (the media/public), culture optimization heading into 2012 was dependent on political acumen and the ability to shape media/public perception as much as, or in some cases more than, expertise in generating sports performance! However, while efforts to optimize the likelihood of success in London reflected the deployment of all of these skills, the context-specific nature of culture change means that the nuances of these critical success factors will change yet again heading into preparation for Rio 2016.

Lying at the heart of the post-London task will be the major loss of funding which some will inevitably experience. Specifically, the loss of the extra resource provided by the government, private sector and the Team 2012 initiative to optimize the likelihood of home success will generate an irretrievable void for all. Again, some sports that have become particularly adept at looking ahead as well as optimizing performance in the present will feel the pinch less severely. For example, British cycling's venture with BSkyB helped deliver the qualification of a five-man road race team for London whilst also, pending the extension of the current agreement, providing their PD with significantly greater scope through assured funding streams than many others preparing for Rio: the classic business principle of diversifying product lines being applied to good effect. For many others, therefore, optimizing the perceptions of UK Sport before the announcement of the 2016 funding programme, including careful negotiation of medal targets, will be a vital first/next step in many PDs' next culture change programme. Beyond this, a focus on early success in 2013 may go a little way towards attracting new private sponsorship. However, coming at the expense of sacrificing long-term development (which many sports have clearly done in the quest for 2012 success), such an approach may have major implications on the culture's orientation and longevity. Furthermore, careful work to ensure that media and public expectation is quickly realigned to match the post-London funding deficit will need to be engaged in by PDs across the board. Accordingly, regardless of each sport's success in 2012, all key culture-building principles (including those not mentioned here) will require significant dissection and remodelling as the new political, economic and competitive conditions unfold.

Conclusions – (how) could things have been better?

As this is written, the UK awaits the London games with mixed feelings. After success in Beijing (fourth in the medals table, with 19 golds and 47 in total), the publicly expressed target of third place, since moderated to fourth and fixed there by the glare of public examination, has served to keep the pressure on as the various personality clashes, organizational machinations and practical problems have rumbled on. Whilst these may be inevitable, and no doubt the whole thing will be presented as a resounding success, we cannot help but speculate on how much better things could have been, were the political clashes, both personal and organizational, to have been solved, and were the 'no compromise/performance-focused' mantras required of the sports people to have been equally required of the organizers. We suggest that, with better, tighter and less point scoring, both performance and structural legacy for sport could have been greater.

As it rests, government assurances of continued investment (although on a smaller scale) have enabled ongoing work towards Sochi and Rio. It remains to be seen how much of the momentum will be retained as the baton is passed. In the meantime, 'it's been emotional'.

Note

1 Because the outcome was so positive, many felt that expectations of outcomes from resource input were accordingly set too high.

References

Baumeister, R. F. (1984) 'Choking under pressure: Self-consciousness and paradoxical effects of incentives on skillful performance', *Journal of Personality and Social Psychology*, 46: 610–620.

Baumeister, R. F. (1995) 'Disputing the effects of championship pressures and home audiences', *Journal of Personality and Social Psychology*, 68: 644–648.

Baumeister, R. F., Hamilton, J. C. and Tice, D. M. (1985) 'Public versus private expectancy of success: Confidence booster or performance pressure?' *Journal of Personality and Social Psychology*, 48: 1447–1457.
Baumeister, R. F. and Steinhilber, A. (1984) 'Paradoxical effects of supportive audiences on performance under pressure: The home field disadvantage in sports championships', *Journal of Personality and Social Psychology*, 47: 85–93.
Boyko, R. H., Boyko, A. R. and Boyko, M. G. (2007) 'Referee bias contributes to home advantage in English Premiership football', *Journal of Sports Sciences*, 25 (11): 1185–1194.
Carter, N. (2007) '"Managing the media": The changing relationship between football managers and the media', *Sport in History*, 27: 217–240.
Collins, D. and Bailey, R. (2012) '"Scienciness" and the allure of second-hand strategy in talent development', *International Journal of Sport Policy*. Online: DOI:10.1080/19406940.2012.656682.
Cruickshank, A. and Collins, C. (2011) 'Culture change in elite sport performance teams: Examining and advancing effectiveness in the new era', *Journal of Applied Sport Psychology*, 24: 338–335.
De Bosscher, V., De Knop, P., van Bottenburg, M. and Shibli, S. (2006) 'A conceptual framework for analyzing sports policy factors leading to international sporting success', *European Sport Management Quarterly*, 6 (2): 185–215.
Department of National Heritage (1995) 'Raising the game', GB Government Publication.
Gibson, O. (2011) 'Sir Clive Woodward draws up lists of 'standards' for GB Olympic athletes', *Guardian*. Online: www.guardian.co.uk/sport/2011/jul/12/sir-clive-woodward-standards-olympic?INTCMP=SRCH (accessed 24 October 2011).
Gilmour, R. (2011) 'London 2012 Olympics: GB table tennis team "lost motivation" after funding cuts, says Steen Hansen', *Telegraph*. Online: www.telegraph.co.uk/sport/olympics/table-tennis/8836779/London-2012-Olympics-GB-table-tennis-team-lost-motivation-after-funding-cuts-says-Steen-Hansen.html (accessed 20 October 2011).
Hassan, G. (2011) 'Olympic "Team GB" is a football farce', *Guardian*. Online: www.guardian.co.uk/commentisfree/2011/jun/24/olympic-team-gb-football (accessed 13 November 2011).
Kim, W. C. and Mauborgne, R. (2003) 'Tipping point leadership', *Harvard Business Review*, 81 (4), 60–69.
Krane, V. and Baird, S. M. (2005) 'Using ethnography in applied sport psychology', *Journal of Applied Sport Psychology*, 17: 87–107.
MacNamara, Á. and Collins, D. (2011) 'Comment on "Talent identification and promotion programmes of Olympic athletes"'. *Journal of Sports Sciences*, 29 (12): 1353–1356.
Pollard, R. (2008) 'Home advantage in football: A current review of an unsolved puzzle', *The Open Sports Sciences Journal*, 1: 12–14.
Railo, W. (1986) *Willing to win*, Utrecht: Amas.
Rosenthal, R. (2002) 'Covert communication in classrooms, clinics, courtroom and cubicles', *American Psychologist*, 57 (11): 839–849.
Schlenker, B. R., Phillips, S. T., Boniecki, K. A. and Schlenker, D. R. (1995) 'Where is the home choke?', *Journal of Personality and Social Psychology*, 68 (4): 649–652.
Wolfson, S., Wakelin, D. and Lewis, M. (2005) 'Football supporters' perceptions of their role in the home advantage', *Journal of Sports Sciences*, 23: 365–374.

10

GOVERNANCE OF THE LONDON 2012 OLYMPIC AND PARALYMPIC GAMES

Vassil Girginov

This chapter addresses the governance of the 2012 London Olympic and Paralympic Games. The 2009 Olympic Congress in Copenhagen recognised governance as a central issue for the Olympic Movement and codified it in a document entitled 'Basic Universal Principles of Good Governance of the Olympic and Sports Movement' (IOC, 2008). The document is underpinned by a moral philosophical position, which was enshrined in the International Olympic Committee's (IOC) Code of Ethics and stipulates that 'the basic universal principles of good governance of the Olympic and sports movement, in particular transparency, responsibility and accountability must be respected by all Olympic Movement constituents' (IOC, 2010, C.1). Naturally, these universal principles of governance also apply to the bidding and organisational processes of the Olympic Games as well as to the planning of the imprint they leave in host cities and countries.

As a cultural phenomenon the Olympic Games belongs to humanity, with its *raison d'être* to celebrate human excellence in all its forms. However, as a legal and economic entity the Games is an intellectual property of the IOC. The IOC is the guardian and ultimate authority of any question relating to the Games. The IOC entrusts to any given city the responsibility of hosting the Games, but the government of the host country must provide legally binding guarantees to underwrite the costs involved. Furthermore, the IOC generates substantial revenue for the Olympic Movement through two global sources of capital – the Olympic Programme (TOP – a sponsorship programme) and the broadcasting rights, which amounted to US$4.960 billion in the 2009–2012 quadrennial (IOC, 2010). The Olympic Movement is made up of three main constituent groups – the IOC, the National Olympic Committees (NOC) and the International Federations (IFs), plus the organising committees for the Olympic Games (OCOG). Hence, the Games-governing environment is inherently complex, institutionally congested and multilayered. It involves local, national and international actors, and an array of private and public interests.

In order to address the main concern of this study, the chapter is structured in three parts. First, it examines the nature of governance and its relevance to the Olympic Games. Second, the chapter analyses the Games as a governance issue, and finally it focuses specifically on the key governance dilemmas exhibited in the organisation of the 2012 London Olympic and Paralympic Games.

Governance as an exchange, institution and instrument

The notion of governance has emerged as a response to the state and market failures to address a number of social and economic problems of modern societies. The state has been traditionally understood to be empowered to pursue public interests versus the egoistic and particularistic interests of private citizens as expressed in the market. The rationality of governance, as Jessop (2000, p. 16) writes, is 'dialogic rather than monologic, pluralistic rather than monolithic, heterarchic rather than either hierarchic or anarchic'. This is in contrast to government, which is associated with command and control. The main concern of governance is with power within the context of changing polity and relations between the state and civil society. The key theme that underpins most of the literature in the field is that of governance as steering, where increasingly governments have to negotiate policy objectives with civil society on which the state depends for resources (Houlihan and Groeneveld, 2011).

In the UK context, the need for governance, or a balance between statisation and marketisation, in the late 1990s and 2000s has been addressed through New Labour's commitment to a 'stakeholder society' and more recently through the Conservative–Liberal Democrat coalition government's declared aspiration towards a 'big society'. In both cases, the primary point of governance, as Jessop observed, is, 'that goals will be modified in and through ongoing negotiation and reflection. This suggests that failure may comprise failure to redefine objectives in the face of continuing disagreement about whether they are still valid for the various partners' (Jessop, 2000, pp. 17–18).

Governance has three core meanings, including a certain type of exchange between the state and society (i.e. political theory or politics), a process of steering concerned with enhancing government's capacity to act by forging strategic partnerships with various actors (i.e. polity) and an empirical phenomenon dealing with the deployment of specific policy instruments (i.e. policy – see Jordan, 2008; Peters and Pierre, 1998; Rhodes, 2007; Treib, Bähr and Falkner, 2007). Governance, therefore, is about achieving common goals through partnerships by steering collective actions towards achieving consensus amongst the parties involved. Its mechanisms provide the framework in which various actors operate in order to achieve agreement over a common vision, while developing solutions to emerging problems.

Governance has always been a central concern for the Olympic Movement, which is reflected in its visions, structures and operations as well as its relations with global political issues. Over the past hundred years it grew from a modest, white male-dominated club to a global social movement incorporating 205 culturally diverse member countries and numerous other stakeholders. Recently, the relevance of governance to the Olympic Movement has become very explicit. The 2009 Olympic Congress in Copenhagen resulted in a number of recommendations and practical steps have been taken concerning polity, politics and policy. In particular, recommendations 32, 33, 37, 38 and 41 make it very clear that the autonomy of sport should be preserved while interacting with government bodies (politics), that broader coalitions and partnerships with various international and national institutions should be forged (polity) and that a range of policy instruments, from legal measures to ethical codes, should be deployed to ensure the success of Olympic visions (policy) (IOC, 2009).

Olympic governance can be discerned at several levels, each providing a different focus of steering. The main concern at local level is with developing the organisational, economic and political capacities of sport organisations to deliver services effectively to their members; at national level the emphasis is on creating systems of rule setting and enforcement to allow for equal participation in sport and fair distribution of resources; while at global level the priority is to develop strategies and regimes for the long-term survival of the Olympic Movement. The next section examines what makes the Olympic Games a governance issue.

The Olympic Games as a governance issue

The Olympic Games is the practical manifestation of Olympism, which is a philosophy of social reform that emphasises the role of sport in world development, international understanding, peaceful coexistence and social and moral education. Olympism claims the status of a social, political and educational ideology, which promotes an idealised conception of the human being. The Olympic Games and the philosophical anthropology on which it is premised have been conceived and promoted as a developmental project based on normative ideas about what constitutes the ideal citizen, the institutions designed to promote such a citizen and the main instruments for achieving these ideals (Girginov, 2010).

Therefore, the Olympic Games, and what it stands for, represents a governance issue for three main reasons. First, contrary to the idealistic view of sport's political neutrality, the Games has always pursued some political ideals, striving for equality, inclusion or more recently sustainable development. Sustainability brings a whole new dimension to the conceptualisation and delivery of the Olympic Games. This is because at the heart of sustainability is an expressed concern with meeting the needs of different people while distributing social and economic benefits equally and fairly across society. Sustainable Olympic Games are premised on three important assumptions: the creation of intersubjective meanings that go beyond individual beliefs; participation; and a mandate for action (Girginov and Hills, 2009). The IOC first introduced the notion of governance to the Olympic Charter in 2004 (IOC, 2004) in recognition of the growing democratisation of the Olympic Movement. The Charter was further amended to accommodate developmental assurances required by governments wishing to host the Olympic Games as to political, economic and security guarantees, as well as committing to the promotion of a positive legacy (IOC, 2007). The IOC's governance commitment was reinforced in its Interim Report of 2009–2010, *Shaping the Future* (IOC, 2010), which makes specific reference to the need to promote good governance and to the contribution of the 2010 Vancouver Winter Olympic Games Organising Committee in developing a new governance model for the Games.

Second, the Games represents a developmental project concerned with promoting a universal normative vision about the ideal citizen. Moreover, the Olympic Charter also prescribes the role of the institutions involved in the organisation of the Games and their conduct. Increasingly, more and more aspects of the Games have been codified including the Host City Contract, some 30 technical manuals, and the ambitious 'Look of the Games' and 'Olympic Games Impact' programmes as well as a structured transfer-of-knowledge process. These specific strategies and instruments serve an important purpose, what Jessop (2000, p. 16) termed 'decentralised intersystemic context steering'. Steering is achieved by communications intended to aid mutual understanding. In this regard, the Olympic Movement's wealth, legal power and knowledge are used as symbolic communication media to modify the structural and strategic context and to ensure compliance. Olympism, and the Olympic Games in particular, promises to develop athletes, communities and sport in general. Thus, those who organise the Games propose to intervene on behalf of others, raising the question of the legitimacy of their claimed trusteeship. The staging of the Games creates institutional difficulties by breaking down the symmetry between decision makers (e.g. the IOC, the UK government) and decision takers (e.g. the communities and people of the parts of East London subject to development). The result is a tendency to neglect the equivalence principle, which is central to governance and at its simplest suggests that those who are significantly affected by a global good or bad should have their say in its provision and regulation.

Third, the Games is inherently a collective exercise, from the bid to the legacy stage and beyond, and involves multiple stakeholders including athletes, clubs, NOCs, IFs, IOC, sponsors, broadcasters and a myriad of local actors. The staging of the Games represents a form of intentional development, which is concerned with the deliberate policy and actions of the state and other agencies, as expressed in the vision and strategic objectives of the Olympic programme. In 2007 the IOC introduced a holistic approach to the management of the Games, called 360°. This approach transcends the narrow idea of 'doing things right' and focuses on 'doing the right things' by considering the wider Games environment, including local culture and the role of various stakeholders (IOC, 2010). In particular, each edition of the Games requires new partnerships to be forged, which are then inserted into the existing national and local systems of governance. Parent, Rouillard and Leopkey (2011) reported that in the case of the 2010 Vancouver Winter Olympic Games, 97 different departments across three levels of federal, provincial and municipal government needed coordinating.

Exchanges, institutions and policy instruments in the governance of London 2012

Bidding and organising the 2012 London Games provides an illuminating example for the interplay between the key characteristics of governance, including the processes of creating shared meaning and visions, mobilisation of public support, participatory decision making and obtaining a mandate for action. These processes involved several years of deliberations and negotiations, the forging of various coalitions and a contested steering of a multitude of diverse actors, locally, nationally and internationally. The London Games also exemplifies the interplay between governance as polity (i.e. constellation of actors), politics (i.e. exchange) and an empirical phenomenon (i.e. policy instruments).

The politics, or exchange between the state and civil society, did not only begin in 2003 when the London Olympic bid was first announced. There is a long history of political disinterest at national level in hosting the Games, allowing regional agendas to be promoted instead. The unsuccessful bids of Birmingham 1992 and Manchester 1996 and 2000, which were given lukewarm support by the government, illustrate the point. The original London bid represented a mixture of national and local concerns, with its international aspirations added at a much latter stage in order to increase its appeal to the IOC. Formulating the national advantages of hosting the Games rested on a well-rehearsed argument that a successful bid would significantly boost the development of sport and bring a range of tangible and intangible economic and social benefits to the UK. Determining the main beneficiaries locally proved much harder, however. Evans's chapter in this volume documents the protracted political struggles in choosing London, and its eastern part in particular, as the main site of the Games (see chapter 4).

By its very nature, the Olympic bid represents a promise made by the city of London and the UK government, both to the international community and to the people of Britain. In exchange, central and local governments have asked for a mandate to organise the Games and to spend significant amounts of public money. The bid was based on a process of consultations with various constituencies including the five host Olympic boroughs of London, the business and sport communities and other stakeholders. The 'Back the Bid' campaign received some 1.2 million signatures from Londoners (Newman, 2007) and a further 68 per cent of the UK population were in favour (Dave, 2005). However, the support from various stakeholders was conditional. Sport England, the agency charged with promoting participation, backed the bid on the understanding that no investment from grassroots sport would be diverted and that was not reliant on Sport England Lottery funding. Both conditions were broken, and in 2007 the former Chair of Sport England, Derek Mapp, was asked to resign by the Secretary of State over his criticism of the Labour government for diverting Lottery money to support London 2012.

Furthermore, the consultation process, as Fussey, Coaffee, Armstrong and Hobbs (2011) demonstrate, had not always been steered according to the fundamental principles of governance. In particular, it was marred by the lack of clarity about aims, sources of funding, legacy and the role of local communities. The Olympic Minister and the Department of Culture, Media and Sport (DCMS) have been criticised for violating a fundamental tenet of governance concerning transparency about funding of the Games. The House of Commons Select Committee expressed concerns that 'so far the process followed by the Government has produced in public no more than a 12 page summary of a 250 page document containing only impenetrable, estimated, aggregated costs ... However, this was of limited use for the purposes of accountability and none whatsoever with regard to public debate' (House of Commons Culture, Media and Sport Committee, 2003, p. 11). Subsequently, the Olympic budget has become a hotly debated topic by parliamentary committees, the National Audit Office (NAO) and the media.

The funding model of the Games was another crucial governance issue, as the resources promised by the government could have been secured in a number of different ways. Eventually, in 2007, a public sector funding package for the Games totalling £9.298 billion was decided, which represents an increase of over 400 per cent over the original estimate given in the bid document of £2.254 billion (DCMS, 2011; NAO, 2007). The public sector contribution includes £6.248 billion from central government, £250 million from the London Development Agency, £625 million from Greater London Authority to be raised in the form of Council tax on local citizens and £2.175 billion from the National Lottery. This arrangement was fixed in a memorandum of understanding between the above stakeholders, which is not a legally binding document and, in line with the reflexive nature of governance, has been reviewed several times to reflect the effects of government spending reviews and other environmental challenges.

As an exchange between state and society, the Games funding model presents a number of issues, which have not yet been satisfactorily addressed. For example, London citizens have not been consulted on whether they support a council tax hike of £20 or £40 per annum per household (depending on property value rather than income). This tax has been particularly unfair to low-income families and those in rented accommodation. The National Audit Office also expressed concerns that £575 million from the National Lottery may be diverted from the non-Olympic good causes such as the arts, health, education and heritage, all of which rely on Lottery funding (NAO, 2007, p. 48).

A central assumption of governance is the creation of intersubjective meanings as the basis for collective action. Getting all 2012 London international, national and local stakeholders to agree on a set of core visions for the Games posed formidable challenges. This is evident from the minutes of the first meeting of the new Olympic Board in 2005. A main item on the agenda was the delivery of the overall Olympic programme where 'it was agreed that high-level workshops would be convened.... The aim of the workshops would be to discuss and agree the common Olympic Programme Objectives for the main Stakeholders; London Organising Committee of the Olympic Games (LOCOG); Government (led by the Department for Culture, Media and Sport, DCMS); The Mayor; the British Olympic Association; and the Olympic Delivery Authority (ODA)' (DCMS, 2005).

The Olympic Games programme vision and strategic objectives (exhibit 1) were inclusive as they promised to meet the needs of all stakeholders – from athletes to local residents (LOCOG, 2009).

Exhibit 1 The Olympic Programme Vision and Strategic Objectives
Vision: To host an inspirational, safe and inclusive Olympic and Paralympic Games and leave a sustainable legacy for London and the UK

Objectives

1 To stage an inspirational Olympic Games and Paralympic Games for the athletes, the Olympic Family and the viewing public.
2 To deliver the Olympic Park and all venues on time, within agreed budget and to specification, minimising the call on public funds and providing for a sustainable legacy.
3 To maximise the economic, social, health and environmental benefits of the Games for the UK, particularly through regeneration and sustainable development in East London.
4 To achieve a sustained improvement in UK sport before, during and after the Games, in both elite performance – particularly in Olympic and Paralympic sports – and grassroots participation.

However, views about what constitutes successful delivery of those objectives differed markedly. For example, the current coalition government quietly abandoned the main deliverable for objective 4 – a further 1 million people playing more sport by 2012 – set by the previous Labour government. For the London Assembly (2010, p. 4), the Games will *only* be successful if they bring about a 'transformation in the life chances of London's most deprived communities'. As the former Mayor of London, Ken Livingstone eloquently put it:

> I didn't bid for the Olympics because I wanted three weeks of sport. I bid because it's the only way to get the billions of pounds off of the government to develop the East End
>
> *(Livingstone, 2008).*

What these views illustrate is that governance entails different time horizons and mechanisms of coordination, and constant modification of goals. While the Games were expected to boost sport participation significantly within three or four years, improving the life chances of the people of East London was going to take 20–30 years (HBSU, 2009). The rift between the central government and the five Olympic boroughs over the legacy of the Games has been well publicised. *(Girginov, 2011)*

The polity of the Games governance reveals a complex tapestry of institutions, numbering over 90 in London alone, as well as several layers of coordination. What is more, LOCOG is expected to issue some 75,000 contracts, thus further complicating the governance landscape. Table 10.1 shows the main institutional actors and their interests. Multiple stakeholders such as the IOC, the international governing bodies whose sports are on the Olympic programme, the National Olympic Committees, clubs, athletes, sponsors and local stakeholders are interconnected not only structurally, through committees and boards, but by proxy through their interests as expressed in different legal and organisational documents. For example, the Olympic Charter stipulates that no venue can be constructed or competition schedules decided without the explicit approval of the IOC and IF (IOC, 2007, R.47). Furthermore, the Charter explicitly prescribes that LOCOG shall not only provide IFs with the requisite premises and facilities but will ensure that particular companies furnish the necessary sport equipment.

Locally, the institutional constellation of actors involved in governance is equally complex and entangled. Catney, Henneberry and Dixon (2006, p. 1) have mapped the institutional congestion regarding the regeneration of the brownfield land, which is one the Olympic sites, and compared it with a maze of policy structures (26 in total) and regimes that 'may undermine the effective delivery of Brownfield regeneration'. The situation is further compounded by the five Olympic boroughs governance framework in the form of a long-term strategy for regeneration of East London (HBSU, 2009).

A major key player in the governance of London 2012 is LOCOG, which is a private company limited by guarantee with responsibility for the delivery of all Games-time operations. The company has no shareholders, and as a private company is neither obliged to apply the principles of corporate governance nor to comply with the Freedom of Information Act to disclose any information. This situation puts in question the main principles of governance as they apply for the public and non-governmental institutions involved in the Olympic Games and makes them hard to enforce. However, LOCOG voluntarily agreed, as a matter of best practice, to comply with the standards of conduct set out in Section 1 of the Combined Code of Corporate Governance published by the Financial Reporting Council (LOCOG, 2011, p. 54). As a result, LOCOG has kept an open Statutory Register of all companies they have been dealing with and have published regular annual reports and accounts. LOCOG has also systematically applied the sustainability standards established in 'Towards a One Planet 2012' Games sustainability plan (LOCOG, 2009) to all aspects of their operations and to those of their partners. This has not always been successful, however, and with regard to the first low-carbon torch, by the admission of LOCOG's own Chair, 'in simple terms, we didn't quite get there' (Coe, 2012). Many aspects of the governance process remain confidential, and although LOCOG has agreed to hand over all Games documentation to the National Archives, there will be a 15-year embargo before the public can scrutinise the handling of the Games.

Table 10.1 Key actors in the governance of London 2012 Olympic and Paralympic Games and their interests

Actors	*Strategic interests*
International	
IOC	Promote Olympic values and revenue generation
IFs	Establish state-of-the-art sport venues and revenue generation
TOP Sponsors	Brand promotion
Broadcasters	Provide spectacle, entertainment, promote national agendas
National	
ODA	Deliver facilities and infrastructure
LOCOG	Staging the event successfully
BOA	Promote elite sport
LDA	Enhance skills, employment, regeneration, legacy
GLA	Ensure good policy and governance for London
HMG	Ensure national policy requirements
NHS	Promote health issues and provide service
Five Host Boroughs	Ensure social and economic regeneration
Local	
NOC	Promote national elite sport systems
Sport clubs	Promote own athletes and sport
Athletes	Promote equitable and ethical participation

Most institutions on the Olympic scene existed well before the Games were awarded to London, but now they had to forge new partnerships with existing and emerging organisations. Rule 36 of the Olympic Charter stipulates that the organisation of the Olympic Games is entrusted by the IOC to the NOC of the country (i.e. the British Olympic Association in the UK) and the host city (IOC, 2007, p. 75). This has turned a voluntary organisation, the BOA, into a key partner of the UK government. Figure 10.1 shows the global governance structure of the Olympic programme and the lead partner for each of the four main objectives. The structure is clearly government led and several commentators (Girginov, 2011; Grix and Phillpots, 2011; Hayes and Horne, 2011; Poynter and MacRury, 2009), including the Audit Commission, expressed concerns that 'government policy has moved from encouraging partnerships to mandating them, even though voluntarism is the key to effective joint working' (Audit Commission, 2009, p. 1). The Department for Communities and Local Government raised another important issue concerning the equivalence principle of governance – that those who are being affected by the Olympic Games have not been adequately involved: 'while "legacy" is often cited as a key dimension in the actions of partners, there appears to be a blind spot around the need to engage people in this process and a lack of imagination in how the very wide range of activities can promote the legacy' (Keogh, 2009, p. 56).

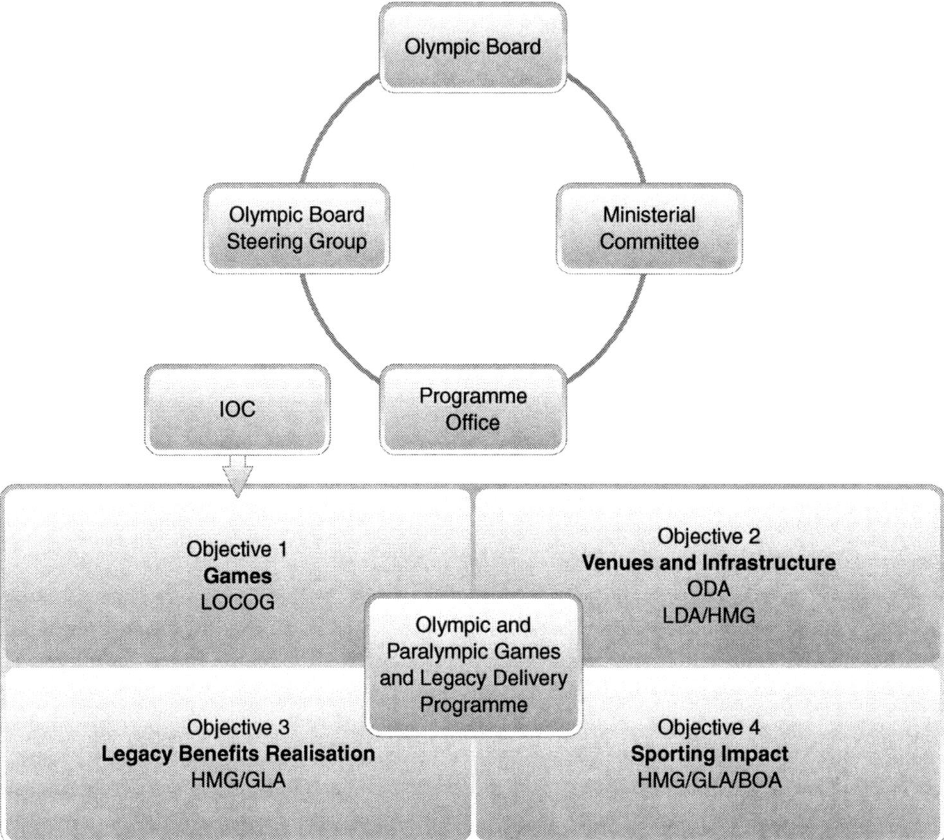

Figure 10.1 Global governance structure of the London 2012 Olympic and Paralympic Games.

Public participation, as a central tenet of governance, has been problematic for London 2012, as has been demonstrated in the context using the local communities and small businesses of East London (Fussey *et al.*, 2011; Hayes and Horne, 2011; Raco and Tunney, 2010). A central plank of the London bid and subsequent government promises (DCMS, 2007) was that the Games would be used to inspire young people and to transform their lives. However, as a representative study of the Department for Children, Schools and Families revealed,

> The spontaneous assumption made by young people is that involvement in the London 2012 Olympic Games & Paralympic Games will constitute either competing in the events or watching the events live. This in itself perhaps contributes to the perception that getting involved will be difficult, as young people assume that both of these activities will be hard to achieve.
>
> *(Johnson et al., 2008, p. 28)*

Not surprisingly, 45 per cent of these 5–19-year-olds stated that they would focus on watching the Games on television. Furthermore, young people overwhelmingly consider playing sport as a critical condition for getting involved with the Olympic Games, which automatically precludes many from associating themselves with this event.

The legacy promise of the Games set out in the UK government's *Our Promise for 2012* (DCMS, 2007) presented a separate set of governance issues. While the delivery of the Games was mainly concerned with ensuring good governance practices, including transparency and accountability, the legacy challenged Olympic developers' ability to shape the future of society, and the lives of young people in particular. The governance of the London Games sport legacy has been discussed in some detail elsewhere (Girginov, 2011). What is worth noting here is the fact that the UK government's original legacy visions articulated in three separate policy documents (DCMS, 2007, 2008, 2009) made only a passing reference to governance, while the current coalition government's 14-page legacy plan that replaced them mentions 'governance' only once in relation to modernising the work of sport governing bodies.

Considered as politics, the London Games saw the deployment of four main modes of governance – coercive, voluntary, targeting and framework regulation – and a wide range of policy instruments. The chief example of an explicit and highly prescriptive (coercive) mode of governance has been the passing of the London Olympic Games and Paralympic Games Act (2006), designed to control the work of the ODA, Regional Development Agencies and the use of Olympic insignia. While the need for the Act has never been questioned, the speed with which it was passed through Parliament in order to honour the government commitments to the IOC has been unprecedented. This raises a number of issues concerning the public participation process and the main beneficiaries of this Act (see chapter 6, James and Osborn's contribution to this volume).

Most policy instruments deployed in steering the Olympic programme have been voluntary in nature. Examples include strategy development at regional, local and institutional levels and specific public engagement programmes such as 'Get Set' and the Inspire mark promoted by LOCOG (www.london2012.com). What unites those programmes from a governance point of view is their declared aspirations to develop others. In that, they have become powerful instruments of cultural governance (Fairclough, 2000), concerned with shaping meaning and promoting specific discourses about how organisations should operate and how individuals should act.

The targeting mode of governance has been concerned with identifying groups and sectors from society and then devising non-binding but detailed recommendations for policies to affect change. The two main explicit targets subject to intervention have been East London, as a geographic, economic and demographic area, and young people. To that end a range of flagship social, housing, skills development and sport programmes have been initiated. The London Mayor's Economic Development Strategy – objective 5, action point C – aspires to bridge different areas and

> the Mayor will fully seize the unique regeneration opportunity offered by the 2012 Olympic and Paralympic Games, managing investment so that it contributes to the broader aim of 'convergence', or raising quality of life across the five host boroughs to the London average.
>
> *(GLA, 2010, p. 61)*

Sport England's 'Places People Play' strategy specifically targets 'iconic, inspired and protected facilities' as well as a new generation of 40,000 young 'sport makers', volunteers to promote Olympic values (Sport England, 2010). However, several target programmes, such as free swimming for the over 60s, were discontinued due to lack of funding.

The framework regulation mode of governance carries a law-binding spirit but allows participants some leeway in the implementation of decisions. The overall governance of the Olympic programme was established in 2005 with a 32-page Master Framework Memorandum of Understanding between the Secretary of State, the Mayor and the BOA, and to which LOCOG is also a party. The Memorandum is not legally binding, but was drawn up with the intention that it would be developed into a binding Master Framework Agreement. The main policy instrument within the framework mode of governance with regard to national governing bodies of sport (NGBs) has been the Public Service Agreement 22 (PSA 22). Its main purpose has been to ensure that UK government sport promises are delivered as measurable and tangible results. The PSA is premised on the idea of target-setting and audit mechanisms where public funding for sport organisations is contingent on the delivery of certain results. Non-delivery of targets is sanctioned by the withdrawal of funding to NGBs. As Grix and Phillpots observe, through the above mechanisms the government has been able 'to shape resource-dependent organisations involved in sport policy' (Grix and Phillpots, 2011, p. 5). There is a problem in that this model reinforces hierarchical relations, which runs against the governance ethos based on a multi-agency approach to sport delivery.

Governance dilemmas of London 2012

This section identifies some of the major governance dilemmas presented by the London Olympic Games by taking a lead from Jessop's (2000) analysis of governance failure. Staging the London 2012 Games has involved a multiplicity of public, voluntary, private and international actors. The implications of the new governance arrangements will be far-reaching and cannot be easily reduced to the 'love–hate' relation implied by London Mayor Boris Johnson, who predicted that 'people will hugely enjoy it and for those who don't enjoy it, it'll all be over in a flash' (Warner, 2010).

These dilemmas emerged as a result of the efforts by government, the city of London, LOCOG and the BOA to find a consensual approach to the delivery and legacy of the Games, by adding a new form of partnership to an already highly complex area of urban politics, and reflect the inherited limitations of governance. A consensual approach incorporates the three key elements of governance and implies creating a shared understanding about the role of the Games (i.e. common goals), ensuring participation of all those affected by the Olympic Games (i.e. partnerships) and steering collective actions in achieving the goals (i.e. steering). Forging consensus and steering collective actions has to be achieved in a very turbulent political, social and economic environment, as was marked by a change in government in 2010 followed by unprecedented public spending cuts, public sector strikes and social unrest in London in 2011.

Although the UK government is a key player, it has to be noted that government and governance mechanisms exist on different scales. This difference was exemplified in the case of the UK government's fifth promise, 'to demonstrate the UK is a creative, inclusive and welcoming place to live in, visit and for business' (DCMS, 2007). Despite modifications of this promise by the current coalition government, it is at its heart an attempt to create a favourable image of the UK and London in particular (DCMS, 2010b). To that effect, out of the £9.32 billion Olympic budget, £32 million has been allocated for the 'look and feel' of London away from the Olympic Park. The same national-scale strategy, to do with visualising the UK as a welcoming place, has resulted in a very different scenario in East London. Raco and Tunney's study on the competitiveness of a community of over 200 small businesses that existed on the proposed Olympic Village site demonstrated that 'development agendas often reflect and reproduce dominant imaginations and *visualisations* of how cities function and should appear. Narratives are constructed in which so-called problem places become re-imagined as "blank slates", ready for comprehensive redevelopment' (Raco and Tunney, 2010, p. 2070). The authors contended that, as a result, 'local firms have found themselves on the receiving end of the process of remaking this part of London and the production of new spaces in which they have no part' (*ibid.*, p. 2082).

Another constraint to governance arises from the different time horizons and corresponding coordination mechanisms involved in organising the Games and in ensuring its legacies. While securing most of the operational costs of the Games has been a responsibility of a private company (i.e. LOCOG) supported by global flows of capital in the form of sponsorship and broadcasting rights, the capital cost of the event, including an escalating security bill that currently stands at £600 million, has been borne mainly by the public purse. The delivery of the Games is essentially an exercise in project management over seven years, with non-negotiable starting and finishing times. The two main agencies responsible for its delivery, LOCOG and the ODA, will cease to exist shortly after the Games closing ceremony. In contrast, providing a sustainable infrastructure for the Games and its legacies as part of the Thames Gateway regeneration project has been a much longer process spanning over 30 years, one that is contested and lies beyond the control of any single agency.

A third constraint has been the ability of the UK government to monitor effectively the effects of various governance mechanisms on its capacity to secure social cohesion, particularly in London, which is home to 43 per cent of the country's non-white population. The governance mechanisms deployed for the Games have largely reasserted the asymmetrical power relations between the UK government and other parties concerned. The government's six promises for the Games and comprehensive implementation strategy 'provided the framework for thinking and acting' (DCMS, 2008, p. 3). Local social movements and community groups such as TELCO (across London) and NOGOE (Greenwich) have been gradually marginalised as consultation partners to the government, and have had to resort to pressure and public actions to have their concerns acknowledged and acted upon (Fussey *et al.*, 2011; Hayes and Horne, 2011). The NGBs have also been put in a dependent position, and their performance subjected to the new culture of managerialism with its insistence on strategic planning, targets, effectiveness and efficiency, so alien to many NGBs steeped in long-established voluntary traditions. For the first time in history, the UK government has also undertaken a longitudinal three-year meta-evaluation of the Olympic Games legacy across four themes: sport, economy, community engagement and East London regeneration (Grant Thornton *et al.*, 2011). Although the purpose of this evaluation is not specifically to understand governance mechanisms, it will nonetheless offer interesting insights into the relations and coordination mechanisms between different institutions involved in the Games.

Finally, the new partnership arrangements outline five dilemmas that have affected the governance of the London Olympic and Paralympic Games. As noted, the good governance of the Games was premised on creating a wide range of partnerships and cooperation between diverse actors. This in turn entails shared goals and trust. At the same time, the Games have stimulated significant competition – for Olympic contracts, official training camps designations and projects funding – between businesses, schools, universities and local authorities. A resulting governance issue has been how to ensure the balance between the commitment to cooperation and partnership and the myriad of self-interested behaviours. The well-publicised falling out between LOCOG and the BOA, the two key partners, over the distribution of Games profits, which was taken to the International Court of Arbitration for Sport in Lausanne in 2011, illustrates the point. Similarly, in 2010 the five Olympic Boroughs publicly vented their frustration with the government for the lack of financial support and clarity about the legacy of the Games in East London.

A related dilemma concerns the balance between openness and closure. Real heterarchic (horizontal) government arrangements dictate that partnerships should remain open to the environment while securing the closure needed for effective coordination amongst the partners. The choice is often between expanding the membership and maximising the range of possible actions or selecting a small core group of members and concentrating on more focused actions. The case of the Sport Legacy Delivery Board (SLDB) exemplifies this dilemma. The SLDB is made up of senior representatives from 17 public and voluntary organisations, including eight government departments. However, this body only managed to meet twice in five years and, as a government report has revealed, it suffered from 'paralysis by analysis' (Bose, 2010).

The Games has created a new policy space for interaction between the state, civil society and the market, and has helped expand governability (the capacity for effective guidance). However, this expansion has been countered by reducing flexibility (the capacity to adapt to changing circumstances). Since London was awarded the Games in 2005, the political and economic circumstances in Britain have significantly changed, to the point where former Olympic Minister Tessa Jowell has admitted that 'had we known what we know now, would we have bid for the Olympics. Almost certainly not' (Osborne and Kirkup, 2008). The role of the British government in the governance of the Games was very pronounced, formulating the main goals of the Olympic programme and establishing the operational rules. In that it has challenged a major tenet of governance, suggesting a 'hollowing out' (i.e. less government and more horizontal partnerships) of the state (Rhodes, 2007), as in fact the state was 'rolled out'. However, in attempting to reduce complexity, the government has alienated a number of local and national actors, as well as a significant portion of the very young people whose lives it set out to transform, and has failed to mobilise their resources.

As a form of public–private partnership, the Games also presents a dilemma between serving the public interest versus delivering private benefits. The huge amount of public money invested urged the government to insist on accountability at every level of governance, but this has also proved non-efficient in the pursuit of common goals. Reconciling social inclusion with economic performance has presented a challenge. The extraordinary measures taken to protect the investment of the global Games sponsors by barring any association with Olympic symbols and words by non-sponsors have created a barrier for the inclusion of communities and small businesses in the spirit of the Games (see James and Osborn in chapter 6 of this volume).

Sustainable Games governance is predicated on learning. As previous dilemmas have demonstrated, the delivery of the Olympic Games has been marked by a tension between universalising development visions and locally meaningful ideas and practices. A great deal of effort has been expended, both in the form of a government-commissioned meta-evaluation concerned with collecting evidence for 'what works' and through the IOC 'Knowledge Transfer' programme, to ensure that knowledge about the process of Games organisation is captured and shared. What tends to be overlooked is that alongside the process of knowledge creation always exist patterns of ignorance production as well. This is because the official visions and records of the Games produced by the government and LOCOG privilege rational scientific knowledge as enhancing democratic governance by ensuring greater transparency and accountability. Thus, knowledge produced by professionals is preferred, while the knowledge of 'laypeople' is ignored. The Olympic Charter requires organising committees to produce an official report of the Games. This is an expensive publication comprising several volumes, which serves a very narrow organisational purpose. Its usefulness to future Games organisers, sport managers and researchers is questionable as it is only descriptive, narrating what happened, but not how and why it happened. For example, the finance chapter of the 2008 Beijing Games Official Report contains virtually no figures (BOCOG, 2010) or budget structure.

Ignorance is produced not only through privileging certain forms of knowledge but also by failing to capture and share knowledge. Advances in digital technology have presented a great opportunity for quick and cost-effective ways of information dissemination through the web. Equally, they pose a challenge about how to preserve Olympic digital history as it unfolds on the Internet. An initiative led by the British Library and other UK legal deposit libraries urged the government to enact the digital legislation passed in 2003, which would allow the legal capture and preservation of much of the story of the London 2012 Olympic and Paralympic Games as told through the websites of sports associations, cultural organisations and online contributions from the general public. An appeal was made to the government to move swiftly to ensure there is no further loss to our digital heritage and to avoid an even greater 'digital black hole'. As a result of this and other pressures, in January 2012 the DCMS has announced that they have plans to publish a public consultation on Legal Deposit Regulations by the end of the month. It is hoped that the consultations will provide the impetus needed to enact the legislation and prevent further losses of knowledge.

The 2012 London Olympic and Paralympic Games represents a normative developmental project concerned with hosting an inspirational, safe and inclusive event that will leave a sustainable legacy for London and the UK. Delivering this vision requires achieving consensus amongst a diverse number of international, national and local actors, steering collective efforts and mobilising significant public and private resources. The UK government and LOCOG have made consistent efforts to put in place governance frameworks and to ensure that the principles of sustainability be followed by all partners. In that regard, new standards of transparency and accountability in the work of public authorities and organising committees have been set. However, the analysis also demonstrates some of the inherited limitations of governance, and that key Games governance dilemmas still persist and have not been satisfactorily addressed.

References

Audit Commission. (2009). *Working Better Together? Managing Local Strategic Partnerships: Cross-Cutting Summary*. London: Audit Commission.

BOCOG. (2010). *Preparation for the Games: New Beijing Great Olympics. Official Report of the Beijing 2008 Olympic Games*, Volume III, Chapter 5. Beijing: BOCOG, 89–105.

Bose, M. (2010). Infighting at Top is Threat to London Olympics Legacy, Warns Government Report. *London Evening Standard*, 22 January.

Catney, P., Henneberry, J. and Dixon, T. (2006). Navigating the Brownfield Maze: Making Sense of Brownfield Regeneration Policy and Governance. Paper presented at the SUBR: IM Conference on 29 March.

Dave, C. (2005). *The 2012 Bid: Five Cities Chasing the Summer Games*. Bloomington, IN: Author House.

DCMS (Department of Culture, Media and Sport). (2011). *Government Olympic Executive London 2012 Olympic and Paralympic Games Annual Report, February*. London: DCMS.

DCMS. (2010a). *London 2012 Olympic and Paralympic Games Annual Report, February*. London: DCMS.

DCMS. (2010b). *Plans for the Legacy from the 2012 Olympic and Paralympic Games*. London: DCMS.

DCMS. (2009). *London 2012: A Legacy for Disabled People: Setting New Standards, Changing Perceptions*. London: DCMS.

DCMS. (2008). *Before, During and After: Making the Most of the London 2012 Games*. London: DCMS.

DCMS. (2007). *Our Promise for 2012: How the UK will Benefit from the Olympic and Paralympic Games*. London: DCMS.

DCMS. (2005). Minutes, First Olympic Board Meeting, 28 July. Online: http://www.london2012.com/mm/Document/Publications/General/01/24/55/98/olympic-board-minutes-july-2005_Neutral.pdf (accessed 3 March 2012).

Fairclough, N. (2000). *New Labour, New Language?*. London: Routledge.

Forster, J. (2006). Global Sports Organisations and their Governance. *Corporate Governance*, 6 (1), 72–78.

Fussey, P., Coaffee, J., Armstrong, G. and Hobbs, D. (2011). *Securing and Sustaining the Olympic City: Reconfiguring London for 2012 and Beyond*. Farnham: Ashgate.

Girginov, V. (2011). Governance of London 2012 Olympic Sport Legacy. *International Review for the Sociology of Sport*, 27 June, 1–16.

Girginov, V. (2010). Studying Olympism, in V. Girginov (ed.). *The Olympics: A Critical Reader*. London: Routledge, 9–23.

Girginov, V. and Hills, L. (2009). The Political Process of Constructing Sustainable London Olympics Sports Development Legacy. *International Journal of Sport Policy*, 1 (2), 161–181.

Girginov, V. and Hills, L. (2008). A Sustainable Sports Legacy: Creating a Link between the London Olympics and Sports Participation. *The International Journal of the History of Sport*, 25 (14), 2091–2117.

Girginov, V. (ed.) (2008). *Management of Sports Development*. Oxford: Elsevier.

GLA. (2010). *The Mayor's Economic Development Strategy for London*. London: GLA.

Grant Thornton, Ecorys and Loughborough University (2011). *Meta-Evaluation of the Impacts & Legacy of the London 2012 Olympic and Paralympic Games Summary Reports 1 and 2*. London: DCMS.

Grix, J. and Phillpots, L. (2011). Revisiting the 'Governance Narrative'. 'Asymmetrical Network Governance' and the Deviant Case of the Sports Policy Sector. *Public Policy and Administration*, 26 (1), 3–19.

Hayes, G. and Horne, J. (2011). Sustainable Development, Shock and Awe? London 2012 and Civil Society. *Sociology*, 45 (5), 749–769.

HBSU. (2009). *Olympic and Paralympic Legacy: Strategic Regeneration Framework*. London: HBSU.

House of Commons Culture, Media and Sport Committee. (2003). *A London Olympic Bid for 2012. Third Report of Session 2002–2003*, London: The Stationary Office.

Houlihan, B. and Groeneveld, M. (2011). Social Capital, Governance and Sport, in Groeneveld, M., Houlihan, B. and Ohl, F. (eds). *Social Capital and Sport Governance in Europe*. London: Routledge, 1–21.

IOC. (2010). *Shaping the Future. IOC Interim Report 2009–2010*. Lausanne: IOC.

IOC. (2009). *XIII Olympic Congress. Follow-Up*. Lausanne: IOC.

IOC. (2008). *Basic Universal Principles of Good Governance of the Olympic and Sports Movement*. Lausanne: IOC.

IOC. (2007). *Olympic Charter*. Lausanne: IOC.

IOC. (2004). *Olympic Charter*. Lausanne: IOC.

Jessop, B. (2000). 'Governance Failure', in Stoker, G. (ed.). *The New Politics of British Local Governance*. London: Macmillan, 11–32.

Johnson, F., Fraser, J., Ganesh, G. and Skowron, L. (2008). *London Olympic Games and Paralympic Games – Children and Young People's Perceptions and Involvement*. Research Report DCSF-RR010, London: DCSF.

Jordan, A. (2008). The Governance of Sustainable Development: Taking Stock and Looking Forwards. *Environment and Planning C: Government and Policy*, 26, 17–33.

Keogh, L. (2009). *London 2012 Olympic Legacies: Conceptualising Legacy, the Role of Communities and Local Government and the Regeneration of East London*. London: Department of Communities.

Livingstone, K. (2008). My 2012 Bid was to Snare Billions of Pounds for London. *Evening Standard*, 24 April. Retrieved from www.thisislondon.co.uk/standard-mayor/article-23480071-livingstone-my-2012-bid-was-to-snare-billions-of-pounds-for-london.do, 20 January.

London Assembly (Economic Development, Culture, Sport and Tourism Committee). (2010). *Legacy Limited? A Rreview of the Olympic Park Legacy Company's Role*. London: Greater London Authority.

LOCOG. (2011). *One Year to Go: Annual Report 2010–2011*. London: LOCOG.

LOCOG. (2009) *Towards a One Planet 2012* (2nd edn). London: LOCOG.

NAO. (2007). *Preparations for the London 2012 Olympic and Paralympic Games – Risk Assessment and Management*. London: NAO.

Newman, P. (2007). 'Back the Bid': The 2012 Summer Olympics and the Governance of London. *Journal of Urban Affairs*, 29 (3), 255–267.

Osborne, A. and Kirkup, J. (2008). Tessa Jowell: Britain Would Not Have Bid for 2012 Olympics if we Knew about Recession, *Telegraph*, 13 November.

Owen, G. (2011). 2012 Olympic Torch Ignites Row over Games' Green Credentials. *Guardian*, 8 June 2011. Online: www.guardian.co.uk/uk/2011/jun/08/2012-olympic-torch-greencredentials (accessed 20 January 2012).

Parent, M., Rouillard, C. and Leopkey, B. (2011). Issues and Strategies Pertaining to the Canadian Government's Coordination Efforts in Relation to the 2010 Olympic Games. *European Sport Management Quarterly*, 11 (4), 337–369.

Peters, G. and Pierre, J. (1998). Governance without Government? Rethinking Public Administration. *Journal of Administration Research and Theory*, 8 (2), 223–243.

Poynter, G. and MacRury, I. (eds) (2009). *Olympic Cities: 2012 and the Remaking of London*. Farnham: Ashgate.

Raco, M. and Tunney, E. (2010). Visibilities and Invisibilities in Urban Development: Small Business Communities and the London Olympics 2012. *Urban Studies*, 20 (10), 1–23.

Rhodes. A. (2007). Understanding Governance: Ten Years On. *Organisation Studies*, 28 (8), 1243–1264.

Sport England. (2010). *Places People Play*. London: Sport England.

Treib, O., Bähr, H. and Falkner, G. (2007). Modes of Governance: Towards a Conceptual Clarification. *Journal of European Public Policy*, 14 (1): 1–20.

Warner, A. (2010). *Boris Johnson's Vision for 2012 is Short-Sighted*, 29 March. Retrieved from www.bbc.co.uk/blogs/adrianwarner/2010/03/boris_johnsons_2012_vision_is.html, 20 January 2012.

Werther, C. (2011). Rebranding Britain: Cool Britania, the Millennium Dome and the 2012 Olympics. *Moderna sprak*, 1, 1–14.

PART 3

Engaging the UK public

11

INVOLVING EAST LONDON COMMUNITIES

The evocative Olympic Games and the emergence of a prospective 'legacy'

Iain MacRury

Mega-events such as the Olympic Games operate within a number of cultural and political frames. The relatively rapid and spectacular intervention in the built environment characteristic of such events serves complex practical, social and politico-aesthetic functions. The 2012 Games has delivered iconic buildings. It remains to be seen if the London Olympic project will contribute to transform neighbourhoods sustainably, to renew socio-cultural engagement in the city and to support improvements in health, the economy and sports.

London 2012 is concurrently conceived as a now-imminent global sporting event *and* as a legacy-driven urban project – with horizons in 2015, 2020 or even 2040. Notable is the Five Olympic Host Boroughs of East London Strategic Regeneration Framework, intimately linked to the Olympic project and proposing that

> Within 20 years the communities who host the 2012 Games will have the same social and economic chances as their neighbours across London.
>
> *(Five Boroughs Strategic Unit, 2009: 1 (note that there are now six recognised boroughs))*

The London 2012 Games continues to open up questions of value and values: costs, benefits, aspirations and anxieties circulate in the discourse about the event and its projected legacies. The agenda is very much a 'live' one. Indeed this liveliness is a key component and contribution of the Games and its relation to the city. The 2012 Olympics will be an event that, as well as providing a frame for sports, competition and global cultural exchange, also affords an extended space in which to think about evolving models and methods in urban development planning (Muñoz, 2006). This chapter seeks to explore how and where this debate agenda has developed – in terms of the formal and less formal spaces of reflection upon, assertion of and articulation in relation to the value and values of the 2012 Games, particularly in relation to the communities of East London.

Legacy: promise, hypothesis and projection

The daily discourse around the Olympic Games binds city-scale projects and the 'long view' to urgent pragmatism and the local politics of place and community. The Strategic Regeneration Framework places 'community' to the fore.

> The most enduring legacy of the Olympics will be the regeneration of an entire community for the direct benefit of everyone who lives there.
>
> *(SRF, 2009: 2)*

A discourse of promise-making[1] circulates the 2012 Games (DCMS, 2007; LERI, 2007). Lasting benefits are touted alongside speculative projections about future successes and failures (MacRury and Poynter, 2009). The mystique of the Games, backed by specialist legislation, serves both to inspire and to overcome planning obstacles. Local critique can be suspended or deferred in the face of Olympic diplomacy – local and international. Olympic host cities link complex governance structures to multidimensional projects. Governments must work with organising committees and delivery bodies to engage public, commercial and community interests. The 2012 organisers have sought to do this, while retaining focus in relation to a clear set of project outcomes.

In a period where 'legacy' has come to script the Olympic-city narrative (MacRury, 2008; MacAloon, 2008; Gratton and Preuss, 2008), Games-time, preparation and future legacy are *telescoped*. In London 2012 the city-future is placed at once near and far away. Buildings spring up and London gears itself up for the event, felt as imminent and urgent, and as immanent, pressing up against everyday London life. At the same time the Games and its more numinous aftermath, the 'transformed' city, emerge in image and in iconic architecture, as complex objects (see MacRury, 2009: 61–65) mustered by planning, city branding, imagination, debate and consultation. London is foregrounded against backdrop promises and undertakings linked to urban development, city branding and economic success.[2]

'Legacy' does a good deal of emotional and rhetorical work in the Olympic city discourse, with London perhaps the major instance exploring an explicit Olympic city 'legacy' script from the start of its bidding and planning. 'Legacy' formally entered the IOC lexicon only at the turn of the twenty-first century – just as London was framing its host-city pitch. Perhaps as a consequence of the prominence of 'legacy' in the London Olympic bid, 'legacy' is projected to an extent where doubt and critique tend to adumbrate any too-enthusiastic appeals to the Games as vector for credible or desirable urban transformation. East London author Iain Sinclair is both pithy and characteristic in his typically sceptical definition of 'legacy'. He describes it in his memoir/novel *Ghostmilk: Calling Time on the Grand Project* as: 'The invention of something that will never happen by people who won't be there when it does' (Sinclair, 2011). The idea of legacy readily produces polarisation. Both pessimists and boosters play on the necessarily prospective nature of 'legacy'. Legacy is, by definition, an unproven or partly proven hypothesis: a promise dressed up as a contract with the city-future. The notions of 'catalyst' attaching to the idea of an inevitable and extensive transformation on the back of the Games are by no means certain, perhaps especially in a period when London is dealing with economic downturn and recession.

Since the bid was won there has been a change in the economic climate, as well as changes in municipal and national government. And there has been the spectacle of Beijing 2008 – an event confirming characterisations of the Olympic Games as, in some respects, a resource-intensive, internationally focused spectacle at risk of becoming disconnected from the lives and needs of the communities of host cities. At the same time, it is by no means clear that – in the absence of the intensive and programmatic investments entailed to the 2012 Games – East London would have found other reliable means to redress or stall some aspects of socio-economic decline connected to the credit crunch and the global financial crises that have followed. The Games has served to legitimate large public expenditure, against the grain of government policy elsewhere. Nor can London ignore its place in the global-city market place. No longer the workshop of the world, and with finance a less reliable economic staple, London needs a shop window.

The form and disposition of the Olympic investment, however, remains, necessarily caught between the highly specified needs of the Games-as-event and the more widely hoped-for 'legacy' outcomes promised in the original bid. The cost, the effort and the sheer size of the mega-event intervention in the city and nationwide demands a rhetoric of legitimation and a vocabulary of motives – this needs to be inflected by real engagements.

Communities: real and imagined

'Community' becomes an important concept and a pressing concern in the Olympic city (Hiller, 2006). Always at risk of reification and romanticism, 'community' registers (amongst many things) the instituted sense of engagement in the remade Olympic city quarter: the settlement between a rapid, top-down event plan and build, and, as it emerges, a place-making project tagged as 'legacy'. It is through community engagement and community action that legacy can become an instituted process of change, rather than a set of more general undertakings and priorities. The communities of East London will bear witness to the unfolding legacies – positive and negative, intended and unintended (Gratton and Preuss, 2008).

The incentives to deliver a lasting, tangible legacy are multiple. East London is seeking to accommodate a dynamic and variously deprived population. Local authorities are serving an increasing population and accommodating rising population density. There is rapid growth in relative and absolute numbers of young people – a key focus for Olympism and legacy. A traditionally multicultural area, East London is home to an expanding black and minority ethnic community. There is an opportunity to explore and expand the prospect of London as a centre for creative cosmopolitan culture (MacRury and Poynter, 2010; Carrington, 2004).

At the same time, and as a consequence of deindustrialisation, the area faces high levels of 'worklessness' within its resident communities. In a city committed to a post-industrial economic strategy since the 1980s, the area's populations exhibit relatively low levels of skills and qualifications compared to London as a whole – notably disbarring many East Londoners from benefiting directly from the previous large regeneration project in the region, the financial services district at Canary Wharf. Economic exclusion feeds and sustains high levels of social deprivation across the sub-region, manifest in high levels of overcrowding and the need for improved diversity in housing provision. In addition, there are relatively high levels of crime and of perception of crime within the resident population. The health agenda in East London reflects the general picture of relative deprivation. As Girginov and Hills (2008) outline, work remains to be done to assure a sporting legacy in East London.

In the Summer of 2011, less than a year before the 2012 opening ceremony, the urgency of the task – evident to project managers and planners in terms of logistics, construction and test-ready venues, became apparent again in another form. Sporadic rioting by young Londoners underlined the importance of the socio-economic and cultural changes entailed to the London 2012 project. In this context there is a special incentive to ensure that 'legacy' promises are not forgotten after the 2012 Games closing ceremony, when attention and energy may become diverted elsewhere.

The East London 'community' stands as a significant protagonist in the Olympic-city drama. As one respondent in a recent community project[3] outlined:

> I'm just so looking forward to 2012, to make Newham a better area, and obviously the surrounding areas, like Hackney and Greenwich. Because, sometimes, I think, why do I live in Newham? But sometimes I really appreciate it, and I hope the Olympics will make it better. I appreciate it all. Because I – like, already you can see the impact – impact

> that it's having. Like, I live in Stratford, so, like, the hub of it. And it's kind of changed, like, the behaviours of people, and – and what – how things are run. And I just really want it to be, like, a better place to live, which hopefully it will be.
>
> *(Respondent, East London Legacies 2012 Focus Group: Young Athletes)*

'Community' becomes a kind of talisman, invoked before, during and after the Games. In legacy discourse, 'community' is the subject and the object of the social narrative. In the abstract, 'community' stands as counterpoint to the Olympic boosterism often linked to the idea of the games serving an 'entrepreneurial' city-development strategy (Harvey, 1989; Hall and Hubbard, 1996; Beriatos and Gospadin, 2004; Hiller, 2006). 'Community' stands too as a redress against an overly economic conception of the Olympic Games – a conception that measures success purely in terms of the event balance sheet (MacRury, 2008).

At the same time, it is important to recall that 'community' refers not (only) to abstract principles but to the real lives and fortunes of a city's inhabitants. In particular, capturing, constructing and engaging 'community' – instituting dialogic and reciprocal frames for engagement and community development – stands as an imperative project: a mission running parallel to infrastructure and city-branding work. While it is clear that Olympism and the 'legacy' discourse recognises 'community' in some sense, it is also evident that pressures on budgets, for fast delivery and on 'imagineering' can relegate the 'community' agenda, leading to charges of marginalisation, exclusion and even exploitation of places and people.

'Legacy' is by no means a straightforward or automatic process. It requires and relies upon investments in registers other than financial. The emotional, the memorial, the affective elements of the Olympic Games are not adjuncts to, or preludes for the emergence of legacy-as-plan. Instead, the sense of community engagement, ownership, even pride and joy in the Olympic Games are crucial sedimentary layers upon which the legacy architecture depends. In a seminal account of 'legacy' Richard Cashman, reflecting on the Sydney 2000 experience (1998), points out:

> Given that the local community invests so much in the Games, it is important that the wider benefits of legacy should be canvassed and articulated. Too often, costs and benefits narrowly focus on economics. Legacy involves casting the gaze wider, to poetry and art, architecture, the environment, information, and many other non-tangible factors.
>
> *(Cashman, 1998: 112)*

Communities bear witness to the Games, as fans, as citizens, as neighbours, as activists, as volunteers and as global and local tourists: in place, across London's various neighbourhoods and quarters, and via multiple media-based engagements.

The development of a city necessarily provokes disagreements and controversies over territory, priorities and means of development. These amount to various kinds of 'crisis' in the discourse of development and change. A successful community development process must manage tensions between municipal and national agendas, between various tiers of local government, between communities and market priorities, between different segments of the community and between competing conceptions of the 'good' city. The Olympic Games offers a powerful vector to carry forward such debates, with the tightness of the seven-year schedule facing a successful host city focusing minds, but also, at points, amplifying anxieties and differences of opinion.

Backing the bid: early polls and current views

The London Games have been a focus for both excitement and controversy. Over the Olympic year it is likely that there will be fluctuations in fortunes of the 2012 Games, as athletic triumph, civic pride, pre-event anxieties, hitches and unanticipated problems jostle for headline space and bandwidth. The Olympic Games have stood 'front of mind' for national newspapers and broadcasters since 2005, with a rich news agenda covering back and front pages – and with local incidents abutting international-level controversies. As John MacAloon proposes:

> In one way or another, at one time or another, to one degree or another, nearly everyone cares about the Olympics.
>
> *(MacAloon, 1982: 98)*

The collocation of the Games and the city-in-transition touches news agendas in sport, politics, economy and culture. The Games highlights and cuts across sensibilities and sensitivities around place, community, governance, inclusion and exclusion. As such, a kind of proto-public conversation emerges around the mega-event; public anticipation, contemplation and reflection abound – framed, often, by the discursive tropes of indignation and investigative scepticism – notably, in the case of London 2012, around the uncertainties about the future use of the Olympic stadium.[4]

Throughout the period of bidding and planning there have been various efforts at capturing and representing general public opinion. Partly, this overview stabilises the 'overall' sense of the place of the games in the popular imagination – up and against specific controversies (e.g. ticketing issues) or successes (e.g. the UK team's sporting performance in Beijing 2008). Partly, too, market surveys and similar tools are expected in relation to an event in many ways conceived as a promotional, 'branded' intervention – for London, for the UK and aimed at local, national and international audiences. Ersatz 'audience testing' for the Olympic 2012 'brand' is a natural part of the dynamic production of the Games as image and as event.

Finally, too, preoccupation with public opinion reflects a host-city commitment. The IOC requires of bidding cities that public support is clearly in place and that it is documented. Thus London's bid document reported 'overwhelming' public support, 'both in the city itself and in the United Kingdom as a whole'. This bid questionnaire describes 'an extensive consultation process' with an Olympic bid initially proposed in 1997. Bid advocates sought inputs and canvassed opinion from the public, from the business community and from local authorities. More concerted work was undertaken for the purposes of formally capturing the public mood.

At the end of 2002, the market research company ICM carried out an independent national poll. The bid questionnaire reports on 'the strength of public support across all age groups and through every region of the UK' and quotes figures from a 320-strong sample. In response to the question: 'Do you think a bid should be made for London to host the 2012 Olympic Games?' The following results emerged: 81 per cent agreed London should bid; 82 per cent living within in London itself agreed with the plan to bid. The poll revealed that support was strong across the entire country, 'with Northern Ireland (87 per cent) and Scotland (84 per cent) the most supportive'. Nowhere did the support fall below 75 per cent (London 2012 Ltd, 2003: 3).

Other surveys: capturing engagements

It is instructive to compare two YouGov polls conducted nearly a decade apart. In a 2002 report commissioned by the London-based paper the *Evening Standard*, 69 per cent of respondents supported the bid and majority responses anticipated positive developments for sports facilities (78 per cent) and transport improvements (45 per cent). Respondents were sceptical about positive impacts on sports participation and health, with a marginal majority disagreeing that the Games would increase sports participation and improve health. Nearly a decade later, in July 2011, with the UK economy seeking to recover from an extended period of poor performance in the aftermath of the banking crisis and with considerable cuts to public services in the news, 44 per cent of respondents felt London should have bid for the games (42 per cent disagreed). Fifty-five per cent felt that the Games would be good for London, though 65 per cent did not feel that 'the Games would be good for people like me'. Only 40 per cent of respondents claimed to be 'interested' in the Olympic Games in this 2011 survey – just 12 months before the Games. Central office of Information (COI) reports in 2007, 2008 and 2009 show higher levels of interest (67 per cent, 73 per cent and 75 per cent, respectively).[5] The different sampling frames are a likely explanation for this discrepancy. Again, it is useful to relay some of the more sceptical responses to the polling and consultation work that has gone on around 2012. Sinclair dismisses much polling as 'Leaflets on the street with boxes to tick. Managed populism. Subverted dissent' (Sinclair, 2011: 65).

This is consistent with a broader critique of the means and modes of public engagement around urban change that sees community opinion utilised as a substitute for instituted dialogue and engagement. Furthermore, as Marike van Harskamp (2006) has suggested, in the 'telescoping' of Olympic planning and other long-term regeneration projects (e.g. in the Lea Valley) the discourse has occluded and confused some other longer-standing regional development planning, with the glamour of the event crowding out some important potential consultative work on the Lea Valley redevelopment. As van Harskamp suggests:

> ...numerous interesting efforts to public involvement were certainly made, some serious doubts about the consultation process remain. Among many other, broader and perhaps more ideological issues, the tight timescale, the top-down use of masterplans, and an uncertainty about the actual consultation focus can be seen as examples of the weaknesses of the exercise.
>
> *(van Harskamp, 2006: 1)*

Nevertheless, within the terms afforded by polling and market research-style engagement, there is a detailed record of public responsiveness.

There has not been any large-scale opinion specifically isolating opinion within the six local Olympic boroughs – with panel samples typically too small to disaggregate localised opinion reliably within these areas.[6] However, there are a number of specific issues where local opinion has indicated concern about aspects of the 2012 Games. In Greenwich, a significant local campaign against the use of Greenwich Park for equestrian events has provoked and captured local concern – and numerous petition signatures (Gibson, 2010).

In Tower Hamlets there was significant local disappointment at the 2010 decision to reroute the marathon event outside the east London borough – taking the spectacle into more central, tourist-friendly areas (BBC, 2010).

An informal online poll (n = 854) undertaken by Newham council at the end of 2011 registers some of the issues linked to attending the 2012 games. Of the 854 respondents polled, 18.9 per cent intended to attend the 2012 Games, 56.8 per cent said they were not attending and 24.3 per cent were undecided.[7]

Engaging people: consultation and community

The ODA, LOCOG and Olympic Park Legacy Company (OPLC) have developed a strategy and practices for community consultation. A programme of events aimed to develop connections and networks in the community, with visits, information sharing and the display and discussion of plans. The wide-ranging approach sought to include faith groups, schools and other stakeholders. This work has been monitored quite closely; as part of the host city's commitment to the IOC it must agree to undertake research under the rubrics of the IOC's evaluation for the Olympic Games Impact Study (OGI). OGI is a means to try to generate systematic evidence across host cities and between Games to provide comparative and summative data on the global and local impacts of the Games on an array of aspects of economy, society and environment.

One element of the report considers the important question of engagement. This is helpful in providing a reminder to organising committees and government of the need to consult and assess opinion at a local and citywide level, and also to consider national public responses to the Games. In this regard, OGI provides a basic 'audit' of host cites' responsibilities to engage with communities. While the OGI data is certainly not detailed, it reveals, as in the case of London, that a degree of consultation and opinion polling has been systematically undertaken in relation to the park development. Thus in the OGI study the IOC requires data on consultation with specific groups (this is social variable number 28). The pre-Games report identifies 221 consultations in London linked to Olympic plans (Table 11.1).

As the OGI pre-Games report sets out, LOCOG, the ODA and lately the OPLC undertake consultation activities in line with planning law, but this does not meet the HMG standard, known as COMPACT. In recent decades, UK planning methods have increasingly highlighted 'citizen, stakeholder and service user involvement' as a key prelude to decision making and project completion. It is clear that in formal terms at least the Olympic Games has progressed in line with requirements for public participation and engagement, as outlined in statutory guidance such as *Creating Strong, Safe and Prosperous Communities* and *Duty to Involve* (see ESRC/LOCOG, 2010: 75). Certainly the bodies responsible for Olympic planning and delivery are able to point to some concrete engagements and to a degree of dialogue and input on key themes. The OPLC offers detailed accounts of engagement and response in relation to some of the key themes raised in consultations around the Olympic Park. Responses captured in the consultative processes included concerns about:

- housing stock and affordability;
- waterways;
- local links and local connectivity in and across the park;
- the prospect of more tall buildings;
- the future care and maintenance of the park;
- environmental and sustainability questions;
- spaces to play;
- community amenities;
- provision for faith communities;
- future use of sports facilities.

Table 11.1 Olympic community consultations

	Public drop-in sessions	*Community meetings and events*	*Public information displays*	*Stakeholder meetings and events*	*Total*
Number of consultations	44	38	44	95	221

Source: OGI 2010/LOCOG.

The OPLC is able to highlight responses and practical plans that promise to address such concerns. Notably there are quite specific commitments to community matters.

> We are intending to provide 12 new local schools and nurseries and 3 health care centres throughout the five new neighbourhoods within the Park. In addition to this, we are also working towards providing community centres, an Ideas store, play spaces, local shops and Safer Neighbourhood Teams.
>
> *(OPLC, 2010: 1)*

Certainly, too, however, caveats remain, notably around the affordability of housing stock. Thus the commitments to and definitions of affordability are not stipulated in promises for:

> Up to 6,800 new homes. A target of 35% affordable housing (*subject to viability*). *Indicative* 42% family homes (3 beds and above).
>
> *(OPLC, 2010: 1, italics added)*

The outline response to the community concern leaves some space for future changes in the level and kind of legacy commitments made in response to the community consultation. Sinclair offers a characteristic critique of the Olympic project and the consultative processes attached to it. He records commentary in the run-up to the games at one consultative event:

> most of the development will be buy to let investments ... Huge amounts of Russian and Saudi money. Tenants will move in and out constantly. There will be no community at all.
>
> *(Sinclair, 2011: 72)*

Projects: work on the ground

Olympic organisers invest heavily in both the cultural-ethical power and the economic power of the Games, investing the Games with capacities to alleviate deep-seated social problems. Thus, 2012 will 'transform the heart of East London'. Sport is presented as a major vector for such change. As Sebastian Coe asserts:

> Sport is the hidden social worker in our communities. It does so much more to help children from deprived communities than any government department or quango can achieve.
>
> *(Coe, 2009: 18)*

The high-level overviews from opinion surveys and local consultations capture a significant degree of engagement, while also showing (in different samples and at different periods) a waxing and waning of the intensity and kind of 'interest' in the Games.

A significant complementary aspect of engagement also needs to be considered. There is a panoply of local and national projects linked formally to the Games organisation (e.g. via the LOCOG 'Inspire' mark scheme), or, more indirectly, through connections to major Olympic themes, such as youth sport, disability, skills, volunteering and urban community development. Indeed, it should be noted that Coe's (2009) comment about sport as social worker is a shorthand which (unfortunately) brackets off a major truth about the success of prospective legacy: that sustained and enduring development in relation to any and all of the themes and promises will depend upon real person power; the development and institution of enduring, if informal, structures to hold, contain and convey the 'contents' of legacy aspirations in sports, health and civic development.

An example of a macro-level sports legacy initiative is Sport England's programme, 'Places People Play'. This £135 million framework seeks to place the spirit of the games at 'the heart of local communities'. The project seeks to transform the places where people play sport. Through this suite of initiatives, London 2012 will reinvigorate sporting life 'in cities, towns and villages across the country'. The project operates via investments in new and upgraded facilities and in reinvigorating extant facilities and structures. The Places People Play initiative also promises to protect playing fields and other sporting spaces in towns and cities – areas otherwise likely to be under pressure in the face of emergent planning regulations linked to the new localism bill and from ongoing pressure on local authorities to release land as a way to offset cuts to public government funding.

Such examples represent an array of 'legacy' projects spanning sports, health and economic development. The projects feeding the legacy are provided via a mixture of public and private funds, with some 134 separate initiatives listed within the ambit of the DCMS's official legacy evaluation framework (DCMS/Grant Thornton, 2011); many of the projects stand as headlines for suites of subprojects and funding streams.

The advantage in project-based community engagement lies in the connection between the project, practical activity and collective commitments to the main area of legacy work, be it sport, health or other aspects of legacy development. This kind of concrete community engagement is more substantive than polling or more active consultation exercises. Evaluation and strategic investment will be needed to assess the enduring contribution of many of these 134 projects – many directing large investments – to legacy and urban transformation.

Consultation matters: planning, community engagement and legacy

> If we keep emotional connectivity at the centre of what it is we are trying to achieve, then we will create emotional appeal . . .
>
> *(Coe, 2009: 37)*

Sinclair, as outlined, is a close observer of all things Olympic. He has sought to chart historical and contemporary changes over a period of decades around the Lea Valley and Hackney Wick territories 'regenerated' by Queen Elizabeth Park and 2012. Sinclair casts a sceptical eye over the community engagement activities he has witnessed, identifying a tendency, in amongst an extensive consultative frame, to 'unchallenged monologue', and 'coshing the public with years of upbeat publicity' (Sinclair, 2011: 197). He is particularly concerned that the places in and around the Lea Valley and Hackney Wick are recognised as having histories, communities and residents, and that these should not be marginalised. His commitment is to place and to history – an important counterpoint to some regeneration rhetoric. To the extent that the Olympic regeneration retains its flavour as the *destruction* of place – rather than as a re-making – then it is likely that the aimed-for sense of community will be patchy and unsustained.

Community and the 'entrepreneurial city'

London's Olympic plan was conceived in a period during which a well-established urban development script was in place – adopted in and adapted to cities seeking to reposition themselves as global competitive 'players', attractive to residents and standing as potential hubs in an emergent global network characterised by rapid flows of capital investment and labour linked to the 'knowledge economy'. This strategic approach has been well described (Hall and Hubbard, 1996) and explicitly connected to Olympic-city development in a number of studies (Andranovich *et al.*, 2001; Burbank *et al.*, 2001; Beriatos and Gospodini, 2004). As David Harvey points out in this regard, entrepreneurial cities engage in redevelopment planning demanding that they 'negotiate a knife-edge path between preserving the values of past capital investments in the built environment and destroying these investments in order to open up fresh room for accumulation' (Harvey, 2001: 247).

While the Olympics stands, iconically and in the values attached to it, as a force for and an assertion of creative human potential, it is also the case that as a contemporary global mega-event the Games plan necessarily becomes tied to actual or potential destructiveness – within the very cities and communities that the Olympic Movement seeks to support and develop. This is part and parcel of contemporary city building.

Psychoanalyst Christopher Bollas, in a sensitive discussion of the emotional life of urban change, makes a pertinent observation:

> Destruction and creation bear an intimate proximity to one another. In the inner city most new builds are developed after the demolition of the former structure, one body standing where the other once stood. For those who live through these moments there will always be two buildings in mind: the obliterated and the existent.
>
> *(Bollas, 2009: 48)*

In London, and as recorded most vividly in critical commentaries such as Sinclair's memoir *Ghost Milk*, the community bears grief as well as excitement in the face of the projected and prospected Olympic regeneration projects. Sinclair documents this in detail in relation to some key sites: Clays Lane housing association, Manor Garden allotments and, from an interesting historical perspective, Eton Manor sports club. It is evident that these have been flashpoints in relation to questions of legacy and consultation. Bollas's gloss is again helpful:

> Once notice is given to a community that a sector will be destroyed and something new will be built, even if the project is promising, there is always a certain dread of witnessing the efficiency of these wreckers.
>
> *(Bollas, 2009: 50)*

It is here that community consultation, as a well-framed and enduring dialogue, becomes important to the decision-making processes linked to regeneration and to the emotional life of the places made and remade through mega-event regeneration. Bollas contends:

> If a building goes too far into the future – as the Eiffel Tower may have done in its day – the people feel a reverse effect: the future has invaded the present and casts scorn on that present's sensibilities.
>
> *(Bollas, 2009: 51)*

Such ambivalence is captured in responses to focus groups conducted as part of the ELL 2012 East London Legacies project. One respondent spoke for a number of ambivalent young people, who felt caught between a present that was in some ways unsatisfactory and a future that threatened to bypass, exclude or make strange the 'homeish' places he had grown up with.

> I do think about it a lot, 'cos I probably will be around the area during 2012. But I think it's probably gonna bring quite a lot of negative effects because there's gonna be lots of different sorts of people in the area, and that like kind of homeish feeling that we have around here – it's gonna kind of go. But I think it'll probably help with the recession going on in the country, . . . 'cos there's gonna be so many people around for the Olympics, the new shopping centre's gonna be packed full of people, so we're gonna have more money, but I don't know if that's better than feeling homely, and, like, ruin our neighbourhoods just for money.
>
> *(Respondent, ELL 2012: focus group at Eastlea School)*

Bollas makes an unlikely connection between planning processes linked to architectural projects and the phases of early infancy – a period of development that is seen as fundamental to the formation of human subjectivity within Bollas's psychoanalytic frame of reference. The process he describes links to the community and its role in metabolising change – with its members as active participants. Leaders of change projects must give this opportunity, with care.

> One of the mother's tasks . . . is to present objects to her infant. This is something of an art, for if she forced a new object upon the infant, the child would inevitably turn away; but if she allowed for 'a period of hesitation' during which the infant would turn away, presumably from lack of interest, the infant would soon return, with heightened interest and desire toward the new object. In this respect cities continue to present their inhabitants with new objects – and the planning stage, when proposals are floated in the press, may constitute an important psychic element in the population's relation to the new.
>
> *(Bollas, 2009: 55)*

As outlined above, there is cause for optimism in some regards. Certainly the Olympic glamour has ensured that the redevelopment of the East London sites has been widely discussed, canvassed, debated and thought about – even if direct community input has not been systematically in evidence at every step. However, as Bollas suggests, it is important that the 'new' is presented in the manner of an extended period of negotiation and consultation.

This avoids a further risk: the feelings attached to the famous 'white elephant' syndrome have their roots in hastily managed – even forced – presentation of the new architectural objects and infrastructures upon unengaged populations and across 'old familiar' places. It is crucial not to disregard the emotional and practical requirements or the powerful value of local interpretations of and historical sense within a city's developmental narrative – to fail here is to reduce the 'evocative' (Bollas, 2009) power of urban places. The 2012 Games should (with its iconic buildings) be able to capture a sense of history and place, intelligible to and exciting for its communities – evocations of a transforming legacy.

From a different perspective, and affording some practical conclusions in keeping with Bollas's insights, a recent report on health linked to the development around Stratford City and the community work in that area highlights some lessons which might be readily applied, post-Games, to ensure a continuing structure for dialogue and community involvement in the place-making work around the Olympic Park. The authors, Hardin and Sampson, suggest:

- Aligning community engagement more closely with community development.
- Having a clear purpose or 'end game' for the community engagement.

- Setting up structures and processes for ongoing engagement as opposed to 'one-off' engagement.
- Using outreach workers and community members to go 'deep' into communities and produce better local intelligence.
- Ensuring that community engagement is inclusive of 'harder to reach groups'.

(Newham NHS, 2010: 108).

Such an instituted approach is consistent with the need to negotiate and construct legacy polices (see Girginov and Hills, 2009) – a crucial component in a community-alert legacy programme. While the extensive polling and consultations undertaken in the pre-Games period, by the ODA, OPLC and LOCOG in particular, point to a genuine commitment to responsive engagement on at least some questions and developments, it is important to note that durable, instituted structures, community development trusts and such formats for framing engagement, as recommended above, alongside an alertness to the emotional and evocative aspects of place-making, are important in maintaining and enhancing dialogue in development. This is likely to be needed in the work of community building that will be required in the Olympic Village and in the rapidly emerging housing developments connected to the Games legacy plan – and to ensure the place-making work linked to 'legacy' develops for vibrant and engaged communities.

Conclusion: 'legacy planning as reflective space'

The recent 'credit crunch' has left London to reconstruct and re-evaluate elements in its position as a global financial centre, reliant upon a wavering financial services sector. The summer riots of 2011 pointed up concerns about the city's young people and about London's ongoing capacity to provide a satisfactory future and a home for segments of its population. The Olympic Games and the 'legacy' debates frame wider questions. What type of city is London? What type of place should it seek to become? In ways barely thought of in the run-up to the successful bid in 2005, the 2012 Olympic mega-event provides a focus for broader considerations about development, governance, engagement and habitation within a London seeking to rearticulate and reassert local and global narratives linked to social and economic success.

This chapter has sought to underline the importance of the Games as a way to support and provoke engagements from across the city in debate about 'London', and in particular highlighting the importance of 'communities' in the long term.

Notes

1 The Games and 'legacy' form part of a plan in London, East London and the Thames gateway. The plan has further elements outlined in these promises.

- To make the UK a world-class sporting nation, in terms of elite success, mass participation and school sport.
- To transform the heart of East London.
- To inspire a new generation of young people to take part in local volunteering, cultural and physical activity.
- To make the Olympic Park a blueprint for sustainable living.
- To demonstrate that the UK is a creative, inclusive and welcoming place to live in, to visit and for business (DCMS, 2007: 3).

Additional emphasis was given to disability, amounting to a sixth promise and tying the legacy more closely to the paralympic games.

A post-election rethink in 2010 has led to some refinement and rephrasing of the promises, towards a more general set of priorities.

- Harnessing the United Kingdom's passion for sport to increase grassroots participation, particularly by young people – and to encourage the whole population to be more physically active.
- Exploiting to the full the opportunities for economic growth offered by hosting the Games.
- Promoting community engagement and achieving participation across all groups in society through the Games.
- Ensuring that the Olympic Park can be developed after the Games as one of the principal drivers of regeneration in East London.

(DCMS, 2007)

2 Thus the regular update visits from the IOC to track progress make headline news, in London and throughout the UK. Similarly, coverage of both Beijing and Vancouver – and their controversies and successes – was 'read' as an example of the kind of attention London was likely to receive. The commitment to reputation building is linked to a conception of the Games as a component of London as a global city 'brand'.

3 East London Legacies 2012 is an archiving project seeking to capture voices and experiences linked to the unfolding 2012 legacy. As part of this work, I conducted a series of 15 focus groups, mostly in East London secondary schools, to examine emergent desires and anxieties linked to the prospect of the 2012 Games.

4 A detailed archive of the controversial plans about ownership and legacy use of the 2012 stadium is available at www.guardian.co.uk/sport/olympic-stadium.

5 A Populus poll commissioned by *The Times* (n = 2052) presents the following levels of agreement on key statements:

- will improve Britain's standing in the world = 51 per cent;
- will make the country feel a greater sense of period in Britain = 60 per cent;
- will benefit British business = 69 per cent;
- will show Britain is able to complete large-scale projects on time and on budget = 62 per cent;
- represents a waste of time and money in the current economic climate = 40 per cent.

Notably, London opinions are marginally more positive than other UK regions in this survey (Populus, 2011: 1).

6 Ipsos Mori, Populus and YouGov have been commissioned by major media and broadcasters to undertake polling. However, the geographical breakdown of samples has tended to divide London (as a whole) from the other UK regions, rather than identifying variant opinion in different parts of the capital.

7 The panel works through online surveys: see www.newhampanel.com.

References

Andranovich, G., M. Burbank and C. Heying (2001) Olympic cities: Lessons learned from mega-event politics. *Journal of Urban Affairs*, 23: 113–131.

BBC (2010) London 2012 Olympic marathon route a 'travesty'. BBC News, www.bbc.co.uk/news/uk-england-london-11471541, accessed December 2011.

Beriatos, E. and A. Gospodini (2004) 'Glocalising' urban landscapes: Athens and the 2004 Olympics. *Cities*, 21 (3): 187–202.

Bollas, C. (2009) *The Evocative Object World*, London: Routledge.

Burbank, M., G. Andranovich and C. Heying (2001) *Olympic Dreams: The impact of mega-events on local politics*, Boulder, CO: Lynne Rienner Publishing.

Carrington B. (2004) *Race, Sport and Politics: The sporting black diaspora*, London: Sage Publications Ltd.

Cashman, R. (1998) *Olympic Legacy in an Olympic City: Monuments, museums and memory*. Fourth International Symposium for Olympic Research, pp.111–112.

Cashman, R. (2002) Impact of the Games on Olympic host cities. Univeristy lecture, International Chair in Olympism (IOC-UAB), Centre d'Estudis Olímpics, Barcelona. Online: http://olympicstudies.uab.es/lectures/web/pdf/cashman.pdf> (accessed 2 January 2011).

Coe, S. (2009) *The Winning Mind: My Inside track on great leadership*, London: Headline.

DCMS (2007) *Before, During and After*, London: DCMS.
DCMS/Grant Thornton (2011) Olympic Meta Evaluation Report 1: Scope, research questions and data strategy, in *Meta-Evaluation of the Impacts and Legacy of the London 2012 Olympic Games and Paralympic Games*, London: DCMS.
ESRC/LOCOG (2010) *Olympic Games Impact Study – London 2012 Pre-Games Report*, London: ESRC.
Five Boroughs Strategic Unit (2009) Olympic and Paralympic Legacy Strategic Regeneration Framework: Summary document. Online: http://www.hackney.gov.uk/Assets/Documents/strategic-regeneration-framework-report.pdf (accessed January 2011).
Gibson, O. (2010) London Olympics row over Greenwich Park role reaches climax. *Guardian*, 23 March.
Girginov, V. and L. Hills (2009) The political process of constructing a sustainable London Olympics sports development legacy. *International Journal of Sport Policy*, 1 (2): 161–181.
Girginov, V. and L. Hills (2008) A sustainable sports legacy: Creating a link between the London Olympics and sports participation. *International Journal of the History of Sport*, 25 (14): 2091–2116.
Gratton, C. and H. Preuss (2008) Maximizing Olympic impacts by building up legacies. *The International Journal of the History of Sport*, 25 (14): 1922–1938.
Hall, T. and P. Hubbard (1996) The entrepreneurial city: New urban politics, new urban geographies?, *Progress in Human Geography*, 20: 153–174.
Harvey, D. (2001) *Spaces of capital: Towards a critical geography*, Edinburgh: Edinburgh University Press.
Harvey, D. (1989) From managerialism to entrepreneurialism: The transformation in urban governance in late capitalism. *Geografiska Annaler. Series B, Human Geography*, 71: 3–17.
Hiller, H. (2006) Post-event outcomes and the post-modern turn: The Olympics and urban transformations. *European Sport Management Quarterly*, 6 (4): 317–332.
London 2012 Ltd (2003) *London 2012: Response to the questionnaire for cities applying to become candidate cities to host the Games of the XXX Olympiad and the Paralympic Games in 2012*, London: London 2012.
London East Research Institute (2007) *A Lasting Legacy?*, London: London Assembly/LERI.
MacAloon, J. J. (2008) 'Legacy' as Managerial/Magical Discourse in Contemporary Olympic Affairs. *International Journal of the History of Sport*, 25 (14): 2060–2071.
MacAloon, J. (1982) Double visions: Olympic games and American culture. *The Kenyon Review*, 4 (1): 98–112.
MacRury, I. (2009) Branding the Games: Commercialism and the Olympic city, in G. Poynter and I. MacRury (eds), *Olympic Cities: 2012 and the Remaking of London*, London: Ashgate, 43–72.
MacRury, I. (2008) Re-thinking the legacy 2012: The Olympics as commodity and gift. *Twenty-First Century Society*, 3 (3): 297–312.
MacRury, I. and G. Poynter (2010) Team GB and London 2012: The paradox of national and global identities. *The International Journal of the History of Sport*, 27 (16–18): 2958–2975.
MacRury, I. and G. Poynter (2009) *Olympic Cities: 2012 and the Remaking of London*, London: Ashgate.
MacRury, I. and G. Poynter (2008) The regeneration Games: Commodities, gifts and the economics of London 2012. *The International Journal of the History of Sport*, 25 (14): 2072–2090.
Muñoz, F. (2006) Olympic urbanism and Olympic villages: Planning strategies in Olympic host cities, London 1908 to London 2012. *Sociological Review – Keele*, 54: 175.
Newham NHS (2010) *Creating and Maintaining a Healthy Stratford*, London: London Borough of Newham/UEL.
OPLC (2010) How we listened, at www.legacycompany.co.uk/legacy-communities-scheme/how-we-listened-2/, accessed December 2011.
Populus (2011) *The Times* Olympic survey, www.populus.co.uk/Poll/Olympic-Survey/ (accessed December 2011).
Poynter. G (2011) Mega events and the urban economy: What can Olympic cities learn from each other? Unpublished working paper, London East Research Institute, UEL.
Sinclair (2011) *Ghost Milk: Calling time on the grand project*, London: Hamish Hamilton/Penguin.
Van Haars M. (2006) Lost in translation, *Rising East* online, www.uel.ac.uk/risingeast/archive03/essays/vanharskamp.htm (accessed December 2011).
YouGov (2011) *YouGov Olympic Results – One Year To Go*, London: YouGov.

12

REGIONAL INVOLVEMENT WITH THE OLYMPIC AND PARALYMPIC GAMES

Ian Jones

Introduction

The hosting of any Olympic and Paralympic Games throws up an interesting paradox. Bids are made by the host city, which, it is argued, will receive the majority of the benefits (particularly in terms of economic benefits and improvements to infrastructure) associated with hosting such an event, while, of course, taking most of the associated risks. As Blake (2005) has demonstrated, for example, the benefits for London would seem significantly to outweigh those benefits for the rest of the country. Such bids, however, require national government to provide support and commitment, given, as was the case with the London bid, on the basis that the Games will benefit the wider nation, a claim that does not always stand up to close scrutiny. With events of such scale requiring subsidization by governments, and with such subsidies having to be financed either out of government revenue or, as has been widely reported in the case of London 2012, reductions in other government spending, it could be argued that the Games are a mixed blessing for regions within the United Kingdom, with the exception of London and perhaps the South-East. Deccio and Baloglu (2002), however, use social exchange theory to suggest that groups will be willing to engage in an exchange with another party (allowing resources to be diverted to the host city) if there is perceived mutual benefit from the exchange. Thus, it is argued, regions outside the capital will be prepared to view the Games positively if there is some perceived gain for them. This need for regions outside London to perceive a sense of benefit has been acknowledged by the organizing bodies. As Garcia suggests, "When historians look back at these Games, they will see the most extensive commitment to nationalize an event that is often considered city based" (Garcia, 2010, p. 5). This follows a set of examples (albeit limited) of previous sporting events that have demonstrated major benefits for the wider nation, with the 1995 Rugby World Cup in South Africa as perhaps the clearest. As Chalip notes:

> The Rugby World Cup came to South Africa as it was endeavouring to create national unity in the aftermath of its apartheid history ... Mandela's government recognized that the liminoid character of the event could be used to alter public perceptions of relations between White and Black South Africa. As the event approached, the government promoted the event's "One Team, One Nation" theme. Then, in an act designed to drive home the new narrative, Mandela appeared at the event wearing a

> replica of the (White) South African team captain's uniform. The effect was palpable, fostering extensive discourse about a new national unity.
>
> *(Chalip, 2006, p. 121)*

Whilst it could be argued that the 1995 Rugby World Cup was unique in terms of the social and political context within which it was held, there are still parallels in the need for the whole of the United Kingdom to capitalize on the potential impacts and legacies of the Games, given that the event is taking place within a global economic environment of relative austerity and uncertainty. Such potential benefits do, of course, require the regions to develop appropriate strategies to capitalize on the Olympic and Paralympic Games. Rather than evaluate the short-term impacts and longer-term legacies of the Games for the various regions of the United Kingdom, this chapter will examine three key aspects:

- A brief outline of the involvement of different English regions with the Olympic and Paralympic Games.
- An examination of the various strategies employed to capitalize on the opportunities presented by the Games.
- A discussion of some of the specific issues that are being addressed in different regions.

The chapter will make reference to a number of existing schemes that are being undertaken, and also present case study material to illustrate the involvement of the various regions in the Olympic and Paralympic Games.

The Nations and Regions Group

From an Olympic perspective, the United Kingdom is divided into 12 regions – nine regions within England, alongside Scotland, Wales and Northern Ireland. The establishment of the Nations and Regions Group addressed the need for a coherent strategy among these various regions of the United Kingdom, and the requirement to ensure that all such regions are involved in and benefit from the Games, in terms of receiving a legacy. Under the chairmanship of London 2012 Organising Committee board member Charles Allen, the Nations and Regions Group consists of representatives from various stakeholders, such as regional cultural consortia, regional development agencies, regional sport boards and local government, as well as representation from various sporting, arts, cultural, commerce, tourism, education and health-related organizations within the specific region (London, 2012a).

The Nations and Regions Group – terms of reference

- Creating and facilitating a UK-wide network in relation to the Games.
- Identifying and sharing best practice.
- Joining up regional activity and initiatives.
- Dovetailing with/enhancing existing non-Olympic programmes and initiatives.
- Raising/registering local issues and interests and facilitating a UK-wide network in relation to the Games (London, 2012a).

The creation of a Nations and Regions Group is not to ensure consistency across regions. Instead, each region will have its own vision in terms of exploiting the potential benefits of the Games, while at the same time mirroring those of the government and LOCOG (North-West RDA, 2009). For example, the North-West will use the Games "as a catalyst to derive the maximum economic, sporting, health and social benefits, and provide our people with opportunities to engage with the pride, passion and spirit of London 2012" (London 2012, 2011b), focusing on three key themes: sporting (getting active); social (delivering a cultural programme, inspiring young people, improving health and well-being, encouraging volunteering, engaging stakeholders); and economic (growing business, staging major events, developing tourism, improving skills and employment) – aspirations that are consistent across all of the regions of the UK.

Developing regional legacies within a changing landscape

As the chapter below outlines, much of the initial momentum for change has been through the various regional development agencies (RDAs). The recent Public Bodies and Localism Bills, passed in November 2011, have made a significant change to the regional landscape. The aim of the bill was to shift power from central government back into the hands of individuals, communities and councils. One of the key outcomes of the bill has been the abolition of the nine regional development agencies. Thus, whilst many of the initiatives described here have gained momentum through the relevant RDAs, the long-term development and outcomes of these regional strategies are difficult to judge.

The Olympic and Paralympic Games and the regions – direct involvement

Although initial plans by the Department for Culture, Media and Sport (DCMS) suggested that the Games should be distributed across the United Kingdom as far as possible (House of Commons, Welsh Affairs Committee, 2009), the requirements of the International Olympic Committee (IOC) make this an unrealistic strategy, and indeed the bid document was explicit in locating the majority of the events in and around London, with the main exceptions being sailing (to be held in Weymouth and Portland in Dorset), the football tournament (held at various venues throughout the United Kingdom, including Wales and Scotland), mountain biking (held in Essex) and Paralympic road cycling (in Kent). Thus, direct involvement for the regions in the hosting of specific Olympic and Paralympic events is limited.

There has been, however, the opportunity for all regions to become involved in the training camp programme. Over 600 training camps have been identified for teams to use in preparation for the Games in all regions of the UK, to fine tune strategy, overcome travel fatigue, adjust to time differences and acclimatize to the conditions they will face in competition. All regions have taken up this opportunity, although the South-East and South-West, perhaps unsurprisingly given the geography of the Games, are most utilized. Table 12.1 provides an illustration of some of the venues being used as training camps.

The benefits to those regions involved in the hosting of teams before the Games potentially extend beyond the pre-Games and Games-time phases. Such legacy initiatives and opportunities from training camps have been highlighted by a number of regions. Wales, for example, has identified a number of possibilities resulting from hosting training camps:

- Wales becoming a natural venue for future Olympic and Paralympic teams to prepare for events in Europe, both before and after the Games.
- The opportunity for volunteers from higher education establishments in Wales to work with the Olympic and Paralympic medical staff and sports teams as part of the support service provision before the Games, resulting in a subsequent legacy for the provision of quality physiotherapy services to sport (particularly disability sport) in Wales.

Table 12.1 Regional examples of pre-Games training camps

Region	*Team/committee*	*Facility*	*Total Pre-Games training camp agreements made in the region (as of 31 August 2011)*
East Midlands	Japanese Olympic Committee	Loughborough University	13
East of England	National Olympic Committee of Mozambique	Comberton Village College, Cambridge	9
North-East	National Olympic Committee of Sri Lanka	Durham University	3
North-West	USA Basketball	Amaechi Basketball Centre, Manchester	6
Northern Ireland	Paralympics Ireland	Antrim Forum Complex, Carrickfergus Sailing Club, South Antrim	2
Scotland	National Olympic Committee of Zambia	Palace of Art Centre for Sports Excellence, Scotstoun Leisure Centre, Glasgow	2
South-East	Papua New Guinea Paralympic Committee	Sevenoaks School, Stoke Mandeville, Bucks	28
South-West	Diving Canada	Plymouth Life Centre, Devon	24
Wales	Chinese Weightlifting Team	Bangor University	6
West Midlands	Jamaica Amateur Athletics Association	Birmingham University	2
Yorkshire and Humber	Olympic Committee of Serbia	Various facilities in Sheffield and Leeds (agreement with local authority)	11

Source: Pre-Games Training Camp Guide (2011).

- A school/community and cultural engagement programme during the camp in 2012 and during sports-specific camps leading into the Games.
- Cooperation between Disability Sport Wales (DSW) and the Australian Paralympic Committee to provide cross-cultural, sports-related information and knowledge exchange and transfer.

(*Visit Wales, 2011*)

In addition to the more generic legacies, specific sport-development legacy opportunities have also been identified. For example, the Welsh Amateur Boxing Association has identified the following legacies as a consequence of hosting boxing teams in the run-up to the London Olympic and Paralympic Games:

Boxer recruitment and development

- To increase grassroots participation in boxing.
- To inspire the next generation of Welsh boxers.
- To link pre-Games training activity with boxing clubs across Wales, with initiatives such as open viewing sessions and question-and-answer sessions with coaches, boxers and boxing officials.
- To allow sparring opportunities for Welsh boxers.

Coach, referee and judge development

- To use the camp and coaching, refereeing and judging seminars to identify future coaches, referees and judges and develop existing volunteers.
- To create a pathway for tutor, referee and judge development.

To raise the profile of boxing in Wales

- To raise the profile of the Welsh Amateur Boxing Association, as well as boxing in Wales in general.
- To raise the profile of the Welsh Amateur Boxing Association in terms of its ability to stage major boxing events.
- To develop a pathway for and portfolio of local, regional and national events.

(*Visit Wales, 2011*)

Thus, despite the lack of events outside London, the training camps still provide a strong opportunity for involvement and opportunities for impacts and legacies, both specific to the sport itself and also in terms of wider legacies such as those related to volunteering and knowledge exchange.

Indirect regional legacies from the Games

Much of the impact and legacy of the Games will come as an indirect result of hosting the Games, and different regions have identified a number of different strategies to capitalize upon the opportunities presented by the Games. Grant Thornton, for example, summarizes the key issues for the East of England Development Agency, suggesting that "Maximising legacy benefits will be the overarching key success measure. Forward planning and partnership working across the private and public sectors will be essential to maximize a myriad of economic, social, community, organisational and cultural opportunities" (Grant Thornton, 2006, p. 4). Although, as highlighted by the strategy of the North-West outlined above, each region will have its own specific strategy to benefit from the Games, the objectives in terms of legacy are broadly similar for each region. The East of England Development Agency identifies a number of targets in terms of what "success" actually means to this particular region (Grant Thornton, 2006):

1. To raise the profile of the region to visitors – tourist growth is identified as a key legacy, both in terms of visitor and business tourism. To achieve this, the key strategy is to showcase the region through the events being held in the area, and specifically through cultural events related to the Games.
2. To develop the region's businesses – this involves not only being awarded Olympic-related work through the Olympic Development Authority (ODA) and the London Organising Committee of the Olympic Games (LOCOG), but also building on future partnerships developed through undertaking such work. The Nations and Regions East's Regional Business Plan (East of England Development Agency, 2006) highlights some key priorities for developing a business legacy, including supporting an increase in new business start-ups and survival rates, supporting small and medium enterprise (SME) growth, enhancing the use of the region's research and development capability, continued professional development and the raising of productivity in key sectors.
3. Skills improvement and capacity building – the Games are seen as a potential catalyst to provide training for a range of sectors including construction, logistics, culture, media, creative industries, hospitality, languages, sport and leisure and security.
4. Improve sporting performance and aspirations – raising sporting aspirations for people within the region and maximizing opportunities for hosting major sporting and cultural events.
5. Maximize opportunities for engagement in culture – involvement in the cultural events, using the London Games as a catalyst for greater interest in cultural organizations, and maximize opportunities for capacity building within cultural organizations and businesses.
6. Stimulate improvement in infrastructure – investment in infrastructure, most notably in terms of investment in training and pre-Games training camps, and tourism infrastructure.
7. Maximize opportunities for participation and social inclusion – to allow all people within the region to have an opportunity to participate in a related cultural event; increase sports participation particularly in disadvantaged locations and areas with poor health, to increase the quantity and quality of coaching (paid or unpaid), and to raise the aspirations of volunteers and improve their workforce prospects.

An examination of the broad strategies developed by other regions shows that they have, on the whole, outlined slightly different but relatively consistent themes. For example, the West Midlands has identified five broad themes: business opportunities; volunteering; culture, tourism and regional image; and sport and physical activity (West Midlands Leadership Group, 2011).

As well as the themes identified by each region, the key elements of the overall strategies within the regions acknowledge that there are three broad phases in terms of impact and legacy planning: before, during and after the Games. Figure 12.1 summarizes the key regional priorities throughout those themes:

Case study Using the pre-Games period to leverage impacts and legacies in the regions – Regional Educational Legacy for the Arts and Youth Sport

One specific regional legacy project that addresses the three Games phases and cuts across a variety of themes, such as participation, volunteering and business development in the South-West of England, is that of RELAYS (Regional Educational Legacy in Arts and Youth Sport). The RELAYS programme was cited by Charles Allen, Chair of the Nations and Regions Group, as a best-practice example at the Local Government Group's London 2012 Legacy Conference in London. The RELAYS project is delivered through universities and cultural organizations across the South-West region, with involvement from a range of stakeholders such as the South-West Regional Development Agency (SWRDA), Arts Council England, Sport England, the Association of Colleges, and the London Organising Committee for the Olympic Games (LOCOG). The RELAYS project aims to inspire young people and their communities to participate in, create and promote cultural and sporting activities, engaging the region with the London 2012 Olympic and Paralympic Games and creating a lasting legacy beyond 2012. The scheme focuses on three main areas of engagement – sport, culture and business – working with various partners to support a variety of sports and arts-related festivals, events and activities. In the first two years of the scheme, almost 330,000 young people and community members participated in sporting and cultural activities, with sports activities and competitions focused on those young people not competing for their school.

All RELAYS events have incorporated elements or activities from more than one sector and this has enhanced the opportunities open to young people and community members – for example, through allowing people who already have a keen interest in sport to understand the cultural offer that is open to them and vice versa – as well as providing opportunities to try out new activities and encourage participation in unfamiliar sports and cultural activities. For example, young people and community members who attended the Devon Games to Inspire sporting competition as audience members were also able to engage with poetry slams and storytelling. By June 2010, 4,837 people had participated in cultural activities, while 101,105 people had been attracted to cultural events as audience members (Dingle, 2011).

Up to the end of September 2011, the RELAYS scheme achieved the following (Laura Phelps, 2011, personal communication):

- events/festivals held – 1,022;
- volunteering opportunities offered – 4,056;
- attendees at events/festivals – 330,915;
- young people engaged with and up-skilled – 69,192;
- businesses supported – 1,072.

RELAYS and legacy planning

As well as its focus on activity during the pre-Games stage, the RELAYS programme has also concentrated on developing sustainable events that are embedded in the community to inspire lifelong participation, thus promoting a longer-lasting legacy within the region. The strategies adopted to achieve this are as follows.

- The encouragement of matched funding to be provided for any event, and to ensure that the RELAYS programme is not the sole funder of any activity. This strategy should ensure the sustainability of such activities once any funding ceases.

- The involvement of key stakeholders, such as students, volunteers and community members, in the planning, organization and promotion of events. This strategy has been developed to raise the confidence, skills and abilities of the relevant communities and to ensure that stakeholders within the community can take ownership of such activities and continue to support and deliver them, thus enhancing the sustainability of any event.
- The creation of an event evaluation toolkit to allow partners such as local businesses to assess the benefits of hosting events in the region, thus helping support the legacy through encouraging partners to support future activity by making them aware of the benefits.

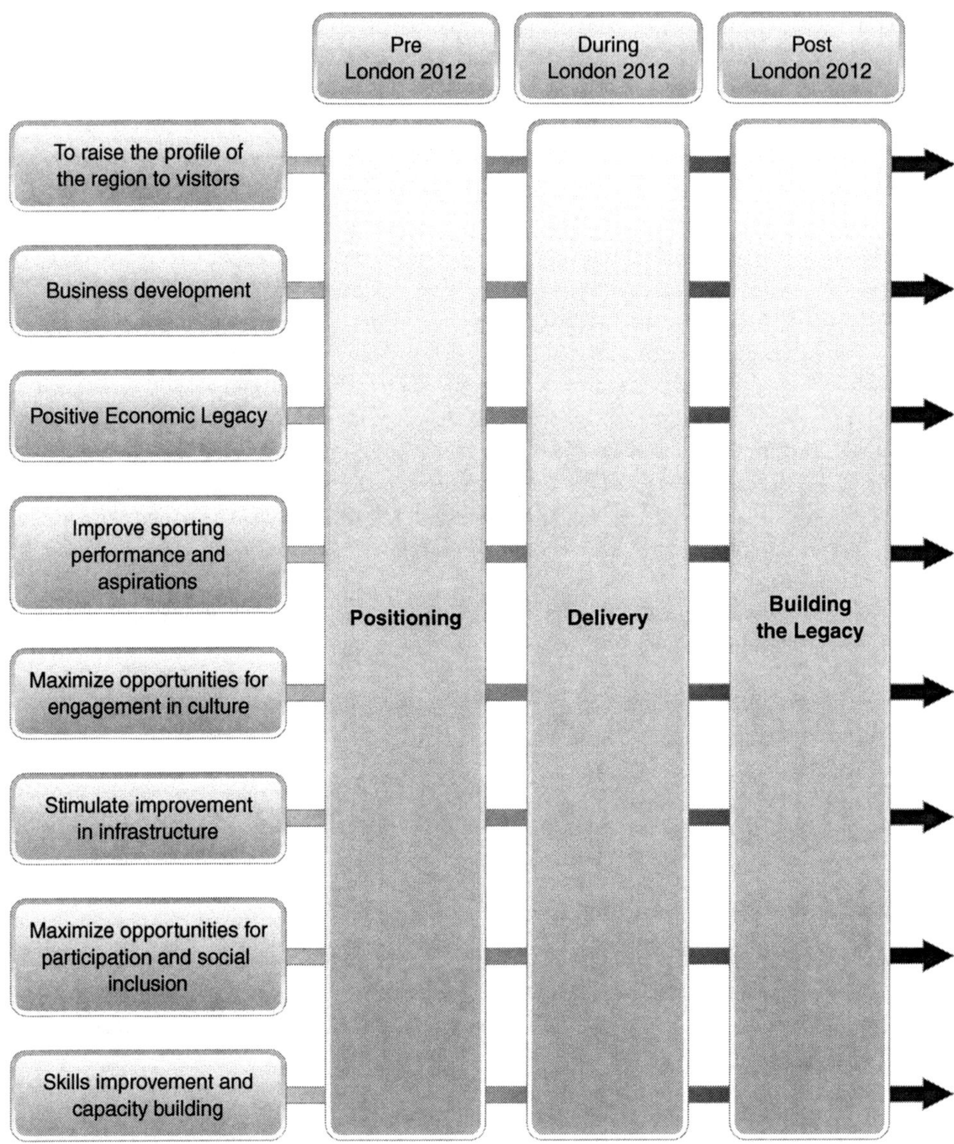

Figure 12.1 Regional priorities pre-, during and post-London 2012.

Legacy Trust UK and the regions

One agency with a key role in the delivery of benefits for the regions is Legacy Trust UK. Legacy Trust UK is an independent charity, created to help develop both a cultural and sporting legacy from the London 2012 Olympic and Paralympic Games, with a mission "to support a wide range of innovative cultural and sporting activities for all, which celebrate the London 2012 Olympic and Paralympic Games and which will leave a lasting legacy in communities throughout the United Kingdom" (Legacy Trust UK, 2011a).

Of the total funding budget for the Games, Legacy Trust UK is allocating over half to 12 programmes across the regions of the UK. The allocation for each region is calculated using an initial baseline of £500,000 per region, subsequently weighted by population and socio-demographics. All programmes supported by this funding are selected and managed at regional level. The 12 regional programmes are unique, but all of them share three key aims:

- to unite culture, sport, knowledge and learning, in line with the values and vision of the Olympic Games;
- to make a lasting difference to all those involved;
- to be grassroots projects, often small in scale, and uniting communities of interest at local and regional level.

All funded programmes are expected to meet the "legacy standards" set by Legacy Trust UK (these are outlined in Table 12.2).

The impact of Legacy Trust UK funding has been categorized into four themes: children and young people; community engagement; accessibility and inclusion; and partnerships and innovation (Legacy Trust UK, 2011a). Each theme involves the use of both sport (for example, 1,600 people taking part in the UK School Games programme) and culture (for example, the Tate Movie Project, which engaged over 9,000 children across 80 separate locations).

Table 12.2 "Legacy standard" requirements of Legacy Trust UK funded programmes

1. To fit at least one of the three key themes of sport, education and the arts: we welcome projects which encourage a joined-up approach across these themes .
2. To be highly visible and wide-reaching: we want to offer diverse communities across the UK the chance to take part in cultural, educational and sporting activities in the build-up to 2012 Games
3. To be distinctive, new or innovative: we encourage new ideas, approaches and collaborations and exemplar projects.
4. To offer a coherent programme of high-quality activities with clearly defined outcomes.
5. To demonstrate a lasting legacy by making a sustained difference to the community.
6. To enjoy public support and demonstrate community engagement.
7. To keep overheads low and make best use of existing community resources and facilities.
8. To be accessible to all and foster community inclusion by encouraging active citizenship and greater participation in community life.
9. To encourage the development of participants, which will help build their personal capacity, thereby helping them to achieve their potential.
10. To be able to lever significant resources: we look to support projects which can expand their reach and impact.
11. Not be for profit and revenue projects (although some capital expenditure may be considered for cultural projects at the discretion of the Trustees).

Source: Legacy Trust UK, 2011b.

Engagement in the projects has been significant, with over a quarter of a million young people being involved in Legacy Trust UK-funded projects in 2010/2011, over 8,500 volunteers taking part, and over 50,000 hard-to-reach young people participating nationwide (Legacy Trust UK, 2011c), with many of these being in regions outside London.

One of the key regions to benefit from Legacy Trust UK funding has been Scotland, which has received £4.7 million of funding to support four main strands of activity (Legacy Trust, 2011b). These are:

People Making Waves

People Making Waves is a volunteering programme focusing upon a range of cultural activities, made up of three strands. *Wave of Friendship* is a volunteer exchange programme that encourages and supports the exchange of volunteers between Scotland and London. Bursaries are provided to cover the costs involved in the exchange and support any volunteer exchange that demonstrates one of the values of friendship, respect, courage, determination, equality and inspiration. *Make A Splash!* is a series of information and training events, run by Voluntary Arts Scotland, encouraging people to think about how they can increase participation in volunteering, either by attracting new volunteers to existing schemes or through the development of new schemes. Finally, *My Volunteering* is an ongoing project to capture the actual experiences of volunteers in the lead up to the Games.

Conflux

The second Legacy Trust UK theme supported in Scotland is that of Conflux. This theme focuses upon the delivery of master classes and outreach work based upon street arts, circus and physical theatre. This work has led to a number of productions and subsequent festivals building upon this outreach work, such as Surge, a festival that took place in Glasgow in July 2010 and again in July 2011, featuring international and Scottish work, both indoors and on the street, as well as offering professional development opportunities and a chance for young people to try new skills.

Curious?

The third theme to receive support is Curious?. The focus of Curious? is on celebrating Glasgow's multicultural communities, culminating in an exhibition and conference, with an outreach programme for schoolchildren based upon celebrating cultural diversity, which is anticipated will be rolled out to other organizations and community groups.

Human Race

The final theme is Human Race, a three-year project to explore Scotland's global impact on the history, culture and science of sport through a series of exhibitions and specially commissioned artworks. These exhibitions will run alongside an accompanying outreach programme that will tour various venues in Scotland during 2012. A key focus of the project is to encourage the people of Scotland to connect with London 2012 and with the core values of the Olympic Movement – excellence, friendship and respect – through exhibitions, events, talks, workshops, films and discussions.

The relationship between the regions and the legacy promises

There are six legacy promises that have been identified for the Games, four of which are important from a regional perspective: to make the UK a world leading sporting nation; to inspire a generation of young people; to develop choices and opportunities for disabled people; and to demonstrate that the UK is a creative, inclusive and welcoming place to live in, visit and do business (DCMS, 2008). The link between the legacy promises can be summarized as shown in Figure 12.2.

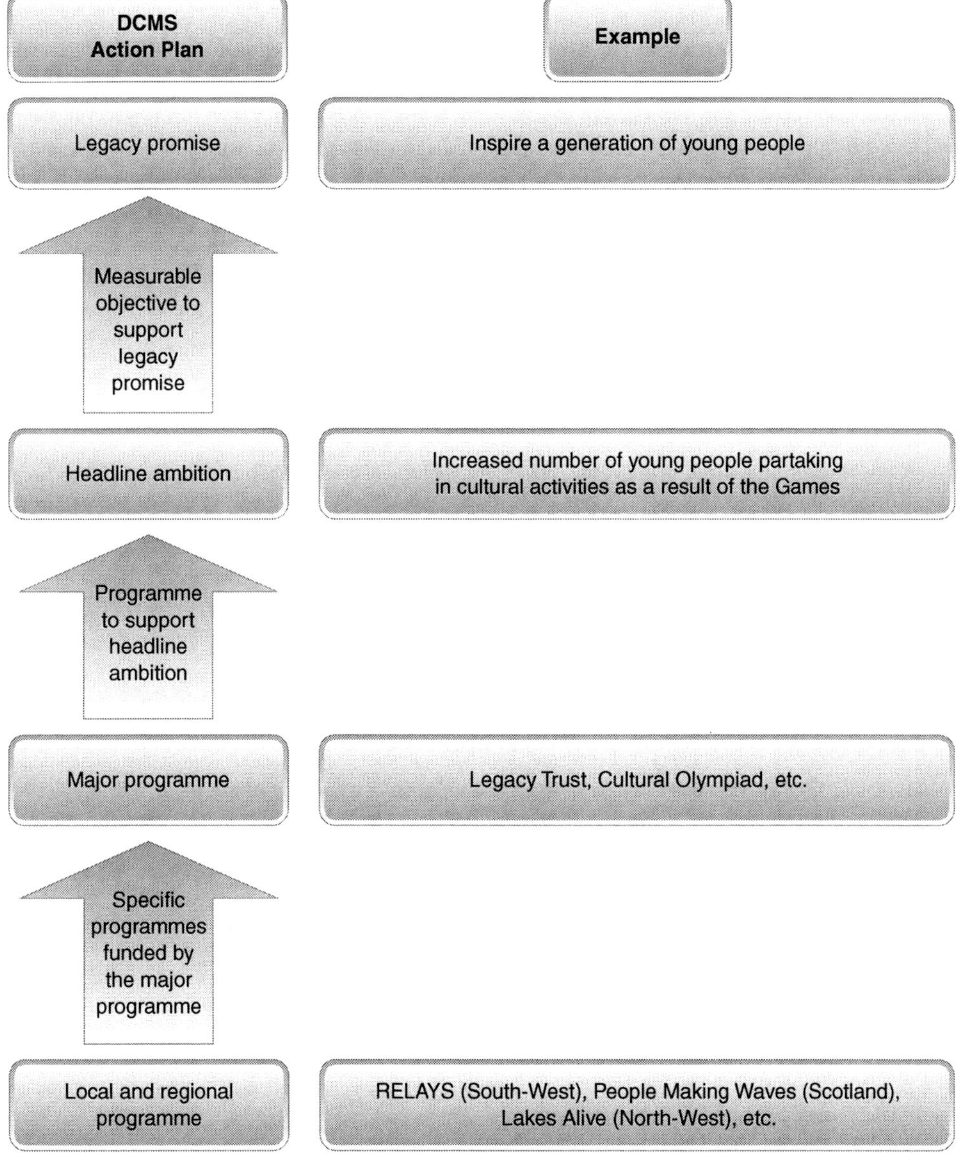

Figure 12.2 An example of links between regions and legacy promises.

The presence of such programmes and strategies does not, however, guarantee success. As Coalter notes with reference to the key aspiration of increasing participation, simply hosting the Games will not lead to increases in activity, and to have any chance of success the underlying mechanisms of participation need to be more clearly conceptualized and understood, and appropriate strategies implemented. This will clearly be the case with the other headline ambitions, and key stakeholders would certainly need to follow Coalter's suggestion that such strategies, "like competing in the Olympics, [will require] sustained hard work, based on a coherent strategy with no guarantee of success" (Coalter, 2007, p. 110).

Conclusions

This chapter has demonstrated that, although there is undoubted emphasis upon London as the focal point of the 2012 Olympic and Paralympic Games, there are a number of clear strategies that have been adopted by the regions to capitalize on the event itself. From direct involvement, such as hosting training camps or Legacy Trust UK-funded projects, to more indirect, long-term legacies, the Games does provide an opportunity for the wider nation to be involved, and to achieve sustainable benefits. These benefits may be in areas such as increased regional awareness, business development, skills and capacity building, infrastructural improvements and social inclusion, as well as the more obvious aspirations of increased participation in sport and cultural activities. To date, the most clearly visible outcomes seem to have been those focused upon participation and social inclusion, especially with the young or other target groups, as evidenced through initiatives such as Curious? in Scotland and RELAYS in the South-West. In terms of the more business-focused initiatives, many of the schemes and strategies outlined have yet to show any clear outcomes, and are, by their very nature, unlikely to do so until after the Games. In terms of assessing actual outcomes, only time will tell the extent to which the Games have been of true benefit to the regions outside London and the South-East. There is debate about the extent of the legacies, given the dismantling of the regional development agencies, and the focus towards localism may well result in an inconsistent approach to the achievement of desired regional legacies across the United Kingdom. It is apparent, however, that an initial impetus has been generated. The extent to which this will be exploited will only become clear at a regional level after the Games.

References

Blake, A. (2005) The economic impact of the London 2012 Olympics, working paper No. 5, Christel DeHaan Tourism and Travel Research Institute, Nottingham University Business School.

Chalip, L. (2006) Towards social leverage of sport events, *Journal of Sport and Tourism*, 11 (2), 109–127.

Coalter, F. (2007) London Olympics 2012: the catalyst that inspires people to lead more active lives?, *Journal of The Royal Society for the Promotion of Health*, 127 (3), 109–110.

DCMS (2008) Before, During and After: making the most of the London 2012 Games, London: DCMS.

Deccio, C. and Baloglu, S. (2002) Nonhost community resident reactions to the 2002 Winter Olympics: the spillover impacts, *Journal of Travel Research*, 41: 46–56.

Dingle, L. (2011) *Relays: Final Report Phase One (May 2008–June 2010)*, Exeter: Universities South West.

Dwyer, L., Forsyth, P. and Spurr, R. (2006) Assessing the economic impacts of events: a computable general equilibrium approach, *Journal of Travel Research*, 45: 59–66.

EEDA (2006) *Draft Regional Business Plan for the London 2012 Olympic Games and Paralympic Games*, Cambridge: East of England Development Agency.

Pre-Games Training Camp Guide (2011) The official pre-Games training camps website for London 2012. Online: http://trainingcamps.london2012.com/ (accessed 8 September 2011).

Grant Thornton (2006) *Economic Impact Study of the London 2012 Olympic Games and Paralympic Games*, report prepared by Grant Thornton, Torkildsen Barclay and the Christel DeHaan Tourism and Travel Research Institute, Cambridge: East of England Development Agency.

Garcia, B. (2010) Introduction, *The Cultural Olympiad, The UK Wide Picture*, London: Legacy Trust UK.

House of Commons, Welsh Affairs Committee (2009) *Potential Benefits of the 2012 Olympics and Paralympics for Wales: eighth report of session 2008–09*, report, together with formal minutes, oral and written evidence, London: Stationery Office.

Legacy Trust UK (2011a) Leaving a lasting legacy from London 2012 in communities throughout the UK. Online: www.legacytrustuk.org/info/About_Approach/ (accessed 20 September 2011).

Legacy Trust UK (2011b) *Annual Review 2010/11*, London: Legacy Trust UK.

Legacy Trust UK (2011c) Our legacy standard. Online: www.legacytrustuk.org/info/About_Legacy-Standard/ (accessed 21 September 2011).

London 2012 (2011a) Nations and regions group. Online: www.london2012.com/about-us/the-people-delivering-the-games/the-nations-and-regions-group/ (accessed 10 September 2011).

London 2012 (2011b) Nations and regions group North West. Online: www.london2012.com/about-us/the-people-delivering-the-games/the-nations-and-regions-group/north-west.php (accessed 10 September 2011).

North West Regional Development Agency (2009) *Everyone's 2012 – North West Legacy Framework for the 2012 Games Update*, Warrington: NWRDA.

Visit Wales (2011) London 2012 pre-games training In Wales. Online: www.visitwales.co.uk/upload/pdf/PGT.pdf (accessed 27 August 2011).

West Midlands Leadership Group (2011) West Midlands regional plan for London 2012. Online: www.london2012.com/documents/nations-and-regions-group/west-midlands-2012-games-regional-plan.pdf (accessed 20 August 2011).

13

INVOLVING SCHOOLS

Get Set – a model for a more open approach to Olympic education?

Charlie Tims

The world as it is, and how it can be

The Olympic Games offers the world a moment to see itself – both as it is and how it could be. This mixture of dreams to aspire to and interrogate is the basis of the educational value of the Games. Pierre de Coubertin, founder of the modern Olympic Movement, viewed the Games as a cultural and an educational event – a legacy that is reflected in an Olympic Organising Committee's obligations under the terms of the Olympic Charter to further Olympic education during the host city's Olympiad. All host nations are committed to providing an education programme in schools, but the way in which this programme is created is left up to host organising committees (for 2012, the London Organising Committee for the Olympic and Paralympic Games – LOCOG) who are relatively free to design the programme as they wish.

Get Set, the official London 2012 education programme, has attempted to provide a framework to realise this learning opportunity in schools across the country by providing a supportive structure and incentives for schools to learn about the Olympic and Paralympic Games through a specially designed website.[1] The programme has developed its own approach, which reflects the diversity of education providers for 3–19-year-olds in the UK, the norms within the country's education system and the new ubiquitous access to broadband-enabled devices. The programme has aimed to be more 'open' than previous Olympic education programmes in three key ways. First, it has bought the Olympic and Paralympic Games into one combined set of resources for schools. Second, it has forefronted the Olympic and Paralympic values and offered them to schools[2] as a starting point for projects, but has not been proscriptive about how they are to be used. Third, it has offered learning providers incentives, resources and instructions through a specially designed website and has aimed to facilitate their learning in a network.

At the time of writing, this model has produced impressive levels of interest from schools, but it also raises questions about the depth of young people's learning and the type of relationships that schools have gained through the programme. The nature of supporting education through a network, especially one that has touched so many schools, is such that it is hard to account comprehensively for what young people have done and how much they have learned. But in any case, at a time when the Olympic Movement has increased its efforts to reach out to young people through the Youth Olympic Games, Get Set should be seen as an attempt to 'open up' and involve wider groups in the experience and creation of London 2012. Lessons could be drawn from the Get Set experience and applied to other areas of the educational and cultural work related to the Olympics.

The Get Set Network

In 2008 a report by MORI commissioned by the Department for Children, Schools and Families (DCSF) to investigate young people's engagement with the Olympic and Paralympic games concluded that 'face to face channels' are the most effective way of engaging young people with the Olympic Games (Fraser *et al.*, 2008). Young people's need to learn about the Games face to face means that an Olympic education programme cannot be delivered by an organising committee alone; it has to be made by teachers and others who work face to face with young people. The Get Set education programme is more than just a set of teaching resources – it is a strategy to mobilise teachers and schools all over the country to 'live the Olympic and Paralympic Values' (London 2012, 2009). This strategy has been characterised by the organising committee as a network – the 'Get Set Network'.

The Get Set Network is organised through the Get Set website, which was launched in September 2009. The website communicates the education programme, provides resources to teachers and enables schools to communicate with one another. Teachers are guided through a process of registering with the website, using its resources and then being officially rewarded with 'membership' of the Get Set Network for completing an activity linked to the Games. This can become confusing – while schools are 'registered' with Get Set and using the resources of the network, they have not yet become 'members', which will entitle them to rewards and benefits, even though all users of the Get Set website and resources could, to all intents and purposes, be considered as part of a general 'Olympic education network'! At the time of writing, of the approximately 30,000 schools in the country nearly 22,000 have registered with the website, of which 17,009 have been officially admitted to the network as members.[3]

Leaving the semantics of 'registration' and 'membership' to one side, schools are under no obligation to engage with the Get Set Network, and when they do engage there is no line manager to look after them and guide their learning. This means that the network has to make an appealing offer to encourage schools to get involved, and has to offer them support in the form of resources and relationships once they do engage. This gives the Get Set Network its key features. They are as follows:

Incentives to participate

Get Set's key message to schoolteachers is that officially becoming a member of the Get Set Network is rewarded with tickets to the Olympic and Paralympic Games – the website currently has a holding page with the slogan 'Get Set to go to the Games'.[4] These tickets will be provided through the Ticketshare scheme, which will see 50,000 tickets distributed to schools outside London, and 50,000 to schools inside London.[5] The Mayor of London's office has also secured a further 75,000 tickets to be distributed to schools admitted to the Get Set Network in London (BBC, 2011b). Other advertised incentives to join the network include visits from mascots, athletes, Olympic officials and invitations to involvement in celebrating key moments during the preparations for the Games.

Resources for learning

Schools can apply to join the Get Set Network when they have completed a project in school that draws on the Olympic and Paralympic values, namely respect, excellence and friendship (the Olympic values) and equality, inspiration, determination and courage (the Paralympic values). The Get Set Network is the first Olympic education programme developed by a Games organising committee to combine the values of the Olympic and the Paralympic Games and offer them as a starting point for schools.

As well as providing online games and exercises, the Get Set website offers teachers a range of different ideas for ways that the Olympic and Paralmypic Games can be incorporated into key stages 0–5 (although using these materials is not actually a prerequisite for attaining 'membership' of the Get Set Network). These resources draw clearly on the staging and creation of the London 2012 Games. Suggested areas of focus for key stages 0–4, with some variations in emphasis at different stages, are: the Winter Games; using Olympic values in assembly; the torch relay; the countdown to 2012; and the construction of the Olympic Park. Olympic mascots is a particular area of focus for primary year groups, while secondary year groups have a clearer focus on modern languages, personal presentation techniques and volunteering. Activities for key stage 5 are undefined.[6]

The website also provides access and pointers to 'Get Set Plus' – a series of 33 affiliated 'partner' education programmes drawing on the Olympic and Paralympic values, arranged in different thematic areas (sustainability, enterprise, community/collaboration/citizenship, practical learning, culture and creativity, PE and sport, healthy and active lifestyles, the Paralympic Games) available to schools nationally, provided by Olympic sponsors, cultural organisations and community groups.[7] For example, the British Natural History Consortium offers 'Meet the Species', an education resource drawing on the Olympic Park that helps children to find and identify creatures near their schools. Coca Cola offers the 'Real Business Challenge', which invites schools to tackle a business challenge set by Coca Cola Enterprises; while Radiowaves, a network of free school websites, offers 'Supporter 2 Reporter', which supports young people to report on sporting events in their local areas.[8] Get Set Plus also points schools towards opportunities for young people in the Cultural Olympiad, including the London 2012 Festival and the Open Weekend.[9] Taking part in a Get Set Plus project is another way for a school to be admitted to the network.

The resources available on the Get Set website have been augmented since its 2009 launch. During 2011, the Get Set Network introduced a new area of focus, 'Get Set Goes Global', which provides specific resources to schools on the areas of the Olympic Truce, World Sport Day and the different countries competing in the Games. LOCOG also provides a set of teaching resources in different languages for schools in other countries.[10]

A community

As well as providing incentives to participate and the means to do so, the Get Set Network aims to generate collective efficacy amongst schools. To this end schools who are registered with the Get Set website are able to access stories of other schools' work on the Olympic values, in the form of case studies, on their own blogs and through emails from the London 2012 education team. Since September 2010, Get Set has highlighted a 'school of the month' to draw attention to exemplary practice in the Get Set Network. Schools are also able to connect with others in their area through the Get Set website.

Although the Get Set Network has not yet been subject to public scrutiny, Nielsen, an international consumer insight agency and sponsor of the Olympics (providing support in kind), conducted an evaluation of participating schools between 2010 and 2011. This involved interviewing a sample of 1,799 schools, of which 76 per cent were taking part in Get Set activities, involving an average of 159 pupils per school. Other headline results include the following: 85 per cent of teachers would recommend the programme; 81 per cent of schools had found the values useful and would be using them after the games; 78 per cent of teachers believe it has had a positive impact on behaviour; 83 per cent believe it has improved attainment; and 75 per cent believe it has enriched learning and teaching.[11]

It is beyond the scope of this chapter to evaluate the effectiveness of a project that is currently incomplete and has touched more than 20,000 schools in the country, assuming a different form in each school in which it has taken place. Rather, I will try to describe the character of the network and the nature of its impact on learning outcomes, which would need to be interrogated were the project to be evaluated and built upon in future Olympic education work.

Learning networks

The last decade has seen a burgeoning of different types of educational network. Protest networks like Occupy, support networks like MumsNet, mass-creative projects like National Novel Writing Month and fundraising initiatives like Movember[12] are all recent examples of networks of interest that have used modern communications technologies to bring people together to learn and create in different ways. Like Get Set, these networks provide groups of people with the instructions, recipes and resources to enable them to learn from one another.

In the United States in 2003 the artists Miranda July and Harrel Fletcher launched the project Learning to Love You More. For five years they posted quirky assignments, using instructions on a website, for anyone to complete. The assignments ranged from simple exercises such as 'climb a tree and take a photo from the top of it' to 'interview someone who has experienced war'. The project has since become a book, an online community and an exhibition.[13] This model of bringing dispersed groups of people together to complete creative exercises has been repeated across the web in numerous different ways; National Novel Writing Month, which also began in the United States, enables tens of thousands of people every year to complete a novel in a month (BBC, 2011a).

In some instances, the ease with which people who share an interest can come together has changed their relationship to big organisations, especially organisations whose goal is supporting learning and education. Five years ago, TED was an isolated, exclusive annual event in California that bought together designers, academics, scientists and artists to give pithy 20-minute talks about 'big ideas'. When the organisers of the conference started sharing videos of these talks online, 'TED talks' turned out to have a broad appeal across the English-speaking world. Very rapidly it became clear to the organisers of the conference that there was a mismatch between the amount of people who wanted to attend the conference and the amount of people who could physically get there and afford to go. So TED created TEDx – a conference that fans of TED can curate and organise for themselves, provided they follow certain rules. Now most days see a TEDx event happen somewhere in the world, and the fringe is bigger and better known than the original conference.[14]

Like TEDx, National Novel Writing Month and Learning to Love You More, Get Set has used communications effectively to channel the energy and enthusiasm of a community of people. The DCFS's research into children and young people's perceptions of involvement in London 2012, concluded in 2008, showed that although young people across the country were excited and had a natural interest in the Games they did not 'spontaneously feel involved' (Fraser *et al.*, 2008). Providing the resources and guidelines to teachers through the Get Set Network in a way that apes the charateristics of these educational movements has provided a highly effective way to close this gap between their interest and their ability to act on it. In the Nielsen evaluation cited earlier, the top reasons schools gave for engaging with Get Set were a desire to feel part of the Games (86 per cent) and that it was an opportunity to engage pupils and teachers (78 per cent).

These educational networks are also successful because they offer similar ways to channel energy that frames how learning happens. First, they offer a *clear goal* – be it 'learning to love other people' or organising a conference for ideas that can change the world. Second, they offer *ways to pursue the goal* – be that the instructions for organising a TEDx event, or for completing a Learning to Love You More exercise. Third, they offer a *sense of community* – all the examples here generate an awareness of other people in the network, by email, picture sharing, blogging and videos, to create a sense of common purpose. These devices offer a balance of freedom and rules within the community that help it towards its goal.

As outlined in the second section of this chapter, Get Set has used similar devices to those used by these other open educational networks but with one key difference: the offer of incentives to participate, separate from the learning experience itself – namely, the offer of tickets for schools in exchange for evidence of completed work responding to the Olympics. But of course, Get Set is also different to the projects outlined above in that it targets schools and teachers, not enthusiasts and volunteers. This use of incentives is justified on the basis that only very proactive schools will take on a new project for the sake of learning alone, but the vast majority will engage if additional incentives are offered. As anyone knows who has ever tried to work on a project like this, schools tend to need considerable support and time to fit new ideas into their curriculum. The Nielsen research also found that 57 per cent of schools taking part in Get Set cited rewards and access to tickets as key reasons for taking part.

The pretext for a broad-ranging education programme that would touch every child in the country was created in London 2012's bid application to the International Olympic Committee, which placed inspiring young people in the UK and across the world at the heart of the bid.[15] The offer of incentives propsed by the small education team (less than 20 staff) within LOCOG, which aims to work with every school in the country, is a rational response.

The danger, of course, is that a learning network that could be the start of an 'Olympic educational movement' starts to look more like a membership club, where schools trade minimal evidence of engagement with the Olympic values for tickets. Schools secure tickets and the Organising Committee secures the numbers it needs to prove that it has fulfilled the promises made to young people in Singapore in 2005. Meanwhile, children miss out on the considerable learning opportunities offered by the Olympic Games, and what began as a project to extend the learning experiences offered by the spectacle of the Games becomes just another way to access the event.

So, it is vital that that future open approaches to Olympic education strike the right balance, between encouraging people to become members of the network and ensuring that young people are still having meaningful learning experiences, in a network that makes the most of the web's capacity to bring dispersed groups of enthusiastic people together in pursuit of learning outcomes.

Striking the right balance

It is beyond the scope of this chapter to prove whether the offer of rewards to take part has created a glitch in the community or not. There are, however, several areas of enquiry that it might be interesting to probe further. A network distorted by the offer of rewards would fail to challenge schools to work differently, to help them get their teeth into the Olympic Games or to build relationships that might endure after the Games; but there is considerable evidence that the Get Set Network has achieved all of these aims.

Do the values challenge schools and partners enough?

According to Nielsen's research, 66 per cent of schools cited a match between the Olympic and Paralympic values and the ethos of the school as a key reason for taking part in the Get Set Network. Churchmead School in Windsor reports on the Get Set website that it has

> completely transformed its rewards system, pastoral form groups and aspects of the curriculum to embed the Olympic and Paralympic values. Student diaries now include a page for counting up house points awarded for displaying one of the Values and house groups represent nations competing at the Games. Individual forms are competing in a house 'race' to travel from Beijing to London earning 'miles' by competing in a variety of different events.
>
> *(http://getset.london2012.com/en/join-us/join-us-case-studies/churchmead-c-of-e-va-school)*

Hastings High School reports 'an Olympic overhaul' where 'the school rewards system now offers students "Championship Points" which are collected to qualify for certain rewards. More points can be earned for demonstrating a commitment to the Olympic and Paralympic Values' (http://getset.london2012.com/en/join-us/join-us-case-studies/hastings-high-school). Mill Chase Community Technology College reports that 'A London 2012 display board has been created using photos of every student to make the numbers 2012. Any Olympic work completed which demonstrates the Values is put up on the board. An Olympic passport forms part of every student's planner' (http://getset.london2012.com/en/join-us/join-us-case-studies/mill-chase-community-technology-college).

The promotional video on the Get Set website explains to teachers that to join the Get Set Network, 'anything goes, as long as the values are at the heart of it'.[16] A strength of Get Set has been its adaptability to different contexts – schools do not want to be hectored at – but could it be *too* adaptable? The Olympic and Parlaympic values are, after all, the values that most schools would be aiming to foster in young people anyway.

Some of the Get Set Plus projects illustrate how loosely connected the Get Set Network can be to the Olympic Games itself – projects organised by official Olympic sponsors are some of the most tangentially related to the Games. For example, Get Set Plus includes: the BP Trading Challenge Roadshow, which describes itself as offering 'fast paced sessions where students trade oil, react to market news and manage a budget while using teamwork and developing skills in decision making'; Coca Cola's Real Business Challenge, which 'challenges students to tackle a business challenge set by Coca Cola enterprises'; and General Electric's Design My Break competition for Olympic tickets, which involved school pupils redesigning their break time in ways that would 'boost emotional well-being'.[17] While it is not hard to see how such projects connect to the values of determination or excellence, it is harder to see how they connect to the Olympic Games. If these projects are a part of the Olympics, what is *not* part of the Olympics?

Projects in Get Set Plus that are more convincingly connected to the Olympic Games do more than just draw on Olympic values; they also make a tangible connection to the Olympics in London in 2012 and place an emphasis on thinking about cultural difference and diversity. For example, Lets Get Cooking, a national network of cooking clubs, ran Lets Get Cooking Around the World, which encouraged pupils across the country to cook a dish from a nation competing in the Games.[18] In the main collection of Get Set leaning resources, the Get Set Goes Global projects – covering the themes of truce, internationalism and nations around the world – are also likely to guide schools towards projects more closely related to the Olympics.

Since the Get Set education programme was conceived, the International Olympic Committee has published the Olympic Education Toolkit, which brings together a set of educational resources for 'Education through Olympism' for teachers and others working with young people. Rather than working directly from the Olympic and Paralympic values, it defines the 'educational values of Olympism' as: the joy of effort; fair play; respect for others; pursuit of excellence; and balance between body, will and mind. Although these values are not necessarily more suited to education than the basic values of the Olympic and Parlaymic Games, they are explained against a bespoke curriculum directly connected to the Olympics, which ensures that work based on these values does become decoupled from its Olympic foundations (Binder, 2007).

Ultimately, the acid test for whether the 'values' can provide a sufficient basis for guiding schools towards work about the Olympic Games is whether any given project could have happened without the Games. If the answer is yes, then it is probably insufficiently 'Olympic' to justify entry to the Get Set Network.

Are enough resources provided to explore the Olympic Games?

The connection between the Olympic Games and education is set out in the second fundamental principle of the Olympic Charter. It describes Olympism as

> a philosophy of life exalting and combining in a balanced whole the qualities of body, will and mind. Blending sport with culture and education, Olympism seeks to create a way of life based on the joy of effort, the educational value of good example and respect for universal fundamental ethical principles.
>
> *(IOC, 2007, p. 11)*

The IOC's educational mission, which it endorses and furthers through the International Olympic Academy, national Olympic committees, the Olympic Values Education Programme and organising committees, is to instill these values in young people through all educational settings. The majority of discussion about Olympic education starts from this point (Binder, 2005). The trouble with an approach that emphasises the development of values alone is twofold. First, it is unrealistic to expect an isolated project in a school to change young people's values.[19] Second, the quixotic focus on values creates a separation between the way that the Olympic Games are publicly discussed and how young people are experiencing them in schools.

The Olympic and Paralympic Games is extraordinary, both as an event and in the way that it brings our era into sharp focus. Janie Hampton's account of the 1948 London Olympic Games, *The Austerity Olympics*, is a book about the Games, but it is also a story about the kind of place Britain was in the immediate aftermath of the Second World War (Hampton, 2008). It is this coming together of the Olympic Games with the times in which we live that makes the event so interesting and engaging, and creates public debate in newspapers, radio phone-ins and works of art. It is what gives colour to the Games.

In summer 2010, I was involved in running a School of Olympic Research – a series of workshops for teachers and pupils at London schools that helped them to think about different questions raised by the Olympic Games. Each day had a theme that reflected a different set of questions. The aim was to find a balance between finding out about the Olympic Games and values and the questions they raise today. The first day, 'Dreams of Something Better', explored perfection as it is expressed in Olympic films, art and architecture, and the different personal and social barriers that can stand in the way of our dreams. The second day, 'The Changing City', looked at processes of urban change bought about by the London Games and explored how residents cope with the loss of places and buildings in cities and how different interests are accommodated in new ones. On the third day, 'Stories of London' looked at the identity of London and the stories that bind the city together. The fourth day, 'Connections to the World', looked at the connections between inhabitants of the United Kingdom and people who live in different countries.

These types of discussions combine the promise of the Olympic Games with real events today and in the past. This way of thinking is not easily accessible through the resources on Get Set – in order to get to this point, teachers would have to find their own way to the Olympic Museum website, or to the work currently being done by cultural institutions as a part of the cultural Olympiad. Some examples are: the Museum of London's Stories of the World project, exploring shared collective and personal stories in the UK; the Photographers Gallery's The World in London project, which photographs people from all the competing nations who are living in London; and the Free Word Centre's forthcoming exhibition on the history of politics and the Olympic Games.

This restriction of young people's exploration of the context in which the Olympic and Paralympic Games occur is less a product of the Get Set Network, and more a product of the squeamishness by the International Olympic Committee about being associated with anything that could be regarded as 'politics'. In future, if Olympic Education programmes are to truly support teachers to do 'anything' in response to the Olympics, teachers should be supported to look at the wider social context of the Olympic Games past and present.

Has Get Set helped schools to form new relationships?

The CfBT Educational Trust recently reviewed the legacy of 52 educational programmes running alongside mega-events. They identify the benefits of educational programmes as a mixture of learning outcomes for young people such as the 'increased awareness and ideals of the movements' and benefits for educational establishments themselves, such as making 'practical international links' (Gaver *et al.*, 2010). This is a helpful distinction for Get Set – its legacy will be in the learning outcomes and behaviours of young people who have taken part in the programme, and also in the capacities of schools themselves: what young people can do, and what schools can do too.

Through Get Set some schools will have been able to form new relationships that they can continue after the games. For example, the Organising Committee's International Inspiration programme, which aims to support sport around the world, has encouraged 200 UK schools to make connections with schools in other countries.[20] It is also possible that over the coming year, through Get Set Goes Global, schools may be stimulated to make relationships with schools in other countries. When Get Set is over, these relationships could endure, leaving a legacy for those schools.

On the Get Set Network website, Priory Special School in Bury St Edmonds reports how after

> a successful visit by two Rwandan head teachers, who spoke about their hopes for the Olympics and about schools in their country, there are plans to organise a teacher exchange. As the Rwandan athletics team are using Bury St Edmunds as a base there

> is great excitement at the prospect of setting up an event with the athletes. Activities based on the Olympic and Paralympic Games and Values have created opportunities for cultural work both in school and the community, and have driven links with Rwanda which look set to continue through the planned teacher exchange.
>
> *(http://getset.london2012.com/en/join-us/join-us-case-studies/priory-special-school)*

St Mary's Sport College in Leeds reports being involved in

> a unique and exciting collaboration with Mnyakanya School in South Africa. This partnership has gained international acclaim for the way it has used sports and particularly London 2012, to promote education, health, leadership and global learning. Sports Leaders from St Mary's are visiting Mnyakanya School to mentor students and an Olympic Festival will be delivered to South African primary school children by students from the two schools. Both schools are also embarking on a 'Spirit of the Olympics/Power of Sport' creative writing and art competition, with the best work to be published just before the start of the Games.
>
> *(http://getset.london2012.com/en/join-us/join-us-case-studies/st-marys-Catholic-Comprehensive-School)*

Stretford High School in Trafford reports a link to Habib Public School in Karachi, Pakistan and with the Pakistan Hockey team – it says that it is 'now becoming one of the few schools in the UK to teach Internationalism as a specific subject and one of the units of work in the summer term is devoted entirely to London 2012. Every single subject across the curriculum is making links to the Games' (http://getset.london2012.com/en/join-us/join-us-case-studies/stretford-high-school).

It is this kind of relationship that could endure beyond the conclusion of Get Set. If Get Set is to be understood as a learning network, it is one where most of the connections are directed inwards, towards LOCOG, and not outwards, towards other education establishments and resources that could endure after LOCOG has been dissolved. For example, rather than Get Set acting as a gatekeeper to Paralympians, Olympians and other athletes, a web-based platform could have been established to help schools connect to athletes training for the Olympics in their local area. Another platform might have encouraged schools to participate in a project to 'collect the Olympic Games' from the huge panoply of films, ephemera, photography and other resources available all over the internet, in order to help make it searchable for schools in Get Set and other schools around the world after the Games.

Conclusion: a more open approach to Olympic education

The Get Set Network should be viewed as the first attempt to create an Olympic educational movement alongside the London Games that shares common principles with other recent attempts to use communications technologies to help dispersed groups of people organise and learn from one another. It has shown the potential of using online tools to engage with a vast number of schools in a relatively short period of time. It seems likely that it has helped some schools build relationships and connections that otherwise would not have been possible, and has created ways for schools to look at some of the most intriguing aspects of the Games.

The challenges for those seeking to create more open models of Olympic education will be to build on the best of what Get Set has achieved. First, they should focus on projects that support schools to develop relationships with athletes, schools in other countries and Olympic resources that will help them to be 'more Olympic' during and after the Games. Second, they should be prescriptive about what is and what is not a project based on the Olympic values; Get Set Goes Global and some of the resources within the IOC's Olympic Values Education Programme may show the way forward here. Third, education programmes should make it easier for teachers to make a connection between how the topic of the Olympic Games is taught in schools and how it is publicly discussed and debated, by helping schools to make connections to the panoply of projects and resources across the world, in foundations, museums, libraries and on the web. A focus on these areas will act as a counterweight to influences – such as political pressure to demonstrate high levels of engagement with young people, commercial pressure to fit sponsors into Olympic education and the related offer of rewards for learning – that might distort Olympic education away from the learning opportunity. These measures would make it more likely for schools to engage in work that otherwise would not have been possible, and they might also ensure a better balance between learning and rewards, making the network less orientated inwards, towards the Organising Committee, and more distributed amongst teachers and schools.

This search to find the right formula for types of network that can do this is part of finding a model for the Games that is more open, participatory and democratic. We are living through times in which consumers, citizens and audiences with new technologies at their disposal are realigning their relationship to organisations of all kinds. The same formula behind a more open education programme could provide the basis for a more open reporting of the Games, a cultural programme that could go beyond providing free entertainment and other opportunities and take learning beyond schools, to wherever young people are (IOC, 2007). As a Games that often claimed to 'belong to everyone', identifying this formula would be a fitting legacy for London 2012.

Notes

1 The Get Set Network: https://getset.london2012.com/ (last accessed 10 December 2012).
2 In the context of this chapter, 'schools' refers to all learning providers for 3–19-year-olds.
3 The rolling total of schools registered with the Get Set Network, and members who have been admitted is available online: http://getset.london2012.com/en/join-us/registrations-in-your-region.
4 This can be found at: https://getset.london2012.com/ (last accessed 10 December 2012).
5 For more details about ticketshare: https://getset.london2012.com/en/join-us/why-join-the-get-set-network/tickets-to-the-Games (last accessed 10 December 2012).
6 For more details on teaching resources, see: http://getset.london2012.com/en/resources (last accessed 10 December 2012).
7 For more details regarding Get Set Plus, see: http://getset.london2012.com/en/get-set-plus (last accessed 10 December 2012).
8 These can be viewed online: Meet the Species (www.bnhc.org.uk/home/meet-the-species/events/schools.html, The Real Business Challenge www.therealbusinesschallenge.co.uk/), Supporter 2 Reporter (https://www.radiowaves.co.uk/s2r).
9 For more on the Cultural Olympiad, see: www.london2012.com/get-involved/cultural-olympiad/index.php (last accessed 10 December 2012).
10 For more on Get Set Goes Global, see: http://getset.london2012.com/en/get-set-goes-global (last accessed 10 December 2012).
11 The Nielsen findings are quoted in the 'Benefits of Get Set', part of the Get Set Network website: http://getset.london2012.com/en/resources/educators/benefits-of-get-set-1 (last accessed 10 December 2012).
12 Mumsnet – www.mumsnet.com/; National Novel Writing Month – www.nanowrimo.org/; Occupy Movement – http://en.wikipedia.org/wiki/Occupy_movement.
13 Learning to Love You More is online at: www.learningtoloveyoumore.com/index.php (last accessed 10 December 2012).

14 For more on Tedx, see: www.ted.com/tedx.
15 For more on the commitment made to young Londoners, see Tims, 2007.
16 This can be found online – 'How do I apply?' (1 min. 50 secs), at http://getset.london2012.com/en/join-us/how-do-i-apply (last accessed 10 December 2012).
17 These are all online: Trading Challenge Roadshow – www.enterprisingscience.com/about_02.jsp; Design My Break – www.designmybreak.co.uk/; Real Business Challenge – www.therealbusiness-challenge.co.uk/ (last accessed 10 December 2012).
18 Lets Get Cooking Around the World is at: www.letsgetcooking.org.uk/CookingAroundtheWorld (last accessed 10 December 2012).
19 For a recent review of research into changing values, see The Common Cause Handbook published by the Public Interest Research Centre, which is supported by the Campaign to Protect Rural England, Friends of the Earth, Oxfam and WWF-UK (http://valuesandframes.org/downloads/& http://valuesandframes.org/).
20 For more on International Inspiration, see www.london2012.com/get-involved/education/international-inspiration/where-is-it-happening/united-kingdom.php29. For more on other thinking about opening up the Olympics, see Miah, 2010.

References

BBC (2011a) NaNoWriMo Challenges Authors to Write a Novel in a Month, www.bbc.co.uk/news/entertainment-arts-15209915 (last accessed 10 December 2012).

BBC (2011b) Schools Urged to Claim Olympic tickets, 3 November, at: http://news.bbc.co.uk/democracylive/hi/house_of_commons/newsid_9629000/9629551.stm.

Binder, Deanna L. (2007) *An Olympic Education Toolkit*, Lausanne: IOC.

Binder, Deanna L. (2005) *Teaching Olympism in Schools: Olympic Education as a focus on values education: university lectures on the Olympics*, Bellaterra: Centre d'Estudis Olímpics (UAB)/International Chair in Olympism (IOC-UAB).

Fraser, J., Ganesh, G., Johnson, F. and Skowron, L. (2008) The London 2012 Olympic Games and Paralympic Games – Children and Young People's Perceptions and Involvement, report, MORI/DCFS.

Gaver, A., Cammiss, L., Charlton, C. and Plantak, J. (2010) What Lasting Educational Benefits can be Created by Mega Events?, Reading, Berkshire: Centre for British Teachers Educational Trust/Sky Blue Research.

Hampton, J. (2008) *The Austerity Olympics: When the Games came to London in 1948*, London: Aurum.

Holmes, Tim, Blackmore, Elena and Hawkins, Richard (2011) *The Common Cause Handbook: A Guide to Values and Frames for Campaigners, Community Organisers, Civil Servants, Fundraisers, Educators, Funders, Politicians and Everyone Inbetween*, Public Interest Research Centre.

IOC (2007) *Olympic Charter*, Lausanne: IOC.

London 2012 (2009) London 2012 Launches Get Set Network as New Education Logo Infill is Unveiled, 15 September, at: www.london2012.com/news/2009/09/london-2012-launches-get-set-network-as-new-education-logo-infill-is-unveile.php (last accessed 10 December 2012).

Miah, A. (2010) Media Blueprint for the London 2012 Games, at: www.culturalolympics.org.uk/2010/07/media-blueprint-for-the-london-2012-games/ (last accessed 10 December 2012).

Tims, C. (2007) *The Biggest Learning Opportunity on Earth*, London: Demos.

14

FURTHER AND HIGHER EDUCATION INVOLVEMENT WITH THE OLYMPIC AND PARALYMPIC GAMES

Dikaia Chatziefstathiou

Coubertin, education and the early Olympic Games

The involvement of universities and colleges with the modern Olympic and Paralympic Games dates back to the late nineteenth century, when founder Baron Pierre de Coubertin was inspired to start the event after visiting several institutions, mostly in England, Ireland, the United States and Canada.[1] Coubertin joined the liberal, republican classicist intellectuals by writing in the journal *La Reforme Sociale* (the combined organ of two organisations, the Société d'économie sociale and the Unions de la paix sociale), where his first thoughts and expressions about *l'education athlétique* and *la pédagogie sportive* were expressed. Both organisations were founded and led by Frédéric Le Play, a sociologist and social philosopher of the mid-nineteenth century whom Coubertin admired. Le Play's work had raised much criticism but also received much recognition for its emphasis on the methods of 'fieldwork' and 'observation', with the modern meaning of the terms, in sociological research (MacAloon, 1981). Pierre de Coubertin related strongly to Frédéric Le Play because they both shared a desire to reform French education.

Having the ambition to improve the use of recreation time and introduce sport in schools, colleges and universities in his native France, Coubertin visited English and Irish universities in 1883. He used Le Play's method of observation and explored the qualities of English education in order to transfer them to France.[2] In 1889 the French government sent him to the United States, where he observed the early programmes of intercollegiate athletics and was impressed by the excellent facilities that colleges and universities had made available to their students. His thoughts and ideas about those visits were expressed in his books *Education en Angleterre* and *Universités Transatlantiques*, as well as in numerous articles and presentations (Müller, 2000; Guttmann, 1992).

The revival of the modern Olympic Games, officially conceived in 1894 at the first Olympic Congress, which was actually held at an educational institution, the Sorbonne University, should therefore be seen as a part and extension of Coubertin's plans for an educational reform.

> Wishing to revive not so much the form but the very principle of this millennial institution, because I felt it would give my country and mankind as a whole the *educational stimulus they needed*, I had to try and restore the powerful buttresses that had supported it in the past: the intellectual buttress, the moral buttress and, to a certain extent, the

> religious buttress. To which the modern world added two new forces: technical improvements and democratic internationalism.
>
> *(Coubertin, 1997: lines 31–57, emphasis added)*

The tight links between universities and his idea of 'Olympism' were also emphasised later (1919) by Coubertin.

> But it is also useful to him [the university student] in carrying out the social task which will lie ahead of him in the new society ... *University students, messengers of knowledge and imagination, will constitute the most active battalions in this great task; let us say if you wish that they will have to be us aviators.* Now I have said, and I repeat, that sport by reason of its potent physical and moral effects will be an inestimable instrument in their hands for the establishment of social peace. They must therefore know how to handle it with tact and how to derive the maximum effect from it. *Popular Olympism is about to be born; let the students prepare to serve it.*
>
> *(Coubertin, 1919: lines 5–25, emphasis added)*[3]

Undoubtedly, university and college students played a significant role in the Olympic Games even from the early years of the movement. Cashman and Veal have identified several types of involvement (Cashman and Toohey, 2002: 12–14):

- *university students as athletes* – especially during the first three Olympic Games (Athens 1896, Paris 1900 and St Louis 1904), a high contribution was made by student athletes;
- *academic staff as IOC members* – a close collaborator of Coubertin and member of the first IOC was Professor William Milligan Sloane from Princeton University in the USA;
- *organisers* – the London Polytechnic Institute played a significant role in the organisation of the 1908 London Games;
- *volunteers* – the Swedish Olympic Committee cooperated with a private company that recruited '120 undergraduates to act as stewards in the stadium during the Games', a similar role to spectator service volunteers in today's Games (Official Olympic Games Report 1912, cited by Cashman and Veal, 2002: 13);
- *university facilities* – the Royal Gymnastic Central Institute provided accommodation for 80 competitors at the Stockholm 1912 Games, while the main auditorium of Berlin University was the venue for the exhibition 'Sport in Hellenic Times' at the Berlin 1936 Games.

It was not only Coubertin who supported the links between universities and the Games. For example, Carl Diem from Germany, one of his close collaborators who played a key role in the movement, especially between the 1930s and 1960s (Chatziefstathiou, 2006; Chatziefstathiou and Henry, 2012), reinforced the links between universities and the Games with his efforts to establish a 'University of Olympism'. This opened in Greece in 1961 right next to the archaeological excavations of Ancient Olympia and was named the International Olympic Academy. Diem emphasised that the establishment of the academy also fulfilled Coubertin's dreams for the operation of a pedagogical centre of Olympism.

> We can say simply that the 'Olympic Academy' which is to arise here will be on the one hand a continuation of the old academy – an 'Elis' of our times – and on the other hand the fulfilment of Coubertin's plans to put Olympism on a scholarly basis.
>
> *(Diem, 1961: lines 3–8)*

And again the emphasis on universities and colleges is quite apparent.

> The Olympic Games bred a spiritual force which made them the focal point of ancient culture and the bond which united firstly the Greek peoples and later the whole Mediterranean. Thus they became part of the foundations of that western culture out of which modern sport has blossomed. These foundations are being continually studied and widened today in the world's universities, and especially in those faculties and colleges of education, which point the way of education through the body.
>
> *(Ibid.: lines 32–48)*

The academy still operates today, and organises conferences, seminars and other activities beyond universities and colleges involving schools, athletes, administrators, etc. with an aim 'to create an international cultural centre in Olympia, to preserve and spread the Olympic Spirit, study and implement the educational and social principles of Olympism and consolidate the scientific basis of the Olympic Ideal' (International Olympic Academy, 2011).

A commitment to Olympic scholarship and research is also the priority of several Olympic study centres worldwide, which usually operate within a higher education institution.[4] Some of those centres were created as a legacy of a successful bid (at least eight major centres for Olympic studies were founded in China after Beijing Games in 2008, with another example being the Olympic Studies Centre (CEO-UAB), Autonomous University of Barcelona, Spain) or of an unsuccessful one (e.g. Centre for Olympic Research and Education (CORE), University of Tsukuba, Japan). However, the involvement of further and higher education (FE and HE) with the Olympic and Paralympic Games is not limited to the 'study' of the subject in scholarly terms. It extends to activities such as skills and vocational education, volunteering, community engagement, etc., especially as part of the host cities' Olympic education programmes.

Olympic education programmes of host cities

Although the term 'Olympic education' is somewhat ambiguous in what it means and embraces (Chatziefstathiou, 2011b), when it comes to the programmes of the host cities during an Olympiad (the four-year cycle between editions of the Games) its meaning becomes clearer. People often recognise as 'Olympic education' the programmes traditionally offered to primary and secondary schools (often in the form of an educational pack, as at Sydney 2000 or Athens 2004), but Olympic education programmes also include other sectors, such as staff and voluntary training, teacher education, community education and the involvement of FE and HE. Figure 14.1 illustrates some of the most common aims for educational legacies as found by Graver and colleagues (2010) from looking at candidature files of previous hosts.

Although the staging and delivery of each Games has common characteristics in terms of management and running, there are some distinctive differences which reflect the cultural, economic, political and social conditions of the host nations. Such disparities are also found in the different Olympic education programmes of the host nations, hence also in the involvement of the FE and HE sectors with each Games. In terms of FE and HE, engagement can take many different forms, such as delivery of vocational training, use of volunteers, use of facilities and course development. In the following sections the role of FE and HE in the Sydney and Beijing Games will be discussed before looking more closely at London 2012.[5]

Sydney 2000[6]

Although education was not included in Sydney's candidature file (PcW, 2008), Cashman and Toohey (2002) argue that the HE sector had the highest contribution to Olympic and Paralympic Games than ever before. However, they note that this was mostly due to a gradually closer relationship between the universities and the Olympic organisers through the years. Indicatively they refer to the host Broadcast Training Programme, which provided 630 students from six universities and North Sydney Technical and Further Education colleges (TAFE) with valuable practical experience in radio and television broadcasting. However, the host Broadcasting Training Programme had begun at the Barcelona 1992 Games in order to offer vocational opportunities to young people and was then carried out at the Atlanta 1996 Games with great success. As Cashman and Toohey comment, 'the strengths of the links between the higher education sector and the Olympic Movement was widely recognised by 2000' (Cashman and Toohey, 2002: 72). They continue, 'there is no doubt that the contribution of the higher education sector to the success of the Sydney 2000 Olympic Games was impressive and substantial in every respect' (*ibid.*). In *University Business* (USA) it was stated that 'the Olympic Games in Sydney saw unprecedented involvement from the higher education sector', while the *Times Higher Education Supplement* (UK) reported that

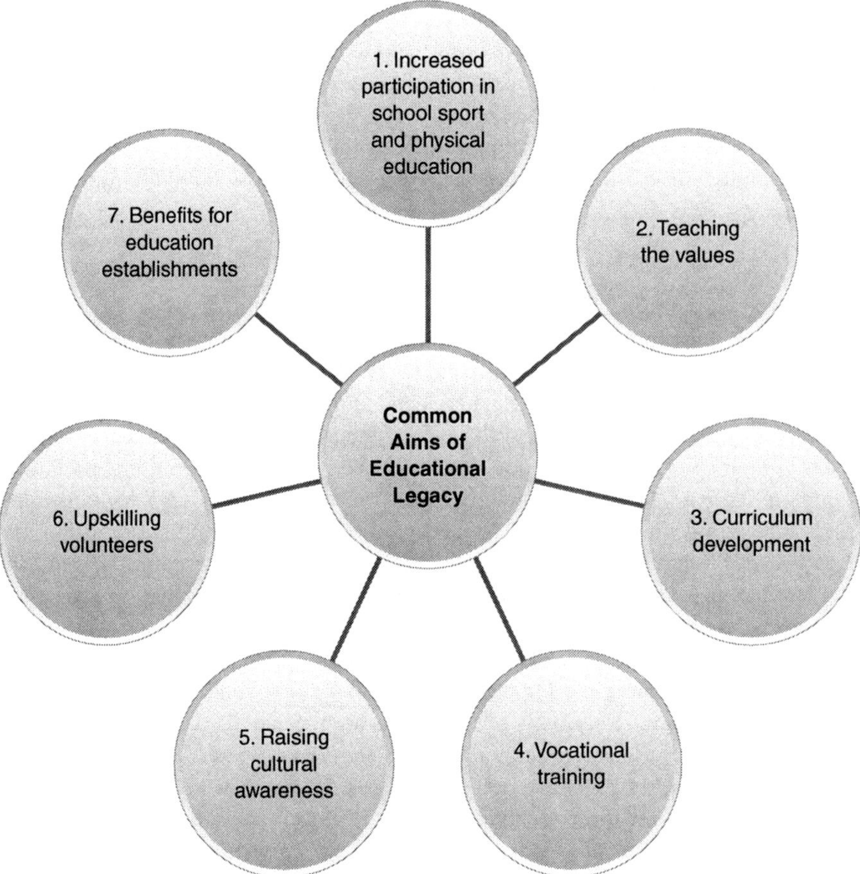

Figure 14.1 Recurring common aims of educational legacy (Graver *et al.*, 2010: p. 8).

> from designing the Olympic site to keeping it mosquito-free, from illuminating the 100,000-capacity stadium to predicting visitor numbers, academics – in their thousands – are getting involved in what one describes as the 'biggest peacetime event to take place in Australia'. And they are advancing research and developing new insights in the process
>
> *(cited in Cashman and Toohey, 2002: 72)*

The NSW universities provided *circa* 6,000 students as volunteers with posts related to their courses and with course credits awarded to them in many cases, while some of those volunteers were human resource management students and assisted in the interview process of 65,000 potential volunteers (Cashman and Toohey, 2002; PWC, 2008). In some cases students also received valuable experience with international companies (e.g. the Advantage International for IBM Surf Shack) or paid contracts (e.g. with the National Broadcasting Company, NBC). According to Brendan Lynch, Programme Manager, Volunteer Recruitment and Coordinator and University Liaison for the Sydney Organising Committee for the Olympic Games (SOCOG), 'the intention of involving the universities in the volunteer programme was to ensure that the students received valuable experience, that the universities were able to provide real practical experience for their students, and that SOCOG received well-trained volunteers' (cited in Cashman and Toohey, 2002: 31).

Eventually more than half of the total 45 Australian universities in Sydney, NSW and the regions became involved with the Games on a variety of activities. Over twenty memoranda of understanding were signed between higher education institutions and SOCOG, the Sydney Olympic Broadcasting Organisation (SOBO), the Australian Olympic Committee (AOC) and the NSW government. Three Olympic study centres were established in joint partnerships between universities and the AOC: the Centre for Olympic Studies at the University of South Wales in May 1996; the Centre for Olympic Studies at the University of South Australia in June 1996; and later in 2000 the Centre for Olympic Studies at the University of Queensland.

However, what has been perhaps the most successful story in terms of the Sydney 2000 Games was the involvement of the FE with the training for the Olympic and Paralympic Games employees and volunteers, a total of approximately 110,000 people. The technical and further education (TAFE) institutions are key providers of vocational education and training (VET) in Australia. TAFE NSW (a consortium of all eleven NSW colleges) was selected in 1997 to become 'the official training services support for the 2000 Olympic Games' and in 1999 it was announced that it would also be 'the official training partner of the 2000 Paralympic Games', together with the workforce training team. Key organisations such as Adecco and Westpac developed strong links with TAFE NSW and training was provided to public and private sector companies, including Coca-Cola, Carlton United Breweries and State Rail. Up to today they have secured multi-million dollar contracts for providing training services; examples include the Athens 2004 and Beijing 2008 Olympic and Paralympic Games, Sydney 2003 World Cup, All Africa 2003 Games, 2006 Doha Asian Games, Shanghai World Expo 2010 (Premier of NSW, 2008).

Although it is obvious that the FE and HE sectors were highly involved with the preparation and the staging of the Sydney 2008 Games, it is argued that institutions of HE and TAFEs mostly worked separately and failed to develop joint collaborations and partnerships which could have been mutually beneficial (Cashman and Toohey, 2002). Also, the majority of the institutions involved were based in Sydney while universities and colleges outside Sydney and NSW were uncertain about the role they could have or develop in relation to the Games (PcW, 2008) or they found distance to be a major issue in terms of a closer participation (Cashman and

Toohey, 2002). Another factor that determined universities' engagement with the Games was whether they had become successful in winning an Olympic contract. Several institutions showed a decline in their Olympic-related activities after a lack of a formal collaboration with the Olympic organisers (e.g. the Institute of Transport Studies at the University of Sydney).

Therefore, although HE and FE sectors contributed to the Games in different ways, it cannot be claimed that a collective, systematic and coherent Olympic programme was developed across the country in involving universities and colleges.

Beijing 2008

The different political systems of China and Australia naturally led into some major variances in the way that FE and HE were involved with the Games in these two cases. China's system of political parties is a system of multiparty cooperation and political consultation under the leadership of the Communist Party of China (CPC), rather than a Western-style multiparty system. The CPC is at the core of the country's leadership and the ruling party, while the non-Communist parties are participating parties (Lo, 1999). The education system in China and other sectors of civil society is largely 'top down', which means that Olympic education was also centralised and overseen by the central ministries and the Communist Party bodies through Olympic Education Affairs and Olympic Training Affairs steering groups at national, provincial and local level (Henry *et al.*, 2008).[7]

Without doubt, one of the areas in which the FE and HE sectors were highly involved was volunteering. Volunteers directly involved in the games totalled 77,169, with another 44,261 for the Paralympics.[8] There were also 4 million city volunteers, and over 10 million social volunteers. Venue volunteers mainly consisted of university students, while elderly volunteers from communities made up the majority of social and city volunteers. Li Mingying, a volunteer from Beijing Technology and Business University who served at the Laoshan Venue Cluster, said: 'The Olympic Games have greatly improved us psychologically. By being a volunteer for it, we have also honed our work abilities and obtained much social work experience' (cited in Wei and Cui, 2011: 22). Mo Qiong, a student majoring in public utilities who was enrolled into Beijing Institute of Technology in 2006, saw his Olympic volunteering experience as a catalyst in developing team awareness and explains how he still maintains close friendship links with his group of the former 'Wukesong Venue Volunteers' (cited in Wei and Cui, 2011: 22). Wei (2010) argues that such claims are not isolated cases but express a general feeling of the majority of student volunteers.

The Chinese institutions also adapted their curriculum to the new Olympic-related needs and a high number of institutions introduced elective and required courses. A part of all four sections of education (staff and voluntary training, teacher, community and school education) took place in universities, with a range of training courses being developed (e.g. since 2006, a training course for Olympic volunteers has become a general course for all first year and graduate students at Beijing University). Moreover, six Olympic venues were located in universities (four new and six existing), eight major Olympic research centres were established, a range of conferences and cultural activities were organised, over 200 textbooks (academic, populist, basic, professional and subject-specific on Olympic venues and volunteer/staff positions) were published, about a range of topics (e.g. *Beijing Olympic Games Text Book for University Students, Beijing Olympic Games Text Book for Volunteers, Beijing 2008 Language Text Book for Medical Service Staff, A Guide to the Olympic Culture for College Students*), and various partnerships and contracts were established with Chinese and international universities and the media.

Although China's government stirred controversy over human rights issues,[9] a subject which won't be discussed here as it extends beyond the scope of this chapter, the centralisation of decision making in relation to education had some obvious advantages. As Henry and colleagues argue,

> The system has several advantages. First and foremost, the education resources of the whole country can be rationally allocated; Olympic programmes and initiatives can be efficiently and widely implemented and the enthusiasm of involved personnel (e.g. teachers, volunteers, students, staff etc.) can be stimulated and harnessed by this system.
>
> *(Henry et al., 2008: 5)*

The Chinese state was committed to using the Games as a vehicle for showcasing China's emergence as a world force on the political, economic and cultural scene. China made a concentrated effort to achieve such global recognition, therefore, which, as shown above, also entailed educating and spreading the Olympic message across the Chinese population including colleges and universities.

London 2012: the engagement so far

As can be seen from the candidature file for London 2012, the education sector was intended from the start to play a role in the Games. The dates for hosting the event (27 July to 12 August 2012 for the Olympic Games, and 29 August until Sunday 9 September 2012 for the Paralympic Games) were chosen in order to coincide with the annual summer holiday for schools and universities, both to enable the use of university accommodation facilities and to facilitate the engagement of students as volunteers. 'London's large stock of student accommodation will be available to house many groups, such as volunteers', but also because 'the timing of the Games will ensure a plentiful supply of volunteers and provide an opportunity for Britain's youth to see the greatest athletes in the world in action on their doorstep' (London 2012 Candidate File, 2004a: 1). More specifically, the following plans were proposed in relation to education:

- To create an athlete ambassador programme for schools and community groups to personify the values of the Olympic ideal. Athlete ambassadors will be drawn from the UK's past and potential Olympians.
- To work with the Department for Education and Skills to create a range of educational materials that will support the National Curriculum while spreading Olympic values throughout the nation's schools.
- Schools were also mentioned in the plans for community engagement in terms of sport and non-sport cultural activities: 'Recognising that the Games will have their greatest impact on local communities, the LOCOG will embark on an extensive community engagement programme. This will include programmes tailored for relevant audiences such as sports clubs, schools, NGOs and businesses' (London 2012 Candidate File, 2004a: 25).
- One of the most ambitious educational programmes mentioned in the bid was the 'Olympic Friend-ship', which would include a physical and a virtual vessel sailing in the seas of the world and through the internet and would form the basis of a four-year education programme linked to the National Curriculum for schools in the UK. As stated in the bid file, 'The Olympic Friend-ship's voyage will be a journey of discovery, carrying a cargo emblematic of the UK's cultural riches' (London 2012 Candidate File, 2004b: 17).[10]

During the period 2003–2007, London Higher, the umbrella body representing more than 40 universities and colleges in London, was the core institution in overseeing the involvement of HE with the Games (during the bid and in the early years after winning the bid). As Jane Glanville, Chief Executive Officer of London Higher, said

> Our involvement with the London 2012 team was rather organic. We had an interest in helping the bid and we knew we could help when no other organisation had shown any interest apart from some individual institutions like Loughborough. What we were mostly working on during the years of preparation for the bid was to secure accommodation by making agreements with a list of universities in London.
>
> *(Interview with Jane Glanville, 2011)*

After the Games were awarded to London, London Higher commissioned a consultancy company to identify an inclusive and effective structure for the Higher Education contribution to the 2012 Olympic and Paralympic Games.[11] The findings of this study suggested that 'a dedicated sub-group of London Higher and Association of Colleges London Region (AoC London) should be established, which would liaise with the Mayor's Office and report to its key funder(s) including London Development Agency' (PA Consulting Group, 2006, p. 6–2). Consequently, London Higher submitted a funding proposal to the Higher Education Funding Council for England (HEFCE) and the Learning and Skills Council (LSC) for the establishment of Podium, an organisation that would act as the further and higher education unit for the 2012 Games. The proposal was successful, and Podium was established in 2007 with two major aims:

> - to communicate both within the sector and with outside agencies the potential for universities and colleges to support the successful staging and delivery of the 2012 Games;
> - to coordinate development of activity within the sector that maximises the benefits of hosting the 2012 Olympic and Paralympic Games in this country, contributing to the building of a sustainable and wide-reaching legacy.
>
> *(HEFCE, 2007: 4–5)*

Podium is a division of London Higher and is funded by HEFCE[12] and the successor organisation of LSC, the Skills Funding Agency. It operates as a platform aiming to build the nationwide engagement of FE and HE with London 2012, and the aims and mission of the organisation have not much changed since 2007. As stated by Gareth Smith, head of Podium, 'Working with key stakeholders and alongside the Games authorities, Podium's role is to communicate Games related opportunities, support the development of programmes and share examples of good practice across the sectors. Simply put, Podium's core functions are to communicate, collaborate and enhance' (Weed *et al.*, 2011: 2).

Podium's activities in relation to Olympic education represent a wide range of initiatives and projects for students, academics, other professionals and the public, such as: 'Knowing Sport', a public engagement programme as part of ICSEMIS 2012, the International Convention on Science, Education and Medicine in Sport, supported by the Scottish government and Podium. Knowing Sport will consist of: ten events in the run-up to the Games that will engage the public with science, research and academic disciplines associated with sport; a web-based resource of Olympic experts for the media and other clients; and collaboration with the Higher Education Academy Network's Special Interest Group on the Olympic and Paralympic Games, aiming to develop Olympic learning legacies.[13]

Weed and colleagues (2011)[14] have shown with regards to opportunities offered by London 2012 that the three opportunities with the highest scores were 'education, volunteering and sport'. 'Volunteering' was seen as a tangible opportunity for students to get involved with the Games; 'sport' was particularly emphasised by respondents with a role focused on sport promotion or development, while it was noted that their organisations do include a wider range of London 2012-related activities. In terms of 'education', it seemed that FE institutions (FEIs) had a stronger interest to integrate Olympic themes into their curricula than the higher education institutions (HEIs), with the number of FEIs listing education-related projects and activities being 40 per cent higher than that of HEIs. As Weed and colleagues (2011) explain, this heightened interest in education-related projects shown by colleges can be seen in connection with the London 2012 education programme Get Set, which targets the 3–19-year-olds across the UK.[15] As stated by one college,

> As part of the Get Set programme, Jessica Ennis came to speak to 100 students on her experience as an athlete, whilst incorporating/identifying with the Olympic and Paralympic Values. Jess also presented the Get Set plaque.
>
> *(Weed et al., 2011: 16)*

In relation to the involvement of colleges with the Get Set programme, Nick Fuller, Head of Education for the London Organising Committee of the Olympic Games (LOCOG), commented:

> Colleges have been at the forefront of engagement with Get Set. There are now over 200 colleges in the Get Set Network, approximately 50 per cent of colleges in the UK. The Get Set logo itself was designed by Reiss Evans, an 18-year-old student from Canterbury College in Kent. His work is showcased in the form of the logo given to the thousands of schools and colleges across the country when they join the Get Set Network ... We have also engaged college students through other elements of the programme, such as the Get Set to Exercise your Taste Buds competition to design a signature dish that will be served to athletes, spectators and VIPs at Games time.
>
> *(Interview with Nick Fuller, 2011)*

It seems, therefore, that when opportunities offered by official programmes of LOCOG are reinforced by Podium's 'communication, collaboration and enhancement' strategies, the outcome could be a positive one. Without doubt, some of the greatest contributions from FE and HE to the organisation and running of the Games are the following.

- The use of Universities as training camp facilities. This is a very sizeable contribution, with most of the pre-Games training camps agreements (PGTC) being with universities, e.g China with Leeds and Leeds Metropolitan, USA with the University of East London, Korea with Brunel and Team GB with Loughborough. LOCOG is offering up to £25,000 to every national Olympic committee (NOC) and national Paralympic committee (NPC) that brings its team to prepare in an approved pre-Games training camp in the UK.
- The second is the 'Bridging the Gap' security programme, an initiative developed by the British Security Industry Association (BSIA), Skills for Security, Buckinghamshire New University and North Hertfordshire FE College. The project has been funded by the Home Office, BIS (Department for Business, Innovation and Skills) and LOCOG, and has been created in liaison with Podium, the Security Industry Authority and Skills Active. Bridging

the Gap provides a formal qualification for further education students from across the UK, leading to a guaranteed job interview with a BSIA member and, for some Bridging the Gap graduates, the opportunity to assist in the security arrangements for London 2012. The initiative has been awarded the London 2012 Inspire mark. This mark recognises innovative and exceptional projects that are directly inspired by the London 2012 Games. The project is seen as a major contributor to the security challenge at the Games. As a result, more than 4,000 students and unemployed people have completed stewarding and/or door supervision qualifications

- Third is the use of the Olympic Stadium by British Universities and Colleges Sport (BUCS) Outdoor Athletics Championships as a major London 2012 test event in May 2012. This event helped the London Organising Committee of the Olympic and Paralympic Games (LOCOG) to test key aspects of the venue, such as the field of play, results, scoring and timing systems, as well as operational procedures and functions.
- Fourth, the involvement of colleges and universities with volunteering has been vital. Hackney Community College is the principal training centre for Games Makers, and there has been extensive involvement of students and use of university facilities in the recruitment process. Human Resource Management and Business Studies undergraduates from 18 universities have helped to interview the 100,000 people who have been shortlisted for the 70,000 Games Maker positions at nine volunteer selection centres.[16]

Beyond LOCOG's programmes there is a whole range of activities and projects that are taking place around the country and are also communicated by Podium. Such activities include: the organisation of Olympic-related seminars, workshops and conferences nationwide (e.g. the Olympic-related student conference in Bournemouth in 2010 organised by the Olympic Special Interest Group of the Higher Education Academy Network); calls for special Olympic-related issues of academic journals and book series (e.g. the one by Taylor and Francis); regional programmes of education (e.g. Kent 2012); national competitions (e.g. the Coubertin Olympic Awards); and the involvement of individual institutions (e.g. the University of Bath hosted BBC Radio 5 Live to mark one year to go until London 2012).

Conclusions

The liaisons between the Olympic Games and education have strong roots in the history of the modern Olympic Movement. Coubertin's interest for an educational reform coupled with the globalising forces of his time led him to the conception of an international sport festival for the celebration of peace, fraternity and other humanist values, which he called 'Olympism' (Chatziefstathiou, 2006; Chatziefstathiou and Henry, 2012). In our time, the IOC Executive Director for the Olympic Games, Gilbert Felli, acknowledges and emphasises the links between education and the Olympics:

> Together with sport and environment, culture and education make up one of the three founding pillars of Olympism. The creation and dissemination of knowledge therefore is a primary and essential component of the success and perpetuity of the Olympic Games ... Through a multitude of educational teachings, the history of the Olympic Movement, its values, inspiring stories about the Olympic Games and its athletes are shared with students of all ages. New working relationships between private and public entities, training and work opportunities for a city's inhabitants, the use and promotion of new and state-of-the-art sustainable technologies, enhanced

> environmental awareness and increased community involvement, all illustrate the range of educational opportunities that the staging of an Olympic Games can provide to a host city and country.
>
> *(Gilbert Felli, cited in Graver et al., 2010: 4)*

There is no doubt that there are wide and numerous opportunities for the involvement of the FE and HE sectors, ranging from small-scale projects to larger ones, those within London and outside, in and beyond sport, at an institutional level or in partnerships, etc. Podium is an innovation of the London 2012 Games and 'its work is valued in the further and higher education sectors', but 'there remains a significant role for it throughout and in the immediate aftermath of the Games' (Weed *et al.*, 2011: 26). As Weed and colleagues found, '92 per cent of further and higher education institutions expect to be involved in some way in activities relating to London 2012 in the run up to the Games' (*ibid.*: 4), but

> There appears to be a divide in the higher education sector between those institutions that see both sport and London as a high strategic priority linked to their institutional mission and strategy, and those for whom the Games are much less significant strategically, but that would like further help and support in understanding how they might engage with London 2012-related opportunities.
>
> *(ibid.: 5)*

It is difficult to draw any parallels with Beijing, due to the very different political and educational realities of the two cities. The centralisation of decision making with respect to education brought some positive results in terms of institutional involvement across China (Henry *et al.*, 2008). However, development of curricula in relation to Olympic and Paralympic courses in the sector across the UK has been very scarce and limited. A similar picture was also found in Sydney. As Cashman and Toohey point out,

> While some institutions had very elaborate and well-organised Olympic courses and programmes, others did not; while some institutions clearly articulated their aims and expected outcomes, others were less well prepared and focused . . . as a result while some institutions believed that they gained considerable ongoing benefit . . . others reported no great institutional benefits and even a sense of disappointment that an opportunity had been missed.
>
> *(Cashman and Toohey, 2002: 42)*

Thus, as Weed and colleagues (2011) also suggest, FEIs and HEIs should also seek opportunities for involvement with *local projects and partnerships* as well as *beyond sport* (e.g. in cultural activities). In Sydney, many institutions lost interest after the rejection of their proposal for some kind of involvement with SOCOG (Cashman and Toohey, 2002). Podium can play a significant role in keeping such institutions engaged (and also those for whom the Games are less significant strategically) by identifying and showcasing a wider range of *smaller-scale projects that do not require extensive resources*,[17] as well as in promoting *the benefits from smaller-scale involvement and collaborations* (Weed *et al.*, 2011).

Given that the top-rated expected legacy of FEIs and HEIs is 'lasting partnerships' (Weed *et al.*, 2011: 21), establishing more and better partnerships between FEIs and HEIs should also be a priority for London 2012. Again, it is difficult to make comparisons with Beijing because 'the separation of the FE and HE sectors in China is far less marked than is the case in the UK. Much that falls under the heading of further and technical and vocational education is actually carried out in the university sector' (Henry *et al.*, 2008: 3). However, Sydney also experienced a lack of collaboration between colleges and universities: 'HEIs and TAFEs did not work together during the Sydney Olympics and a more linked and cohesive approach would have been beneficial to both sets of organisations' (PWC, 2008: 4). Weed and colleagues found that, in terms of London 2012, 'there was an acknowledgement that further and higher education do not work together as well as and as often as they could' (Weed *et al.*, 2011: 27). Jane Granville from London Higher agrees that this is an area for further improvement for London 2012 but saw the existence of a joint unit like Podium as a positive drive for enhancing collaborations between the two sectors.

To conclude, a major challenge in terms of the long-term legacies in FE and HE is Podium's rather short and limited lifespan, as the unit is scheduled to close after the end of the Games. Jane Granville of London Higher revealed that no certain plans are yet in place in relation to the future of the work delivered by Podium, but emphasised that it is important that more collaborative projects and lasting partnerships in the FE and HE sectors shall continue to grow, an area which Weed and colleagues (2011) also see as being potentially one of the most significant sustainable legacies of London 2012. Finally, since the London 2012 Olympic and Paralympic Games, while hosted in London, concerns the whole of the UK, such partnerships should be sustained countrywide and not limited to the London HE and FE institutions.

Notes

1 For a fuller account of Coubertin's work and ideas, see Chatziefstathiou and Henry, 2012.

2 Coubertin was convinced that Thomas Arnold's methods at Rugby School and the British sport ethic of Muscular Christianity practised in elite private schools had been responsible for Britain's success as a world superpower in the nineteenth century, and that a similar approach should be exported to France (Hill, 1992; Guttmann, 1992; Toohey and Veal, 2000).

3 As I have argued elsewhere (Chatziefstathiou, 2006, 2011a) Coubertin's turn to a more inclusive Games and 'Popular Olympism' were responses to the threats and challenges posed by the pressure groups of Worker's and Women's Olympics in the 1920s. Nevertheless such claims are beyond the scope of this chapter and what is significant here is his emphasis on youth and especially university students as key agents for social transformation and peace.

4 Examples include: Centre for Olympic Studies and Research (COS&R), Loughborough University, UK; Olympic Studies Centre (CEO-UAB), Autonomous University of Barcelona, Spain; International Centre for Olympic Studies (ICOS), University of Western Ontario, Canada; Centre for Olympic Studies, University of Canterbury, New Zealand; Centre for Olympic Studies, Sydney, University of New South Wales (UNSW), Australia; Humanistic Olympic Studies Centre, Renmin University, China; Centre for Olympic Research and Education (CORE), University of Tsukuba, Japan. For a list of the Olympic study centres worldwide, go to: www.olympic.org/Assets/OSC%20Section/pdf/OSCs%20in%20the%20world.pdf.

5 These two host cities were chosen based on two criteria: availability of resources in terms of the involvement of FE and HE with the Games; and their different approaches in implementing Olympic education programmes.

6 Our knowledge about the contribution of the further education and higher education sectors to the Olympic and Paralympic Games in Sydney 2008 derives mostly from two reports: the first focused only on HE and published in 2002 by the Centre for Olympic Studies of the University of New South Wales in Australia, and the second published in 2008 by Podium, the Unit for FE and HE for the London 2012 Games (to which we shall return later in more detail) and London Higher (Podium's parent body).

7 Podium commissioned the Centre for Olympic Studies and Research (COS&R) at Loughborough University and the Irish Institute of Chinese Studies (IICS) at the University College, Cork to research the contribution of the further and higher education sectors in China to the staging and delivery of the 2008 Games. The discussion in this chapter about the case study of the Beijing Games 2008 relies upon the findings of this research, which is the only comprehensive research in relation to the role that FE and HE played in those Games.

8 For a detailed account of the different types of volunteers, volunteer education and participating institutions, read the report by Henry *et al.* (2008).
9 This tended to overshadow accusations about the human rights abuses perpetrated by the West in terms of detention without trial in Guantanamo Bay, and the use of torture interrogation techniques on prisoners (Worden, 2008).
10 The Olympic Friend-ship was later replaced by the Get Set programme.
11 London Higher commissioned PA consultants to 'outline possible structures and ways of working by which HEIs institutions in London and the UK can best contribute to the London 2012 Olympic and Paralympic Games' (PA Consulting Group, 2006, pp. 1–2). They administered two surveys (one covering the entire UK HE sector and one covering all the London-region FE colleges), as well as interviews and focus groups with heads of HE and FE institutions and key stakeholders, including: the Olympic-related committees; sports bodies; regional and national agencies; and central government departments.
12 HEFCE is still part of the steering group for the Olympics in the renamed Department for Education, which has replaced the DCSF.
13 Podium's website, www.podium.ac.uk, provides detailed information about the organisation's various activities countrywide.
14 Podium commissioned the Centre for Sport, Physical Education and Activity Research (SPEAR) at Canterbury Christ Church University to research the engagement of further and higher education with the London 2012 Olympic and Paralympic Games.
15 The programme has recently expanded its reach through international partnerships and activities, with'Get Set Goes Global'.
16 Such volunteer selection centres include Queen's University (Belfast), Warwick University, University College Plymouth St Mark and St John.
17 For more examples of smaller-scale projects, see Podium's *Spotlight Magazine.*

References

Cashman, R. and Toohey, K. (2002) *Contribution of the Higher Education Sector to the Sydney 2000 Olympic Games*, Centre for Olympic Studies, UNSW Press, Sydney.

Chatziefstathiou, D. (2006) 'All Sports for All People: The Socialist Challenge, Coubertin and the Ideology of "Popular" Olympism', *Kinesiologia Slovenica*, 12 (2), 13–22.

Chatziefstathiou, D. (2011a) 'Changes and Continuities of the Ideology of Olympism in the Modern Olympic Movement', *Sport in Society*, 14 (3), 332–344.

Chatziefstathiou, D. (2011b) 'Olympism: A Learning Philosophy for Physical Education and Youth Sport', in K. M. Armour, *Introduction to Sport Pedagogy for Teachers and Coaches: Effective Learners in Physical Education and Youth Sport*, London: Sage, 90–101.

Chatziefstathiou, D. and Henry, I. P. (2012) *From the Sorbonne 1984 to London 2012*, Basingstoke: Palgrave.

Coubertin, P. ((1919) 2000) 'Olympic Letter XI: The Sporting Spirit of Students', in N. Müller, ed., *Pierre de Coubertin 1863–1937 – Olympism: Selected Writings*, Lausanne: International Olympic Committee, 172–173.

Coubertin, P. ((1997) 2000) 'The Inclusion of Literature and the Arts', in: N. Müller, ed., *Pierre de Coubertin 1863–1937 – Olympism: Selected Writings*. Lausanne: International Olympic Committee, 620–622.

Diem, C. ((1961) 1970) 'An "Elis" of Our Time', in Carl Diem, ed., *The Olympic Idea. Discourses and Essays*, Schorndorf, Germany: Verlag Karl Hofmann, 113–118.

Graver, A., Cammiss, L. Charlton, C. and Plantak, J. (2010) 'What Lasting Educational Benefits can be created from Mega Events?', CfBT Education Trust. Online: www.cfbt.com/evidenceforeducation/pdf/FINAL%20Launch.pdf (accessed 15 October 2011).

Guttmann, A. (1992) *The Olympics: A History of the Modern Games*, Urbana: University of Illinois Press.

HEFCE (2007) 'The HE Sector and the 2012 London Olympic Games', report to the Secretary of State for Innovation, Universities and Skills, The Rt Hon. John Denham MP, London.

Henry, I. P., Fan, H. and Lu, Z. (2008) 'The Contribution of the Further and Higher Education Sectors to the Staging and Delivery of the 2008 Beijing Olympic Games', report by the Centre for Olympic Studies and Research (COS&R), Loughborough University, and the Irish Institute of Chinese Studies (IICS), University College Cork, commissioned by Podium, the Further and Higher Education Unit for the London 2012 Games. Online: www.podium.ac.uk/resources/academic-research?page=2 (accessed 15 October 2011).

Hill, C. (1992) *Olympic Politics*. Manchester: Manchester University Press.

International Olympic Academy (2011) 'Mission of the International Olympic Academy'. Online: http://ioa.org.gr/en/ioa-information/mission (accessed 15 October 2011).

International Olympic Committee (2011) 'Olympic Study Centres in the World'. Online: www.olympic.org/Assets/OSC%20Section/pdf/OSCs%20in%20the%20world.pdf (accessed 15 October 2011).

Lo, C. W. (1999) 'Political Liberalization in the People's Republic of China: Its Linkage to the Mainland-Taiwan Reunification', *East Asia: An International Quarterly*, Winter 1999 (17), 78–110.

London 2012 Candidate File (2004a) 'Theme 1. Olympism and Education'. Online: www.london2012.com/documents/candidate-files/theme-1-olympic-games-concept-and-legacy.pdf (accessed 15 October 2011).

London 2012 Candidate File (2004b) 'Theme 17. Olympism and Culture'. Online: www.london2012.com/documents/candidate-files/theme-17-olympism.pdf (accessed 15 October 2011).

MacAloon, J. (1981) *This Great Symbol: Pierre de Coubertin and the Origins of the Modern Olympic Games*, Chicago: University of Chicago Press.

Müller, N. (2000) *Pierre de Coubertin, 1863–1937. Olympism – Selected Writings*. Lausanne: International Olympic Committee.

Official Olympic Games Report (1912) *The Fifth Olympiad: The Official Report of the Olympic Games of Stockholm 1912*, Stockholm: Swedish Olympic Committee.

PA Consulting Group (2006) 'London Higher: Identifying an inclusive and effective structure for thr Higher Education contribution to the 2012 Olympic and Paralympic Games. Final Management Report'. Online: www.londonhigher.ac.uk/fileadmin/documents/OlympicScoping.pdf (accessed 1 July 2012).

Premier of NSW (2008) Press release, 20 May, New South Wales. Online: www.tda.edu.au/resources//260508–3.pdf (accessed 15 October 2011).

Price Waterhouse Coopers (2008) 'Impacts of the Olympic Games on HE in the Host City', report commissioned by Podium, the Further and Higher Education Unit for the London 2012 Games. Online: www.podium.ac.uk/resources/academic-research?page=3 (accessed 15 October 2011).

Toohey, K. and Veal, A. J. (2000) *The Olympic Games: A Social Science Perspective*. London: CAB International.

Weed, M., Wellard, I., Dowse, S., Mansfield, L., Swain, J. and Gubby, L. (2011) 'The Engagement of Further and Higher Education with the London 2012 Olympic and Paralympic Games', report by the Centre for Sport, Physical Education and Activity Research (SPEAR), Canterbury Christ Church University, commissioned by Podium, the Further and Higher Education Unit for the London 2012 Games. Online: www.podium.ac.uk/resources/academic-research?page=1 (accessed 15 October 2011).

Wei, N. (2010) 'Experience, Value, Influence. A Research Report on the Volunteer work Legacy Transformation of the Beijing 2008 Olympic Games and Paralympics Games', Beijing, China: Renmin University Press.

Wei, N. and Cui, Y. (2011) 'The Development of Volunteerism in China: Context, Role of Government and Influences', *Journal of Cambridge Studies*, 6 (2–3), 12–26.

Worden, M., ed. (2008) *China's Great Leap: The Beijing Games and Olympian Human Rights Challenges*, New York: Seven Stories Press.

15

THE LONDON 2012 CULTURAL OLYMPIAD AND TORCH RELAY

Beatriz Garcia

By the time of the London 2012 Olympic and Paralympic Games it will be exactly a hundred years since the first official presentation of an Olympic cultural programme. London has placed a strong emphasis on its cultural and creative narrative since the bid stage, building on its reputation as a 'creative city' (Landry, 2005) and a world leading centre for the cultural and creative industries. London has also been keen to claim that the Games will leave a long-lasting legacy, not only for the host city – and its East End in particular – but for the rest of the UK. The UK-wide dimensions of the legacy have often been articulated in cultural terms, with a focus on commitment to a national cultural programme as well as the expected national torch relay celebration. Some of the central claims of London's cultural programme – the Cultural Olympiad – are a promise to use culture and the arts to expand engagement from young people and help overcome barriers to participation for people with disability. Advancing the engagement of the youth and disabled people are two central commitments from the 2012 Games at large; by promising that the Cultural Olympiad will expand opportunities at a national level, London is positioning the programme as an essential Games component to fulfil its inclusion promises.

Attempting to present a strong cultural narrative for the Games is not a new endeavour. However, most Games editions have struggled to position their official cultural programme as central to the Games experience due to ongoing tensions in terms of media profile, sponsorship and branding regulations, let alone a challenging sense of rivalry between the sports and arts agendas of key stakeholders. This chapter provides a reflection of London's experience of bidding for, designing, promoting and managing its Cultural Olympiad in a context of heightened expectations about the host's cultural offer. London's cultural proposal was built on the unique positioning of the city and the UK as a leading hub for the cultural and creative industries worldwide, and on the expectation by national and international stakeholders that the Games should benefit from such cultural reputation as well as contribute to its long-term sustainability. The chapter also offers some reflection on the relationship between the Cultural Olympiad and the torch relay as the most iconic programme dedicated to nationwide involvement within the Games.

What is the Cultural Olympiad?

Beyond its role as the world's largest and most successful international multi-sport event, the Olympic Games is also embedded within a centenary movement, the Olympic Movement, founded back in 1894 with the purpose of advancing a humanistic agenda, building on the ambition to pursue human excellence by 'blending sport with culture and education' (IOC, 2011: 10). The Paralympic Games have followed a slightly different route, but its framing ideology is increasingly aligning itself with that of the Olympic Movement and placing a similar degree of emphasis on the role of culture and education as essential dimensions of the Games experience. While the Paralympic Games has only staged official cultural programmes in recent editions, by the time of London 2012, both sets of Games are effectively integrated as a single entity managed by the same team, in this case the London 2012 Olympic and Paralympic Organising Committee (LOCOG). For the purposes of clarity, and given the short-lived history of distinct Paralympic cultural programming, this section will focus on offering an overview of the background to the Cultural Olympiad as a historical component of the Olympic Games.

The official Olympic cultural programme has evolved from its original inception as an Olympic arts competition into non-competitive Olympic arts exhibitions and festivals and, since 1992, a four-year cultural Olympiad (Garcia, 2008). The history of this programme is not to be confused with other cultural components of the Games, from the opening and closing ceremonies to the torch relay. These components are more closely in line with the notion of 'ritual' and come with distinct regulations by the International Olympic Committee (IOC). In contrast, the cultural programme has traditionally been a broadly unregulated area, where the only explicit requirements from the IOC are:

> The OCOG shall organise a programme of cultural events which must cover at least the entire period during which the Olympic Village is open. Such programme shall be submitted to the IOC Executive Board for its prior approval.
>
> *(IOC, 2011: 74)*

Such a lack of explicit guidelines and supporting technical manuals (ubiquitous for almost all other official Games programmes) has allowed host cities to interpret their cultural and arts priorities quite openly but, at the same time, has made the programme vulnerable to funding cuts and subsequent changes to its vision and key deliverables. In general, this has also translated into a poor integration with other Games activity, which is closely monitored by the IOC and thus understood as more essential to the delivery of successful Games. The traditional lack of priority given to the Cultural Olympiad by organising committees is apparent in the frequent marginalisation of the team appointed to deliver it, and is further evident in its poor positioning to attract mainstream media and global Olympic corporate support. Typically, Olympic media rights-holders and global sponsors (who commit millions of pounds for the right to use the rings) have paid minimal attention to the Cultural Olympiad, which is instead left to find non-conflicting sources of funding (mainly via public bodies) and fragmented local media coverage (often through specialist arts or cultural outlets) (Garcia, 2008, 2012a). In turn, this has resulted in very low levels of awareness about the programme by the general public and poor or negative expectations by its closest stakeholders (cultural organisations and artists), who tend to feel that previous Games have not succeeded in positioning arts and culture as central to the hosting process and assume that they will be affected negatively by the diversion of media attention, funding and interest towards sports activity and related infrastructure (*ibid.*).

Despite these ongoing challenges and limitations, the Cultural Olympiad has also brought opportunities for important cultural policy advancements – for instance, by providing long overdue mainstream recognition to contemporary Aboriginal arts activity in the lead to and during Sydney 2000, a practice that has been sustained throughout Australia ever since (Garcia, 2012a). In parallel to this, artists have also used the Games to push their creative practices, from

Leni Riefenstahl's seminal exploration of film techniques in *Olympia* (a Berlin 1936 commission) to avant-garde graphic design advancements in Tokyo 1964, Munich 1972 and particularly Mexico 1968 (Zolov, 2004). Disappointingly, however, the media have been reluctant to tell these stories and they do not form part of the historical Games narrative within official Olympic sources such as the IOC website.

The torch relay

In stark contrast with the low media profile of the Cultural Olympiad, the torch relay is one of the most iconic and widely recognised cultural dimensions of the Games staging process. Its origins differ greatly from those of the cultural programme: the first official staging took place in Berlin 1936 and was envisaged by Carl Diem, a German sports administrator and renowned historian who became the Secretary General of the Berlin Games Organising Committee. While the requirement to host a cultural (or, rather, arts) programme was proposed by the founder of the modern Games, Pierre de Coubertin, as an integral part of his human excellence vision, the relay became a way to add to the Games pageant by connecting it with a romantic vision of the Ancient Greek Games. The idea of a relay was thus entirely conceived by Diem and a German IOC member, who in turn convinced the IOC to establish this as a new Olympic Games ritual (Lennartz, 1997).

With the advent of the commercialisation of the Olympic symbol in the 1980s, mainly through the selling of television rights and exclusive single-product category deals for global sponsors, the torch relay became one of the most desirable assets of the Games, and is currently staged under the close supervision of corporate sponsors acting as its 'presenting partners'. This means that, beyond the protection of a series of symbolic rituals as originally envisaged by Diem (i.e. the lighting of the flame in Ancient Olympia framed by a traditional Greek performance), the actual relay is a noticeably commercialised venture (Tomlinson, 2005). The latter involves a large number of heavily branded vehicles, the selection of a considerable proportion of torch bearers via sponsorship promotions, and the setting of 'celebration stages' throughout the torch route under strict commercial and branding guidelines to maximise the visibility of official sponsor messages.

Perhaps partly due to the marked disparity in terms of their commercial versus non-commercial appeal and status, the Cultural Olympiad and the torch relay do not tend to be directly connected. Although it is not uncommon for the Games bid documents to request information about the vision and plans for both programmes under the same chapter, they are rarely implemented by the same teams and, as suggested above, in the context of contemporary branding guidelines they are staged and promoted following very different operational plans. London has tried to bring a degree of proximity, mainly by encouraging links between the torch relay regional coordinators and the activities managed by appointed Cultural Olympiad regional creative programmers, as discussed in the sections below. All the same, these programmes and their promotion follow completely separate paths and their ability to engage with the general public is also noticeably different.

Bidding for culture

The London 2012 Games bid was not as high profile or widely supported as other competing 2012 bids in the early candidature years. Cities like Madrid and Paris were presenting their second consecutive bid to the IOC and counted on visible and enthusiastic public support from day one, having started their campaigns earlier than London. Within the UK, the decision to bid was not publicly announced until late 2003 and the profile of the bid was low until the final countdown, gaining momentum from the end of 2004 (only half a year before the final presentation to the IOC), possibly on the back of the UK's successful performance at the Athens 2004 Games.

Following established bid regulations, London was asked to respond to a candidature procedure and questionnaire by the IOC (2004) and to set up separate teams to address each of the main questionnaire chapters. Jude Kelly, MBE was appointed to lead on the 'Olympism and Culture' chapter, which also included questions about the torch relay, ceremonies and education programmes. In common with previous candidates, particularly since the Barcelona 1992 bid, London saw in its culture chapter an opportunity to present a distinct vision and propose innovative ideas about how to experience the Games and define what the Olympics and Paralympics mean for youth today. Since early in 2004, Jude Kelly has embarked on an ambitious journey to attract high-profile artists and intellectuals as cultural programme advisors, conducting a wide range of workshops and speaking at public events to involve the views of arts organisations around the country (see Garcia, 2005a; London 2012, 2005a). Ideas circulated at the time ranged from how to link the largest sport event in the world with the largest arts festival (the Edinburgh festival), which were to coincide in the UK over August 2012, to discussion about the meaning of internationalism and interculturalism, and ways of ensuring that the Olympiad provided a platform to 'keep this [Olympic] Movement moving' (Kelly, in Garcia, 2005: 19) and in touch with contemporary youth concerns.

During the writing-up process, which involved feedback from International Olympic Committee advisors, it became apparent that there were certain limitations to the kind of language that was most appropriate to use in order to appeal to and engage IOC members. Terms such as 'fusion' (of cultures, of artforms) were discouraged on the grounds that they would be difficult to appreciate or understand universally by all members. This exercise and the need to question the jargon that has become commonly attractive within UK culture and creative circles was an interesting process for the bid team to engage with, in order to appreciate what it takes to convey a message that is fresh and distinct as well as easy to understand by an organisation with such ties to tradition and such international (and non-English-dominated) representation.

The eventual chapter narrative focused on youth, the diversity and global connections of host communities and the strength of London and the UK as a world centre for creative industries and entrepreneurship. Beyond this, the aspects most distinct to the cultural programme were the commitment to engaging the whole of the UK and the promise of a seamless transition with and building upon the preceding Games, Beijing – two aspects not explored by any of the competing bids. The education programme was also distinct in the richness of detail (e.g. its emphasis on the concept of Friend-ship, described below), and the rare proposal to create a national Olympic Institute as a key legacy. For the torch relay, the main proposal was to use it to advance peace and promote the IOC's 'Olympic Truce' narrative, involving an international route touching on the homes of Nobel Peace Prize laureates around the world. These are all examples of initiatives unmatched by rival candidates, which tended to present cultural proposals that were much more vague. The London culture bid was also the only one to emphasise a clear commitment to bring the programme into the Olympic Village to engage athletes, and was ambitious in its promise to stage the first 'World Culture Fair in honour of the Olympic Games' (London 2012, 2004).

Culture in action – making a difference at the bid stage

London's final bid presentation in Singapore in July 2005 has been widely presented as successful and memorable for its emphasis on youth and the distinct take on 'Olympic values', credibly presented by a veteran Olympian, Sebastian Coe, as head of the bid team and organisation. This was in stark contrast with the more managerial tone of other presentations, which focused on technical aspects or used less distinct (and ethnically diverse) styles to represent people's engagement with the bid (Hart, 2005). The involvement of 30 children from the East End of London (who made up a considerable proportion of London's delegation) and the use of a small local (East End) creative company to produce the main presentation films were all hints at London's credentials as a city with great confidence and expertise that was supporting the creative talents of its population, particularly new and emerging talent.

Within the UK, in the lead to this final presentation, London committed to supporting a nationwide programme of cultural activity involving young people acting as ambassadors for their local identity. This was part of the so-called 'Friend-ship' programme, which connected with an initiative already in place via the Liverpool 2008 European Capital of Culture programme (see London 2012, 2005b). These activities were all ways of demonstrating London's commitment to youth and using cultural expression as a platform to expand the appeal of the Games to young people. From a policy perspective, the value of these initiatives was also to show how the Games would link to existing or emerging nationwide programmes. As suggested by the Friend-ship collaboration, a common narrative at this point in time was for the Cultural Olympiad to build on and extend the experience and legacy of the European Capital of Culture programme – using 2008 (ECoC year) as the gateway to the Olympiad.

Delivering the cultural programme – from promises to reality

As is common within any Games hosting process, once the Olympics was awarded to London some major changes were required, and this had a significant impact on the set-up for the cultural programme. During the bid stage, the team was formed as a coalition between culture, ceremonies and education. Most bid staff members were seconded from other organisations, ranging from the UK Department for Culture, Media and Sport to the Arts Council England. During the initial years of OCOG formation these secondments changed regularly, particularly within the culture section, thus threatening the team's continuity of vision and the steep learning process in terms of Olympic delivery needs. Interestingly, this was not the case for the education team, which retained the same staff members it had inherited from the bid stage.

Beyond the regular changes to team composition, the main challenge to retaining aspects of any Games bid original vision is about managing the transition in senior positions or 'director roles'. For London, the high-profile lead of the culture bidding team became Chair of the original Cultural Olympiad Advisory Board, but was gradually removed from the day-to-day operations, which would be led instead by a specially appointed Head of Culture and a joint Culture, Ceremonies and Education Director. For a period of time, the Chair retained a public leadership and championing role and continued close conversations with key advisors – however, such involvement diminished with time. The role of the Advisory Board became unclear for a while and this group was eventually disbanded, to be replaced by a considerably different group of individuals and Chair. In other host cities, although it is common for the director's role to change and for the board to have a slightly different emphasis after the bid stage, it is usual for the culture bid leader to retain a chairing role throughout, which eases the protection of the most aspirational aspects of the original Games proposal. In London, these changes resulted in a marked departure from the original underlying narrative about 'keeping the movement moving' and the abandonment of some of the project's most iconic priorities.

Major changes included the elimination of the Friend-ship as the main flagship initiative that was to offer a continuum between Beijing and London, and the explicit commitment to an

Olympic Institute for Research. However, other important aspects, such as the idea of a nation-wide programme with strong regional involvement and the emphasis on youth as creators and users of activity, were retained throughout. This is to the credit of the original bidding team as well as the transition teams, who had to grapple against ongoing budgeting and structural team modifications.

The vision for the torch relay changed considerably as well, particularly as, on the wake of Beijing's noticeably controversial international relay, the IOC decided that future hosts would no longer be allowed to programme an international leg for the relay, focusing instead on the established tradition of a brief relay in Greece (after the lighting in Ancient Olympia) and a direct transfer into the UK, for a nationwide relay. This effectively meant that the original concept of a relay visiting the locations of Nobel Peace Prize winners had to be dropped. The emphasis on peace as the motif for the relay has also faded, with references being made in passing to the traditional rhetoric presented via the Olympic Charter, but with no distinct 2012 narrative about this issue. Instead, the emphasis is on the originality of the torch design, as has been the case in most previous Games.

Management challenges and innovations

One of the most challenging aspects for the delivery of a Cultural Olympiad is choosing the most appropriate management framework. Given the now-established commitment of host cities to deliver a four-year programme, this means in practice that the cultural programme is the earliest Olympic programme to go into delivery mode, and one of the first tests for an OCOG to prove that it has a clear operational structure and clear roles and commitments agreed with its key stakeholders. In London, the culture team was originally integrated with the ceremonies team, which had responsibility to deliver the very first high-profile global Olympic statement for London 2012: the staging of an eight-minute segment within the closing ceremony of the previous Games host, Beijing. This counts as part of the 'ceremonies' rather than of the 'culture' commitments for the OCOG, but was all the same a key statement that required a degree of coordination with London's main cultural vision. As already noted, at this early stage the team was small and fluid, with constant staff replacements and few full-time appointments, but the pressure to deliver the eight-minute segment helped to solidify the team's visibility.

By 2008, however, it became apparent that each part of the team had a very different set of pressures and priorities to attend to. The culture team lost its original head in 2008, two years after his appointment, and did not get a new director until January 2010, once a new board and chair had been established. Thus, after considerable transition in the period 2005–2008, it was not until late 2009 that the culture team became more stable and grew significantly. The appointment of Ruth Mackenzie as director, a well-known and respected figure with experience managing large-scale events and advising government on cultural policy priorities, has been seen as a positive measure to ensure confidence amongst national and international arts peers. Some of the activities coordinated by the team within the London 2012 offices involve a series of high-profile national programmes (a range of which build on the original bid proposal), as well as a distinctly branded series of cultural events during the Olympic year, the London 2012 Festival, presented as the 'culmination of the Cultural Olympiad' (see the next section, on promotional issues). Since late 2008 and 2009, the role of the team has mainly been to keep abreast of the wide range of Olympic-driven or other Games-related activities taking place in London and throughout the UK, and to help determine what should be considered part of the Cultural Olympiad and how to make this operationally feasible. A considerable part of this task is of a promotional/branding negotiation nature and is covered in following sections.

Within this section, it is relevant to consider some of the most ambitious management innovations for culture. As has been the case now for a number of Games editions, London 2012 is designed as an organisation that manages both the Olympic and Paralympic Games and has promoted both events simultaneously from day one. While this is an established requirement, previous Games had opted to present their Olympic and Paralympic cultural activity as two separate consecutive programmes, as with the sporting events. In London, both cultural programmes are fully integrated, which means that all funding streams, dedicated staff and related promotions refer to both sets of Games. As discussed in following sections, this has strengthened the visibility and centrality of disabled arts activity, which cannot be disassociated from any dimension of the Cultural Olympiad.

In addition to the above, another important innovation brought by the 2012 Games was the decision to establish a UK-wide structure, with 13 creative programmers being appointed in late 2007 and 2008, two for London and one for each UK region and nation. These posts have enabled considerable growth and consolidation of Games-inspired cultural activity throughout the country. However, the capacity of programmers to shape initiatives varies quite a lot from area to area. While in the northern parts of the country programmers have felt empowered to steer or commission projects, building on generous, purpose-specific funding (allocated by the Legacy Trust UK – see below) and thus drive new activity and priorities, in the southern parts, despite also counting on special funding allocations, programmers have mainly operated as coordinators of activity defined by other organisations rather than taking a leading role in defining a vision for their region (Garcia, 2012b).

Programming overview and funding sources

As suggested above, in order to make the Cultural Olympiad feasible and as inclusive as possible, it has been conceived as a series of programming layers managed under slightly different frameworks within and outside LOCOG. In the lead to its original launch in 2008, the core values and main themes of the Cultural Olympiad were presented as follows:

> Core values: 'Celebrate London and the whole of the UK welcoming the world [...]; Inspire and involve young people; Generate a positive legacy'.
>
> *(LOCOG, 2008: 4)*

> Main Themes: 'Bringing together culture and sport; Encouraging audiences to take part; Animating public spaces through street theatre, public art, circus skills and live big-screen sites; Using culture and sport to promote environmental sustainability, health and well-being; Encouraging collaborations and innovation between communities and cultural sectors; Enhancing the learning, skills and personal development of young people by linking with education programmes.
>
> *(LOCOG, 2008: 5)*

According to LOCOG, the estimated audience up to the end of 2011 is 16 million people.[1] The combined budget for four years of activity has been presented tentatively as £100 million, but LOCOG is not the budget holder. Instead,

> the structure of the Culture Programme [has been] designed so that LOCOG would be the catalyst rather than the funding source for the Cultural Olympiad and LOCOG

> would open up opportunities for the cultural sector to exploit – and to do so in a far more open way than perhaps has been possible in previous Games.
>
> *(LOCOG, 2008: 11)*

The Cultural Olympiad principal funding bodies are listed as 'Arts Council England, Legacy Trust UK and the Olympic Lottery Distributor', and the programme's 'Premier Partners' (meaning London 2012 domestic corporate sponsors associated with the Olympic cultural programme) are British Petroleum (BP) and British Telecom (BT). The British Council 'support[s] the international development' of projects, and Panasonic, a global Olympic sponsor, is noted as a presenting partner of the project 'Film Nation'.[2] The Legacy Trust UK, one of the three principal Cultural Olympiad funders, has committed £17 million towards four national programmes and £24 million to 12 regional programmes[3] (each of them coordinated by a different regional creative programmer). This brings a distinct angle to the work presented, as it is designed to last beyond the Games period and become a sustainable venture. It is the first time that such an emphasis has been placed on the sustainability of the Games cultural programme, an approach that is consistent with the decision to appoint a legacy steering committee for the Olympiad, as well as to fund a Cultural Olympiad legacy evaluation programme.

In order to understand the multiple dimensions and scope of the programme, Figure 15.1 presents an overview of activities, core teams in charge and main funding sources. Table 15.1 goes on to outline the different Cultural Olympiad sub-programme descriptions and (where available) their respective estimated audiences. Finally, Table 15.2 reproduces the first, tentative

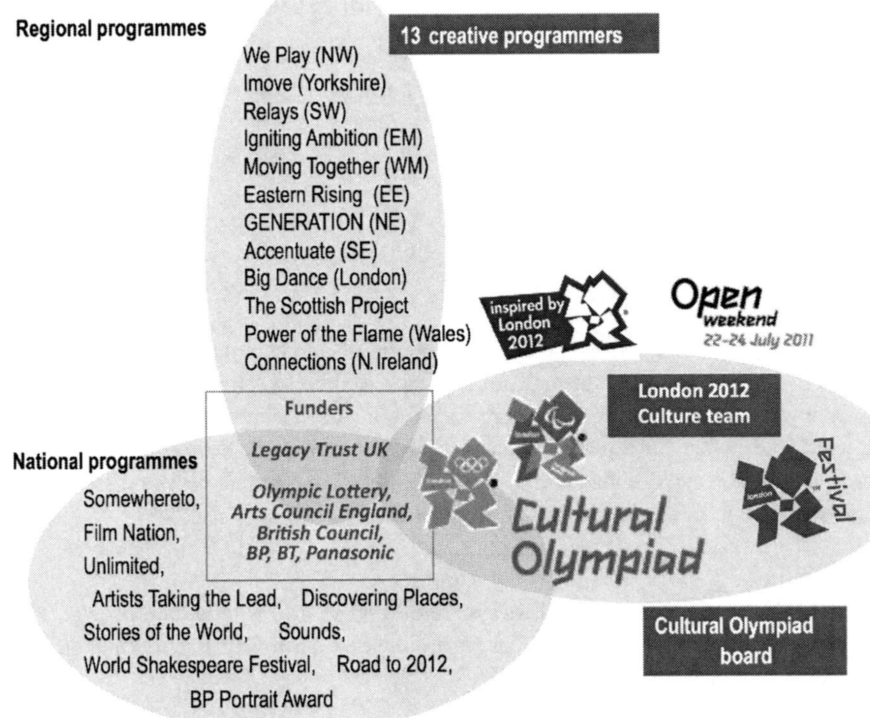

Figure 15.1 Overview of cultural programmes.

Table 15.1 Cultural Olympiad, key programme components

Major national programmes/signature programmes, different start dates 2008–2012	Description: 'Large-scale programmes with nation-wide reach and impact which will form the centrerpiece of the Cultural Olympiad between [2008] and 2012 and which are being produced in partnership with leading arts and cultural organisations in the UK.' A range of these were first outlined within the original bidding documents. Funding: estimated up to £60 million from all main funding partners.
Regional programmes (12 major programmes), different start dates 2008–2012	Objectives: 'To unite culture, sport, knowledge and learning, in line with the values and vision of the Olympics; to make a lasting difference to all those involved; to be grassroots projects, often small in scale, and uniting communities of interest at local and regional level.' Funding: Legacy Trust UK (£24 million).
Inspire mark (2,000 individual projects, UK-wide), 2008–2011	Description: 'An Olympic and Paralympic first, the London 2012 Inspire programme enables non-commercial organisations across the UK to link their events and projects to the London 2012 Games in an official scope. From Wales to the East of England, from the South West to Yorkshire and Humber – more than 2,000 projects and events have been awarded the coveted Inspire mark for their work in one of six areas: sustainability, education, volunteering, business, sport or culture.' Funding: no specific funding has been allocated. Organisations apply to LOCOG and justify how they meet their selection criteria to obtain the Inspire mark.
Open Weekend (thousands of individual projects, UK-wide), one weekend per year (2008–2011)	Description: 'London 2012 Open Weekend is an annual event happening each summer leading up to 2012 to celebrate the countdown to the Opening Ceremonies at the London 2012 Olympic Games and Paralympic Games.' Funding: no specific funding has been allocated. Organisations apply to LOCOG to be listed under this programme. Estimated audience outreach: over two million people up to 2011 taking part in sport, arts and culture events across the UK.
London 2012 Festival (over 1,000 events UK-wide), 21 June – 9 September 2012	Description: 'The culmination of the Cultural Olympiad, [...] Leading artists from all over the world will come together in the UK's biggest ever nationwide festival – a chance for everyone to get into the spirit of London 2012 through dance, music, theatre, the visual arts, film and digital innovation and leave a lasting legacy for the arts in the UK.' Expected audience outreach: ten million people. Some of the events will be ticketed, the majority will be free to attend.

Source: London 2012 website and programme-specific press releases.

Table 15.2 Cultural Olympiad outcome framework (consultation paper)

Legacy type	*Cultural Olympiad legacy*	*Timescale*	*Range*
Economic	Culture is featured in £1.6 billion worth of Games-related positive media coverage of Britain in 2012, as measured by Visit Britain.	2012	National
	For the UK to have improved in its ranking by an average of one place across relevant national brand index markets.	2012	National
	Ten new artistic pieces co-commissioned as part of the Cultural Olympiad have been presented overseas, raising the international profile of the UK's creative and cultural sector.	2013	National
	Within ten years the creative and cultural workforce of the host boroughs will have grown by 7.5 per cent, representing 2,000 new jobs.	2020	Host boroughs
	To have increased the number of creative businesses in the host boroughs by 500.	2020	Host boroughs
	20,000 more residents to have degree-level qualifications in creative/arts-related courses	2010–2030	Host boroughs
Social	Increased levels of volunteering and a more diverse volunteer base in London's cultural sector, with 10,000 of Games volunteers going onto longer-term volunteering in the cultural sector.	2010–2020	London
Cultural	20 new partnerships, with cultural organisations and other bodies coming together for the Cultural Olympiad and establishing several major new creative relationships, activities and festivals.	2012	National
	A knowledge-exchange programme between the Cultural Olympiad and counterparts at Derry, UK City of Culture and the Glasgow Commonwealth Games.	2012–2014	National
	A cross-borough annual festival – Create – working towards increasing cultural engagement across the boroughs.	2012	Host boroughs
	Within five years all the host boroughs will exceed the current figures for culture engagement, as measured by the DCMS 'Taking Part' survey.	2015	Host boroughs
	Creative partnerships between ten cultural organisations and institutes in Brazil and London to have been initiated.	2016	International

Source: LOCOG (2011) London 2012 Cultural Olympiad. Creating the Legacy Consultation.

Note

Please note that these outcomes were presented as indicative, aimed at generating an 'informed discussion so that final measures can be refined and agreed upon' between all programme stakeholders (LOCOG, 2011: 7).

outline of core output aspirations as presented within a public consultation paper distributed by the LOCOG Culture Team in May 2011 to all their core stakeholders in order to agree priority legacies.

This multiplicity of stakeholders and need for agenda coordination has made the Cultural Olympiad possible on a grand scale but it has also brought about one of its main challenges. Due to the need to rely on a wide range of funding sources, many organisations take a stand on what the Olympiad should be about, with the consequent risk of having to make decisions 'by committee', which may ensure policy consensus but rarely achieves truly original and memorable cultural interventions. As Charlotte Higgins put it in 2009,

> One person I spoke to, who is running a Cultural Olympiad project, said: 'It's very labyrinthine. There are one or two good people, but the meetings last for ever. You need a benign dictator to bang some heads together. There are too many fiefdoms.'
>
> *(Higgins, 2009)*

With the appointment of Ruth MacKenzie in 2010, the right balance may be achieved after all. At the time of writing, with just one month to go before the start of 2012, a lot seems to depend on how the distinct London 2012 Festival is conceived, promoted and understood by partners and the general public, and whether this contributes to, diminishes or simply ignores the credibility and value of a four-year UK-wide Cultural Olympiad concept.

Promotional issues

From a promotional point of view, London 2012 has inherited the challenges that have been common to Games cultural programmers since the establishment of the very successful but utterly restrictive Olympic global brand guidelines (London 2012, 2010).[4] I stress the term 'Olympic', as within the Paralympics there is a greater degree of flexibility. The main issue to overcome is the conflict of interest that exists in the use of the Olympic rings, the most prized Games commercial asset, which the IOC has monetised by offering it as an exclusive right to a very limited number of global sponsors using the Olympic Partner programme (TOP programme) and broadcasters. For cultural organisations, this means that unless their activity is sponsored exclusively by one of the TOP sponsors, they are not allowed to use the rings nor associate themselves with the Olympic programme. This situation tends to apply to the majority of Cultural Olympiad contributors as, typically, most art organisations receive some degree of support from non-IOC-sanctioned organisations, be it in the commercial or public sector.

The London team was keen to consider options to address this issue from the start. Since 2005, they worked on the creation of a parallel 'brand' or visual icon that could be used to signify an association with the 2012 Games without breaching IOC global partner branding exclusivity rights. This resulted in the creation of the 'Inspired by 2012' mark, originally seen by some as the main vehicle to label Cultural Olympiad activity, though eventually this is a mark that welcomes applications from culture as well as voluntary, educational and grassroots sport organisations.[5] Organisations throughout the UK have been encouraged to apply for the Inspire mark, on the condition that their work is non-lucrative and takes place before 2012. This has resulted in a unique layering of branding, where activities have been tagged as related to the 2012 Games, even though they are not part of the IOC-led Olympic global branding. This technique has also been valuable in the sense that it breaks the Olympic/Paralympic branding division that has been common to previous Games.

In parallel, the appointment of 13 creative programmers with differing levels of affiliation and access to funding pots has also resulted in the creation of an additional layer of 'brands' or associated programmes that present themselves as respective regions' contribution to the Games cultural programme. The most visible layer is that funded by the Legacy Trust, resulting in twelve programmes around the country, each of which involves a number of specific events or festivals, which also bring their own distinct branding style.[6] Not all of these programmes are promoted individually (via separate websites or brochures) but many of them are, and the styles of communication vary greatly, not always presenting a clear narrative of Games association. The resulting picture is confusing, therefore, and makes it difficult to capture the attention of the media and ensure a clear understanding for the average public or even interested audiences (see Figure 15.1 and Table 15.1).

Furthermore, up until late in 2011, the term Cultural Olympiad was not used beyond stakeholder documents and reports or the LOCOG website. Due to its being property of the IOC (effectively, a variation of the term Olympic) the term (or any recognisable logo) was absent from the brochures designed to promote specific activity – particularly in the regions. The Inspire mark logo has been growing in use since 2009 but this was not clearly associated with the Cultural Olympiad until 2011, and has not been used consistently in parallel with this term in most event materials. Instead, activity is varyingly promoted, following very different design styles and often ignoring any kind of Games-related narrative.[7]

The Cultural Olympiad national programmes tend to be a bit more consistent in their promotion of Games association – some, such as Film Nation, going as far as to adopt the London 2012 visual look.[8] However, there is no overarching style of communications and up to the end of 2011, some of them, such as the Tate Movie Project, fail to highlight clearly (either visually or textually) their London 2012 relationship.

Overall, it is expected that branding coherence and Games narrative will not be in full operation until well into 2012. The creation of yet another 'brand' for Games-time cultural activity, the London 2012 Festival, will assist in creating an overarching look and coordinated promotion during the final months leading to the Games. The need to create a different title for Games-time activity is not uncommon, but it tends to happen when host cities have created non-obvious Games link titles for their festivals. For instance, Sydney's year-long festivals were named 'Festival of the Dreaming', 'A Sea Change', 'Reaching the World' and 'The Harbour of Life'. The choice to change the title of the final, Games-time festival into 'Olympic Art Festival' was successful in promotional terms – it attracted the right kind of attention from the media and attained greater recognition from the public (Garcia, 2012a). In the case of London, given that the term 'Cultural Olympiad' was not used widely by anyone other than boards and committees in advance of 2012, it was less obvious that a different name would be required for Games time, and the elimination of an explicit Olympic reference does bring the risk of a loss of clear association. However, some arguments in favour are the desire to distinguish different activities and distance them from any negative preconceptions associated with the difficult (communications as well as managerial) build-up.

On a separate note, the torch relay has followed a completely different promotional journey. As an activity that needs no introduction and enjoys iconic status and high demand from corporate as well as public partners, there has been no need to start from zero explaining 'what it is' (an exercise of considerable importance in the case of the Cultural Olympiad) and instead has simply had to focus on negotiating the route and related timeframes. A major difference with the Cultural Olympiad is that this is a highly commercialised programme, with corporate partners dominating presentation styles. Coca-Cola, Lloyds TSB and Samsung are the three London 2012 partners for the Relay and they have led the promotional strategy, enacting UK-wide torch showcases and encouraging 'torch bearer nominations' by the general public.

Figure 15.2 shows the essential differences in branding style and opportunity for the cultural programme and the torch relay. While the pictogram for the torch incorporates the logos of its corporate presenting partners, the Cultural Olympiad simply combines both Olympic and Paralympic logos (it is the only official Games programme to do this, which could be considered highly advanced and symbolic of the Olympiad role, advancing full Games integration), while the 2012 Festival pictogram and the Inspire mark essentially demonstrate that it is possible to recognise London 2012's iconography without need for the rings, which in turn is also symbolic of Olympic and Paralympic programming integration.

Engagement and legacies beyond 2012

The London 2012 Cultural Olympiad has tried to advance the Olympic and Paralympic cultural agenda and attempted to prove that it is possible to expand the Games experience nationwide and coordinate activity with diverse stakeholders, from grassroots to world-class organisations. It has also claimed that activity will be sustainable and leave a long-lasting legacy, and has committed to achieving this by establishing the Legacy Trust as main funding body, conducting a detailed evaluation into the main lessons learnt and assisting knowledge transfer within the UK as well as to future Olympic hosts. By the end of 2011, some of these promises seem to have been met. The creation of a nationwide network of programmers, with appointed individuals retaining their posts from 2008 onwards, is a Games first that has enabled new kinds of collaboration, particularly within respective regions. Although many programmers would note that it has been difficult to interact at a national level or sustain a clear relationship with the London 2012 team and its vision, there is consensus over the range of opportunities to explore new synergies within their respective areas and, in many cases, also agreement that new subjects have been explored or received additional attention thanks to the Games. Key examples include the innovative approaches to exploring the concept of 'play' in the North-West, or explorations around 'movement' in Yorkshire.[9] Programmers also note that they have been encouraged to be more ambitious in their uses of open spaces in order to attract more diverse and younger audiences (Garcia, 2012b).

Figure 15.2 Cultural Olympiad and torch relay branding (printed with permission from London 2012).

Another major achievement has been the clear integration of the Olympic and Paralympic message in the context of the cultural programme. London's ingenious conception of a single design for both the Olympic and Paralympic logo, with an emphasis on the number '2012' has been paramount to achieving this integration, which is extended in the creation of the Inspire mark (equally valid for both) without depending on the Olympic rings. Predictably, this is an initiative that may be encouraged in future Games – although it puts into question the relevance of the 'rings' as the most prized symbol or identity in the local and national context. London may in fact have opened a new era for Games cultural programming, where the association is created with the Games as a unified Olympic and Paralympic entity, rather than the IOC or the rings as an Olympic-only mark of prestige.

Despite these achievements, some major challenges remain. The multiplicity of brands, funding body agendas and the ongoing barriers to using the terms 'Olympic' or 'Paralympic' – let alone any attempt at using the rings – in association with the diverse range of activity that supposedly constitutes the Cultural Olympiad means that in the four years leading up to the Games, events and initiatives have been extremely fragmented and have not achieved a unifying narrative to be captured by the media or understood by the general public. Lack of message integration and public awareness are still major limitations for the Cultural Olympiad that London has not been able to overcome in the years preceding 2012. This has been so despite major advancements with the Inspire mark, and may be indicative of the amount of time required to experiment with such a potentially revolutionary new Games identity. With the Inspire mark finally in full swing, a national programme launch in November 2011 and regional programme launches in the early part of 2012, these are challenges that may be finally overcome during the Games year, just in time for the sporting competition fortnight and the concentration of global media attention on the UK.

Transfer of knowledge

Cultural programming remains an ambiguous area of delivery in the context of an otherwise extremely structured and regulated event hosting process. However, both local hosts and the IOC or International Paralympic Committee (IPC) as umbrella organisations seem to be paying greater attention to this programme and considering options to extend its influence and visibility as part of the Games experience. This involves a marked evolution, from the origins of the concept as part of an 'ideal' or philosophy of Olympism but not backed by any clear operational guidelines (Garcia, 2008), into more pragmatic recent rediscoveries as an opportunity to maximise engagement, assist in the projection of local and national identities and as a distinct branding asset that can help to position the Games as a global event with a history, values and social agenda more credible and extensive than other multinational sporting events such as the World Cup (Miah and Garcia, 2012). The latter considerations have grown since Barcelona 1992, which created a narrative of success around its cultural offerings, even though its Cultural Olympiad was flawed from a managerial and promotional point of view (Moragas, 2008). Sydney and Athens were also insistent on the centrality of their cultural programmes to demonstrate the value of hosting the Games, though they were less successful in generating media attention around the Games-time cultural offerings and equally limited in their Cultural Olympiad management structure – in Sydney as a result of lack of funds, in Athens because of excess of bureaucracy and dependence on agendas alien to the organising committee for the Games (Garcia, 2012a, 2008).

With London, an opportunity has emerged both to strengthen the generic international narrative (e.g. the UK as a world creative centre) and make real progress in terms of managerial and promotional structures. The creation of the Inspire mark and the creative programmers' network provide two alternative models for delivery that could be taken up and developed as a Games requirement in the future. In contrast, the relationship between the nationwide cultural programme and the torch relay remain an underdeveloped area, reliant on ad hoc decisions and challenged by commercial versus artistic interests. Other popular programmes, such as the Live Sites (a legacy from Sydney 2000), are also still poorly connected with the Cultural Olympiad, despite original (bid-stage) attempts at exploring options for greater integration.

Conversations have already started with representatives from Rio 2016, which is the first Games to respond to a bidding proposition where culture is not treated as a separate chapter, but an integral part of the Olympic experience (IOC, 2008). Their ability to build on London's achievements and learn from their limitations will depend on the degree of transparency and extent of documentation over the 2012 experience. The commitment towards extensive and varied research, observation programmes and evaluations, from a DCMS-led meta-evaluation to a specific Cultural Olympiad evaluation and multiple event-specific monitoring and research projects, offers a strong indication that this will be possible and is a good reference for future Cultural Olympiad hosts. Despite the ongoing challenges and limitations, London's approach to its cultural programme shows a clear commitment to making it sustainable and sharing lessons learnt, which is already an important step forward and is raising the expectations of key Olympic and Paralympic stakeholders so that this aspect of the Games is not overshadowed in future editions.

Notes

1 London 2012: www.london2012.com/cultural-olympiad (last accessed January 2012).
2 Cultural Olympiad webpage: www.london2012.com/cultural-olympiad.
3 See: www.legacytrustuk.org/.
4 See: www.london2012.com/about-us/our-brand/frequently-asked-questions.php.
5 Inspire mark website: www.london2012.com/about-us/our-brand/inspire-programme.php.
6 Legacy Trust website: www.legacytrustuk.org/.
7 As an example, in the North-West, 'We Play' is the main Games cultural programme and consists of three large-scale events within the region, all funded via the Legacy Trust. Of these, Lakes Alive does not include any London 2012-related visuals within its 2011 website, nor any reference to its links with the Games or Cultural Olympiad; 'Abandon Normal Devices' includes the 'Inspired by 2012' logo but not any reference to its being part of the Cultural Olympiad. In Wales, the range of events and activities framed as Legacy Trust funded omit any Games-related visual identification and only a few are explicit in their reference to a relationship with London 2012, while references to the Cultural Olympiad have not been found within their 2011 webpages. In contrast, in the West Midlands, the 'Dancing for the Games' programme utilises a visual style that is very strongly reminiscent of London 2012 communications, and the Inspire mark is clearly displayed.
8 See: www.filmnation.org.uk/.
9 See programme websites for 'We Play' (http://tinyurl.com/cut9qj3) and 'Imove' (www.imoveand.com).

References

Garcia, B. (2012a) *The Olympic Games and Cultural Policy*, New York: Routledge.

Garcia, B. (2012b) 'London 2012 Creative Programmers Network: A new model to advance the nationwide cultural legacy of the Olympic Games', *Culture @ the Olympics*, 14 (2): 20–35.

Garcia, B. (ed.) (2005) 'Exploring Internationalism', *Culture @ the Olympics*, 7: 1–55. Online: www.culturalolympics.org.uk/volume/vol-07–2005/.

Hart, S. (2005) 'Coe Struck Gold by Playing the Youth Card', *Telegraph*, 10 July. Online: http://tinyurl.com/4525nbt.

Higgins, C. (2009) 'Is the Cultural Olympiad a Runner?', *Guardian*, 25 March. Online: http://tinyurl.com/d4krly.

IOC (2011) *Olympic Charter*, Lausanne: International Olympic Committee.

IOC (2008) *Candidature Acceptance Procedure. Games of the XXXI Olympiad in 2016.* Online: http://www.olympic.org/Documents/Reports/EN/en_report_1213.pdf.

IOC (2004) *2012 Candidature Procedure and Questionnaire.* Online: http://www.olympic.org/Documents/Reports/EN/en_report_810.pdf.

Garcia, B. (2008) 'One Hundred Years of Cultural Programming within the Olympic Games (1912–2012)', *International Journal of Cultural Policy*, 14 (4): 361–376.

Landry, C. (2005) 'London as a Creative City', in Hartley, J. (ed.) *Creative Industries*, London: Blackwell: 233–243.

Lennartz, K. (1997) 'The Genesis of Legends', *Journal of Olympic History*, 5 (1): 8–11.

London 2012 (2010) 'London 2012 Statutory Marketing Rights – Brand Protection'. Online: http://tinyurl.com/35wgwxp.

London 2012 (2005a) 'London Launches Cultural Conference Programme'. Online: http://tinyurl.com/3ltgo7b.

London 2012 (2005b) 'Liverpool Backs London 2012 Bid'. Online: http://tinyurl.com/c63kg7w.

London 2012 (2004) 'Theme 17: Olympism and Culture', in London 2012, *Candidate File,* London: London 2012 Candidate City: 170 – 177.

LOCOG (2011) *London 2012 Cultural Olympiad. Creating the Legacy Consultation*, London: London Organising Committee for the Olympic and Paralympic Games.

LOCOG (2008) 'The Cultural Olympiad. Background Briefing Paper', London: London Organising Committee for the Olympic and Paralympic Games. Online: www.sel.org.uk/uploads/LOCOG-Cultural-Olympiad-Background-Briefing.pdf.

Miah, A. and Garcia, B. (2012) *The Olympic Games. The Basics*, London: Routledge

Moragas, M. (2008) 'The Cultural Olympiad of Barcelona in 1992: Good points and bad points', Barcelona: Centre d'Estudis Olímpics UAB. Online: http://olympicstudies.uab.es/pdf/wp049_end.pdf.

Tomlinson, A. (2005) 'The Commercialisation of the Olympics: Cities, corporations and the Olympic commodity', in Young, K. and Wamsley, K. (eds) *Global Olympics: Historical and sociological studies of the modern Games*, Oxford: Elsevier.

Zolov, E. (2004) 'Showcasing the "Land of Tomorrow": Mexico and the 1968 Olympics', *The Americas*, 61 (2): 159–188.

16
VOLUNTEERING FOR THE GAMES

Geoff Nichols

Introduction – the importance of Olympic volunteers

Mega-events involving sport almost invariably rely on a large number of volunteers, and a key aspect of the resourcing for an Olympic Games event is 'the donation of work of volunteers' (Preuss, 2004: 182). The Olympic Games is the epitome of sporting mega-events – defined as 'large-scale cultural (including commercial and sporting) events which have a dramatic character, mass popular appeal and international significance' (Roche, 2000: 1), yet many reviews barely mention volunteers, if at all (e.g. Horne and Manzenreiter, 2006; Poynter and MacRury, 2009; Sadd and Jones, 2009; Toohey and Veal, 2007). The study of event volunteering has grown (Auld *et al.*, 2009) and there have been several studies of volunteers at relatively large events, but not as many as one might have expected covering the Olympic Games. Perhaps this is because of the difficulty for researchers in gaining access. A detailed assessment of the income and expenditure of the Olympic Games merely notes that the labour freely given by volunteers is 'difficult to evaluate' (Preuss, 2004: 182), while recognizing that their importance is 'not only the work they do, but also the image of the host nation they create…'. Volunteers contribute significantly to the experience of participants and spectators through frequent interactions, and to the public image of the event. If the hours of work provided by the volunteers at the Sydney Games had been paid for it would have added AUD $140 million to the cost of the event – about 5 per cent of the organizing committee's total Games expenditure (Haynes, 2001). Official reports of Olympic Games make little evaluation of the contribution of volunteers to the 'event experience'. In contrast, Cashman's (2006) account of the Sydney Olympic Games emphasized the importance of volunteers to the quality of the event and the emotional legacy, although this is hard to quantify. As a volunteer himself, Cashman had a strong emotional engagement with the Sydney Games and its potential volunteering legacy.

While the use of volunteers at Olympic Games reduces costs and contributes to the 'ambiance' of the event, the Olympic Charter (International Olympic Committee, 2007), stipulating the conditions under which international Olympic committees (IOCs) organize the Games, does not explicitly require the use of volunteers. This has been a tradition consistent with the ethos of amateurism predominating at the inception of the modern Olympic Games in 1894, although London pioneered the use of volunteers at the 1948 Games. Volunteers are mentioned in the IOC *Technical Manual on Workforce*, which gives both guidance and contractual requirements of the host city, and volunteers were the subject of an international symposium promoted by the IOC (Moragas *et al.*, 1999).

The Sydney Olympic Games in 2000 used 70,000 volunteers (Cashman, 2006), Athens 2004 used 65,000 (Karkatsoulis and Michalopoulos, 2005), Beijing 2008 used 100,000 (Auld *et al.*, 2009) and the London 2012 Games will require 70,000 volunteers. Care has to be taken in comparing these figures, as information varies between different sources, including IOC documents, and volunteers may take different roles at different venues. Another source reports the Beijing Olympic Games as including not only 70,000 volunteers at the events themselves but also 1,000,000 'society' volunteers, whose role was mainly related to ensuring good order in society at large, and 200,000 'cheerleading' volunteers, whose role was to enhance the atmosphere of Olympic venues by cheering at appropriate times during events. Cultural traditions in different societies mean that the notion of 'volunteering' will also differ (for example, for China see Zhuang, 2010).

Mega-event volunteers' motivation, satisfaction and management style

A study of 942 volunteers at the Sydney Games, building on previous research into event volunteers, showed that their initial motivations for volunteering were the prestige of the event, the potential to learn, excitement and altruistic motives of 'wanting to put something back into the community' (Green and Chalip, 2004). At the UK 2002 Commonwealth Games in Manchester, the most important reasons for volunteering, as measured by 698 volunteers' responses to rating scales on 30 statements, were (in order of those 'strongly agreeing' with them): 'chance of a lifetime', 72 per cent; 'it will be an exciting experience', 66 per cent; 'it will give me satisfaction to help others', 46 per cent; 'I will be supporting sport', 45 per cent; 'I will meet interesting people', 44 per cent; 'I will be part of a team', 41 per cent (Downward and Ralston, 2005). There are inherent problems in obtaining an accurate view of motivations because of the value-laden nature of statements (for example, people are quite likely to say they want to help the community if they are asked), and these methods also fail to measure the strength of motivations. However, the fact that by January 2008, within a short period of it being advertised, over 120,000 people registered their interest to volunteer at the London 2012 Games supports the view that motives are very strong, and that the prestige/status/high profile of the event is a strong motivator.

Interestingly, both these studies found that motives changed during the course of the experience of volunteering. During the event, challenges include long shifts, the problems of commuting at difficult times, being allocated tasks that volunteers feel unsuited to and other practical problems (Lumsdon *et al.*, 2003). However, a sense of community with the organization and with other volunteers grew to be one of the most important satisfactions. This could be enhanced by team-building initiatives, as in Sydney. In both studies, 'a sense of camaraderie, shared purpose and pulling together' (Green and Chalip, 2004: 64) was what made the experience worthwhile at the end. This suggests that effective volunteer management needs to incorporate awareness of changing motivations into an event volunteer lifestyle approach to ensure that volunteers are managed in a manner conducive to influencing satisfaction, commitment and retention. This could extend to post-Games retention if that is an objective.

These motivations have implications for management. The complexity of the event and the need to ensure effective organization of one of the highest-profile events in the world means that management is likely to adopt a 'rational systems perspective', in which the goal of effectively running the Games is paramount. This guides the organization's structure, design and allocation of resources, including which tasks are performed, formal role definition, what kinds of personnel are employed, and how resources are allocated (Schulz *et al.*, 2011). In terms of events, this is a 'programme management' approach – defining the roles required and slotting volunteers into them. This is in contrast to 'membership management', in which volunteers are allocated roles to match their aspirations (Cuskelly *et al.*, 2006). The very strong motivation of volunteers for high-status events makes a programme management approach possible. However, there may be a delicate balance between this and maintaining volunteers' enthusiasm. Further, to nurture a longer-term commitment, possibly to enable a volunteering legacy, it may be important to provide activities to enhance the emerging sense of camaraderie. A frustration apparent in Cashman's account (2006) of the Sydney Olympic Games is that while this sense of camaraderie was very strong it was not capitalized on and volunteers felt a post-Games vacuum. Volunteers created their own social networks as a focus for their emotional attachment.

Practical considerations also play a role. For example, in Beijing, 83 per cent of Games-time volunteers were university students in Beijing, which facilitated recruitment and political vetting of the potential volunteers and their families. Educational establishments were associated with particular events run close to them, thus avoiding problems related to transport and accommodation for volunteers.

Managing volunteers at London 2012

At the time of writing (November 2011) limited public information is available for the operational details of the London 2012 Games. IOC contractual requirements of host countries and specific IOC guidance are not publicly available, and specific management practices in the host country are considered confidential. LOCOG members with access to them are required to sign a confidentiality agreement, and this extends to publishers of official accounts. This confidentiality prevents media criticism of details that are kept secret, and may also aid security. But a negative implication is that such secrecy may invite ill-informed speculative criticism. Thus any pre-event account of management at the 2012 Games is inherently limited in terms of what it can contain, and must take pains to avoid criticism that might not have arisen were the full picture open to scrutiny.

Recruitment and selection

London 2012 has dubbed its Olympic volunteers 'Games Makers'. By January 2011, far more people than required had applied for the target 70,000 places, which allowed recruitment to be highly selective. Discussions with rejected applicants suggest that their rejections may have been because of conditions they indicated on the application form. For example, a couple that appeared very suitable requested they be allocated roles together, as volunteering would be their summer holiday. Similarly, a doctor experienced in managing multiple accidents requested some remuneration for giving up his hospital work, and this would have made him unacceptable.

Thus responses on the application form must have been used as initial criteria to secure an interview. It is not known whether Criminal Record Bureau (CRB) checks were also used at this stage. Interviews were conducted from February 2011, in London and (some) in the regions. Interviews were conducted by 'Event Trailblazers', who were themselves volunteers (London 2012, 2011a). Since January 2009, over 400 Trailblazers have been recruited to help with preparation for the Games, so interviewing potential volunteers was only one of their tasks. They work a minimum of one day a week for four months. Wherever possible they can choose the day they work. Trailblazers do not necessarily have previous interviewing experience, but they were provided with training. They probably had to take a CRB check – but, as with Games Makers, it is not known what level of offending history would debar an applicant from volunteering. Trailblazers were provided with refreshments and a shirt with a Games logo on it, but not with tickets for the Games or travel expenses. It is an IOC policy that volunteers are not remunerated. Thus the commitment required, in both time and travel costs (Trailblazers might come from a wide area), could be considerable. Consistent with LOCOG policy, Trailblazers had to sign a confidentiality agreement before their first shift.

Guidance stated that 'it's important that you reflect our values. Selection event volunteers should be inspirational, open, respectful, team-focused, distinctive and have a "can do" attitude' (London 2012, 2011b), so these are the values that would also be looked for in potential Games Makers.

Related volunteer programmes

Personal Best

Funding for the Personal Best programme associated with the 2012 Olympic and Paralympic Games came from the European Social Fund, the London Development Agency and the London boroughs themselves. Personal Best was a programme of personal development aimed at people disengaged from the labour market and those who are the most disadvantaged in their communities. The programme ran from 2006 to 2011 and was modelled on the pre-volunteer programme (PVP) developed for the 2002 Commonwealth Games in Manchester, with the same individual responsible for designing, developing and running both programmes. This model was also rolled out across the nine regions of England and a pilot delivered by Glasgow East Regeneration, preparing for the Commonwealth Games in Scotland in 2014.

Personal Best's objectives were to provide participants with vocational training and a qualification to help them enter employment, to enable some of them to secure roles as volunteers for the Olympic and Paralympic Games, and to provide a long-term pool of volunteers that would be available for future events.

The aim of producing a pool of volunteers to act at events reflected the way the PVP at the 2002 Commonwealth Games had led to a volunteering legacy in the form of a volunteer–event broker organization called Manchester Event Volunteers (Nichols and Ralston, 2011a, b). Manchester Event Volunteers (MEV) evolved to provide not only a broker service between a pool of trained and experienced volunteers and events, but also to contribute to the development of good practice in volunteer management by advising event managers new to using volunteers and only promoting events that met good standards of volunteer management. Between 2002 and 2009 MEV directed volunteers towards over 1,000 events, with associated economic benefits for the region (Nichols and Ralston, 2011).

Personal Best participants were engaged by paid outreach workers. They completed a programme of 120 guided learning hours, over a maximum period of 12 weeks. This included two units (out of nine), entitled 'Becoming a Volunteer' and 'Volunteering and the Olympics'. A final unit was 'Preparing for and Reflecting on a Voluntary Placement'. At completion, participants were awarded a Level 1 award in Event Volunteering.

The catalyst inspiring people to take part in the programme was the opportunity to secure an interview to be a 2012 Games Maker. This was the incentive and the 'hook' at the 2002 Commonwealth Games PVP. However, many participants were more strongly motivated by the opportunity to develop their employment skills. This reflected the PB programme's London launch in 2007, five years before the London 2012 Games, when the opportunity to volunteer at the Games was less immediate – the PVP was developed and delivered closer in time to the 2012 Commonwealth Games, which provided a much greater association with games-time volunteering opportunities.

Personal Best aimed to engage 20,000 participants, and for between 7,000 and 10,000 to complete the programme. PB was obliged to provide LOCOG with 7,000 names for potential interviews as Games Makers. If all had been selected these would have accounted for 10 per cent of the Games Makers. PB graduates were supported through the Games Maker application process to ensure that all relevant sections of the application form were completed to satisfy the initial criteria for selection. Most PB graduates needed help to do this. One-to-one support was provided by British Telecommunications (BT) as a corporate social responsibility (CSR) programme, and by Learn Direct Centres across London.

The PB strategy and business plan had to be written before the Olympic volunteer strategy was developed, as the Mayor's office was keen to pilot the programme and maximize the opportunity for Londoners. The application window to be Games Maker opened and closed in 2010, nearly two years before the 2012 Games. This was to allow sufficient time for recruiting/selecting and training the 70,000 Games Makers. Therefore, only PB graduates completing the programme by October 2010 would have had a chance to apply.

Experience of the PVP in Manchester showed that, as the date of the Games drew nearer, the incentive of being able to apply to become a Commonwealth Games volunteer had a stronger impact on motivating those most disengaged from the labour market. Further, the close liaison between the PVP and the Commonwealth Games organizers allowed late applications for Commonwealth Games volunteering roles to be made by those completing the PVP.

PB plans had envisaged being able to continue operating through 2011, and still being able to offer participants the incentive of being able to apply to be a Games Maker. However, the earlier cut-off time for applicants for the Games Maker programme reduced the effectiveness of PB in targeting the most 'hard to reach' groups, and meant that from October 2010 recruitment to PB ceased. Public funding for the London PB programme ceased in December 2010.

Sport Makers

Sport Makers is one of several programmes predicated on the assumption that the Games in London would provide a catalyst for individuals to become involved in volunteering – in this case, to promote sport. This programme is run by Sport England, funded by £4 million from the National Lottery (Sport England, 2011b). It aims to engage 50,000 new volunteers in sport: 40,000 will attend an orientation workshop and be deployed through county sport partnerships to opportunities to give ten hours of volunteering each. These will be through sports events, sports clubs, or to act as individual animators who will promote sport in an informal manner. A target of 20,000 volunteers will continue to volunteer after the initial ten hours. The launch information (Sport England, 2011b) announced that those completing the ten voluntary hours might be eligible for a ticket for the Olympic or Paralympic Games, and the programme started recruiting in October 2011. Up to 25 November, 3,735 people had booked to attend orientation workshops and 2,427 had attended 62 workshops. By December 2012, Sport England had negotiated a link between Games Makers and Sport Makers. LOCOG will promote the opportunity to take part in Sport Makers to Games Maker applicants who are not invited to an interview to be a Games Maker. LOCOG will also promote Sport Makers on their website, and on a Games Maker social network site, which 'went live' in early 2012.

The Sport Makers programme will be evaluated. However, it will be challenging to monitor the sports opportunities offered and the number of hours that volunteers contribute because new volunteers will not want to be burdened by a complex recording system, and because of the informal nature of some of the volunteering and participation. The possibility of an Olympic ticket may provide an incentive for volunteers to record their time contributed, but this will only apply before the Games, and the programme is due to run until March 2013. If successful, Sport Makers will provide 20,000 new volunteers in sport. If a third of these are in sports clubs it will go some way towards alleviating the problems that 53 per cent of clubs experience in recruiting new volunteers (Sport and Recreation Alliance, 2011) and thus add to their capacity to provide sports opportunities. Across the UK this would equate to about two new volunteers per club. These new volunteers will be able to expand clubs' capacity to offer opportunities to participate in sport, if they bring specific skills – such as sport coaching or team administration – and if their contribution can be rapidly built into the club structure. One hopes that this will be the case. However, as only 2,427 had attended an orientation workshop by November 2011, there will probably be a further drop-out between attendance and deployment and only some volunteers will bring the skills that can significantly add to clubs' capacity, the programme's ability to expand participation opportunities offered by sports clubs in time to meet a potential surge in demand for participation stimulated by the Olympic Games may be limited.

It is difficult to speculate on the impact of Sport Makers as the programme is developing at the time of writing, December 2011. (An update provided by Sport England in May 2012 reported that 29,000 people had registered with Sport Makers; 15,205 had attended an orientation workshop and 2,000 had completed a minimum of ten hours of 'Sport Making'. County Sport Partnerships report a considerable difference between actual hours of sport volunteering and hours recorded on the web-based system. Thus about 2,000 new volunteers may be in place to facilitate extra sports participation inspired at the time of the Olympics.) For example, ten national governing bodies of sport have already made links between their own volunteer promotion schemes and the Sport Makers website (www.sportmakers.co.uk), and more are starting to do this. Each county sport partnership may have different deployment opportunities. It is not known how much impact the work of Sport Makers acting as individual animateurs will have. Will recruitment peak around the time of the Games? If the Olympic Games stimulate significant numbers of new volunteers this will be against the national trend, which has seen a decline in formal volunteering since 2001 (National Statistics, 2011).

Other programmes

Several other programmes appear to be similarly predicated on an assumption that the Olympic event will generate a surge of enthusiasm for volunteering: 'The London 2012 "Changing Places" programme encourages volunteers to get out and transform their local area' (London, 2012, 2012c) – for example, by removing graffiti; 'London Ambassadors' are volunteers who will welcome visitors to London. By November 2011, 12,000 people had been interviewed for these roles. Young volunteers were recruited to help act as competitors at practice events. The 'Inspire' programme allows non-commercial organizations to link new events and projects officially to the Olympic and Paralympic Games, although only some of these are concerned with volunteers.

Apart from Sport Makers, it is not clear whether any of these programmes have a direct method of connecting with the large number of people who volunteered to be Games Makers, but who will not be accepted. With respect to sport, in 2008 it was suggested that the extremely large number of people registering an interest in becoming Games Makers offered the opportunity to channel these applicants towards volunteering in sports delivery organizations, such as sports clubs or through sport event broker organizations. This could enhance opportunities for others, especially young people, to participate in sport, while a record of volunteering could have been taken into consideration in selecting Games Makers (Nichols and Ojala, 2008). However, the fact that Sport England and LOCOG did not make a formal link between Sport Makers and Games Makers until three months after Sport Makers was launched does not suggest a strategic approach to using the Games to stimulate sports participation. In relation to youth sport, Lord Moynihan, who will manage the British team for the Games,

> said that since the UK won the 2012 bid in 2005 politicians have failed to honour pledges to drive through a national, sporting revolution at school and grassroots levels … barring a last minute 'step change' in policy to build better links between schools, local sports clubs and volunteers, the Games would spur precious little improvement.
>
> *(Guardian, 2011)*

A strategy for a volunteering legacy, or an opportunity lost?

The experience of the 2002 Commonwealth Games was that, before the Games, the plans for a volunteer legacy were a vague aspiration, discussed up to two years before the Games, but with no details in terms of who was responsible, what creating a volunteer legacy would involve and who would pay for it. It was impossible to make detailed plans less than two years before the Games, as the priority was to make the Games function. The legacy that emerged in the form of a volunteer development and broker organization – Manchester Event Volunteers, linking volunteers with events – was unanticipated, and in some respects fortuitous (Nichols and Ralston, 2011). However, it provided an example of a potential legacy for the London 2012 Games.

Claims for an anticipated legacy have become an essential part of bids to host the Olympic Games and other mega sports events (Gold and Gold, 2007). But, as the aptly titled 'After the Gold Rush' conference (Vigor *et al.*, 2004) noted, the evidence for several of these claims is not strong. This is partly because, as Gold and Gold put it in relation to the Olympic Games, 'what is certain is that the circus will have left town long before the day of reckoning arrives' (Gold and Gold, 2007: 320). The point is that, similarly to the 2002 Commonwealth Games, the organization responsible for delivering the Games – the London Organizing Committee for the Olympic and Paralympic Games (LOCOG) – will not exist after the Games and did not exist when the bid to run the Games was made.

During 2005–2006 a volunteer strategy group prepared detailed plans for generating a volunteering legacy from the 2012 Games. A team of five part-time and full-time officers, seconded from government, non-department public bodies and Volunteering England, was supported by a strategy group of approximately 30 members, representing a wide range of organizations. These included the Learning and Skills Council, Cabinet Office, DCMS, Department for Education and Skills, Youth Sport Trust, British Olympic Association, Sport England, UK Sport and CCPR (now Sport and Recreation Alliance). The group had a Chair, who was passionate and visionary about the potential of the Games to make a step-change to volunteering. Under the leadership of the Chair, the strategy development process had a strong sense of purpose and collaboration, which had the potential to be maintained beyond the Games – a legacy in itself! The strategy was developed around three phases – pre-games, Games and post-games – in the recognition that these phases had to be connected if a legacy were to be achieved. This approach had not been taken before.

Within the strategy some proposals might have appeared 'bold' but were designed to develop volunteering. For example, it proposed that recruitment would be devolved to the nations and regions. This would encourage a regional legacy as groups of volunteers returned to their regions after the Games and carried on expressing a collective enthusiasm and sense of camaraderie through local volunteering, as was demonstrated by Manchester Event Volunteers after the 2002 Commonwealth Games and the experience of Sydney. Devolving recruitment in this way would be at the expense of central control. Similarly, to promote youth volunteering a minimum age of 14 was recommended, with a small target of carefully selected volunteers in the age category 14–16. The carefully selected group would be recruited from existing youth volunteering/leadership programmes and, as such, would be some of the most gifted and trustworthy young leaders in the country, who it was felt deserved the opportunity to participate in the Games and were perfectly capable of performing certain volunteering roles. By November 2006, 15 sets of detailed project plans had been drawn up for the following year for areas of the strategy, including: volunteers' roles and numbers; engaging young people; event volunteering (to develop a plan for events volunteering linked to 2012); volunteer accommodation and hosting; research and evaluation (devising an action plan for research and evaluation to cover pre-Games initiatives, the Games-time programme and legacy); and designing a pre-volunteer programme. In addition, job descriptions were written for a staffing structure to implement the plans. The project plans were designed to support the implementation of the strategy with immediate effect, with many of the organizations involved in strategy development being invited to play a role.

While the strategy was presented informally to LOCOG senior management in late 2006, it is unknown how it was used to influence LOCOG's thinking, the influence it might have had over the final volunteer strategy and how the final strategy was devised. In early 2007 LOCOG appointed staff that had been involved in the Sydney 2000 volunteering programme. This allowed expertise and experience from previous Games to be used in planning for London 2012; however, this coincided with a 'tailing off' of goodwill and collaboration amongst volunteering partners, which had been achieved via the strategy process up to that point. It may have signalled the start of LOCOG focusing purely on the Games-time programme (i.e. the middle third of the strategy) rather than the strategy as a whole, in which the three linked phases were seen as important in generating a volunteer legacy.

Conclusion

Volunteers are used at the Olympic Games because it is traditional to do so, because it is expected by the IOC that volunteer enthusiasm will add to the atmosphere of the event and the quality of experience, and possibly because the contribution of volunteers enables the event to be run more cheaply. For many volunteers, the rewards of being an Olympic volunteer are valued as a 'once in a lifetime' experience. The extremely strong motivations of volunteers and the complexity of the event means that a 'programme management' approach to organizing volunteers is always likely to prevail, but management still has to balance this with recognizing the motivations of volunteers and showing they are valued. If a volunteering legacy was a LOCOG objective it might be reflected in a strategy for managing volunteers before, during and after the Games. But the details of any such strategy are not known. However, the priority of LOCOG is to run the Games successfully, and this is reflected in IOC advice. The London 2012 Games may generate a surge of volunteering activity that may be taken advantage of by other programmes – time will tell. This chapter has been limited by the confidential nature of LOCOG's organization and has had to interpret only data that is in the public domain. It was completed in December 2011, while programmes such as Sport Makers were still developing and while LOCOG was still completing its volunteer selection and deployment. Gaps in information may be filled as the event unfolds.

Acknowledgement

Thank you to Mumtaz Bashir, head of the Personal Best programme, London 2012, for information.

References

Auld, C., Cuskelly, G. and Harrington, M. (2009) 'Managing volunteers to enhance the legacy potential of major events', in T. Baum, M. Deery, C. Hanlon, L. Lockstone and K. Smith (eds) *People and Work in Events and Conventions: A research perspective*, Oxfordshire: CABI (pp. 181–192).

Cashman, R. (2006) *The Bitter-Sweet Awakening: The legacy of the Sydney 2000 Olympic Games*, Petersham, NSW: Walla Walla Press.

Cuskelly, G., Hoye, R. and Auld, C. (2006) *Working with Volunteers in Sport: Theory and practice*, London: Routledge.

Green, C. and Chalip, L. (2004) 'Paths to volunteer commitment: lessons from the Sydney Olympic Games', in R. A. Stebbins and M. Graham (eds) *Volunteering as Leisure: Leisure as volunteering*, Wallingford: CABI (pp. 49–67).

Downward, P. and Ralston, R. (2005) 'Volunteer motivation and expectations prior to the XVII Commonwealth Games in Manchester, UK: A quantitative study', *Tourism and Hospitality: Planning and development*, 2 (I): 17–26.

Guardian (2011) 'London 2012 will fail to deliver lasting legacy for young, says Lord Moynihan', 19 November. Online: www.guardian.co.uk/sport/2011/nov/19/moynihan-attack-on-olympic-missed-opportunities#start-of-comments (accessed 24 November 2011).

Gold, J. R. and Gold, M. M. (eds) (2007) *Olympic Cities: City agendas, planning and the World's Games, 1896–2012*, London: Routledge.

Haynes, J. (2001) *Socio-Economic Impact of the Sydney 2000 Olympic Games*, Barcelona: Centre d'Estudis Olimpics UAB. Online: http://olympicstudies.uab.es/pdf/wp094_eng.pdf (accessed 17 December 2009).

Horne, J. and Manzenreiter, W. (2006) *Sports Mega-Events: Social scientific analysis of a global phenomenon*, Oxford: Blackwell.

International Olympic Committee (2007) *Olympic Charter*, Lausanne: IOC.

Karkatsoulis, P. and Michalopoulos, N. (2005) 'The national identity as a motivational factor for better performance in the public sector: the case of the volunteers of the Athens 2004 Olympic Games', *International Journal of Productivity and Performance Management*, 54 (7): 579–593.

London 2012 (2011a) 'Making the games happen', www.london2012.com/get-involved/volunteer/other-ways-to-volunteer/trailblazers.php (accessed 11 November 2011).

London 2012 (2011b) 'Selection event trailblazer — questions and answers', www.london2012.com/documents/volunteering/trailblazer-faqs.pdf (accessed 11 November 2011).

London 2012 (2011c) 'Changing Places', www.london2012.com/making-it-happen/sustainability/changing-places/ (accessed 11 November, 2011).

Lumsdon, L., Ralston, R. and Downward, P. (2003) 'An Evaluation of the Motivations, Expectations and Experiences of Volunteers prior to and during the XVII Commonwealth Games, Manchester, UK, Report 1: Quantitative analysis', UK Sport.

Moragas, M., Moreno, A. and Puig, N. (eds) (1999) *Volunteers, Global Society and the Olympic Movement*, Lausanne: IOC.

National Statistics (2011) *Citizenship Survey: April 2010 – March 2011, England*, www.communities.gov.uk/publications/corporate/statistics/citizenshipsurveyq4201011 (accessed 8 November 2011).

Nichols, G. and Ojala, E. (2008) 'A model for volunteering', *Recreation*, January/February, 67 (1): 28–29.

Nichols, G. and Ralson, R. (2011a) *Manchester Event Volunteers: A role model and a legacy*, University of Sheffield Management School. Online: www.mgt.dept.shef.ac.uk/ResearchReports/2011-11MEV_REPORT.pdf.

Nichols, G. and Ralston, R. (2011b) 'Lessons from the volunteering legacy of the 2002 Commonwealth Games', *Urban Studies*, January, 49 (1): 165–180.

Poynter, G. and MacRury, I. (eds) (2009) *Olympic Cities: 2012 and the remaking of London*, Farnham: Ashgate.

Preuss, H. (2004) *The Economics of Staging the Olympic Games: A comparison of the Games 1972–2008*, Cheltenham: Edward Elgar.

Roche, M. (2000) *Mega-Events and Modernity*, London: Routledge.

Sadd, D. and Jones, I. (2009) 'Long-term legacy implications for Olympic Games', in R. Raj and J. Musgrave (eds) *Event Management and Sustainability*, Wallingford: CABI (pp. 90–98).

Schulz, J., Nichols, G. and Auld, C. (2011) 'Issues in the management of voluntary sports organisations and volunteers', in B. Houlihan and M. Green (eds) *Handbook of Sports Development*, London: Routledge (pp. 432–445).

Sport and Recreation Alliance (2011) *Survey of Sports Clubs 2011*, London: SARA.

Sport England (2011a) 'Be a sporting hero', www.sportengland.org/about_us/our_news/sport_makers.aspx (accessed 7 November 2011).

Sport England (2011b) 'Sport Makers', www.sportengland.org/about_us/places_people_play/sport_makers.aspx (accessed 15 April 2011).

Toohey, K. and Veal, A. J. (2007) *The Olympic Games: A social science perspective*, Wallingford: CABI.

Vigor, A., Mean, M. and Tims, C. (eds) (2004) *After the Gold Rush: A sustainable Olympics for London*, London: Demos Institute for Public Policy Research.

Zhuang, C. (2011) 'Volunteer selection and social, human and political capital: a case of Beijing 2008', presentation at Sport Volunteer Research Network, 7 April 2011: www.sportandrecreation.org.uk/campaigning/policy-areas/community-sports-clubs/sports-volunteering-research-network.

Zhuang, J. (2010) 'Beijing 2008: volunteerism in Chinese culture and its Olympic interpretation and influence', *International Journal of History of Sport*, 27 (16): 2842–2862.

PART 4

Engaging sports

17

NATIONAL OLYMPIC AND PARALYMPIC GOVERNING BODIES OF SPORT INVOLVEMENT WITH THE GAMES[1]

Vassil Girginov and Nick Rowe

Introduction

This chapter examines the involvement of the UK national governing bodies of sport (NGB) with the 2012 London Olympic and Paralympic Games. This is an underexplored topic, which has been further relegated to a back-seat position as the main focus of most policy, economic and sport analysis has been on the effectiveness of the public investments and the legacies of the Games. Despite increased government and academic interest in the potential of mega events to contribute to the political, social and economic agenda, very little is known about the role of mega events in enhancing NGBs' capacity and operational effectiveness.

NGBs' role in helping to deliver a successful Olympic Games is multifaceted and crucial over the three phases of the event. Before the Games, NGBs are responsible for the development of the whole sport, including preparing athletes, coaches and referees, volunteers and other technical personnel and providing a range of services. During the Games, it is largely NGBs' members who staff the events in various capacities and provide valuable expertise, without which there would be no competitions. After the event, NGBs analyse athletes' performances and summarise the learning that has taken place in the run-up to and during the Games, and draw strategies for the next Olympic cycle and beyond.

NGBs are also central to the governance of sport in each participating country, as they constitute the backbone of National Olympic Committees, which are responsible for entering athletes in the Games. Moreover, NGBs' representatives sit on various governing bodies of international sport federations (IF), which control and run the Olympic programme for each sport. To be able to undertake their work successfully, NGBs have to forge partnerships with various public and commercial agencies to enhance their capacity.

In the context of the UK sport system, NGBs have a wider sports-development role to grow and sustain participation in their sport and to deliver a community sport-participation legacy that draws on the inspirational effect of the London Olympic and Paralympic Games. NGBs have been considered by the government as the main sport delivery agencies, with funding from Sport England supported by a 'Whole Sport Plan' to deliver increased participation and to nurture and develop talent (Sport England, 2008). NGBs' central position in the delivery system has recently been reinforced by the government's new youth sport strategy, 'Creating a Sporting Habit for Life' (DCMS, 2012).

Despite NGBs' historically established voluntary roots, increasingly they have been under pressure to modernise and become more professionalised through building their organisational capacities to sustain sport and deliver a range of social and economic benefits (Houlihan and Green, 2009; UK Sport, 2003). Mega sporting events such as the Olympic Games present NGBs with unique opportunities to capitalise on their symbolic and material power. Mega events possess three essential characteristics that can be strategically utilised to enhance the capacity of NGBs. First, mega sporting events have a liminoid character, which is marked by a sense of celebration and camaraderie (Chalip, 2006). Second, they can generate a sense of community and foster social interactions across groups, ages and geographical locations. Third, mega events can mobilise a great deal of public and private investment and can address a range of longstanding issues in a relatively short period of time. These three characteristics are central to the work of any NGB and have direct implications for their organisational capacity and operational effectiveness. Mega sporting events, therefore, present not only a platform for showcasing athletes' achievements but a valuable resource, which can be leveraged to enhance NBGs' overall capabilities. The UK has hosted around 80 major international events in the four years up to London 2012, and typically the country hosts over 100 major international events each year.

Strengthening the work of NGBs is of strategic importance as they have been described as 'custodians of their sport' (UK Sport, 2003) and entrusted with managing significant public funds and with providing services to a vast network of sport clubs, members and millions of participants. The latest 'Active People Survey' shows that there are 6.927 million regular adult sport participants in England (people participating three times a week for at least 30 minutes at moderate intensity) (Sport England, 2011). Those sports boost an active membership of over 5,200,000 people and support a network of an estimated 150,000 affiliated clubs, and over 3 million adults in England or 7.3 per cent of the adult population who volunteer in sport for at least one hour a week (Sport England, 2011). Tables 17.1 and 17.2 show the public funding of NGBs for mass and elite sport respectively. Between 2009 and 2013, Sport England is investing £450 million through 46 NGBs to deliver its strategy, 'Growth, Sustain, Excel'. In addition to allocations to individual NGBs, there is over £3 million for improving their governance and £16 million for coaching development. UK Sport is the government agency responsible for elite sport and through its 'World Class' programme funds only sports on the Olympic and Paralympic Games programme. Both agencies make their funding available against agreed targets, and failure to deliver may result in a withdrawal of or reduction in funds.

London 2012 and NGBs: an evolving relation

The link between the Olympic Games and NGBs is not as straightforward as it may seem. This is because of different sports' histories, structures and capacity to perform at the Games, as well as their international development and contribution to the Olympic programme. There are over 300 NGBs recognised by the five sports councils in the UK (i.e. England, Scotland, Wales, Northern Ireland and UK Sport), with large variations in size, turnover, organisational structure, and the number of member clubs and individual members. The UK 'sportspace' is dominated by three 'off the scale' NGBs, with the largest of these having a turnover of around £120 million. The majority of NGBs are small-scale organisations, with a quarter having a turnover of under £50,000 and the remaining 75 per cent of under £1 million. Forty-five per cent of NGBs have less than 100 member clubs and only 11 per cent over 1,000, with a further 11 per cent having between 500 and 1,000 member clubs. NGBs with a turnover of £100,000 rarely have full-time management staff. It is only when an NGB has a turnover of over £500,000 that a core management team becomes present (UK Sport, 2003). NGBs' structural and functional variations mean that their engagement with the Games will also vary. Given this diversity, it is only to be expected that NGBs will be variously placed to harness the resources offered by the Olympic and Paralympic Games.

The place of the 26 sports on the London Games' programme is not a 'given' and has to be established and maintained in competition with other sports. Another important consideration is that in order to enhance their chances for success at the Olympic Games many countries, including the UK, have categorised sports on the basis of their potential to win medals. Table 17.3 shows how the three main priority group sports in the UK were categorised in 2004. As can be seen from the table a number of sports on the Olympic programme, such as handball, wrestling and weightlifting, did not even feature in any of the three categories. Such categorisations have significant implications for NGBs' funding, media presence and public awareness, as well as for building their organisational capacities. It should be noted, however, that the 2004 UK sports categorisation was superseded by a new funding process for 46 NGBs, which is in line with Sport England strategy (2008–2009). UK Sport also developed a new 'No Compromise' approach designed to support sports in winning medals. The wider point is that the Olympic Games both creates and limits the opportunities for NGBs and sports development nationally. Sports on the Olympic programme inevitably receive greater public and commercial support and media exposure, while other sports struggle to compete for the same resources.

Table 17.1 Sport England funding for mass sport 2009–2013

Angling	£1,561,906	Modern pentathlon	£886,496
Archery	£857,989	Mountaineering	£1,287,850
Athletics	£20,447,169	Movement and dance	£741,552
Badminton	£20,800,000	Netball	£17,658,116
Baseball and softball	£2,700,000	Orienteering	£2,275,000
Basketball	£8,200,000	Rounders	£2,200,000
Basketball (wheelchair)	£727,683	Rowing	£9,100,000
Boccia	£8,126,041	Rugby (wheelchair)	£480,000
Bowls	£756,750	Rugby League	£29,408,341
Boxing	£4,700,000	Rugby Union	£31,219,542
Canoeing	£8,470,577	Sailing	£9,619,542
Cricket	£38,003,357	Shooting	£750,000
Cycling	£24,288,000	Snowsport	£985,000
Equestrian	£4,268,002	Squash	£13,096,192
Fencing	£1,041,413	Swimming	£20,875,000
Football	£25,635,000	Table tennis	£9,301,404
Goalball	£354,000	Taekwondo	£750,000
Golf	£12,851,500	Tennis	£26,800,000
Gymnastics	£11,388,481	Triathlon	£4,700,000
Handball	£645,300	Volleyball	£5,600,000
Hockey	£11,511,000	Waterskiing	£95,1373
Judo	£10,241,001	Weightlifting	£609,094
Lacrosse	£2,210,993	Wrestling	£331,824
		Subtotal	£402,102,950

Source: Sport England (2009).

There is also a positive correlation between international success and public funding for sport. As Tables 17.1 and 17.2 demonstrate, the four top-funded elite and mass sports are athletics, cycling, rowing and swimming, each receiving over £25 million for the 2009–2013 Olympic cycle. These four sports delivered 4, 14, 6 and 6 medals from the 2008 Beijing Olympic Games respectively, or 30 out of 47 medals won by Team GB.

The relationship between NGBs and the London Games can be described as evolving. The London bid was launched after three previous unsuccessful attempts by the cities of Birmingham (1992) and Manchester (1996 and 2000). Following a comprehensive analysis of the lessons learned from those bids, the British Olympic Association (BOA) arrived at the conclusion that only a London bid stood a chance of winning. But the BOA's 1995 decision to nominate London had to be approved first by the 35 NGBs of which it is constituted. NGBs have always been supportive of an Olympic bid but they also sought assurances that if successful it would be used to stimulate the development of mass participation as well as elite sport. Sport England represented the collective voice of NGBs and clearly articulated this position at a Parliamentary Select Committee hearing in 2003 as a condition for backing the bid (House of Commons, Culture, Media and Sport Committee, 2003). At the time when the bid for the 2012 Games was being put together the government published one of its most influential policy documents, 'Game Plan' (DCMS, 2002). This document was designed fundamentally to reshape the UK

Table 17.2 UK Sport funding for elite Olympic and Paralympic sport 2009–2013

Sport	*Award*	*Sport*	*Award*
Archery	£4,408,000	Modern pentathlon	£6,284,800
Athletics	£25,073,000	Rowing	£27,240,700
Badminton	£7,428,900	Sailing	£22,926,600
Basketball	£8,575,000	Shooting	£2,450,866
Boxing (amateur)	£9,542,400	Swimming	£25,096,600
Canoeing	£16,161,700	Synchronised swimming	£3,389,300
Cycling	£26,390,300	Table tennis	£1,207,848
Diving	£6,523,700	Taekwondo	£4,829,600
Equestrian	£13,382,100	Triathlon	£5,285,200
Fencing	£2,519,335	Volleyball	£3,508,077
Gymnastics	£10,752,600	Water polo	£2,902,039
Handball	£2,896,721	Weightlifting	£1,360,157
Hockey	£14,981,200	Wrestling	£1,435,210
Judo	£7,484,100	**Total**	**£264,036,053**
Paralympic sport			
Adaptive rowing	£2,324,300	Judo (visually impaired)	£1,289,400
Boccia	£2,324,300	Para-cycling	£3,776,500
Disability archery	£2,147,700	Para-equestrian dressage	£3,600,500
Disability athletics	£6,685,000	Powerlifting	£1,087,700
Disability sailing	£1,742,900	Sitting volleyball	£764,961
Disability shooting	£2,072,900	Wheelchair basketball	£4,469,930
Disability swimming	£10,428,650	Wheelchair fencing	£545,892
Disability table tennis	£1,686,400	Wheelchair rugby	£2,350,600
Goalball	£502,453	Wheelchair tennis	£799,600
		Total	**£48,599,686**

Source: UK Sport (2011).

sport system. It also made a specific reference to the role of mega sporting events in promoting sport and states, that 'hosting events is not an effective, value for money method of achieving ... a sustained increase in mass participation...' (DCMS, 2002, p. 75).

Although sport administrators have always been aware of the potential of the Games to boost sport nationally, at the time the bid was publicly announced the political climate was not particularly conducive for establishing the link between the Olympic Games and the mission of NGBs to develop the whole sport. This position, however, was gradually about to change. In 2004, Sport England published its policy document 'The Framework for Sport in England', in which it declared its commitment to make England the most successful sporting nation by 2020. The framework was based on three main pillars: providing strategic leadership; introducing whole sport plans for NGBs; and putting in place a robust evidence-based investment policy. The framework also clearly identified the role of a London Games in helping deliver this new vision: 'Backing the bid to host the 2012 Olympic and Paralympic Games in London, to enhance the national sporting infrastructure, create a sustainable legacy for sport, and deliver impact on economic and social issues within London' (Sport England, 2004, p. 6). Although the document makes no specific reference to the link between the Games and NGBs, it nonetheless highlighted the importance of building NGBs' capabilities so they can better respond to the challenges of modernisation. By putting sports in three main categories, the framework also implicitly established one of the main criteria for funding – being an Olympic NGB.

As the economic and social impacts of sport have increasingly been recognised globally (Preuss, 2004), in 2005 UK Sport developed a guide for major sports events. The guide specifically puts forward a set of criteria for a successful event and encourages NGBs to use them in determining their approach to an event. These include: using mega events to help improve athlete performance (i.e. medals); to raise awareness of sport; facility development or upgrade; financial gain; gaining international profile; training of personnel/volunteers; achieving positive local economic impact; attracting new sponsors/supporters/partners; and helping the development of grassroots sport (UK Sport, 2005, p. 2). It is worth mentioning that although an earlier major UK Sport policy document, *Investing in Change* (UK Sport, 2003), clearly recognises governance and strategic planning as central issues for NGBs, the guide for major sports events does not establish a link between the role of mega events and improvements in these two areas.

More specifically, in relation to London 2012, UK Sport in 2007 followed up with 'Mission 2012' (see http://www.uksport.gov.uk/pages/mission-2012/), which focuses on the performance of Olympic sport NGBs in three dimensions: athlete (focusing on athletes' performances, development, health and well-being); system (covering issues such as staff, structures, facilities and processes); and climate (relating to the culture, feel and day-to-day operation of the training environment). UK Sport's 2010 report on Mission 2012 (http://www.uksport.gov.uk/news/

Table 17.3 UK sports categorisation

UK-wide priority sports	*England priority sports*	*England development sports*
Athletics, swimming, cycling, rowing, sailing, canoeing, triathlon, judo, gymnastics, equestrian.	Football, tennis, cricket, rugby union, rugby league, golf, hockey, badminton, squash, netball.	Basketball, rounders, softball, baseball, movement and dance, table tennis, volleyball, lacrosse, outdoor pursuits (mountaineering and angling), bowls, karate, boxing.

Source: Sport England (2004, p. 8).

latest-mission-2012-report-shows-british-sport-on-track-for-london) suggested that of the 27 Olympic sports assessed, 12 were rated as green overall (i.e. progress was on track), 15 amber (i.e. increased support/attention was needed) and no sport was given an overall rating of red (i.e. immediate remedial intervention required). The 2011 report largely confirms those performance results that were replicated across the 18 Paralympic sports assessed, with eight having an overall rating of green and no sports with an overall red assessment (UK Sport, 2010, 2011). Despite Mission 2012 being concerned only with the performance of 28 Olympic and 18 Paralympic sports on the Games programme, it nonetheless provides a strong impetus for NGBs to think about making the most of hosting London 2012 for the overall development of their sports.

The UK government's 'Creating a Sporting Habit for Life' policy (DCMS, 2012) recognises that the link between London 2012 and sport development should not be taken for granted. In the words of Jeremy Hunt, Secretary of State for Culture, Olympics, Media and Sport, 'what we've learnt over the last six years is that there can be no "plug and play" sporting legacy from the Games' (DCMS, 2012, p. 1). As a result, the policy envisages a greater and more targeted role for NGBs in delivering the Olympic promises of getting more young people to play sport.

The UK has successfully played host to major sporting events in the past, including the 2002 Manchester Commonwealth Games, which have yielded a great deal of experience and organisational learning. However, nothing could have prepared the sport community for the challenges and opportunities presented by London 2012. For about a year after the Games were awarded in 2005, NGBs collectively experienced the 'now what' moment where everybody was talking about 'the once in a lifetime opportunity' but nothing really substantial was done (Girginov and Hills, 2008). The next section explores more specifically NGBs' involvement with the Games. It draws on an online survey, with 39 out of 54 Sport England funded and other organisations of Olympic, Paralympic and non-Olympic sports carried out in October–November 2011. In total, there were responses from 25 sports on the London 2012 programme and 14 not on the programme, including three Winter Olympic sports and one disability sport. The questionnaire was piloted with two NGBs that provided valuable feedback. The structure of the questionnaire included eight core areas of NGB operations and specific involvement with the Games. The next section presents the results of the study.

NGBs harnessing of the Games

Eight main themes related to NGBs' involvement with the Games are discussed in this section, including general effects, strategy, media and communications, resources, governance, contribution to running the Games, involvement with Games-related programmes and long-term prospects. The main themes of investigation were formulated on the basis of an analysis of the various roles performed by NGBs in running their sports. Good governance is the key that underpins the effectiveness of all NGBs' operations, and funding organisations such as Sport England have been helping them to develop their role holistically, and to make the connections between their different functions more effectively. NGBs' operations are not confined to growing participation and helping athletes excel. Increasingly they also have to forge various public and commercial partnerships, improve their performance planning, bid for major events and be active in international sports politics. To be able to perform their role successfully, NGBs need constantly to build their organisational capacity, and London 2012 presents a rare opportunity in this regard. This study considers a range of NGBs, because the 2012 London Olympic and Paralympic Games provide a catalyst for organisational capacity building, not only for those sports on the Games programme but to sport in the UK in general. Moreover, the Olympic Games was conceived to promote the universal message of sport, as opposed to 26 specific images of it that feature in London 2012. Similarly, the UK government has made a promise to use London 2012 to create a world-class sporting nation, with a combination of government resources and commitment from the sporting community (DCMS, 2007).

The overwhelming majority of the NGBs surveyed (73 per cent) agreed that the Games presented unique opportunities for the development of their sport. However, when probed into the specifics of the inspirational effects of London 2012, answers start to differ along the lines of Olympic or non-Olympic and sports for able-bodied or disabled people. Furthermore, 83 per cent of Olympic and 64 per cent of non-Olympic NGBs stated that they have been able to use the inspirational effect of the Games to increase participation in their sports. Those increases have been achieved mainly through bringing new people into sport (nine and four NGBs respectively) and by getting existing participants to do more (seven NGBs). A much smaller percentage of NGBs (51 per cent) agree that they have been able to use the effect of the Games to increase participation among people with a disability. While 18 Olympic NGBs say they have been successful in attracting more disabled participants, nine non-Olympic NGBs state that they have been unable to capitalise on the opportunity. This difference would suggest that non-Olympic sports have a reduced capacity to promote participation for people with disability, or for seeing the inspirational effect of the Olympic Games. The inspirational effect of the Games to increase the number of affiliated club members was felt by only 18 per cent of NGBs, all of which are on the Olympic programme. For many it would appear that the potential for increases in participation has not been achieved through the formal network of clubs but more on an ad hoc and 'informal' basis.

The initial visionary gap in how best to use the London Games for a nationally coordinated sport development strategy was gradually filled by three consecutive government policy documents. The first document, 'Our Promise for 2012', presented a vision about the role of the Games in society and contained five election-type substantive pledges, one of which was to make the UK a world leading sporting nation (DCMS, 2007).

It was followed by a detailed strategy about how to implement those promises (DCMS, 2008), and since London is hosting both the Olympic and Paralympic Games, in 2009 a legacy plan for disabled people was also produced (DCMS, 2009). Most NGBs (64 per cent) felt that the UK government's positioning and promotion of the Games has provided a positive stimulus for the development of their sport, but some 13 per cent disagreed and 15 per cent neither agreed nor disagreed. All NGBs that disagreed with the positive effects of the government's efforts and two of the undecided were for non-Olympic sports. This is indicative of the divide between these two groups of sports, which was established much earlier (DCMS, 2002; Sport England, 2004), but the Games has reinforced it further.

For nearly ten years, NGBs that have received public funding have been required to develop whole sport plans to help them define their strategic priorities and channel organisational efforts better. NGBs differ markedly in their approach to leveraging the benefits from the Games. Some 18 out of 25 Olympic NGBs saw this as a central part of their overall sport strategy. No NGB of non-Olympic sport considered this to be a strategic issue, but there are a couple of exceptions to developing a strategic approach towards a single issue such as increasing participation in London with the Environment Agency. Under further scrutiny, however, it transpires that only three NGBs have taken a more holistic view of the Olympic Games by specifically incorporating their potential into their whole sport plans. The other NGBs have been using more of a tactical approach by leveraging different programmes, initiatives and areas, thus narrowing the scope of the impact to a limited number of beneficiaries and organisational benefits.

Table 17.4 shows the five areas in which NGBs have developed specific strategies to leverage the Games. It is clear that Olympic NGBs have been more proactive and have, to varying degrees, made concerted efforts to harness the opportunities presented by London 2012, with a particular focus on growing participation and achieving elite success.

There is a strong positive correlation between NGBs' belief in the inspirational effects of the Games and their area-specific strategies for harnessing those benefits. This is particularly evident in increasing participation for the able-bodied (31 NGBs – 23 Olympic and 8 non-Olympic respectively) and people with disabilities (28 NGBs – 20 and 8 respectively), as well as in achieving elite success (24 NGBs – 20 and 4 respectively) and talent development (22 NGBs – 20 and 2 respectively). This finding is supported by NGBs' rating of the impact of the Games on different strategic areas (Table 17.5). In judging the impact of the Games on growing participation, 11 NGBs rated this as low, 11 as medium and 16 as high; 11 NGBs rated the impact on elite success as low, 4 as medium and 17 as high; and 11 NGBs rated the impact on talent development as low, 10 as medium and 11 as high. Table 17.5 shows NGBs' rating of the impact of the Games on their business development. Over a quarter rated the impact of the Olympic Games on their organisational learning and performance management as high, which is close but somehow lower to the felt impact on staff development (23 per cent), as improvements in both areas directly concern the people in the organisation. The area where the lowest impact of the Games was rated is revenue generation, which is discussed in more detail below.

In addition to growing participation and increasing success in elite sport, the Games also provide NGBs with a platform to actively communicate the general message of sport and of their organisation-specific objectives. All Sport England-funded NGBs have well-developed websites and relations with the media, which allows them to use a range of strategies to shape public opinion. As sport is a source of both good and bad stories, 22 NGBs have used the Games to increase positive media coverage. However, this number drops by almost a half, to 13, where disability sport is concerned. Furthermore, only 19 Olympic NGBs managed to secure positive

Table 17.4 NGBs' area-specific strategies for leveraging the benefits of the Olympics

Area	*Olympic NGB*	*Non-Olympic NGB*
Growing sport participation	17	7
Indentifying sport talent	15	0
Developing sport talent	17	1
Achieving elite success	20	0
Improving facilities and equipment	11	4

Table 17.5 NGBs' rating of the impact of the Olympics on their business development

Business area	*Impact*		
	Low	*Medium*	*High*
Staff development	13 (33%)	13 (33%)	9 (23%)
Revenue generation	21 (54%)	6 (15%)	8 (21%)
Organisational learning	13 (33%)	11 (28%)	11 (28%)
Performance management	17 (44%)	6 (15%)	11 (28%)
Innovation	13 (33%)	11 (28%)	10 (26%)

coverage for elite athletes, and 26 NGBs felt that they have been able to increase public awareness of their sport generally, but four NGBs disagreed with the heightened public perceptions. This division of opinion reflects the unequal status and media appeal of different sports, including several on the Olympic programme that are hardly ever televised on terrestrial channels or covered in newspapers. It is worth pointing out that of the 548 hours devoted by the BBC to the UK broadcast of the Beijing Olympic Games, 97 per cent were devoted to the coverage of four sports (i.e. athletics, swimming, gymnastics and cycling) and only 3 per cent to the remaining 22 sports (National Audit Office, 2010).

As chapters 1 and 19 in this volume demonstrate, the Olympic Games provides home NGBs and other organisations with a stimulus for generating additional revenue outside regular government grants and commercial sponsorship. Some of the additional revenue streams include global Olympic and national sponsors' activating budgets, international federations' development programmes, public funding through national, regional and local authorities, as well as targeted support from various charities. A major beneficiary in this regard has been disability sport, as the UK government provides 50 per cent (£95 million) of the cost of the Paralympic Games. The majority of NGBs believe that the Games has further stimulated resources in three main areas – grassroots development (64 per cent), sport talent systems (51 per cent) and international success (59 per cent). However, there are significant variations when the contribution of specific sources of revenue is considered. For example, only 13 NGBs (12 Olympic and 1 non-Olympic respectively) agree that there is increased funding for equipment to support elite athletes, while 19 NGBs (12 and 7 respectively) agree that there is funding to develop outreach participation products and services. A further 15 NGBs (12 and 3 respectively) agree that there is an increase in the level of investment in facility improvement, but 12 NGBs disagree (4 and 8 respectively). Thirteen Olympic NGBs also state that they have been successful in securing increased investment in systems and technology for sport development. What emerges from the findings is that the funding opportunities for sports development presented by the Games have been largely in favour of Olympic sports. Non-Olympic sports struggle to make a case for enhanced financial support, despite the overall potential of the Games for positive inspirational effect.

NGBs' governance has been at the top of the sport policy agenda since 2000. In particular, NGBs that receive public funding are expected to modernise their structures and operations (DCMS, 2002; UK Sport, 2003). The IOC has also recognised improved governance as a critical issue for the Olympic Movement (IOC, 2009). Holmes and colleagues' review of the state of British sport summarises the role of NGBs' governance:

> National governing boards must be structured to ensure their governance is transparent. A governance culture like that of a plc must be adopted, offering public access to accounts, remuneration, compliance and a commentary on major financial decisions. This will allow the public to scrutinise decisions by trustees and ensure they are made by trustees whose interests are those of the sport as a whole rather than narrow, parochial concerns.
>
> *(Holmes et al., 2010, p. 15)*

Effective structures, accountability and transparency of decisions and actions have been defined as the key pillars of good governance (Sport England, 2012).

The enhanced opportunities for organisational development presented by the Games also entail putting in place performance management systems designed to stimulate improvements in governance. Only eight Olympic and one non-Olympic NGB of the 39 surveyed agree that the

Games has helped improve their governance structures and decision-making process. This does not, of course, imply that they have not made these improvements – it is just that these are not seen as being directly connected to the London Games. Seven Olympic NGBs do feel that London 2012 has helped them improve their financial accountability and transparency, but an equal number disagree. Generally, non-Olympic NGBs disagree that the Games has provided any positive stimulus for enhanced governance.

As discussed, NGBs also make significant contributions to the running of the Games. Of the 26 NGBs on the Olympic programme surveyed, 20 have between 1 and 600 of their members directly involved in various capacities. Thirteen Olympic NGBs have between 1 and 500 members contributing to the administration and management of the Games, while no staff from non-Olympic NGBs are involved in this capacity. A further 14 NGBs have between 2 and 35 coaches supporting athletes in the run-up and during the Games; 11 NGBs will see between 2 and 200 members refereeing and officiating; 12 NGBs will contribute between 1 and 50 volunteers, and 10 NGBs between 1 and 100 technical personnel. The use of non-Olympic NGBs' staff and members in the running of the Games has been virtually non-existent, with only one organisation being involved with the Cultural Olympiad. While the highly specialised nature of Olympic competitions clearly requires the top expertise available, certainly there are areas of Games operations, such as volunteering and general administration, where non-Olympic NGB staff could have been involved and benefited from the experience.

NGBs are not only making a valuable contribution to the Games but are gaining various benefits as well: 13 of the NGBs feel that their involvement is worth doing for staff development and organisational learning, and 12 NGBs agree that the Games is helping them enhance their influence on the international administration of sport. Two NGBs disagree, however, and seven neither agree nor disagree. The involvement of 17 NGBs includes dedicated staff time or secondment, but only five have had their staff replaced and seven their staff compensated for.

Another important aspect of the NGBs' involvement with London 2012 concerns participating and running a number of Games-related programmes. Table 17.6 summarises NGB engagement with eight major national and international initiatives. As can be seen, involvement varies significantly across different programmes, with the greatest uptake being in three key priority areas: volunteering (Sport Makers – 24 NGBs); mass participation (Gold Challenge – 17 NGBs); and coaching (Sportivate – 19 NGBs). However, there are a number of Olympic sport organisations that are not part of any of the main Olympic initiatives. Apart from training young people to gain a coaching qualification (Sportivate), non-Olympic NGBs have been largely on the fringes of the organisational efforts to use the Games to promote sport in general and have not been actively involved.

The London Games also presents host-country NGBs with unique opportunities to strengthen their links with the international governing body of that sport (IFs), and other important stakeholders such as regional and local authorities and other NGBs. Such Games-inspired collaborations have multiple positive effects on NGBs' image, governance and organisational capacities. A small number of Olympic NGBs only have collaborated with IFs to organise staff development courses (eight), master classes (four), innovation workshops (two), to pilot new projects (four) and to provide pre-Games training camps (seven). One NGB benefited from an infrastructural project supported by an IF, and one in relationships building. This variance in involvement with IFs can partly be explained by the different positions of the British NGBs internationally. More successful and well-established sports, such as cycling, swimming and athletics, are in a much better position to leverage the advantages presented by the Games compared to less-established sports such as handball, wrestling and weightlifting. This is because they possess greater human, material and know-how capital.

Table 17.6 NGBs' involvement with Olympic-related programmes

Programme	*Owner/description*	*Olympic NGB*		*Non-Olympic NGB*	
		Yes	*No*	*Yes*	*No*
Get Set	LOCOG Inspiring 3–19-year-olds to get involved with the Games	3	14	0	9
Sport Makers	LOCOG Training Games volunteers	17	3	7	3
Inspire mark	LOCOG Awarded to non-commercial community projects inspired by the Games	13	7	1	8
Gold Challenge	Sport England Encouraging the mass participation of adults as a legacy of the Games	17	2	0	8
Cultural Olympiad	LOCOG/DCMS Encourages everyone to get involved with the Games through all forms of culture	4	12	1	7
Sportivate	Sport England Giving 14–25-year-olds access to coaching courses	19	1	7	3
International Inspiration	LOCOG/UK Sport Inspiring young people around the world to choose sport	6	12	0	8
Pre-Games training camps	LOCOG/Sport England/various local agencies	13	6	1	8
Other	Various	2	7	0	6

NGBs' collaboration with regional and local authorities in the UK has been more widespread, including Games-related interventions in the field of promotional campaigns to increase participation (12 Olympic and 4 non-Olympic NGBs respectively), talent identification (7 NGBs), club development (13 and 4 NGBs respectively), cultural activities (3 and 1 NGB respectively), and tourism development (2 NGBs). Eight NGBs have collaborated with other NGBs to share knowledge and expertise on how to leverage the impact of London 2012. Clearly, the Games has encouraged NBGs to engage with other stakeholders to enhance their organisational capacities, but this involvement has been sporadic and limited in scope. This finding is consistent with NGBs' overall approach to the Games, where only three of them included business-related Olympic activities in their strategic whole sport plans. It would appear that relatively little formal organisational learning has been taking place as well. Sharing knowledge and expertise amongst NGBs has yet to become a common practice, with only eight having participated in a Games-related research project, concerned with improving organisational effectiveness (two NGBs), athlete performance (two NGBs), promoting participation (two NGBs) and talent identification (two NGBs). Furthermore, despite the UK Government-led meta-evaluation of the Games impact (DCMS *et al.*, 2011), only seven Olympic NGBs report that they are involved in projects being considered by this evaluation, thus potentially limiting both our understanding of what has been going on across various sports and the opportunities for learning. This is also indicative of the challenges of producing robust evidence for policy making, and specifically in the field of NGBs' leveraging of mega sporting events for capacity building.

Looking to the future after London 2012, NGBs variously rated the overall impact of the Games in three key areas – inspiring participation in sport, increased funding and improved infrastructure. Fourteen Olympic and three non-Olympic NGBs agree that the Games will be a major factor in encouraging more able-bodied and people with disabilities (14 and 2 NGBs respectively) to participate in sport regularly; while injection of increased funding leads 16 NGBs (14 and 2 respectively), and 12 NGBs (9 and 3 respectively) to predict enhanced infrastructure for their sports. The words of an NGB CEO eloquently summarise the overall impact of the Olympic Games: 'A great opportunity to all – a ready-made marketing tool through which sports can use to underpin their ongoing development priorities.'

However, as with other aspects of involvement, not all Olympic NGBs believe in the 'magic power' of London 2012, with non-Olympic NGBs being much less optimistic about the overall positive impact of the Olympic and Paralympic Games. Table 17.7 shows NGBs' main beneficiaries from the Games. Fourteen NGBs (9 and 5 respectively) agreed that their staff and the sport as a whole have benefited the most from the London Games. The main gains for non-Olympic sports have been for their coaches and volunteers.

Conclusions

The 2012 London Olympic and Paralympic Games has presented UK NGBs with a number of opportunities and challenges. The study of 39 Sport England-funded and other NGBs allows for a number of conclusions to be made. First, despite the evolution of UK major sporting event policy from an event that needs to be well managed to a tool for delivering a range of social, economic and organisational benefits, the link between the London Games and NGBs' operations took time to be established so those benefits could really accrue, and has been shaped by several factors. This is mainly because of the power of the Games to mobilise huge public and commercial resources and to engage various stakeholders who otherwise would not have been involved with an event. The UK government has framed the London Games as a national

Table 17.7 NGBs' main beneficiaries from the 2012 London Olympics

Beneficiary	*Very much*		*Benefited*		*Neutral*		*Not much*		*Not at all*	
	Olympic NGB	*Non-Olympic NGB*	*Olympic NGB*	*Non-Olympic NGB*	*Olympic NGB*	*Non-Olympic NGB*	*Olympic NGB*	*Non-Olympic NGB*	*Olympic NGB*	*Non-Olympic NGB*
Whole sport	9	1	7	4	3	2	0	0	0	2
NGB staff	9	0	5	3	4	2	1	1	0	3
Coaches	6	0	10	1	2	5	1	1	0	3
Referees	4	0	7	0	7	3	1	1	0	4
Volunteers	5	0	9	3	3	4	3	0	0	3
County SP	0	0	8	2	9	3	2	1	0	3
Clubs	3	0	5	2	10	5	1	1	0	2
Members	1	0	7	1	10	5	0	1	0	2

project and appealed to all people to get involved. This has inevitably encouraged both cooperation and competition amongst stakeholders and between NGBs in particular.

Second, most NGBs perceive the Games as a unique opportunity for the overall development of their sport. However, these opportunities have varied significantly across Olympic and non-Olympic sports as well as for the able-bodied and people with disabilities. These variations could be down to NGBs' different histories, structures and organisational potential. Third, only a handful of NGBs have taken a holistic approach to the Games and integrated it into their strategic whole sport plans. The others have been using mainly single programmes and initiatives to engage with the Olympic Games on a more tactical basis. Although involvement in any programme is better than non-involvement, a fragmented approach limits the possibilities for organisational capacity building. Fourth, the London Games has already had and will have a positive impact on NGBs' performance in the three key areas of increasing participation, funding and infrastructure of sport.

Finally, the Games has allowed NGBs to leverage their opportunities to various degrees in all nine key areas of competence, as defined by UK Sport (2003), including: (1) preparing and implementing a vision and strategic plan for the sport; (2) promoting the sport; (3) managing the rules and regulations of the sport, including anti-doping; (4) administering officials of the sport; (5) establishing and maintaining links with the international governing body/federation; (6) encouraging participation; (7) developing talent; (8) developing elite athletes; and (9) organising and hosting competitions. However, there is little evidence for organisational learning designed to capture, share and disseminate knowledge, and there is a danger that the opportunity for learning important lessons may be lost. The current study suggests that the time is right for considering a new development in the UK and amongst the governing bodies of sport's mega events policies. Specifically, it requires recognising the potential of mega events for organisational capacity building and more importantly the need for a strategic approach to leveraging the opportunities they present.

Note

1 The authors would like to acknowledge the support of Sport England and UK Sport in conducting the survey with UK national governing bodies of sport, on which this chapter is based. Our appreciative thanks are extended to Jerry Bingham from UK Sport for his valuable comments as well as to Helen Bibby and Alan Dovaston from Sport England for their help in analysing the data.

References

Chalip, L. (2006) Towards Social Leverage of Sport Events. *Journal of Sport and Tourism*, 11 (2), 109–127.

DCMS (Department for Culture, Media and Sport). (2012) *Creating a Sporting Habit for Life*. London: DCMS.

DCMS/Grant Thornton/Ecorys/Loughborough University (2011) *Meta-Evaluation of the Impacts and Legacy of the London 2012 Olympic amd Paralympic Games. Summary Reports 1 and 2*. London: DCMS.

DCMS. (2009) *London 2012: A legacy for disabled people: Setting new standards, changing perceptions*. London: DCMS.

DCMS. (2008) *Before, During and After: Making the most of the London 2012 Games*. London: DCMS.

DCMS. (2007) *Our Promise for 2012: How the UK will benefit from the Olympic and Paralympic Games*. London: DCMS.

DCMS. (2002) *Game Plan*. London: DCMS.

Girginov, V. and Hills, L. (2008) A Sustainable Sports Legacy: Creating a link between the London Olympics and sports participation, *The International Journal of the History of Sport*, 25 (14), 2091–2117.

Holmes, J., Szymanski, S., Ross, S. and Kavetsos, G. (2010) *State of Sport in Britain 2010: A reforming sports policy for the new coalition government*. London: The Sport Nexus.

Houlihan, B. and Green, M. (2009) Modernization and Sport: The Reform of Sport England and UK Sport, Paper for the Political Studies Association.

House of Commons, Culture, Media and Sport Committee. (2003) *A London Olympic Bid for 2012*. Third Report of Session 2002–03. London: DCMS.

IOC. (2009) *Twelfth Olympic Congress: The Olympic Movement in society*. Lausanne: IOC.

National Audit Office. (2010) *The BBC's Management of its Coverage of Major Sporting and Music Events*. London: NAO.

Sport England. (2012) *Governance*. Online: http://www.sportengland.org/support__advice/governance,_finance__control/governance.aspx (accessed 3 March 2012).

Sport England. (2011) *Active People 5*. London: Sport England.

Sport England. (2009). National Governing Body Outcomes 2009–2013. Online: http://www.sportengland.org/media_centre/press_releases/ngb_outcomes_2009-2013.aspx (accessed 1 April 2012).

Sport England. (2008) *Whole Sport Plans*. London: Sport England.

Sport England. (2004) *The Framework for Sport in England: Making England an active and successful sporting nation: A vision for 2020*. London: Sport England.

UK Sport. (2005) *Staging Major Sporting Events: The guide*. London: UK Sport.

UK Sport. (2003) *Investing in Change: High level review of the modernisation programme for governing bodies of sport*. London: Deloitte and Touche.

UK Sport. (n.d.) http://www.uksport.gov.uk/news/latest-mission-2012-report-shows-british-sport-on-track-for-london (accessed 2 April 2012).

18

OTHER SPORTS PROVIDERS AND THE GAMES

Mike Collins

Introduction

This chapter takes stock of the involvement with the Games of providers other than national governing bodies of sport (NGBs). It starts with the regional context of London sport and such details as are available on regional participation, and then looks successively at the London Organising Committee of the Olympic and Paralympic Games (LOCOG), Sport England (national), Greater London Authority (GLA)/Mayor of London and the host Olympic boroughs' programmes, before making some concluding remarks.

The coalition government (Conservative–Liberal Democrat) declared a focus on four areas for Olympic legacy (DCMS, 2010a):

1 *Harnessing the United Kingdom's passion for sport* to increase grassroots participation, particularly by young people – and to encourage the whole population to be more physically active, including £65 million (DfE) for schools to release a PE teacher to organise competitive sports, £10 million (Lottery via Youth Sport Trust) for the new Schools Games, £14 million for development in primary schools (DoH), £130 million for Places People Play – see below – and £8 million for disability sport (Sport England).
2 *Exploiting to the full the opportunities for economic growth* offered by hosting the Games, including £6 billion of building and supply contracts (98 per cent to UK companies), income from 14,700 participants, 320,000 extra visitors and 20,000 accredited journalists in 2012, and the hope of 1 million extra visitors for four years to the UK, leading to spending of £2 billion.
3 *Promoting community engagement and achieving participation* across all groups in society through the Games, including sports leaders (40,000, Sport England/BOA), the Cultural Olympiad hoping for 3 million visitors, and 70,000 Games Maker volunteers (LOCOG).
4 *Ensuring that the Olympic Park* can be developed after the Games as one of the principal drivers of regeneration in East London (new sports and industrial facilities, 2,800 homes, a new park, 8 km of waterways and improved shopping and transport (£125 million locally, plus Crossrail and other works), and a Mayoral Development Corporation to support the Olympic Park Legacy Company and coordinate wider East London projects.

Worried about a hiatus between LOCOG-driven, event-focused actions and the Park Legacy Company takeover, MacRury and Poynter argued that the existing governance framework is sufficient to secure a successful event-phase but is currently unlikely to achieve 'Transformative Momentum'; and suggested that 'steady state regeneration' is the likely outcome, 'where public benefits and private commercial activity co-exist but do not gel into long term transformation' (MacRury and Poynter, 2009, pp. 9–11).

It must be remembered that a unique feature of London is that it contains 43 per cent of the country's non-white population, and the Office of National Statistics classed 23 of the 32 boroughs as 'highly diverse'. Thus, equality, diversity and inclusion issues have to be prominent in any strategy.

The socioeconomic and resource context of London sport

The CASE (Culture and Sport Evidence) programme provided for the first time reasonable regional contextual data for sport and culture. The London data (TBS, 2010) is summarised in Table 18.1. Some main points are:

1 Sport produces quite a high value-added, though sports employment is overshadowed by the concentration of theatres, music venues and galleries.
2 Lottery and local authority revenue investment had already started shrinking, and is the lowest of any region.
3 There had been an above-average increase in local authority capital spending whether catching up on obsolescence or stimulated by 2012 is not possible to tell.
4 Because of density and space, London had fewer outdoor facilities than the average, but twice the England average of gyms and leisure centres; many people travel from inner to outer London and from the outer suburbs to countryside locations beyond the green belt, especially for playing pitches (London Sport, 1990).
5 Participation was average, but curiously slightly above average when recreational walking and cycling are included.

Patterns in sports participation

Despite targets set from 2002, modest rises in participation have been overtaken by the world trends in economic recession and the considerable cuts in welfare and public spending instituted from 2010 by the coalition government.

I have elaborated elsewhere why the *Game Plan* (DCMS, 2002) target to make England (the fourth most unequal country in terms of income) like Finland (the third most equal) in just 16 years was never on, even before the recession (Collins, 2010). The DCMS 'Taking Part' survey further showed that all four key indicator targets had been missed (for women, disabled people, black and ethnic minorities and low-income groups (DCMS, 2010b)). Sport England had set targets for 700,000 new participants via NGB programmes and 300,000 via higher education. It became clear that it was falling behind these targets, and Sport England warned NGBs of grant cuts if sports failed to increase participation (Gibson, O. *Guardian* 16 December10). In 2010 Jeremy Hunt, Secretary of State at the DCMS, admitted that he had quietly dropped the 1 million target, and would announce something 'more meaningful' (Gibson, O. *Guardian Sport* 29 March 11:1,8), but he has not yet done so.

Table 18.2 shows the latest Active People (Survey 4) data on participation. Even with a survey of over 170,000 respondents, small sample sizes for individual activities mean having to

Table 18.1 The regional context of London sport

Themes	*Date/measure*	*Notes – cf. London 15 6% of working population 2008*
ECONOMY		
Jobs: activities (000)[1]	*2008* 40.6	+13% from 2006, 14% of England, 23% new starts 2009, averaging 16 jobs
Businesses: activities (no)	*2009* 1,640	1% of England
Gross value added (£ billion)	*2007* £1.38	25% of England
Volunteers (000)	*2008* 237	12% of England
NON-CAPITAL INVESTMENT[2]	(£ million)	
LA Sport dev./community	*2008–2009*: 47.5	15% of England −10% *cf.* +16% England since 2004–5
LA facilities (£ million)	*2008–2009*: 88.2	9% of England total since 2004, 5–10% *cf.* +2% England
Lottery (£ million)	*2008–2009*: 30.0	15% of England
CAPITAL INVESTMENT[2]	(£ million)	
LA Sport/community dev.	*2008–2009*: 10.5	18% of England
LA facilities	60.9	16% of England
Sport England	1.0	0.6% of England
SPORTS ASSETS	*2009*: 6,617; 38% pitches, 29% tennis courts, 16% gym/leisure centres	8.7% of England total (*cf.* 8% England)
ENGAGEMENT IN SPORT		
Participation (3 × 30min./wk moderate in last 4 wks excl. rec. walk/cycle) (m)	*2008–2009*: 1.04	16.7 *cf.* 6.5% England
Participation 18 (3 × 30min./wk moderate in last 4 wks incl. rec. walk/cycle) (m)	1.3	20% *cf.* 21.8% England
Spectate last 4 weeks (m)	5.4	12% *cf.* 15% England
EDUCATION	*000*	
HE sports science students	*2008–2009*: 3.6	13% of England total
LSC training places in FE	44	14% of England total
GCSE PE students	13	14% of England total

Source: TBS, 2010.

Notes
1 No data on manufacturing.
2 No data on private investment.

look at national rather than regional trends for population subgroups. The features I draw attention to are:

1 London is strong in some indoor sports (basketball, boxing, squash, swimming, table tennis and volleyball), but also in outdoor sports that require high incomes to travel to upland or overseas sites (snowsports, mountaineering) and where there is strong tradition (athletics, cricket, rowing, tennis).
2 Significant increases were more rare (in cycling, swimming and mountaineering for men, canoeing for women, and athletics for all groups) than decreases in 21 sports (confirming the trends already mentioned in Taking Part).
3 Table tennis showed no significant increase, despite the 'Ping' programme placing tables in public spaces, which attracted 30,000 people on 124,000 occasions, of which 27 will become permanent, including tables at St Pancras international rail station, Regents Park and the O2 Arena.

The Mayor's strategy (Mayor of London, 2009) showed sport and active recreation participation averaging 20.2 per cent (three times 30 minutes' moderate exercise a week in 2007–2008, the second lowest in England) and a wide range by borough in quartiles:

1 *low* (13.3–19.4 per cent) – 14 mostly outer and eastern boroughs (City, Tower Hamlets, Newham, Greenwich, Harrow, Enfield, Waltham Forest, Barking and Dagenham, Havering, Bexley, Croydon, Sutton, Kingston and Hounslow);
2 *low–middle* (19.5–21.7 per cent) ten, in three blocks (Hillingdon, Ealing, Brent, Westminster, Haringey, Islington, Hackney, Redbridge, Lewisham and Bromley);
3 *middle–high* (21.8 –23.8 per cent) – three, scattered (Barnet, Southwark, Merton);
4 *high* (23.9–30.9 per cent) Camden and a south-west wedge (Camden, Kensington and Chelsea, Hammersmith and Fulham, Lambeth, Wandsworth, Richmond).

Almost half the population was inactive (less than 30 minutes' moderate activity in the last four weeks).

LOCOG's strategy and programmes

The Olympic Delivery Authority (ODA) had ten threads in its 'Learning Legacy' strategy, one of which was equality and inclusion. Regarding this, LOCOG (2008:1) emphasised the multicultural nature of London, with 50 ethnic communities, over 10,000 people and 300 languages. As Paul Deighton, CEO, confirms: 'diversity and inclusion is a fundamental part of the 2012 Games and must remain at the very heart of everything we do', and 'delivering this vision can't just be about recruiting a diverse workforce, it has to be about partners, suppliers, competitors, officials and spectators; in fact everyone connected with the Games'. As an organisation LOCOG has been delivering on its commitments, and by April 2012 had employed over 500 staff from the six host boroughs; some 325 previously unemployed people and around 6,400 local residents had been made job offers for various contracts offered by LOCOG (www.london2012.com/press/media-releases/2012/03/london-2012-celebrates-diversity-day.php).

The equality and diversity aim was stated as 'to use the power of the Games to inspire change ... Games that welcome the world' (LOCOG, 2008: 8). Themes were:

1 inclusive business methods (communications, decision making and procurement, including encouraging suppliers to diversify their own purchasing chains);

Table 18.2 Sports participation in London

	AP3 2008–2009		*AP4 2009–2010*		*Reg. rank*	*England significant trends + = increase ★ = decrease*				
TOTAL	*000*	*%*	*000*	*%*		*M*	*F*	*BME*	*Dis*	*NC*
3 × 30 mins/wk in last 4 wks			1.04	16.5						
SPORT at least 1/wk										
Angling	4	0.1	2	0.3	9					
Athletics	342	5.6	338	5.4	1	+	+	+	+	+
Badminton	73	1.2	65	1.0	4		★	★		★
Basketball	43	0.7	39	0.6	1	★	★			★
Bowls	21	0.3	17	0.3	8		★			
Boxing	23	0.4	23	0.4	1					
Canoeing	4	0.1	–	–	9		★			
Cricket	33	0.5	26	0.4	2	★		★		★
Cycling	233	3.8	223	3.6	3	+		★		
Equestrian	18	0.3	17	0.3	8	★				
Football	293	4.8	287	4.6	2	★				
Golf	75	1.2	80	1.3	7	★	★			★
Hockey	7	0.1	8	0.1	7		★			
Mountaineering	–10	0.2	11	0.2	5	+				
Netball	15	0.3	15	0.2	3		★			
Rowing	7	0.1	4	0.1	7	★				
Rugby League	6	0.1	4	0.1	7	★				
Rugby Union	17	0.3	22	0.4	4	★	★			
Sailing	7	0.1	5	0.1	5	★	★			
Snowsport	19	0.3	17	0.3	2	★				
Squash	31	0.5	41	0.7	2		★			
Swimming	422	6.9	436	7.0	3	+	★		★	★
Table tennis	14	0.2	19	0.3	1				★	
Tennis	110	1.8	89	1.4	2		★		★	★
Volleyball	8	0.1	6	0.1	2		★			
Weightlifting	25	0.4	11	0.2	4	★				

Source: Active People 3, 4 reports Dec. 2010, Sport England.

2 individual responsibility (in combating bias, influencing behaviour and attitudes, including supporting staff and other leaders);
3 recruitment (including outreach advertising and developmental training for all staff);
4 an inclusive culture, a stakeholder plan and the Cultural Olympiad;
5 a catalyst of legacy for youth (NVQs, school/FE/HE programmes via Podium, volunteer recruitment strategy, participation (supporting Sport England and helping NGBs to diversify their officials' cadre), accessibility (of venues, transport and public buildings, despite only one in four of LT tube stations and a third of public buildings being fully accessible), procurement and participation, including volunteers.

Cutting across these Olympic legacy themes are the areas of sustainability and disability, and wider strategic commitments around equality, inclusion and diversity. Grant Thornton and colleagues showed a logic model and plan for meta-evaluation research for 2011–2013, and listed sport and other legacy activities in the six host boroughs. The Olympic Games Impact group listed 43 indicators each for the social and economic spheres, compared to 13 by the IOC and seven more by LOCOG; whether Grant Thornton and partners will be able to find and gather data on all these aspects in 2012–2013 remains to be seen.

DCMS (2009, 2010b) produced a separate document about 'Putting Disabled People at the Heart' of 2012 (for example, as part of the inclusive ticketing initiatives, a companion seat is included in the cost of a ticket for a wheelchair space, while the 'Ticket Care' scheme will see thousands of tickets funded by LOCOG for carers of those with a high-dependency care need). Dowse (2011), however, saw no strategic focus on social outcomes rather than sports development goals.

LOCOG developed an Olympic-branded programme (An Olympic and Paralympic first) under six headings, including sustainability, education, volunteering, business, sport or culture, of which we will focus on sport. The London 2012 Inspire programme enables non-commercial organisations across the UK to link their events and projects to the London 2012 Games in an official scope. More than 2,000 projects and events across the UK have been awarded the coveted Inspire mark for their work in one of the six areas. As of 1 December 2011, organisations can no longer apply for the Inspire mark. It is worth mentioning that under the education heading there was the Loughborough 'Flames' project, for supporting primary school PE in that town, and under volunteering the 'GoldMark' programme for 16–24-year-old sports volunteers.

Under the sport heading, Inspire comprised 25 projects (24 once free swimming was abolished), of which seven were specifically in London (including the 18 projects in the Mayor's 'PlaySport' programme (see below)), ten outside, and seven that were part of nationwide initiatives. They covered two specifically for primary schools, one for older people, three for people with disabilities, three for youth and sport clubs, one for competition, one for supporting elite athletes, one for informal sport, five for promoting health, including walking and cycling, and seven promotional, including two festivals. The list is in Table 18.3.

National/Sport England programmes

In this section, programmes that support the Olympic effort are summarised. As a context, in just over three financial years, from 2008–2009 to 2011–2012, Sport England distributed £19.85 million in grants in London, the majority being small grants of £10,000 or less and community programme grants, so that excluding facilities the average was only £45,000 (Table 18.4). Boroughs receiving sizeable numbers of grants for mass participation and single sport/club projects were Newham and Tower Hamlets (both London host boroughs), Lambeth, Southwark and Westminster (inner London), and Bromley, Haringey and Redbridge (outer boroughs).

Table 18.3 LOCOG's Inspire sport projects

	Title and purpose/content of project
1.	*Young Ambassadors for Sport* – run by the Youth Sport Trust, seeking 5,500 youths who can go into schools and clubs via the 450 School Sport Partnerships (now disbanded by Mr Gove).
2.	*Active8* – for 7–11s in Northern Ireland.
3.	*Bristol Festival of Sport and Culture.*
4.	*Norfolk Competitive Edge* – pathway for talented youth.
5.	*Championing the East Midlands* – seven iconic images linking sport and tourism.
6.	*City Masters* – five sports for over 45s in the City of London.
7.	*Free Swimming* (abolished as a national scheme in late 2009).
8.	*Getting Ready for the Olympics* – harnessing the power of youth clubs in London.
9.	*Go Enfield Go* – sport and dance for 1,000 primary schoolchildren in the borough.
10.	*Lloyds TSB national school sport week*, involving three million children from 10,000 schools across England.
11.	*New Life New You* – seeking to combat type-two diabetes with sport in Middlesbrough.
12.	*Five Star Disability Sports Challenge* – in 65 Northern Irish primary schools.
13.	*Once in a Lifetime* – showcasing sport in the East End.
14.	*Sports Jam* – 20 community sports clubs in Tower Hamlets.
15.	*Sports Legacy* – athletics in former coalfield communities in Yorkshire and the East Midlands.
16.	*St Helens Club Conference* – for Merseyside sports clubs.
17.	*Street Games: Legacy Leaders* – sport in over 100 inner-city projects across England.
18.	*Surf Life Festival* – promoting surfing, lifesaving and other sports in Cornwall.
19.	*The Suffolk Challenge* – to promote active, healthy lifestyles in families and combat obesity.
20.	*The Virtual Games Village* – NHS website resources to help people to take up sport.
21.	*Time to Get Active* – mass participation initiative by Scope (charity for people with cerebral palsy) for an annual 'Time to get Equal' week.
22.	*Walk England active challenge routes* – to create 2,012 one-mile routes to allow people to test their fitness using the Rockport one-mile walking test.
23.	*Walking and cycling publicity material* – supporting the NHS in its drive to get 1 million people active by 2012.
24.	*Walk London* – free of charge, leading walking weekends in the city.
25.	*Play Sport London* – the Mayor's programme – see pp. 254–255.

Source: LOCOG website – www.london2012.com/get-involved/inspire-sport.php.

The coalition's restoration of sport's share of the National Lottery income from 16 per cent to 20 per cent has allowed some new funding under the £136 million Places People Play (Sport England Press Release, 15 November 2010).

Facilities

Sport England's facilities grants included millions of pounds for: improving playing fields in Hackney, Ealing (three), and Haringey; sports centres in Westminster, Bexley, Southwark, Richmond and Redbridge (two); a velopark and a whitewater course in Enfield; a watersports centre in Kensington/Chelsea; and a riding centre in Lambeth.

The Places People Play programme was to offer £30 million in three waves for 'iconic' multisport facilities. Given local authority cutbacks and reduction in other sources of capital grants, it is not surprising that the first wave received 112 applications for a total of £106 million. Sport England made six awards worth £17 million, including extensions to the Manchester national velodrome, worth £3 million. Nationwide, up to 1,000 clubs were to get grant support for development, while hundreds of playing fields were to be protected and improved across the country (including the improvement of Tufnell Park playing fields in inner North London), and open spaces preserved for sport. These facilities will be the only ones to carry the London 2012 Inspire mark, in permanent celebration of their role in the Games legacy.

Participation

The Places People Play programme is under development through the Gold Challenge, an independent initiative to motivate over 100,000 adults in Olympic and Paralympic sports, and in Sportivate, a campaign providing opportunities for teenagers and young adults to receive six weeks of coaching in the sport of their choice and guiding them into regular participation within their community. It will also offer disabled people additional investment of at least £8 million, to help tackle the barriers they face. Chapter 17 discusses NGBs' involvement with these programmes.

Some major national programmes supported the Games, while not being totally focused on them.

Table 18.4 Sport England grants in London, 2008–2009 to 2011–2012

Type	*6 host LBs*		*Other 10 inner*		*Other 17 outer*		*Total*		
	No.	*£000*	*No.*	*£000*	*No.*	*£000*	*No.*	*£000*	*Aver.*
Facilities	1	500	4	2,033	9	5,190	14	7,723	n/a
Mass participation	18	767	18	2,603	46	2,577	82	5,947	*73*
Girls and women	6	115	8	354	17	409	31	878	*28*
Disabled	4	199	6	600	5	80	15	879	*59*
Older people	1	40	1	5	3	197	5	242	*48*
Club/NGB	27	922	8	366	78	1,925	114	3,213	*28*
Health-related fitness	249	4	249	5	180	12	678	*57*	
Volunteering	–		–		5	256	5	256	*53*
Coaching	–		3	270	4	36	4	36	*9*
Total	60	2,797	52	6,480	172	10,850	284	19,852	*70*
Average £000 excl. facilities		*39*		*93*		*35*			*45*

Source: Personal communication, J. Buller, Head of Shared Service Centre, Sport England, 1 December 2011.

Sport Unlimited was a £36 million programme in 2008–2011, aiming to retain and develop the interests of 900,000 'semi-sporty' young people through offering them activity courses of between eight and ten weeks, promoted and coordinated through county sports partnerships. Sport Industry Research Centre monitoring (SIRC, 2011) found that 1.2 million took part, and 82 per cent – or 7 per cent more than the target – were retained (i.e. attended three or more out of five of their course sessions). One in six was from Black and Ethnic Minorities and 7 per cent from disabled groups, but both groups showed lower than overall retention rates. In terms of longer retention, a second aim was to keep one in three in increased activity or in club membership: online polls showed that 45 per cent had joined clubs in the three months after their courses. The rates for London are shown in Table 18.5.

So 111,600 young Londoners were retained in activity. It can be seen that numbers were highest for the North London and East London sectors encompassing the Olympic Park: SIRC and Sport England attributed this success to strong partnerships, involving the youth in activity choice and delivery, support of sports' NGBs and private delivery organisations, a broad menu of activities and clear exit routes for those wishing to continue. Sport England accepted lessons that a longer set-up phase was needed for such work, along with a lead officer (as the award-winning role played by Nikki Enoch and her team in Active Sports partnerships 1999–2004 – see Enoch, 2010).

Change4life clubs are supported nationwide by the Department of Health for people with and without disabilities, to encourage activity (via badminton, boccia, fencing, handball, table tennis, volleyball, wheelchair basketball) and healthy lifestyles in terms of eating, drinking and giving up smoking. A budget of £5.9 million was allocated for 3,000 clubs in England.

Active Universities was a mainstream £10 million programme following up Sport England's (2008) strategy aimed at involving 300,000 HE students. When it was launched, the aspiration had been reduced to 'tens of thousands' of new participants (typically 3,000 per campus). The original was over-optimistic, given that full-time students are already the most active group in the population, with the proportion participating averaging three out of four. Of the 41 HEIs chosen, eight were in London and five nearby:

Brunel – focusing on low-participant groups (women, disabled students and those from black and ethnic minorities);
City – ensuring continuity of playing and avoiding drop-out;
University of East London – taster and social sports sessions;
Queen Mary – 'Get Active' for the nine out of ten students who said they wanted to play more sport;
Roehampton – 'RoeActive', 10 new and 15 developed clubs, plus coaching for 10,000 students;
Royal Holloway – 'Be Active' in dance, drop-ins and football fives;
Middlesex – sports champions and coaching in surrounding counties;
Bedfordshire – trying to increase the low number of students who take part in regular vigorous activity (7 per cent);
Bucks New – on campus and in the community;
Herts – returners and newcomers;
Canterbury – 'try it' and coaching;
Surrey – tasters, drop-ins and leagues.

Table 18.5 Participation retention rates

Partnership	*Percentage overall retained*	*No. (000)*	*Percentage of three-year target*
Central London	71	17.0	111
East London	81	29.3	92
North London	85	23.1	110
South London	77	21.1	95
West London	75	21.1	86

Source: SIRC, 2011.

'Active Women' was another £10 million mainstream programme announced in 2010, when Active People results showed a gender gap that was widening rather than closing. In London the projects were:

Netball in the City;
Street Games (dance in Hammersmith and Fulham);
Tottenham Hotspur Foundation (seeking 1,000 new females in Haringey, Enfield, Barnet and Waltham Forest);
Women Active 4 Life (offering netball, badminton, boxing, dance, jogging and trampolining for 1,500 mothers of under-16s in disadvantaged areas of Barking and Dagenham).

Coaching and training

The 'people' element of Places People Play will seek to recruit, train and deploy 40,000 volunteer sports leaders. These will run alongside the National Skills Academy's offer of 3,900 bursaries for people taking sports coaching courses at a cost of £1.8 million, and support for 1,800 coach educators, and the Youth Sport Trust's continuing training programmes.

Greater London Authority/Mayor of London's programmes

The Mayor produced 'A Sporting Future for London' (2009) as a rallying call to all partners to celebrate 'sport for sport's sake' while also looking to wider social benefits, labelled 'sport for good' by Labour sports minister Richard Caborn, such as social inclusion, staying healthy and combating obesity, academic underachievement and crime.

The strategy involved £15.5 million to be matched by other sponsors, over four goals and nine themes:

Goal 1 – get more people active, via a diversity and inequality forum:

- tackle inactivity which was costing London £105 million a year;
- tackle inequality, notably among lower socio-economic groups, young women aged 14 to 24, older people, black and minority ethnic people, disabled people, lesbian, gay, bisexual and trans people.

Goal 2 – transform the sporting infrastructure:

- Olympic Park and training facilities;
- a new 'London Facilities Strategy' and new venues, including two mobile swimming pools, green gyms in open spaces, community tennis courts.

Goal 3 – build capacity and skills:

- recruit, retain and 'upskill';
- provide support for clubs and volunteers via the London Federation of Sport and Recreation and the four ProActive partnerships (counterparts to county sports partnerships outside London).

Goal 4 – maximise benefits of sport to our society:

- tackle crime (Mayor of London, 2008), including £1.5 million for anti-bullying programmes in nine boroughs, football and education programmes for school drop-outs in five inner-London boroughs, community programmes London-wide for unemployed immigrant and refugee youth with the city's Federation of Youth Clubs, and sports and business training for youth at risk of offending in Camden, Islington and Haringey;
- promote health and community cohesion, not spelled out.

In his 'Inclusive and Active' action plan of 2007–2012 (Barker and Watson, 2007), the Mayor set a target of helping 40,000–50,000 additional disabled people to become active over five years to 2012. By mid-2011 progress was as follows:

- in facilities – of £7 million, 50 per cent had been allocated and 5 per cent spent, including spending on 26 community venues;
- in participation – of £4 million, 58 per cent had been allocated, 15 per cent spent;
- in skills – of £3 million, 20 per cent had been spent (GL Assembly, Written answer 1337).

By July 2011 the Mayor's spend was £10 million, with match funding of £20 million, so he had already met his target of £30 million. More than 150 organisations benefited from 'Free-Sport' grants of up to £1,500, to provide 10,000 Londoners with a minimum of six hours free coaching (just tasters, not enough to qualify for a basic coaching award).

Facilities

These 26 venues included a BMX track in Walthamstow and a new bouldering wall at Westway in North Kensington. Inclusive design, for able-bodied and disabled people of both genders and all ages and faiths, was a principle embodied in the planning of these venues (ODA, 2011a). The GLA's main concern over the facilities is about who will pick up the bill, estimated at £231 million, when the London Development Agency hands over the Park site to the GLA; the Mayor had assumed that the government would continue to pay the grant, as it had to the LDA, but that is still unconfirmed (GLA *Press Release*, 17 November 2011).

Skills

The Games skills training programme cost £6.9 million, and included:

- job brokerage – in 2009 4,434 worked for construction companies on the Park, 20 per cent from the host boroughs, and 10 per cent from the unemployment rolls (LDA *et al.*, 2011b), and 3,550 training opportunities were delivered by the National Skills Academy (Thrush, Eley and Martins, 2011);

- at a cost of £0.5 million, 430 construction apprenticeships exceeded the target, with 12 per cent from black and minority ethnic groups, and 64 per cent resident in London (Bowler and Martins, 2011);
- ODA and contractors' roll-out of equality practices was monitored (Thrush and Amory, 2011);
- a choice of training programmes via the National Skills Academy (210 for coaching and officiating, but only small numbers for disability sport, community and club management, volunteer training and management, and 15 for health-related fitness).

Participation

Participation is this section's main concern. In two rounds of Play Sport, to the time of writing, 34 projects were initiated across a range very similar to LOCOG's Inspire programme (see Table 18.6). Of these, 16 were wholly and 9 partly in the inner city, with particular targets relating to the policy documents mentioned above for lower-paid workers' households and youth (nine projects), people with disabilities (six), informal activities that are easy to access (five) and youth involved in or at risk of crime (four). Two projects each targeted women, black and ethnic/religious minorities and older people. The criteria were made more specific for phase two, including the category of people at risk of crime (see Table 18.7).

Monitoring of the Street League project showed the following:

1. progression into jobs, education and training – 72 per cent of academy participants moved into long-term employment, education or training;
2. qualifications – 98 per cent of participants completed Street League courses and achieved a qualification;
3. reduced re-offending – while nationally 75 per cent of imprisoned youth offenders re-offended within two years, 75 per cent did not re-offend whilst working with Street League;
4. reduced substance misuse – in 2010, 54 per cent of participants reduced their substance misuse;
5. improved health and well-being – 86 per cent reported a significant increase in health and well-being as a result of working with Street League (www.streetleague.co.uk/impact.php, downloaded 23 November 2011).

LOCOG's community relations teams promoted a London 2012 Forum that works across five main UK denominations, including the More than Gold group, representing Christian communities; the ODA has been running five bus tours a day to the site (20,000 visitors each in 2008–2009 and 2009–2010, later extended by evening trips); consultation meetings have been held with 8,500 people and in particular with 1,800 youth in the host boroughs.

Following DCMS reports (2009, 2010a), and a 2006 report identifying weaknesses in provision for disabled people which raised awareness, the Mayor produced a five-year strategy for disability sport, to extend provision, promote an active/healthy lifestyle for all disabled people, diversify the sport sector so that more than the current 2 in 1,000 jobs are taken by disabled people, and upskill leaders and workers. *PlaySport London: Free Sport* showed that in 2009–2010 one participant in eight was disabled, and one in seven of people receiving six or more hours of coaching, but overall participation had stayed low, at 9 per cent.

Table 18.6 Mayor of London's PlaySport participation schemes

Title	*No. of boroughs*	*Project aims/content*
PHASE 1	£2.3 million	18 projects
Access Sport	4	Up to 50 open-access projects in 6 host boroughs, developing 18 sports clubs
Active Communities networks	6	Building capacity
All Stars boxing club	Kensington and Chelsea	Free boxing and martial arts training for disadvantaged youth
City of London	City	Subsidies for low-paid City workers
Cricket for a change	All	Hit the top – training teachers for after-school cricket, and setting up 16 new clubs for youth with disabilities
England Athletics	12	12 activators, providing inner-city events including car parks, housing estates, shopping centres and setting up new clubs
Federation of London youth clubs	14	Coach training and capacity development in ten sports, at 60 venues.
Fight for Peace	Merton	Boxing academy development
Fitness Industry Association	All	Shift into sport – discounted off-peak sport and fitness for shift workers
London Jewish Forum	Barnet	Sport for inactive people in the Haredi community
Panathlon Foundation	All	Coaching/training for seriously disabled children
Parkrun	All	Free 5 km runs in parks, extending from 13 to 36
Proactive Central	Brent +?	Dare2Dance – street dance for women aged 14–24
Reach and Teach Sport and education	7	Basketball training and new clubs
Rugby Football Foundation	6	Rugby and other sports in 15 high-crime areas
Salmon Youth Centre	Southwark	Education and activities extended to 10 p.m
Tottenham Hotspur Foundation	3	Opportunities for 16–19 school leavers to help get them into education, jobs
Westminster Boating Base	8	Kayaking/sail training in the inner city

PHASE 2	£1.3 million	16 projects
Age Concern Bromley	1	Fit for Life – programmes for older people.
AHOY Centre	Greenwich	Pulling together – sailing for all ages and the disabled.
Dame Kelly Holmes Legacy Trust	(various)	Get on Track athletics and life mentoring for disadvantaged 16–25s to aid employability; seven courses run including Southwark, Haringey.
Drug and Alcohol Service for London	4	DASL Active – programmes for young addicts.
Fight for Change	2	Boxing/weightlifting academy.
GB Wheelchair Basketball	14	London programme officer to develop 9 new clubs, basketball for women and juniors, and 7 school-club links, benfiting over 7,000 players.
Greenhouse School	?	Project 2016 to empower disadvantaged youngsters (from poor and single-parent families and those with learning difficulties) through 8 sports.
Greenwich Leisure Ltd	15	Adult swimming lessons.
London Youth Rowing	?	75 schools and 20 clubs – includes race nights and virtual rowing (machines) for visually impaired youth.
Metropolitan Police	Hounslow +?	Kickz plus – reducing/avoiding crime and a gateway to jobs for 8–19-year-olds via 8 sports in deprived estates.
Rugby Football Foundation	?	London Touch – [details to follow].
Skyway Charity	Hackney	Street leaders in football and other sports for disadvantaged 13–25-year-olds.
Street League	5?	Advanced Street Football, working with 16–24-year-olds not in work or training – 5 academies.
Street Games	?	Engaging neighbourhoods in sport participation in Newham, monitored by Brunel University, plus developing a network of coaches and leaders.
Westway Development Trust	Kensington and Chelsea	Women's World – including Muslim groups.

Sources: GL Assembly Written answers DD3393 December 2010 and DD341, May 2011; personal communication, J. Popat of GBWBA, 25 November 2011.

Table 18.7 PlaySport round two criteria, 2011

Criteria	*Evidence*	*Marks depending on theme*		
		Participation	*Community development*	*'At risk' youth*
Strategic fit	Bring increased participation/support by governing body	10	10	10
Evidence	Adequate demand/aim realistic/commitment to evaluation	30	30	30
Percentage inactive people	At least 10 per cent; higher marks for more	30	n/a	n/a
Value for money	Large demand/lower unit cost/grant realistic	10	10	10
Sustainability, partnership	Have life beyond 2012/clear 'exit route' after funding/strong partnership(s)	20	20	20
Community development	Community designed/part of inclusion/justice/equality process	n/a	30	n/a
'At risk' 16–25-year-olds	Explain 'theory of change' for reducing risk of crime/plan for most at risk/use volunteers, starting 2011/safeguarding in place	n/a	n/a	30

Source: Mayor of London (2011) Sports Participation Fund round 2, pers. com.

London host borough activities

Hespe (2010) set out 14 possible agenda items for local government in supporting 2012, but many of these were existing actions, which he suggested, rather unconvincingly, could be enhanced by incorporating the 'magic of the Games' (Hespe, 2010: 1). Given that two-thirds of the cost of the physical infrastructure of the Games came from central government and much of the rest from the GLA and LDA, local authorities cannot exert much leverage.

Grant Thornton *et al.* (2011) identified some joint sports projects by the six host boroughs, the broadest of which was the Strategic Regeneration Framework, which sought, over 2009–2019, to enable residents to 'enjoy the same social and economic conditions as Londoners as a whole'. Two others were:

- The Four Borough Sports Festival 2009: four FE colleges from Newham, Hackney and Greenwich collaborating in a three-day, ten-sport festival;
- VAULT: a youth film training project for 14–19-year-olds, portraying life in London during the 1948 Olympic Games and the run-up to 2012.

Table 18.8 lists 22 individual projects in the six boroughs, covering, like the Inspire and Play Sport lists, projects for primary and secondary schools, disabled and talented youth but also a cruise ship terminal close to sport venues, and two outdoor multisport areas sponsored by sportswear firm Adidas. Other boroughs also yield projects, like the long-planned 50 m pool in Hillingdon costing £40 million.

A great deal of effort has been extended by a number of providers to improve the sporting infrastructure and participation. But it is somehow ironic to see how the attractiveness of the Games could jeopardise investments worth several state-of-the-art pools. For example, in the bid book Transport for London planned conservatively that summer travel in 2012 would reduce London travel by 10 per cent while the Olympic Games would increase it 5 per cent. But more specific modelling suggests that on the nine busiest days more than 1 million visitors will travel by public transport, with 700,000 on Saturday 4 August for events in the Park, Wembley and the Mall. The chair of GLA's transport committee said, 'in 2012 London is facing extreme demand placed on a network already creaking at the seams' (O. Gibson, *Guardian* 15 April 2011), while traffic congestion caused by the 60 miles of Olympic-only traffic lanes could lead to air pollution breaching European air-quality standards and risking a £175 million or £300 million fine (B. Webster, *Times* 12 April 2–11:15; J. Vidal and O. Gibson, *Guardian* 25 April 2011:7).

Conclusions

In *Tough Times*, the Audit Commission (2011) rather understated the challenges facing English local authorities, with an 11.8 per cent cut in government funding and a 5 per cent reduction in Council Tax and fees income, a total of £4.7 billion in 2009–2010 alone. Culture took the second-largest cut after planning; with 54 per cent of councils looking to reduce service volume, two-thirds increasing fees and a third reducing standards. Although deprived areas had larger central grant sums, they were also the worst hit, in inner London as well as the midlands and north. It is against this context that one has to judge the likelihood of short and long-term 'soft legacies'.

Undoubtedly, LOCOG and the London and peripheral local authorities are making greater efforts than ever before to leave a legacy of mass and youth participation, and many

Table 18.8 Host borough initiatives

Greenwich

Apart from the three Games venues for 12 events:

- two regional sports halls at schools;
- a gymnastics centre and martial arts dojo for local residents;
- a new cycle trail to link the three Olympic venues;
- an annual sportathon for primary schools located on an army site;
- a disability sports programme as part of a wider ODA initiative, with construction companies sponsoring young people with spinal injuries;
- sports tourism events at the O_2 Arena, e.g. the National Hockey League;
- a new cruise ship terminal.

Newham

Besides the major Park Venues and training camps for 14 Olympic and 2 Paralympic squads:

- Newham Volunteers: 800 trained-for-event organisers;
- Newham Council grants offering £2,012 to local groups for activities that bring the community together.

Hackney

Besides seven Paralympic training camps, Sports Arena Three will host handball, fencing and Paralympic goalball, and will be available for community and commercial use, as well as:

- new indoor sports facilities for Hackney Wick alongside leisure retail and office space;
- developments in five disabled sports clubs for boccia, swimming, athletics, wheelchair basketball and goalball;
- 24 Hackney 2012 Youth Ambassadors from secondary schools to promote sports participation;
- Hackney Schools at the Heart – a Games-inspired curriculum for primary schools.

Tower Hamlets

Besides four Paralympic training camps:

- Team Tower Hamlets Gifted and Talented programme has been set up to identify potential athletes and help youth join sports clubs progress to county, national and international standards;
- the Sports Development 2012 programme aims to inspire people to get active;
- the Urban Olympic project visits schools and youth clubs to inform pupils about local clubs, in partnership with Children's Services and the Borough's Outdoor Adventure/Youth Opportunity Fund.

Waltham Forest

With four Olympic sites and an athletics training area, and a Paralympic tennis site and 8 Para training camps:

- the Waltham Forest Tennis Centre will become a regional centre for disability tennis and a centre for tennis development;
- the adiZone in Langthorne Park funded by Adidas is free to use, and includes a streetball court, a tennis wall, a traversing climbing wall and outdoor gym equipment;
- a National Skills Academy for construction in Leytonstone in 2010 is part of a £7.6 million investment.

Barking and Dagenham

Although it has no venues, it was granted host borough status, and:

- an Adizone in Mayesbrook, giving residents access to outdoor exercise equipment, and a giant beach facility in Mayesbrook Park;
- free access for national sportspeople to the borough's sports facilities;
- 'Living the Dream' – Barking and Dagenham Trust raises money to help local individuals develop their sporting talent.

Source: Grant Thornton/Ecorys/Loughborough University, 2011, Appendix B.

Olympic-related programmes have been rolled out (over 1,300 across the UK are mentioned in Grant Thornton *et al.*, 2011). Now, many individual projects will have very positive outcomes; the question is, even if they all do, with all the will in the world, do they add up to a coherent legacy? As Tables 18.3, 18.4, 18.6 and 18.8 show, the types of LOCOG, Mayoral, Sport England and borough projects fall into the same categories in trying to promote participation, club sport and coaching, so it will be very difficult to separate any Games effect. In February 2011 the GLA committee responsible for delivering a legacy (the Economic Development, Sport, Culture and Tourism Committee) suggested that the Mayor's plan had been rather slow to start and made seven recommendations (my comments appear in italics below) for:

1 greater involvement by the Mayor and London Community Sports Board with the education and health sectors (*this seems too late to be practicable*);
2 negotiation with LOCOG to broaden use of the Olympic brand to encourage participation (*LOCOG is required to guard use of the brand very carefully*);
3 the Mayor reporting on how facility grants were helping in areas where sports demand exceeded supply;
4 review of alternative funding to maximise return on the final grant rounds (*unlikely to be able to make major changes at this late stage*);
5 report in December 2011 on outcomes of the grants, and how the Sports Board had encouraged others to fill gaps (*too soon to get mature outcomes rather than 'honeymoon' effects*);
6 indentifying a role for the Sports Commissioner and the Sports Board after 2012;
7 confirming whether he is still committed to his earlier target of 90 per cent community use of the Park facilities after the Games, and whether the Legacy Company will impose such a clause on tenants (some senior GLA members suggested 50 per cent would be a good and feasible outcome – Economic Development, Sport, Culture and Tourism Committee minutes, 19 July 2011, Appendix 1) (*whether an enforceable condition can be included in leases must be doubtful*).

Sports Minister Hugh Robertson described the two Games as 'the biggest peacetime logistical exercise' ever undertaken in the UK (DCMS, 2011b: 2), and the Olympic Delivery Authority reported a final bill for delivering the venues at £7.26 billion, a reduction of £55 million since the government's spending review. There is general agreement that the Games will be a huge, successful spectacle, and maybe a medal success for GB with home advantage. It will be watched live by virtually sell-out crowds, 95 per cent of them the sport-mad British, with 1.9 million people applying for tickets in the first phase of the Olympic ticketing process and a total of 1.1 million tickets being applied for in the first phase of the Paralympic ticketing process (letter to GLA from Paul Deighton, CEO, LOCOG, Appendix 1 to GLA EDSCT committee minutes, 8 November 2011).

Five broader comments going beyond LOCOG's remit must be made, however:

First, some activities, like the three-year Sportivate, are pale shadows of earlier, better-sustained programmes that had better linkages into pathways to club or competitive systems (like Champion Coaching – Collins and Buller, 2000, 2003; Bell, 2010, and Active England – Enoch, 2010). To some extent this chapter is a series of lists of not dissimilar projects by different promoters, and almost all projects will cease to have external funding in 2012 or 2013. There is no overall coordination.

Second, and most critically, no Games has had a positive impact on participation (Brown and Murray, 2001; Coalter, 2004; Culture Media and Sport Committee, 2007: para. 113; Weed *et al.*, 2009). Indeed, Pappous (2011) showed that over the five years after Athens 2004, sport participation in Greece declined below pre-Games levels. In Manchester after the Commonwealth Games there was a 2 per cent decrease and a widening of the gap between rich and poor communities, and new facilities benefited athletes more than local residents (Brown and Murray, 2001). SPEAR (2011a) did show that 1.5 million children did more sport immediately after the National School Games weeks in 2010 and 2011 and through Change4Life clubs, but the question is, how long will such improvements be sustained? No studies showed direct health benefits (McCartney *et al.*, 2010).

Third, focus on the poor and excluded was strong in the Mayor's Play Sport programme, but less so overall. Minnaert (2010), reviewing provisions for socially excluded groups in the seven Games from Atlanta 1996 to Beijing 2008, highlights that five paid no attention to non-infrastructural items, despite mention in the Olympic Movement's Agenda 21. The issue was taken seriously only by Sydney 2000, with:

- training and jobs for locally unemployed, though poorly targeted;
- 735,000 tickets at under AUD $20, but for less popular events;
- a protocol for the homeless in Sydney, which continued after the Games.

Minnaert urged the IOC to give more prominence to 'soft' as well as 'hard' legacies for Rio 2016. London is trying hard to do better than this. The balloting for tickets was controversial, but the Mayor made 75,000 free tickets available to London schools, and LOCOG another 100,000, the latter paid for by a levy on the national and international Prestige hospitality ticket sales (Paul Deighton, GLA question and answer session – Minutes, item 3, appendix 1).

Fourth, some houseboat owners and 425 Clays Lane residents were removed to make room for the athletes' Village, and are unlikely tenants of the post-Games social housing; Cheyne (2009) wrote movingly of the human cost of this upheaval, as did Jaconelli and Porter (2009) of the same process in preparation for the 2014 Commonwealth Games in Glasgow's East End. In Stratford, some small industrial firms and allotment holders also were moved to make the main site available, but this is nothing to the scale of clearances of poor housing and homeless people seen in Moscow or Beijing, or even, as has already happened, in Rio's favelas in preparation for 2016 (T. Philips, *Guardian* 27 April 2011:24).

Fifth, in terms of overall governance, it is clear that neither the IOC nor the DCMS nor LOCOG (Girginov and Hills, 2009) have an overall handle on the 'soft' social legacy and its sustainability once the Olympic caravan and its attendant glamour moves on to Rio de Janeiro – they all have aspirations, many not spelled out in clear and measurable terms. Even the Grant Thornton/Loughborough team (2011) will struggle to measure many of their elements in 2013; the prevailing intellectual climate only values what can be measured, and treats other items as 'nice' but peripheral.

Chair of the Sport and Physical Activity Alliance (the sports confederation, formerly the CCPR) and GB team manager for 2012 Lord Moynihan attacked the government for 'squandering the chances of a legacy' – with Secretary of State Gove's cancelling the school and youth sport strategy, while 50 per cent of medal winners came from private schools that teach only 7 per cent of pupils, and with only half of schools signed up to the national School Games, leaving a 'patchwork' of supportive activity (T. Helm, *Observer* 20 November 2011:9). A former Tory sports minister, Gove had earlier called on government to give local authorities mandatory power to provide sports facilities (O. Gibson, *Guardian* 1 July 2011:11). Keech argues that the buck for legacy stops not with Labour and its aspirations and promises of a legacy of participation, but with the coalition, commenting:

> with far less resources, an emphasis on competition ... it seems unlikely that London 2012 will come close to keeping its legacy promise. No amount of political blame and counter-blame will shield the fact that for young people, sadly London 2012 looks likely to be a missed opportunity. And once the circus has left town, who will be there to clear up the mess after the elephants?
>
> *(Keech, 2011)*

Ensuring legacy is still an early and complex learning process, and from London 2012 there may be as many cautionary lessons as inspiring ones.

References

Audit Commission (2011) *Tough Times: Councils' responses to a challenging financial climate*, London: AC.

Barker, Y. and Watson, A. (2007) *Inclusive and Active Action Plan 2007–12*, London: Greater London Authority.

Bell, B. (2010) Building a legacy for youth and coaching: Champion coaching on Merseyside, in Collins, M. (ed.) *Examining Sport Development*, London: Routledge, 139–168.

Bowler, K. and Martins, L. (2011) *London 2012 Apprenticeship Programme Learning Legacy*, London: ODA.

Brown, A. and Murray, J. (2001) *Literature Review: The impact of major sports events*, Manchester: Manchester Metropolitan University, Centre for Popular Culture.

Cheyne, J. (2009) Olympian masterplanning in London, *Planning Theory and* Practice, 10, 3: 405–408.

Coalter, F. (2004) Stuck in the blocks? A sustainable sporting legacy, in Vigor, A. and Mean, M. (eds) *After the Gold Rush: The London Olympics*, London: Institute of Public Policy Research/Demos.

Collins, M. F. (2010) From 'sport for good' to 'sport for sport's sake'– not a good move for sports development in England?, *International Journal of Sport Policy*, 2, 3: 367–379.

Collins, M. F. and Buller, J. R. (2000) Bridging the post-school institutional gap in sport: Evaluating Champion coaching in Nottinghamshire, *Managing Leisure*, 5: 200–221.

Collins, M. F. and Buller, J. R. (2003) Social exclusion from high performance sport: are all talented young people being given an equal opportunity of reaching the Olympic podium?, *Journal of Sport and Social Issues (US)*, 27, 4.1: 420–442.

Culture, Media and Sport Committee (2007) *London 2012 Olympic Games and Paralympic Games: Funding and legacy*, HC 69-I.

Deloitte Touche Ltd (2004) *Tourism Hospitality and Leisure-Executive Report*, 3, January, London: DT.

Department for Children, Schools and Families (2008) *PESSYP: Creating a world-class system for PE and sport*, London: DCSF.

Department of Culture, Media and Sport (2011a) *Taking Part, 2005–10*, London: DCMS.

Department of Culture, Media and Sport (2011b) London 2012 Olympic and Paralympic Games quarterly report, May, London: DCMS.

Department of Culture, Media and Sport (2010a) *London 2012: A legacy for disabled people*, London: DCMS.

Department of Culture, Media and Sport (2010b) *Plans for the legacy from the 2012 Olympic and Paralympic Games*, London: DCMS.

Department for Culture, Media and Sport (2009) New legacy promise puts disabled people at the heart of London 2012, Press release, 3 December.

Department of Culture, Media and Sport (2008) *Taking Part: The national survey of culture leisure and sport (complete estimates from year 3)*, London: DCMS.

Department for Culture, Media and Sport/Strategy Unit (2002) *Game Plan: A strategy for delivering the government's sport and physical activity objectives*, London: DCMS.

Dowse, S. (2011) Paralympic potential: Opportunities and risks, in Weed, M. and Wellard, I. (eds) *Wellbeing, Health and Leisure*, Publication 111, Eastbourne: Leisure Studies Association.

Economic Development, Culture, Sport & Tourism Committee (2011) *A sporting legacy for London?* London: GL Authority.

Enoch, N. (2010) Towards a contemporary national structure for youth sport in England, in Collins, M. (ed.) *Examining Sport Development*, London: Routledge, 45–71.

European Tour Operators Association (n.d.) *Olympic Report*, London: ETOA.

Girginov, V. and Hills, L. (2009) The political process of constructing a sustainable London Olympics sports development legacy, *International Journal of Sports Policy*, 1, 2: 161–181.

Grant Thornton/Ecorys/Loughborough University (2011) *Meta-Evaluation of the Impacts and Legacy of the London 2012 Olympic and Paralympic Games Summary, Reports 1 and 2*, London: DCMS.

Hespe, C. (2010) *London 2012 Games: Sports legacy agenda for local government*, London: Local Government Association/Kent County Council/ISPAL.

Jaconelli, M. and Porter, L. (2009) 'Just a person in a wee flat': Being displaced by the Commonwealth Games in Glasgow's East End, *Planning Theory and Practice*, 10, 3: 399–403.

Johnson, V., Currie, G. and Stanley, J. (2011) Exploring transport to arts and cultural activities as a facilitator of social inclusion, *Transport Policy*, 18: 68–75.

Keech, M. (2011) Youth sport and London 2012's legacy, in Sugden, J. and Tomlinson, A. (eds) *Watching the Olympics: Power, policy and representation*, London: Routledge.

London Development Agency, DCMS, and Mayor of London (2011a) *Working towards an inclusive Games 2008–09: First annual report of the London 2012 Equality and Diversity Forum*, London: LDA.

London Development Agency, DCMS, and Mayor of London (2011b) *Lessons Learned from the London 2012 Construction Project: Jobs, skills, futures*, London: LDA.

London Organising Committee for the Olympic Games (2008) *Open: The world in a city – diversity and inclusion strategy*, London: LOCOG.

London Sport (1990) *A Playing Field Strategy for London*, London: LCSR.

MacRury, I. and Poynter, G. (2009) *London's Olympic Legacy: A report for the OECD and DCLG*, London: University of East London.

Mayor of London (2010) *Inclusive and Active 2: A sport and physical activity strategy for disabled people in London 2010–15*, London: Greater London Authority/NHS/Interactive.

Mayor of London (2009) *A Sporting Future for London*, London: Greater London Authority.

Mayor of London (2008) *Time for Action*, London: Greater London Authority.

McCartney, G., Thomas, S., Thomson, H., Scott, J., Hamilton, V., Hanlon, P., Morrison, D. S. and Bond, L.(2010) The health and socioeconomic impacts of major multi-sport events: a systematic review (1978–2008), *British Medical Journal*. Online: 2010:340c2369doi/10.1136/bmj2369.

Minnaert, L. (2010) *Non-Infrastructural Impacts of the Olympic Games on Socially Excluded Groups in the Host Cities*, London: Centre for Tourism Research, University of Westminster.

Office for Disability Issues (2011) *London 2012: A legacy for disabled* people, London: ODI.

Olympic Delivery Authority (2011a) *Inclusive Design Lessons learned from the London 2012 Construction Project Learning Legacy*, London: ODA.

Olympic Delivery Authority (2011b) *Everyone: An integrated equality scheme 2009–12, learning legacy*, London: ODA.

Pappous, S. (2011) Do the Olympic Games lead to a sustainable increase in grass roots sport participation? A secondary analysis of Athens 2004, in Savery, J. and Gilbert, K. (eds) *Sustainability and Sport*, Chicago: Common Ground Publishing.

Sport England (2008) *Strategy 2008–11*, London: SE.

Sport Industry Research Centre (2011) *Sport Unlimited: final (monitoring) report*, Sheffield: SIRC for Sport England.

Sport, Physical Recreation and Activity Research Centre (2011a) *The Games in Schools: PE and cross-curricular impacts*, Canterbury: Christ Church Canterbury University. Online: 2011.can22.07.201:0008.

Sport, Physical Recreation and Activity Research Centre (SPEAR, 2011b) *Street Games Additionality Evaluation*, Canterbury: Christ Church Canterbury University.

Surborg, B., Van Wynsberghe, R. and Wyly, E. (2008) Mapping the Olympic growth machine: Transnational urbanism and the growth machine disapora, *City*, 12, 3: 341–355.

Thrush, C. and Amory, J. (2011) *Equality, Inclusion, Employment and Skills: Process and systems case study – learning legacy*, London: ODA.

Thrush, C., Eley, S.-J. and Martins, L. (2011) *Jobs, Skills And Futures Brokerage, Learning Legacy*, London: ODA.

Trends Business Research Ltd (2010) *CASE Regional Insights: London*, London: TBS for DCMS.

Weed, M., Coren, E. and Fiore, J. (2009) *A Systematic Review of the Evidence Base for Developing a Physical Activity and Health Legacy from the London 2012 Olympic and Paralympic Games*, London: Department of Health.

Weed, M. (2008) The relationship between sport and tourism, Powerpoint presentation, Canterbury Christ Church University, Centre for Sport, Physical Education and Activity Research.

Weed, M. E. (2007) Olympic tourism flows keynote paper, at Event Tourism: Enhancing the Visitor Economy conference, Bournemouth, January.

PART 5

London 2012 and the world's participation

19

NATIONAL ELITE SPORT POLICIES IN PREPARATION FOR LONDON 2012

Barrie Houlihan, Jae-Woo Park and Mayumi Ya-Ya Yamamoto

The money invested directly and indirectly by the UK Government in preparation for the Olympic Games and Paralympic Games in Athens in 2004 resulted in the winning of 30 medals at a cost of £5.3 million per medal (see Table 19.1). The funding that produced the medals and placed the United Kingdom tenth in the medals table was part of a steadily increasing expenditure on elite athletes. Following the award of the 2012 Olympic Games and Paralympic Games to London in 2005 the Government 'agreed a funding package of £722 million from April 2006 to March 2013, doubling the direct funding for elite sports and athletes from £300 million to £600 million' (House of Commons, 2008, p. 7). Although this figure was subsequently reduced to £550 million and despite the post-2006 figures not being directly comparable to those in previous years, it is clear that the upward trend in funding evident from the early 1990s has continued and accelerated.

The United Kingdom is not alone in increasing expenditure to buy Olympic success. In one of the first analyses of the cost of winning an Olympic medal, Hogan and Norton (2000) showed how the cost per medal to the Australian Government rose steadily over the period 1980–1996 and concluded that the cost of a medal at the then forthcoming Athens 2000 would be approximately £7 million for a bronze and approximately £19 million for silver or gold.

Not surprisingly, China is also at the forefront of the inflation in the cost of medals. In 2000 the country's annual budget for the sport ministry was ¥1.6 billion. Over the period 2001–2004, the country added ¥100 million on top of the previous year's budget for sports; over 2005–2008 the additions doubled to ¥200 million per year. This did not include special funds for the Beijing

Table 19.1 Funding estimates and Olympic medal success, 1992–2008

Olympic Games	*Funding for elite sport*	*Cost per gold medal*	*Cost per medal*
Barcelona 1992	£62 million	£12.4 million	£3.1 million
Atlanta 1996	£67.4 million	£67.4 million	£4.5 million
Sydney 2000	£171.7 million	£15.6 million	£6.1 million
Athens 2004	£166.6 million	£18.5 million	£5.3 million
Beijing 2008	£394 million	£20.7 million	£8.4 million

Source: Zheng, 2011.

Games, which were estimated at ¥4 billion. In the sport of gymnastics, for example, the investment in medals rose from around ¥20 million per year over 2001–2003 to ¥80 million per year over 2003–2004.[1]

As the global economy struggles to move out of recession it is unlikely that the increased pace of investment will be maintained, but explaining the willingness of governments of a variety of ideological hues to expend public resources so freely over the previous 10–15 years is still surprising: after all, it is *only* sport. Not only is understanding the motives for such heavy government funding a requirement, but it is also important to consider when the upward trend in funding will level off and begin to decline. In relation to the motives for such high levels of expenditure one needs to acknowledge that public policy is rarely the product of the accumulation of evidence, but is more likely to be the product of the interaction between interests, deep-rooted myths, contemporary ideology and selective use of evidence.

As regards the evidence base, the only unequivocal evidence related to elite success is the strong correlation between funding and winning medals. In other words, the impact of public expenditure on elite sport policy objectives has been clearly positive: the more governments spend on the preparation of elite athletes the greater are their chances of winning medals. Needless to say, this bold statement needs some qualification, not least of which is that if the other major sports powers are also increasing their expenditure then 'success' might mean retaining rather than increasing a country's share of Olympic medals. However, if one is searching for evidence then this is one of the few statements that can be made with confidence. Indeed, numerous researchers have indicated the weakness of the evidence base in relation to claims of elite sport's capacity to deliver on objectives, whether those objectives are to increase general participation in sport (Carmichael and Grix, 2011; Feddersen *et al.*, 2009; Girginov and Hills, 2008; Green, 2006) or to increase national morale (what is sometimes referred to as the 'feel-good' factor) (Grix and Carmichael, 2012). The steady climb in investment in elite sport is much more clearly the outcome of the effectiveness of the mythologising about elite sport by politicians, sports administrators and the media (for example, that it reflects the character of a nation and that it develops positive personal qualities related to teamwork, leadership and values of fair play) and the recognition by politicians that elite sport success is a malleable resource that they can use in relation to a variety of diplomatic, welfare and economic objectives in the confident expectation of public acceptance of its legitimacy and potential effectiveness.

Despite the weak evidence base for any general social or other benefits arising from elite sporting success at the Olympic Games, the apparent unwavering depth of governmental and public support for investment in elite sport development provides a very comfortable environment for those athletes and organisations concerned with the preparation of the UK Olympic squad for the London 2012 Games. While the particular socio-political context differs across countries, there is considerable uniformity in the assumptions that governments make about the capacity of elite sport success to achieve a wide range of non-sport objectives, and it is this confidence that underpins their willingness to continue to invest heavily at the elite level and to seek to gain a competitive advantage over their rivals. In the sections that follow three countries – the United Kingdom, South Korea and Japan – are used to illustrate not only the increasing expenditure on elite sport, but also the increasing sophistication in the use of that investment.

In activities such as international sport, where a competitive advantage is sought, it is often the case that domestic policy innovation will be complemented and stimulated by the actions of competitor nations: domestic policy innovation and learning are complemented by policy transfer between countries. While a dramatic breakthrough in training or preparation techniques is sought, progress in improving the quality of an Olympic squad tends to be a slow and relatively gradual process, with performance at the previous Games providing feedback on the effectiveness of medium- to long-term strategies. Thus, performance at Beijing 2008 will for some countries, such as the United Kingdom, provide confirmation that the policy direction is appropriate, while for others, such as Australia, it might begin to raise concerns about the effectiveness of current policy. What will be described and discussed below is often cautious policy refinement, incremental innovation and steady intensification rather than dramatic change. As is the case in the preparation of athletes, the typical pattern is the constant search for minor improvements across a range of factors rather than the revolutionary innovation.

The United Kingdom

As mentioned above, the award of the 2012 Olympic Games and Paralympic Games to London in 2005 prompted an acceleration in the Government's investment in high-performance sport. Prior to 2006 (when the additional funding was allocated) the UK Government had already taken significant steps towards strengthening the infrastructure of elite, and especially Olympic and Paralympic, sport. John Major's Conservative Government prioritised elite sport success in the 1995 policy statement, *Sport: Raising the Game* (DNH, 1995), and introduced the National Lottery as an important source of funding to help deliver medal success. The Government also took the important decision to create in 1997 a specialist agency, UK Sport, to oversee the achievement of the Government's elite sport ambitions. Also in 1997 the newly elected Labour Government published a sport policy document, *A Sporting Future for All*, which accepted the previous Government's prioritisation of elite sport. Evidence of this commitment was the establishment in 1999 of the network of high-performance centres known collectively as the UK Sports Institute, which were designed to concentrate the scarce resources (coaching, medical and sport science) required for Olympic and Paralympic success.

Three years later in 2002 the Government published *Game Plan* (DCMS, 2002), a strategy document which took the privileging of elite sport as unproblematic and uncontroversial. The strategy was designed to establish a more systematic and professional approach to the identification and development of talented athletes. However, as Bergsgard *et al.* note, 'Game Plan does not discuss … *whether* international success should be pursued, it only discusses *how* it should be pursued' (2007, p. 164, emphasis in original). By the middle of the first decade of the present century the reform of elite sport policy had acquired considerable momentum. While it is accurate to identify substantial continuity of goals between the Conservative Government of John Major and the New Labour Government of Tony Blair, the position regarding the means to achieve those ends is more complex. In some respects there is evidence of continuity of means; this is most obviously the case in terms of the utilisation of the proceeds of the National Lottery to fund new initiatives such as the UK Sports Institute and to underpin the purchase of elite coaching expertise from around the world. However, the approach of the Blair Government differed in a number of highly significant respects from that of the Conservative Government.

First, the New Labour Government tightened its control over UK Sport under the guise of fulfilling its commitment to modernise the institutions of government. As Houlihan and Green (2009) noted, modernisation involved greatly limiting the degree of relative autonomy that the agency had previously enjoyed and re-establishing the relationship on a more formal contractual basis which involved, *inter alia*, the reform of the membership of the governing board (replacing members who were frequently representing sports interest with those who had been selected on the basis of their functional skills) and the formalisation of performance targets as the basis for tighter accountability. Second, and as a consequence of the changed relationship between the Government and UK Sport, the relationship between UK Sport and the country's national governing bodies (NGBs) was also subject to modernisation as a condition of continued funding.

NGBs were expected to professionalise, to organise themselves at the board level in a way that mirrored their funder, and to be subject to the same accountability regime. In many ways the re-engineering of the relationship between the NGBs of sport and UK Sport is the most significant change prompted by the desire for more medals. That the transition from a relationship based substantially on an entitlement culture, according to which NGBs assumed an entitlement to public funding, to a contractual resource-dependency culture was achieved so swiftly is indicative less of the resolve of the Government and more of the scale of financial inducements on offer.

The third difference was the increasing organisational, financial and policy differentiation within the sport policy network. What at one time looked like an emergent policy community for sport has fragmented (to place a negative interpretation on the pattern of change) or become more specialised (to interpret the change more positively). The organisational unity within the GB Sports Council has given way gradually to a sharper differentiation of functional responsibilities between Sport England and UK Sport. The organisational differentiation has been reinforced by a more rigid hypothecation of funding with far less scope for cross subsidy. Moreover, the conceptual unity of the sport development continuum has been superseded by a cluster of much more self-contained policy sub-sectors around community sport, youth sport and elite sport. The combined effect of these developments has been to undermine the admittedly weak interdependence and reciprocity between elite, community and youth/school sport interests and replace it with a culture of self-sufficiency (largely delusional given NGBs heavy reliance on UK Sport funding). As will be illustrated later, the production of elite athletes is no longer assumed to depend on a percolation model of talent identification and development. The impact of this growing perception of self-sufficiency at the elite development level is that it has paved the way for the creation of defensive advocacy coalitions which will increasingly see their opponents in the struggle for public resources not in other policy sub-sectors (defence, housing, education, etc.), but other areas of sport such as community and youth sport.

The fourth major difference between the New Labour and Conservative Governments' strategies concerned the willingness to agree to the progressive concentration of funding on the sports which offered the best Olympic medal prospects. Since 1999/2000, when UK Sport funded 40 sports (including non-Olympic sports such as caving, gliding and parachuting), there has been a steady reduction in the sports receiving funding to a point in the mid-2000s when the figure had almost halved. The policy slogan adopted by UK Sport of 'no compromise' was most clearly reflected in its funding policy. However, the concentration of financial resources was also mirrored in the concentration of non-financial resources, such as coaching, sports medicine and sports science support through the development of a network of elite sports institutes.

The final major difference relates to the concentration of resources and to the pursuit of modernisation, and concerns the attempted reform of the coaching infrastructure in the United Kingdom. The publication of the report of the coaching task force (DCMS, 2002) emphasised the need for more full-time coaches and the professionalisation of their education and training.

The award of the Olympic Games and Paralympic Games to London in 2005 led to a sharp increase in public funding for elite sport, announced in 2006, and resulted in a notable acceleration in the momentum of some of the changes listed above and also some arguably tactical innovations which might have more substantial long-term strategic consequences. Acceleration in momentum was perhaps most evident in the extent of oversight of the work of UK Sport exercised by the Government and Parliament. However, the increase in oversight was as much, if not more, to do with the hosting of the Games as with the likely performance of the UK squad. Nevertheless, not only did the Government allocate ministerial responsibility for the

Olympic Games (a responsibility combined with the posts of Secretary of State for Culture, Media and Sport and Minister for Sport), but the House of Commons Select Committee for Culture, Media and Sport held a series of hearings related to the preparations for the Games. Not only does the Committee question the Secretary of State each year on the work of their department, which includes oversight of UK Sport, but the Committee has also held a series of hearings specifically related to the preparations for the Games. The closer scrutiny by Parliament is paralleled by the closer scrutiny exercised by UK Sport over the major Olympic and Paralympic NGBs. However, the financial leverage available to UK Sport (that is, the opportunity to cut the allocations to underperforming NGBs as was the case with swimming following the 2004 Olympic Games) has been reduced due to the substantial increase in funding provided by the Government to help the preparations for 2012. Nevertheless, there is an acute awareness that the Government's generosity is not likely to survive far beyond the Closing Ceremony and that a strong performance in London is likely to reduce the extent of budget reductions. Ironically, for an organisation committed to a tough business approach to improving medal performance, the increase in Government funding for the preparation of the UK Olympic and Paralympic squads has resulted in the funding of a number of sports, such as handball, table tennis and water polo, whose medal prospects are slight but which will add to the visibility of the United Kingdom at the event.

Apart from the substantial increase in funding, the most significant change in UK elite sport policy since the award of the Games to London has been the investment in high-quality coaches, which built upon the earlier attempts to reform the training and development of coaches in the United Kingdom through the work of Sportscoach UK and the report of the coaching task force. However, the main innovation has been to bring in foreign coaches. As de Bosscher (2007) has shown in a comparison of the earnings of coaches in Italy, the Netherlands and the Flanders region of Belgium, UK coaches are substantially better paid, with one-third reporting earnings of over €50,000 by comparison to none in Italy, 5 per cent in the Netherlands and just over 3 per cent in Flanders. According to Hubbard (*Independent*, 2011),

> At least 21 of the 26 sports in which Team GB compete in London will have performance directors or senior coaches who have been expensively head-hunted.... In all there are 52 foreigners working at various levels. Several are on six-figure salaries. In athletics Charles van Commenee, the Dutch disciplinarian brought in to succeed axed Briton Dave Collins [see Chapter 9] as performance director, is believed to earn approaching £200,000 a year.

It is likely that only boxing, hockey and shooting will have British coaches.

These strategic changes, many of which pre-date the Beijing Games, have had a dramatic impact on the preparations of the UK squad for the Games. There have been a number of other innovations that are better described as tactical developments, but if continued after 2012 they might have more long-term significance for the broader aspects of UK sport. It was mentioned above that the percolation method for identifying and developing sporting talent was under threat. The percolation method, according to which talented young athletes are identified at school or in junior club settings and then gradually moved up through district, county, regional to national development squads, has in many sports operated for some time alongside fast-track methods, such as the football academies which remove talented players at a young age from school sport and lower-level club sport. However, the imperative to maximise medals in London 2012 has led UK Sport to introduce a series of talent identification schemes which bypass the percolation process either by fast-tracking potential medal winners into development squads or by encouraging athletes who have not reached the highest level in one sport to transfer to another sport. The recent and current schemes are summarised in Table 19.2.

While some of the schemes listed in Table 19.2 are focused on 2016 rather than 2012 there have been a number of athletes who have been sufficiently successful to be under consideration for the 2012 Olympic and Paralympic squads. From the point of view of UK Sport these innovative schemes are currently exhibiting signs of success although the true test will only come in 2012, 2014 or 2016. However, it is important to consider the longer term possible impact of the schemes. First, what will be the impact on NGB-organised talent identification and development programmes? It remains to be seen whether NGBs and clubs will be willing to invest in talent identification if an elite squad can be (or is being) assembled in parallel and to some extent in competition with their efforts. It would certainly be tempting to abandon NGB and club-based labour-intensive scouting and development structures in favour of nationally marketed schemes that might still deliver gold medals for their sport.

While it might be claimed that clubs would not necessarily suffer as a result of the emergence of a parallel talent identification and development process in their sport, it might also be argued, perhaps more persuasively, that they will be affected negatively by the loss of talented competitors from their sport. In many sports those who reach a high level of proficiency, but fail to reach international standard, often fulfil important functions within their clubs – as coaches, players and administrators – and their loss would be a serious depletion of an important club resource. While this claim might be countered on the grounds that the loss to one sport is a gain for another it is questionable whether an athlete develops the same level of commitment and loyalty to a sport into which they have been parachuted at a relatively mature stage in their career. They may not have developed the same depth of loyalty to a club and to their peers as those who grow up with a club are likely to do.

The drive to improve the performance of UK athletes at the Olympic Games and Paralympic Games received substantial added momentum following the award of the 2012 Games to London. The performance of the UK squad at Beijing 2008 was strong evidence of the rapid impact of the changes to the scale of funding, the concentration of non-financial resources in the UK Sports Institute network and the organisational drive provided by UK Sport. Since Beijing 2008 there has been a substantial acceleration in the effort and resources devoted to ensuring that the UK squad is at least as successful in 2012 as it was in 2008. What is less clear is the long-term impact of this arguable over-concentration on elite success on the health of the NGB club structure in particular and on community sport participation more generally. Not only is there a need to assess the success in achieving the promised legacy of the 2012 Games, but there is also a need to be alert to some of the unintended consequences, particularly for the 140,000 sports clubs in the United Kingdom.

South Korea

South Korea has a long history of success in the Olympic Games and of government support for elite sport. In 1988, when the Summer Games were held in Seoul, the country came fourth in the medals table (33 medals of which 12 were gold). After that peak in performance there was a steady decline (seventh in 1992 and tenth in 1996) to a relatively poor performance at Sydney 2000, where the country only managed twelfth place (28 medals of which 8 were gold). Although this was still a good performance when compared to other countries of similar population and wealth, it was considered a significant disappointment by the Government, who began to put in place a series of policies designed to restore the country to a place among the top ten most successful countries. One of the most obvious changes was a substantial increase in the elite

Table 19.2 UK Sport talent identification schemes

Scheme title	*Description*
Talent 2012: Paralympic potential	The purpose is to find individuals who have undiscovered talents in a number of Paralympic sports. Potential Paralympians need to be between 25 and 35 years of age, have or be eligible for a UK passport and have some experience in sport. At the selection events applicants will be assessed in terms of their suitability for particular Paralympic events.
Girls4Gold	The aim is to identify sportswomen who exhibit potential in one of UK Sport's target sports – cycling, bob skeleton, canoeing, modern pentathlon, rowing and sailing. Applicants need to be: between 17 and 25 years old; competing in any sport at county/regional level; fit, powerful and strong; and mentally tough and competitive.
Talent 2012: Fighting Chance	A talent transfer scheme aimed at athletes in 'kicking oriented martial arts' to take part in trials for inclusion in the 'elite taekwondo academy'.
Pitch2Podium	In conjunction with the football and rugby NGBs the scheme is designed to attract football and rugby academy members who have failed to make the grade in their sport to consider transferring to an Olympic sport such as rowing or track and field.
Talent 2012: Tall and Talented	A scheme to identify potential competitors in sports such as basketball and rowing. Applicants need to be: aged between 15 and 22 years old; exceptionally tall (men over 190 cm and women over 180 cm); competing in any sport at a minimum of county/regional level; quick, agile and skilful and/or fit and powerful and strong; and mentally tough and competitive.
Sporting Giants	Launched in 2007 the scheme is aimed at identifying potential athletes who are tall (a minimum of 190 cm for men and 180 cm for women), young (between 16 and 25) and with 'some sort of athletic background'. Athletes who make it through the selection process are likely to be directed to sports such as handball, volleyball and rowing. The publicity attracted 4,800 applicants of whom 4,000 were eligible to proceed to the next stage in the selection process.
Power2Podium	The selection process is aimed at identifying potential Olympic competitors in a range of sports including athletics, sprint canoeing, sprint cycling, rugby 7s, weightlifting, bob skeleton, bobsleigh.

sports budget from ₩54,059 million (approximately £30,521,300) in 2002 to ₩142,701 million (approximately £80,567,900) in 2007.[2] (For more information see Table 19.3.)

It should be noted that a sharp decrease in the elite sports budget from ₩177,563 million in 2009 to ₩42,404 million in 2010 was due to a considerable increase in the 'Sport for All' budget in the same period.

In 2004 the country finished in ninth place and by Beijing 2008 had consolidated its position among the sports powers by finishing seventh and winning 13 gold medals.

As with the United Kingdom a public perception of underperformance was an important element in prompting a review of elite sport policy and, similarly, a greater concentration of resources on the sports where the country held a comparative advantage was deemed to be the basis for improving success. The priority, as expressed by the Korean Sports Council (KSC), was to maintain a 'top ten' position for the country in the Summer Olympic Games. In 2004 the KSC published Vision 21, which set out a medium- to long-term strategy (2005–2014) for improving elite performance. An important element of the strategy was the system of 'selection and concentration' which was intended to ensure that resources were allocated to those sports that had the greatest potential for medal success. To this end the strategy divided sports into two groups: those where competitors were most likely to win gold medals (which included archery, marathon, badminton, fencing, male gymnastics, judo, shooting, table tennis, taekwondo and wrestling); and those where competitors were likely to win other medals (which included swimming, gymnastics, female basketball, boxing, cycling, handball, hockey, sailing and female wrestling). A second feature of the policy which is similar to that of the United Kingdom is the willingness to import foreign coaches to improve the quality of athlete performance. After the poor performance in track and field events in Sydney 2000, the Korean Athletics Federation began to import foreign coaches, a process that accelerated following the successful bid in 2007 to host the 2011 Athletics World Championships. An example of the introduction of a foreign coach for improving the most vulnerable short-distance events in athletics was Miyakawa Chiaki, the former Japanese national athlete for 100 m and currently professor at Tokai University (Park, 2011). This use of foreign coaches is also observed in other sports such as badminton. For badminton, the nation's men and women single athletes competed in the Athens 2004 and Beijing 2008 Olympic Games under the supervision of Chinese coach, Li Mao. The successful bid for the Athletics World Championships also prompted the Government to invest more resources in the development of a sport science capacity and in elite training facilities (MCST, 2008). Sports science capacity would be concentrated in the existing national training centres and in a new indoor athletics training and competition facility in Daegu city.

Because of the autonomy of the Korean NGBs it was necessary for the KSC to attract their support for the strategy of selection and concentration. While the introduction of greater selectivity in finance was a concern to many NGBs, they were persuaded to accept the new policy in part by the extent of the criticism of national performance at Sydney and in part because it was apparent that many other countries were adopting or had already adopted a similar strategy.

Table 19.3 The elite sports budget of the National Treasury, 2005–2010 (million won)

	2005	*2006*	*2007*	*2008*	*2009*	*2010*
Elite sport	77,718 (£43,879,000)	98,342 (£55,523,123)	142,701 (£80,567,900)	193,058 (£108,999,000)	177,563 (£100,250,680)	42,404 (£23,941,000)

Source: Sports White Paper, Ministry of Culture, Sport and Tourism (2010: 98).

Korean elite sport policy is implemented under the auspices of the Ministry of Culture, Sports and Tourism, by the KSC. While the KSC has a wide remit there is an open acknowledgement that its primary responsibility is the delivery of elite sport success. To this end the KSC funds two national training centres (Taeneung Athletic Village and Taebaek Training Centre), which are modelled on similar centres in Japan. If athletes do not train within either of these two centres it is often because they are completing their military service and, if they are at the elite level, they would train full-time at the Korea Armed Forces Athletic Corps (popularly known as 'Sangmu'). These well-established training centres have been relatively effective in maintaining Korea's position among the world's sports powers, but their success has not prevented recent innovation in talent identification and development policy. For example, in 2007 the Korean Foundation for the Next Generation of Sports Talent (NEST) was established. At first sight NEST would seem to overlap with the work of the KSC, but NEST argues that its remit is broader and more long term than that of the KSC. In its 2009 annual plan NEST identified ten key projects, which included developing programmes for nurturing young talent, fostering coaching and the development of specialists to support disabled athletes. For 2011 NEST reveals its key business projects on its webpage, which include the construction of a specialised sports talent nourishment system, the nurture of global sport leaders, an athlete career programme and the support of national sport schools.

Any discussion of recent developments in Korean sport policy would be incomplete without mention of the importance of the business sector and the role of the Chaebol (the major conglomerates). In his study of athletics, archery and baseball, Park (2011) illustrated the central role of Chaebol in providing these sports with financial support and business leadership. All three sports were led by businesspeople from their major sponsor (for example, Samsung for athletics and Hyundai for archery). The major consequence of the involvement of Chaebol companies is to greatly increase the financial resources available to elite sport, enabling not only investment in expert coaches and sport science support, but also enabling the offer of substantial cash rewards to athletes who win medals at the Olympic Games and other major international events. However, the high level of business involvement also tied the finances of major Olympic sports to the vagaries of the business cycle. For example, during the economic crisis of 1997–2000, which resulted in intervention by the International Monetary Fund, over 60 business sports teams were disbanded and 212 male and 143 female athletes lost their funding (Bang, 1998). However, during times of economic growth a number of businesses remain willing to invest heavily in elite sport. Perhaps the best recent example is the opening of the Samsung Sport Science Centre in 2007, which provides high-level sports science support to athletes from a range of sports (currently over ten) that the company currently supports.

Nonetheless, while the new strategy indicates the strength of the Government's commitment to Olympic success, the strategy also reinforces a growing concern that the pursuit of medals is at the expense of the human rights of the athletes, many of whom are student-athletes. As Yamamoto (2008, p. 69) noted, although the Korean elite development system has been successful, there has been 'growing criticism of the excessive hours of training that athletes of junior, middle and high school age undertake and the "trade off" between studying and training'. The expressions of concern were not just limited to students, but also related to female athletes and the danger of violence and sexual abuse. The nature and extent of abuse was publicised in a series of television programmes which resulted in a resolution being passed by the Korean National Assembly in 2007 to 'normalise school sport' and the publication by the education ministry of a revised strategy (a plan for the revitalisation of school athletic teams) aimed at school sport (MEST, 2008).

Overall there are marked similarities between the elite sport strategies of the United Kingdom and South Korea, especially in relation to the concentration of resources on the best medal prospects, the strategic investment in sport science and the significance of hosting an event for leveraging additional funding. Where South Korea differs from the United Kingdom is in the heavy reliance on the Chaebol and the stronger involvement of the armed forces in elite athlete development.

Japan

Unlike South Korea and the United Kingdom, the award of the 1964 Olympic Games to Japan resulted only in a temporary increase in the Government's interest in supporting elite sport success. Indeed, the promotion of community sport remained a priority (though a modestly supported one) throughout much of the 1970s and 1980s. However, like South Korea and the United Kingdom it was a relatively poor performance at two Olympic Games (Seoul 1988, where Japan ranked ten places behind South Korea, and – more importantly – twenty-third place at Atlanta 1996) that pushed the issue of elite sport performance up the Government's agenda. The publication in 1989 of the report by the Ministry of Education's Advisory Council on Health and Physical Education on sports promotion and the subsequent 1992 white paper had only limited impact, but following the poor performance in Atlanta the government produced a ten-year strategy – the Basic Plan (MEXT, 2000) – designed to enable Japan to regain the position it held (fifth) when it hosted the Games in 1964.

Efforts to improve elite performance were underwritten by a one-off allocation of ¥25 billion (approximately £97.5 million) (the Sports Promotion Fund) in 1990 with the Basic Plan relying more on funding from the lottery (the *toto*) established in 2001. Although the major priorities of the Basic Plan emphasised the development of community sport and school sport as much as elite sporting success, it was soon clear that community and youth sport were in large part means to the achievement of the central priority of elite success. The Basic Plan established or reinforced four elements which continue to define elite sport policy objectives: (1) the ambition to win 3.5 per cent of all medals available at the Summer and Winter Olympic Games; (2) to invest in sports science; (3) to complement the strategic plan of the Japan Olympic Committee (the Gold Plan); and (4) to establish a national training centre. The decision to invest in sport science and medicine resulted in the establishment in 2001 of the Japan Institute of Sport Sciences (JISS) (as a division within the public agency the National Agency for the Advancement of Sports and Health – NAASH), which quickly became the central science and training resource for Olympic athletes. Although JISS contained a small training facility it was inadequate for the number of athletes who needed access to a specialist facility and pressure within sport and the Government mounted for the establishment of a larger specialist training centre for elite athletes.

The rationale for the establishment of the National Training Centre (NTC) in 2007 was not just the shortage of appropriate facilities in Japan, but a recognition that 'nine out of ten countries in the gold medal table at the Athens Olympic Games possess[ed]' a central elite training facility (MEXT, 2006, p. 26). The NTC operates in conjunction with the JISS and is managed by the NAASH, but with the Japan Olympic Committee (JOC) playing a central role in designing the programmes. The degree of complementarity between the objectives of the Government and those of the JOC is indicated by the extent to which the Committee's *Gold Plan II*, published in 2006, echoes the sentiments of the government's *Basic Plan* and also by the fact that the Government has delegated to the JOC responsibility for overseeing the achievement of international success. Just prior to Beijing 2008 an evaluation of the country's elite sport strategy was commissioned by MEXT and concluded that the new arrangements had been instrumental in the success in 2004 and were likely to contribute to success in 2008. As it turned out Japan was only relatively successful in Beijing, coming eighth in the medals table and winning 25 medals, including 9 gold. Rather than consolidate its success in Athens, Japan had slipped from fifth to eighth, won 12 fewer medals and failed to overtake South Korea.

In summary, Japanese Olympic success is the product of the relatively recent adoption of a more systematic approach to talent identification and development. It is only since the early years of the present century that Japan has put in place the organisational infrastructure and the necessary financial support to enable the delivery of a coherent and consistent approach to elite athlete preparation. Recent progress has been made in six key areas. First, the Team Nippon Multi-Supports Project was launched in 2008 and retitled as the National Project for the Improvement in High Performance Sport in 2009, with the specific objective of winning more medals in 2012 and at Sochi in 2014. The objective of the National Project is to strategically invest in the provision of 'comprehensive professional support' for targeted sports and potential medal-winning athletes. It aimed to create 'a unified and consistent multi-support system, unique to Japan' (MEXT press release, 21 June 2010) and comprises a special athlete support programme and a research and development programme aimed at developing tighter collaboration between practitioners and researchers. As part of the special athlete support programme, in 2009 the NAASH/JISS implemented a 'Multi-Support House' intended to provide on-site support to the athletes during London 2012 and trialled during the 2010 Asian Games. The University of Tsukuba was also granted funding to undertake 'cutting edge' performance research. In 2010, eight events were targeted, which was expanded to 16 events (both Summer and Winter Games) in 2011. These initiatives were supported by a substantially increased budget, as shown in Table 19.4.

Second, over the last ten years the country has radically improved the availability of specialist facilities to elite athletes. The opening of the JISS in 2002 was complemented in 2006 by the announcement of plans to build the NTC (the latter partly stimulated by the failure of the Japanese squad at the Winter Olympic Games in Turin, where the country won only one gold medal). While the decision to build the NTC was a significant investment, the budget of the JISS was fixed by legislation which, until the recent increase in budget, prevented it from expanding to meet the increasing demand for its services for athletes, coaches and NGBs.

The third key area where progress has been made is in relation to direct support to athletes and coaches. Of particular importance is the direct funding that goes to athletes. If athletes are within the JOC's Elite A group they would be eligible for a maximum allocation of ¥200,000 (approximately £900). The modesty of this sum forces athletes to seek additional funding from business sponsors who will provide funding often in return for public relations work by the athletes. While this dual-funding approach is often effective in supporting an athlete's

Table 19.4 Budget for the National Project for the Improvement in High Performance Sport, 2008–2012

Year	*Budget (yen)*
2008	204 million
2009	608 million
2010	2.412 billion
2011	2.2 billion
2012	3.2 billion

preparations, it is indicative of the fragility of the funding base. As was the case with South Korea, the heavy reliance on corporations makes athletes vulnerable to the vicissitudes of the economy and introduces a high degree of uncertainty into the long-term preparations required for international success. In addition, the demands from sponsoring companies can be a distraction from systematic training.

The fourth area of progress relates to improvements in the quality of coaching. As was the case in many countries, the needs of coaches have experienced relative neglect when compared to the needs of athletes – ignoring the fact that one of the central needs of athletes is access to high-quality coaching. In the early part of the 2000s the Competitive Sports Division of MEXT introduced a system for supporting and developing coaches working with elite athletes. In 2003 it was announced that two high-level coaches would be allocated to each national federation. It was also decided that the newly established NTC would host coach development training. Despite the progress that has been made in recent years, Japan, like both the United Kingdom and South Korea, still relies on foreign coaches in a range of sports, including football, volleyball, badminton, hockey and handball.

The fifth area of progress is closely associated with the issue of coaching, and concerns the process by which talent is identified and developed. While the recognition of weaknesses in talent identification pre-date the 1964 Games they remained fragmented, relying on corporations and schools rather than national federations. Subsequent to the establishment of the JISS, talent identification gained a higher priority and led to the JISS–JOC-supported Fukuoka Sports Talent Scout Project, which was launched in 2004 and involved the systematic selection of children based on scientific and genetic data. As yet there has been no evaluation of the impact of the project on the selection of talented athletes.

The final recent change is distinctive, although not unique to Japan, and concerns the systematic scanning of the global sport environment for examples of good practice that might be transferable to Japan. In 2001 the JISS formed the Department of Sports Information which, working in conjunction with the JOC's Information and Medical Science Special Committee, is responsible not only for information gathering from around the world, but also for the effective dissemination of that information throughout the national sports network. This policy is complemented by the development of a long-term relationship with Loughborough University. The Japan team will use Loughborough as its base for the London 2012 Games, but has signed a memorandum of understanding on research collaboration. In part the stimulus for these developments is the perception within Japan that it is isolated from the major sports science and coaching networks in Europe and North America.

As regards Japan's ambitions for London 2012, the plan expressed within the JOC is to improve on the country's performance at Beijing 2008 (eighth in the medal table with nine gold medals). While the president of the JOC has also referred to a target of 15 gold medals the official target remains the same as for Beijing 2008 – 3.5 per cent of all medals.

Conclusion

In all three countries the development of a more systematic approach to elite athlete development has either emerged or certainly accelerated in the last ten years. While the acknowledgement by governments of the public relations and diplomatic value of a strong performance at the Olympic Games and Paralympic Games partly explains the increased willingness to invest taxpayers' money in elite sport development, the more particular catalyst for change is a poor performance at a particular Games. To some extent, governments were simply responding to public/media pressure to preserve the sporting self-perception of the country, but it does raise the interesting question of whether public pressure can ever be resisted or ignored, or whether governments are locked on a path of steadily increasing investment. It would be a brave government indeed that announced to its electorate that Japan would aim only for 2 per cent of Olympic medals, that South Korea would settle for being in the top 20 rather than the top ten in the medals table and that the UK Government is content to let Germany, Australia and France overtake the United Kingdom in the medals table.

In the three countries reviewed in this chapter there are clear common features to their respective strategies. Most important of all is a substantial increase in funding, whether from the exchequer, lotteries or corporations. The funding is frequently used in broadly similar ways, namely: to improve the quality of, and access to, sports science; to enable athletes to train full time; to improve the quality of coaching either by developing domestic coaching talent or, more commonly, buying in foreign coaching expertise; and adopting a more systematic approach to talent identification, primarily at the youth level, but as in the case of the UK, developing mechanisms for adult talent transfer. An additional central element in the success of these three countries is the process, aptly described by the South Korean authorities as 'selection and concentration' by which countries identify either the sports in which they already have a comparative advantage or those sports where the standard of competition is relatively low and where comparative advantage can be developed.

One interpretation of the evidence in this chapter is that it provides powerful confirmation of the ability of governments to achieve clear objectives through the investment of public money. However, there has, as yet, been little analysis of the long-term impact of this global preoccupation with Olympic and Paralympic medal success on the wider sport community. There is plenty of self-interested speculation about the demonstration effect of elite success, the positive impact of medal winners as role models to the young and the trickle-down effect of investment in elite-level facilities and support services. However, there is little evidence to support these claims and it is doubtful whether governments are interested in gathering such evidence. In the introduction to this chapter it was noted that it was important to consider when the upward trend in funding would level off and begin to decline. The present global recession notwithstanding, it is hard to identify a government which would have the confidence to downgrade the importance of Olympic success, such is the strength and depth of the symbolism that surrounds medal success.

Notes

1 This information was obtained from: http://chinadigitaltimes.net/2008/08/the-cost-of-gold-medals.

2 This tripling of the budget for elite sport compares to a decline in the allocation for 'Sport For All' from ₩29,654 million to ₩27,248 million over the same period.

References

Advisory Council on Health and Physical Education (ACHPE) (1989) *The Promotion of Sport for the 21st Century*, Tokyo: ACHPE.

Bang, Y. (1998) 'Current crisis in Korean sports: how to cope with it', *Korean Journal of Sport Management*, 3 (2): 217–227.

Bergsgard, N.A., Houlihan, B., Mangset, P., Nødland, S.I. and Rommetvedt, H. (2007) *Sport Policy: A Comparative Analysis of Stability and Change*, Oxford: Butterworth-Heinemann.

Carmichael, F. and Grix, J. (2011) 'The Olympic legacy and participation in sport: an interim assessment of Sport England's Active People Survey', in Grix, J. and Phillpots, L. (eds) *An Assessment of UK Sport Policy in Comparative Context*, London: Routledge.

de Bosscher, V. (2007) *Sports Policy Factors Leading to International Sporting Success*, Brussels: VUBPRESS.

Department of Culture, Media and Sport (DCMS) (2002) *The Coaching Task Force: Final Report*, London: DCMS.

Department of National Heritage (DNH) (1995) *Sport: Raising the Game*, London: DNH.

Feddersen, A., Jacobson, S. and Maenning, W. (2009*) Sports Heroes and Mass Sports Participation: The (Double) Paradox of the German Tennis Boom*, Hamburg: Faculty of Economics and Social science, Hamburg University.

Girginov, V. and Hills, L. (2008) 'A sustainable sports legacy: creating a link between the London Olympics and sports participation', *International Journal of the History of Sport*, 25 (14): 2091–2116.

Green, M. (2006) 'From "Sport for All" to not about sport at all? Interrogating sport policy interventions in the United Kingdom', *European Sport Management Quarterly*, 6: 217–238.

Grix, J. and Carmichael, F. (2012) 'Why do government invest in elite sport? A polemic', *International Journal of Sport Policy and Politics*, 4 (1): 73–90.

Hogan, K. and Norton, K. (2000) 'The price of Olympic gold', *Journal of Science and Medicine in Sport*, 3 (2): 203–218.

Houlihan, B. and Green, M. (2009) 'Modernisation and sport: the reform of Sport England and UK Sport', *Public Administration*, 87 (3): 678–698.

House of Commons (2008) *Preparing for Sporting Success at the London 2012 Olympic and Paralympic Games and Beyond*, London: The Stationery Office.

Independent (2011) 'Team GB banking on foreign legion', 10 July. Available: www.independent.co.uk/sport/olympics/team-gb-banking-on-foreign-legion-2309889.html (accessed 28 October 2011).

Korea Sports Council (2004) *Vision 21: A Long-term Plan for Improving Future Performance, 2005–2014*, Seoul: KSC.

Ministry of Culture, Sport and Tourism (MCST) (2008) *Korean Athletics Development Plan: Run Korea 2011*, Seoul: MCST.

Ministry of Education, Culture, Sports, Science and Technology (MEXT) (2006) *Basic Plan for the Promotion of Sport* (revised), Tokyo: MEXT.

Ministry of Education, Science and Technology (MEST) (2008) *A Plan for the Revitalisation of School Sport*, Seoul: MEST.

Park, J.W. (2011) 'Elite sport development: an analysis of policy change in the sports of athletics, archery and baseball', unpublished doctoral thesis, Loughborough University.

Yamamoto, M.Y. (2008) 'Japan', in Houlihan, B. and Green, M. (eds) *Comparative Elite Sport Development: Systems, Structures and Public Policy*, Oxford: Butterworth-Heinemann.

Zheng, J. (2011) 'An investigation of the UK squad's performance in the five most recent Summer Olympic Games and the correlation between performance and government financial support. Unpublished MSc dissertation, Loughborough University.

20

LONDON 2012 AND THE GLOBAL SOUTH – AN EXPLORATION

A case study of India's Olympic sport

Boria Majumdar

The foundation for Indian Olympic success was created at the Commonwealth Games (CWG) in Delhi in October 2010.[1] With 101 medals, 38 of which were gold, and coming second in the medals table, displacing England for the first time in history, Indian Olympic sports and sports persons had made a statement to the world. Critics, however, drew attention to the relatively lower level of competition at the CWG[2] and suggested that the real test was the Asian Games at Guangzhou in November 2010 – and as India's shooters achieved modest success at the Asian Games,[3] this criticism was fast gathering strength. The CWG, the first week at Guangzhou was deemed to prove, was a false dawn. The national ritual celebrating failure was about to start and, coupled with the CWG scams, which were and still continue to be in focus, Indian sport was staring down the barrel.

But, as with sport, conclusions shouldn't be drawn till the last medal is actually won. India, which had one gold medal from Pankaj Advani in Snooker to show at the end of the first week of competition at the Asian Games, came alive on 21 November 2010, claiming a further three gold medals. Ranjan Sodhi was on target in the men's Double Trap and Preeja Sreedharan and Sudha Singh gave millions of Indian sports fans reasons to celebrate as they raced to gold in the 10,000 m and 3,000 m Steeplechase. Suddenly the Doha 2006 haul of ten gold medals looked achievable, and with the boxers putting on a stunning show – their best ever at the Asian Games – the CWG success did not look so distant.

Just as in the CWG, where Saina Nehwal's gold in Badminton – India's thirty-eighth and last – was more than a medal, at Guangzhou Vijender Singh's gold – India's fourteenth – shone brighter than the metal it was made of. Achieved with a broken thumb in the 75 kg class in boxing, it propelled India to an unprecedented sixth place in the medals table and summed up the story of India's athletes – fighting on despite administrative apathy and bureaucratic red tape at every step. London 2012, it is hoped, will allow these athletes to occupy centre-stage and herald the start of a systemic overhaul in Indian sports that the nation is badly in need of and has been craving for years.

If the Asian Games was any indication, India, for the first time ever, can realistically expect seven medals at London 2012,[4] more than double what India won at Beijing 2008. For the first time the world media has been forced to publish headlines such as 'China and India up, Japan down', when summing up performances at the Asian Games in November 2010.

Talking about a possible Indian sporting renaissance at London 2012, Indian Olympic Association (IOA) Secretary General and India's IOC member Randhir Singh suggests 'It's a Catch-22 situation. You can't produce champions without money, and money doesn't come unless you have champions to flaunt.'[5] Fortunately for Randhir and India's moribund and deeply politicised sports bureaucracy, India now has a plethora of champions in multiple sporting disciplines to market and promote.

What should help in marketing these athletes is the fact that their achievements in Delhi and China were analysed for hours on television and turned them into national celebrities overnight. If the media catharsis that followed was any indication, for the first time, Olympic sports, apart from Hockey, were at the centre of what could be termed the national consciousness. It was an indication that decades of neglect, which had reduced Olympic sport to a footnote in India, could finally change.

That there is a perceptible change is evident from the coverage in the media, the harbingers of such change. In March–April 2009 the leading lights of world badminton were in India to participate in the Indian Open tournament in Hyderabad. Around the same time, the Indian cricket team was playing New Zealand for a bilateral series in New Zealand. Even on the day of the Indian Open finals, coverage of the competition was relegated to the lower half of most sports pages across the country, while items about India's preparation for the third Test of the series in New Zealand were given eight-column banner headlines.[6] This was startling because India now has a handful of players who have made it to the top 25 in world badminton. Saina Nehwal, ranked fifth in the world and India's best bet for a medal at the Olympic Games, trailed off with the following lament: 'A lot of cricket is happening ... nobody wants to take it [badminton] up professionally. It is not easy to be ranked number eight or nine. A lot of sacrifices have to be made and still not many are ready to do that. So maybe once in ten years we will have a Saina Nehwal.'[7]

In a glaring departure from the reality described above, every Indian achievement at Delhi and then at Guangzhou was a front-page headline, while India's triumphs against Australia and New Zealand in cricket were relegated to the sports pages of the national dailies. A successful London 2012 and a sports culture will no longer be an illusion, with India gradually starting to look beyond cricket and turning into a multi-sporting nation.

Amidst this optimism it is important to remember, however, that at least 15 corporate houses turned down pleas to sponsor the Indian shooters before the Beijing 2008 Olympic Games. While the Beijing 2008 medal winners deserved the highest accolades – and corporate coffers had justly opened up for them – the legacy of the victories at Beijing 2008, CWG 2010 and Asian Games 2010 will depend on whether money is made available to build training facilities for the bulk of India's athletes. It will also depend on whether India's sports czars are made more accountable and become more proactive towards athletes' concerns.

Politics over the national sports bill: red tape persists

After much deliberation and careful consideration, the Indian Sports Ministry presented the National Sports Bill before the Union Cabinet on 30 August 2011. The bill, which was years in coming, provoked much outrage among several members of the Union Cabinet and wasn't allowed to be tabled before the Members of Parliament. Sections of the bill were considered too radical and the Sports Minister was instructed to redraft the bill and present it once again at a later date.[8] The leading opponent of the bill was the Union Agriculture Minister Sharad Pawar, who is also the immediate past President of the International Cricket Council (ICC) and a former President of the Board of Control for Cricket in India (BCCI).

Pawar, on losing the BCCI presidential election to Ranbir Singh Mahendra in September 2004, had famously said that he was helpless because 'the bowler, umpire and the third umpire was the same person'.[9] He was referring to his predecessor, Jagmohan Dalmiya, using the BCCI President's vote in levelling the poll count and subsequently using his casting vote to get Mahendra elected. It was, Pawar suggested, 'a classic case of conflict of interest'.[10] Pawar, as mentioned above, is now one of the principal detractors of the National Sports Bill. As immediate past President of the ICC he is an interested party and as Union Agriculture Minister and former BCCI Chief, Pawar, in this case, is the bowler and umpire rolled into one. His opposition to the bill is also a classic case of conflict of interest.

Cases of conflict of interest over the bill don't end with Pawar. Farooq Abdulla, yet another senior member of the Union Cabinet and President of the Jammu and Kashmir Cricket Association and Praful Patel, President of the All India Football Federation, are in the same league. It is natural that they would want to sink the bill, for neither of them can debate it on merit as members of the Manmohan Singh Cabinet. While their opposition as sports czars is understandable, their challenging the bill from within the Union Cabinet is untenable.[11]

While there is little doubt that some of the concerns expressed by both the proponents and the detractors of the bill were/are legitimate and tangible, far more problematic and far more significant, are the ego battles that were/are being fought around the bill. These games of one-upmanship are likely to have an adverse impact upon the fortunes of Indian sport in the immediate future.

Unfortunately, the debates over the sports bill have hardly addressed the core concerns of transparency and accountability. The discussions are limited to the government trying to control the IOA and the association doing its best to protect its autonomy. If there's one body that desperately needs to be made accountable it is the IOA. Its performance graph shows a consistent downward trend, natural in view of the gloom surrounding India's Olympic sports scene for the longest time after independence in 1947. India has won just one individual gold medal in its 88 years of participation at the Olympic Games, and did not win a single medal at Seoul 1988 or Barcelona 1992. The controversies surrounding the CWG have badly dented the IOA's image and its failure to organise the National Games in the last five years has had an adverse impact on Indian sport.

Moving on to specifics, despite a good number of shooters having achieved success on the international stage over the last few years, India continues to rue the absence of a pistol coach, with the shooting federation and the IOA sidestepping such issues and focusing their attention on trying to protect their autonomy. That the CWG opportunity was partly lost was largely due to a dysfunctional IOA and an ineffective Sports Ministry. The CWG, which could have been the game-changer for India's Olympic sport, is remembered more for the associated scams and cases of malpractice.

Indian sport, to take advantage of the opportunities before it, needs to reform itself. Change is needed, both at the top and also at the grassroots, especially with London 2012 just around the corner. London 2012 is India's last opportunity to becoming a sporting nation, an opportunity that might be lost due to ego battles over the national sports bill. Winning medals at London 2012, it must be acknowledged, will provide a huge boost for the athletes and will also result in opening up the possibility of corporate investment in Olympic sport. But the politics over the sports bill has badly impacted preparations for the Games, with administrators engaged in guarding their turf rather than concentrating on athletes training for London 2012.

A firm 'no' to an Olympic bid

A survey of international media reports in the aftermath of the CWG 2010 helped draw attention to one singular strand of argument – that India was finally ready to mount a strong Olympic bid. These arguments were based on assumptions that hosting the CWG was a stepping stone towards bidding for the 2020 Olympic Games.

Put bluntly, India is not ready to prepare a serious Olympic bid. The CWG came to India prematurely in 2003,[12] a decision that explains the problems in the lead-up to the event and the clean-up act currently underway. Most top brass of the Games Organizing Committee are now in jail (or have just been released on bail) on charges of misappropriation of funds. An Olympic bid, which comes at a serious cost to a nation, will divert attention from the athletic achievement at the CWG and Asian Games 2010, which for the first time ever in India's sporting history has offered hope of achieving the objective of sport for all.

If the CWG experience is taken as evidence, an Indian bid will only be a waste of time, energy and money, and will only result in huge sums being spent on non-sporting activities at the cost of our athletes, with little return on the investment.

As Jacques Rogge emphasised during his visit to Delhi in October 2010 when asked about an Indian Olympic bid: 'You have great athletes and you have one overriding sport, which is cricket. But we need more gold medals from the second most populous country in the world before you make a pitch for hosting the Olympics.'[13]

The point the IOC President made is already a well-established paradigm in the West. Only after a country seriously invests in sport and improves its record by winning a handful of medals at the Games can it join the race for hosting the most prestigious global sports spectacle. A strong Olympic bid is premised on winning medals on the Olympic stage, and unless India achieves the latter, the former is a non-starter. In the current context an Olympic bid is a luxury in India, which its sportspersons can ill afford.

The making of a national audience

The CWG 2010, as mentioned above, was an important pit-stop in the journey of Indian sport. It was proof that Beijing 2008 was no flash-in-the-pan success. Abhinav Bindra, India's lone individual gold medallist at the Olympic Games, was only part of a phalanx of world-class Indian shooters that has emerged in the past decade.

Besides the shooters, India has a number of boxers capable of winning medals at London 2012. As the boxers felled their more-famous opponents at Guangzhou, for the second time since Beijing 2008 a national television audience, led by a cheerleading media, focused on Olympic sports. The fact that the entire boxing team had emerged from the small, north Indian town of Bhiwani with few facilities provided too irresistible a story of human triumph against all odds. A poll on Times Now, India's most popular English TV news channel, revealed that the national religion of cricket was sliding in popularity charts. According to the survey, 53 per cent of sports fans in Chennai and 44 per cent in Kolkata were glued to the Olympic competitions. In contrast, 41 per cent of sports fans in Chennai and 29 per cent in Kolkata watched the Indian cricket team in action against the Sri Lankans. In Mumbai an amazing 64 per cent of the fans interviewed were unaware of the ongoing cricket series between India and Sri Lanka.

As Bhiwani hogged the limelight it became evident that attention and achievement was not new to the town, which is used to winning medals at international contests. Today, Bhiwani is home to at least 1,500–2,000 regular boxers and 20,000–25,000 active sportspersons. It alone has produced 14 Arjuna awardees – India's highest award for sportspersons – and is part of an economy that thrives on local sportsmen and -women making it to the sports quotas of the paramilitary forces, the army and the police.

Lessons from Bhiwani: demystifying the revolution

The Bhiwani Boxing Club's iconic coach, Jagdish Singh, is fond of saying 'Geedar ka shikar karna ho to sher se ladna seekho' ('If you want to hunt jackals, learn how to fight a lion').[14] Surprisingly enough, till 2008 Bhiwani was a rather insignificant presence on the Indian sporting map. Despite giving the country multiple Asian Games gold medallists and a slew of medals in other international boxing competitions, the nation hadn't trained its eyes on Bhiwani before Beijing 2008. A few startling days at the Olympic Games changed all of this. As Akhil Kumar punched his way through Sergei Vodopyanov after four gruelling rounds in the 54 kg pre-quarterfinal and Vijender Singh matched up to Emilio Correa in the semi-finals of the 75 kg category, media persons swarmed to make every inch of Bhiwani their own. Apathy soon gave way to unending television glare, and Bhiwani, from being a shantytown, suddenly turned into the cynosure of all attention.

Bhiwani had its first tryst with international sporting success in the 1960s, when Hawa Singh won gold at the 1966 Asian Games. He followed it up with another gold medal at the Bangkok Asian Games in 1970, giving rise to a boxing culture that has since flourished in this village on the Haryana–Rajasthan border. This is a well-established paradigm and one on which the Olympic Games are premised. Performance at the highest level has always served as the best inspiration for new participants wanting to embrace the sport. Despite such success on the international stage, no funding was directed towards developing a boxing culture. But that didn't dampen the gung-ho sporting spirit of the Bhiwani boxers, who continued to pursue their sporting dream. Things hardly looked up in the 1970s and 1980s. Consequently, a section of the youth left Bhiwani for neighbouring states in search of work and livelihood. This was their way of showing discontentment over the central Government's prolonged apathy. Things reached a climax during the 1980s and early 1990s, amidst a growing sense of frustration and uncertainty as unemployment rose. Thousands of Bhiwani youths were left with two options – either take up sport or fall prey to unemployment.[15]

In a desperate act to protect young children from future unemployment, most parents encouraged their wards to embrace sports. To encourage this effort, the Sports Authority of India (SAI) started a training school, giving Bhiwani its first organised sports facility. They were encouraged to do so by the achievements of Raj Kumar Sangwan, who won golds at two Asia-level meets – at Bangkok in 1991 and at Tehran in 1994. However, this solitary SAI facility did little to solve the problems of infrastructure. It was the Bhiwani Boxing Club, hardly a modern facility itself, which ultimately made a perceptible difference. The club, which is in a much better state today, was once described in the *Indian Express* thus:

> Tucked in a corner, almost hidden by fields, the yellow brick building is more a farm outhouse than a possible breeding centre of international sportspersons. If quaintness equalled success, the place would get top marks. And well, now it does.... The Bhiwani Boxing Club is just that, two rooms and a shed. A peepul tree and a Shiva idol stand to the left outside the gate, a sagging volleyball netting graces the right flank. Five punching bags hang next to the room, a huge mirror frames one wall, there is a basic weight-training machine on one side, and a new ring on the other.[16]

Problems of infrastructure were, however, more than counterbalanced by individual passion for boxing, as the turn of the century marked the arrival of a golden era of Bhiwani boxers in the national arena. Despite making a mark in almost every recognised competition, it was at Beijing 2008 that Bhiwani finally scripted an unparalleled success story. The nodal boxing body of Bhiwani – the Bhiwani Boxing Club – was established in 2002 by current coach Jagdish Singh. The *Indian Express* reported it thus:

> Six years ago [in 2002], Singh, one of the many boxing coaches with the Sports Authority of India, decided the daily effort he was putting at the SAI centre in Bhiwani needed to be topped with something more. So, in a move that some would describe as whimsical, he got together his life's savings, took a bank loan, and set about realizing his dream of having his own boxing club. Singh has always had an eye for spotting talent and following an approach that focuses on dealing with the worst-case scenario, he trained a band of boxers who slowly began dominating the national scene.[17]

Almost seven years after its inception, the boxing club has finally spread its wings to the far-flung corners of the state through its policy of decentralisation. In fact, Bhiwani's glittering track record (producing as many as 50 sportspersons who have represented India in international competitions) can largely be attributed to the modus operandi of the nodal organisation, which tried its best to promote a healthy sporting environment. Lack of exposure and absence of recruiters acted against Bhiwani's boxers, while mainstream Indian sport remained unaware of their maturing skills. At the turn of the millennium, a few self-made individuals training under the watchful eyes of Jagdish Singh finally broke all shackles to catapult Bhiwani to the national and subsequently international level. Akhil Kumar, for example, beat all odds to come out stronger from a career-threatening injury and made it to the Olympic Games quarter-finals.[18] Following his example, Olympic medallist Vijender Singh emerged as the biggest name in Indian boxing and is currently one of the most sought after sports celebrities in the country. Inspired by the simple logic that a good showing at the national level is the best bet to securing a government job, a vast array of talented youngsters have now taken to boxing in Bhiwani. In Jagdish Singh's words: 'Parents are keen to bring them here, knowing this is a future they can dream of. Now that they've seen the success stories, it's a reality they want to believe in.'[19]

The problem: we are like this only

While Bhiwani was and is at the centre of national attention, it is important to remember that only a sustained effort at building infrastructure could ensure that the CWG 2010 and Gwangzhou aren't exceptions. In 2004, the ruling Bharatiya Janata Party (BJP) fooled itself into believing that five years of 8 per cent economic growth on paper had all but assured its victory. Sure of sweeping back to power, it overconfidently called a general election six months before time, ran a campaign focused on the catchy tagline 'India Shining' and was duly voted out of power by the majority of Indians who had been left out of the success of the economic reforms. There is now a danger of a generic 'India Shining' kind of discourse subsuming the real achievements and the real resurgence of the CWG athletes. The boxers have emerged from a town which goes sometimes for days without electricity, where the rains have made it impossible to drive a car faster than 5 kmh on most roads and where most people have to rely on inverters to watch the home boys win. In such a setting, sport has emerged as a way out for many.[20] The real success of Bhiwani lies in the rock-solid confidence of the new generation of athletes and a nascent public–private partnership which allowed them to transcend a system used to mediocrity. They have not been content to merely repeat the past. This is the new Indian spirit that needs to be celebrated.

The picture is similar if we turn our gaze to shooting, India's favourite medal event since Bindra's gold at Beijing 2008. While Gagan Narang, Bindra's compatriot in the 10 m Air Rifle, has been on sizzling form since the Olympic Games and has even broken multiple world records, his performances are once again the result of individual flair and brilliance. The fact that Narang could win four gold medals and two silvers at the CWG and Asian Games, respectively, is testament to his skill and mental strength. While Narang's exploits give us ample hope before the London 2012 Games, in a shocking exposé it was brought to the nation's attention in April 2009 that the 15 top coaches engaged in training India's shooters for the CWG weren't paid between January and March 2009, when each of them was entitled to payments of up to Rs.30,000 per month as per the terms of their contracts. Also, at the time of appointment, these coaches were promised advanced-level coaching abroad, but up to April 2009 none had been sent. In an interview with Ajai Masand and Saurabh Duggal of the *Hindustan Times*, one of these coaches, engaged in training at the national camp in Pune, spilled the beans: 'All of us, barring national coach Sunny Thomas, have not received a paisa (penny) from the government for the work we have been putting in to prepare the 150-odd core group shooters.'[21] At the time of writing, with just months left before London 2012, India still doesn't have a pistol coach and the nation's leading shooters are trying to circumnavigate the problem by making use of the facilities at compatriot Gagan Narang's academy in Pune.[22]

These discrepancies, born out of insurmountable administrative apathy at the highest levels of Indian sport, only add to the despondence of India's sportsmen and women. Blaming the media is the shortcut sports administrators often resort to. However, that such a situation has been created in the first place speaks volumes of their efficiency. Unfortunately, in India virtually every sporting body is controlled by a politician or a bureaucrat and, once entrenched, most manage to stay on for years, if not decades. The list, as I have detailed elsewhere, is long: Congress MP Suresh Kalmadi, now in Tihar Jail for alleged misappropriation of CWG funds was President of the IOA for over 15 years; BJP MP V.K. Malhotra, President of the Archery Federation since 1972 is now heading the IOA. Former Congress MP K.P. Singh Deo was President of the Rowing Federation for 24 years. In addition, V.K. Verma, also in jail for his role in the CWG 2010, was in charge of Indian badminton since 1998; the Indian National Lok Dal's Ajay Chautala has been running table tennis since 2001; and Samata Party's Digvijay Singh headed shooting between 2000 until the time of his death in 2010.[23]

What is more alarming is that these men have managed to stay in power despite a High Court ruling which decreed that guidelines on tenure of office bearers of the National Sports Federations are maintainable and enforceable. Suggesting that this is in no way a violation of the principles enshrined in the Olympic Charter, Justice Geeta Mittal, sitting judge of the Delhi High Court, observed that even the IOC had restrictions on the terms of its office bearers.[24] She went on to state:

> Firstly, I see no interference by the stipulation of the tenure condition as a condition for grant of recognition and assistance by the government. Secondly, the same does not enable the government to have any say of any kind in the affairs of running of the sports body.... A limited office tenure will have the impact of minimizing, if not eliminating, allegations, criticism and elements of nepotism, favouritism and bias of any kind.[25]

The court judgement, the *Hindu* noted, had serious ramifications for the tenure of office bearers and stipulated that an office bearer of a federation can have two terms of four years each at a stretch, the second one on a two-thirds majority. However, the same report went on to suggest that 'the IOA took the lead sometime in the mid-1980s to flout the guidelines by amending its constitution and almost all National Sports Federations followed suit'.[26]

Commenting on the impact of the ruling, the *Times of India* reported:

> Most of them do not believe in handing over the baton. Perched securely as heads of various sporting federations, sports bosses have been virtually unmovable. But maybe not for long. The ruling could lead to changes in the Indian Olympic Association as well as other sports bodies.[27]

What the court ruling highlights is that the IOC needs to take into account local peculiarities while trying to push through its agenda of political independence of the NOCs. The ruling demonstrates that in cases like India you need the power of local legislation to force the IOA to get its act together. Unless global policies are mediated by local ground truths it might result in empowering the unworthy and it is important for the IOC to take note of these ground realities.

A more proactive Sports Ministry?

Drawing strength from the High Court ruling, the Sports Ministry under the newly appointed minister Ajay Maken has now suggested in the National Sports Bill that no administrator can continue to head sports bodies past 70 years of age. Following the lead of the IOC, which asks IOC members to retire at 70, the ministry is determined to ensure that Indian administrators give up their posts past this age. Again, this draws attention to the differing realities in particular local contexts. While the ministry's agenda may be perceived as interference by the IOC, the ministry is actually trying to implement a policy laid down by the IOC itself against opposition by the IOA, which, in turn, is drawing strength from the autonomy clause in the IOC charter.

Further continuing with its agenda of sports reform, the Sports Ministry, for the first time in years, sent out a circular to all sports federations whose disciplines were in the 2010 CWG, requesting details of the past and recent performances of all 'core group' athletes. This directive came on the back of growing discord among sportspersons who felt that despite performing at their best they weren't being rewarded in the absence of proper laws and guidelines. Reacting against the groundswell of discontent, a ministry official emphasised that the directive was meant to weed out the non-performers and encourage sportspersons to excel in international competitions.

Carrying on with its objective of identifying talented sportspersons on the eve of the Delhi Games, the Government, the *Telegraph* reported, endowed Rs.5 lakh (£7,000) for the Maulana Abul Kalam Azad Trophy, handed out to the best sporting university in India, to encourage talent at the collegiate level. It also identified Ladakh as a fertile ground for archery, ice hockey and figure skating.[28]

As Anirban Das Mahapatra reported:

> The government has upped financial incentives for successful sportspeople. Former medal winners at international events now have their pensions doubled. Financial assistance for medical treatment is now up a whopping 500 per cent to Rs 2 lakh [£2,800]. The government has also released a grant of over Rs 6.5 crore [£900,000] for upgrading all four training centres of the Sports Authority of India, to provide state-of-the-art training facilities.[29]

It was in 2009, for the first time ever in India's sporting history, that the Government came forward with a grant of Rs.678 crore (£97 million) to enable India's athletes to train abroad with the world's leading professionals. This was to ensure that they were exposed to the best facilities before the 2010 CWG and in the lead-up to London 2012.

While more money for sport is always welcome, the problem lies in the details and in how it is spent. One statistic is telling. Against an allocation of Rs.678 crore for the CWG, the Government had spent just over 35 per cent, only Rs.232.19 crores (£330 million), by November 2009. If the idea of pumping in this money was to create champions for the CWG, to use them as a springboard for greater sporting glory at London 2012, then clearly something went terribly wrong. Unless there is some serious organisational learning and unless there is a realisation that London 2012 is India's last opportunity at becoming a sporting nation, it is impossible to expect radical change in the existing scenario. London 2012 is a potential game-changer and this realisation is crucial to heralding a fundamental transformation of the country's sporting scene.

The London test

Talking about the possibility of a sporting resurgence, the IOA Secretary General Randhir Singh suggested that individual prodigies aside, the connection between modern sport and commerce is undeniable. This is precisely why nascent private-sector initiatives like the Mittal Champions Trust and Olympic Gold Quest, as well as non-governmental organisations formed to stimulate sporting excellence, are much needed.

That Olympic Gold Quest is clearly focused on the job at hand is evident from the following report published in the *Hindu*:

> With exactly a year to go for the London Olympics, Olympic Gold Quest (OGQ) announced that it was putting together the best possible package to help the athletes in their pursuit for the gold medals. Addressing a press conference, the Chief Executive Officer (CEO) of OGQ, Viren Rasquinha, said that five select athletes would get the support of 'performance and mental strength' coach, Abha Maryada Banerjee. Rasquinha mentioned that a personal masseur, Kassenova Kacehoba of Kazakhstan would help the shooters, who often complain of back and shoulder stiffness.[30]

In August 2012 the CWG legacy will be put to its sternest test. If India can double the medal count it achieved at the 2008 Beijing Games, it will give an unprecedented fillip to Indian Olympic sport. A failed effort at London 2012, on the other hand, organisationally and with regards to medals won, will mean that the lush promises of the CWG and Asian Games 2010 will be confined to sports history books by the time of the next Olympic Games and Paralympic Games at Rio in 2016.

London 2012, it is time to accept, is going to be a watershed event in the history of Indian sport. A successful London Games will propel India to the forefront of Asian sport and may even translate into an Olympic bid a decade down the line. A failed Games experience, on the other hand, will mean Olympic sport taking a backward step and the country losing all momentum built at the Delhi CWG and the Asian Games at Guangzhou.

Notes

1 The CWG was held in New Delhi over 3–14 October 2010.

2 In the absence of many star athletes, who had withdrawn from the Delhi Games, the standard of competition in some events was modest to say the least. World stars like Usain Bolt or Yohan Blake did not make it to Delhi, nor did Chris Hoy, Andy Murray or US Open Champion Samantha Stosur.

3 Contrary to expectations, India won only a solitary shooting gold at the Guangzhou Asian Games.

4 India can expect medals in Shooting, Tennis, Boxing, Archery, Badminton and Wrestling.

5 Personal interview with Randhir Singh, 10 November 2010. He said the exact same things to the *Telegraph* reporter Anirban Das Mahapatra on 1 February 2009.
6 This discrepancy was noticeable across the media. I have looked at ten leading national newspapers and not a single one had the Indian Open as its first headline.
7 Quoted in the *Telegraph*, 1 April 2009.
8 For details, see: *The Times of India*, 31 August 2011, p. 1.
9 Quoted in *The Times of India*, op-ed, 5 September 2011.
10 Ibid.
11 Patel even went on to suggest that had the bill been implemented it would mean a joint secretary running the affairs of a National Sport Federation. Quoted in *The Times of India*, 2 September 2011.
12 India beat Hamilton to win the hosting rights for the 2010 CWG at Montego Bay in Jamaica in November 2003.
13 Personal interview with Jacques Rogge in New Delhi, 2 October 2010.
14 Personal interview with Jagdish Singh, 6 September 2008.
15 Personal interview with Raj Kumar Sangwan, 8 September 2008.
16 'Inside India's Fight Club', *The Indian Express*, 24 August 2008.
17 Ibid.
18 His rustic yet pleasant statements to the media have endeared him to the nation's sports fraternity. When I asked him a question in English after his win against the Russian world number one on his way to the Olympic quarter-finals, his candid confession was startling: 'If I could speak English that well, I'd be doing what you are', he retorted in jest.
19 Personal interview with Jagdish Singh, 6 April 2009.
20 There is a telling television commercial which shows village folk sitting huddled together in front of a television set operating on a battery, watching their local lad in action. This inverter advertisement is a pithy comment on the realities of Bhiwani.
21 *Hindustan Times*, 10 April 2009.
22 Several pistol shooters suggested this way out to me on condition of anonymity. The only person who came on record was Samresh Jung, one of India's veteran pistol shooters and one who had won the Best Athlete Award at the Melbourne CWG in 2006.
23 For details, see Majumdar, B. and Mehta, N. (2008) 'Epilogue', in *Olympics: The India Story*, New Delhi: HarperCollins.
24 For details, see the *Hindu*, 7 March 2009; also see *The Times of India*, 7 March 2009.
25 *Hindu*, 7 March 2009.
26 Ibid.
27 *The Times of India*, 7 March 2009.
28 *Telegraph*, 1 February 2009.
29 Ibid.
30 *Hindu*, 28 July 2011.

Bibliography

Majumdar, B. and Mehta, N. (2008) *Olympics: The India Story*, New Delhi: HarperCollins.
Majumdar, B. and Mehta, N. (2009) *India and the Olympics*, London: Routledge.
Majumdar, B. and Mehta, N. (2010) *Sellotape Legacy: Delhi and the Commonwealth Games*, New Delhi: HarperCollins.

21

BEIJING–LONDON–RIO DE JANEIRO

A never-ending global competition

John R. Gold and Margaret M. Gold

> Have you studied the official reports of previous Games and are you prepared to stage the Games equally well?
>
> *IOC, 1957*

Introduction

Competition is almost as natural a part of staging the Olympic Games and Paralympic Games as it is intrinsic to the sporting events themselves. The 23 cities that have hosted the Summer Games since the quadrennial olympiads were reintroduced in 1896 form a chronological sequence within which comparisons are inevitable. Which was the best Games ever? Which offered the most appealing spectacle? Which supplied the benchmarks for efficient organisation, for imaginative planning or for greatest benefits for the hosts? Which supplied the paradigms for financial disaster, nationalistic excess or over-commercialism? The answers to these questions are not purely academic. Quite apart from any formal transfer of knowledge procedures, any new hosts will scrutinise the experience of predecessors to locate examples of good practice that they might emulate or surpass. By the same token, prospective applicant cities will look for whatever pointers they can find to help them in the fierce and never-ending competition to gain the nomination to stage an Olympic Games.

To elaborate, most of the world's major cities, at one point or other in their recent histories, will have toyed with the idea of staging the Olympic Games. At one time, of course, this was an untaxing task. The epigram above is taken from the Host City questionnaire developed in the 1950s (IOC, 1957) and poses a question that could probably be answered with a single word. It was one of 14 such questions, which covered the sports to be accommodated, their timing, facilities, Olympic village, construction plans, legal framework, finance, accommodation for the Olympic family and visitors, the organisational skills and experience which the city had of large-scale events, the fine arts programme and guarantees that the Games would be well run. There was an opportunity for cities to say why they should be considered as a site for the Olympic Games (ibid.: 12). In the questionnaire's preamble, applicants were warned: 'Invitations must have the approval of the Government of the country in which the city is located in order to ensure its cooperation in staging the

Games successfully.' Furthermore, the International Olympic Committee (IOC) pointed out that there should be no political demonstrations in any of the Olympic facilities during the Games and that the Games should be used for no purpose 'other than the advancement of the Olympic Movement' (ibid.: 9).

Cities contemplating applying for the Olympic Games and Paralympic Games at the present time face a process that is worlds away from that of the early Games, when the business of bidding was traditionally shaped by the IOC's concerns with the promotion of sport, education and culture and the ways in which these were expressed through the movement itself and the philosophy of Olympism. Detailed discussion of the subsequent transformation of this gentle exercise into the laborious inquisition of the present day lies beyond the scope of this chapter (Booth, 2005; Theodoraki, 2007). Nevertheless, the changes that have been seen reflect far more than just the confrontation between a nostalgically framed festival and the harsh commercial environment of the early twenty-first century. In the first place, there are new forms of partnership between the IOC and the Host Cities, in which the former accepts that the latter will use the Games as a vehicle for advancing its own agendas. Second, the IOC has accepted the need for greater rigour and transparency in its dealings with the Host Cities – a development made compellingly necessary after the bribery scandal over the 2002 Winter Games at Salt Lake City. Third, the climate of opinion changes and new issues constantly rise to the fore. In the 1990s, for example, the IOC responded to society's environmental concerns and, arguably, accusations about the gigantism of the Games by adding 'environment' to its core philosophy of Olympism alongside sport and culture. From this point onwards, notions of sustainability and environmental auditing were added to the candidature procedures.

The net result is that potential hosts are subjected to a lengthy and arduous process of international scrutiny in which they are vetted to ensure that they are capable of delivering a huge, complex and extremely costly multi-sport festival. They do so at (their own) considerable expense. The US$59.4 million that the Chicago team spent on its abortive 42-month campaign to gain the nomination for the 2016 Summer Games is a case in point (Rogers, 2010). Nevertheless, in recent decades at least, there has still been no shortage of willing volunteers to stage the Games and to mount elaborate campaigns to persuade the IOC and other local and national constituencies that their candidacy is the one to support. Moreover, prospective applicants are willing to make their commitment years in advance. They may well recognise that they need time to convince local interests that some or all of the potential advantages can be realised and to gain adequate support, nationally and internationally. They might also recognise that their cities are unlikely to be successful at the first attempt and thus may make an initial bid primarily to gain experience and make valuable contacts. In approaching this matter, they will be able to select the point at which they wish to enter the fray with some confidence. The timetable is well-known; indeed, there are few more stable aspects of cultural history than the Olympic calendar – not even the minor inconvenience of world wars has been allowed to disrupt calculation of the four-year Olympiads. It is possible, therefore, to decide not to bid for the next available Games but one scheduled for a more distant date. In 2011, for example, no less than eight cities (Amsterdam, Brisbane, Melbourne, Nairobi, Rotterdam, Seattle, Thessaloniki and Vancouver) had already expressed interest in bidding for the Games of the XXXIV Olympiad in 2028 – for which the Host City will not be chosen until 2021.

The nature and ferocity of the resulting competition for the Games speaks volumes about the perceived benefits, for the Olympic Games have become a development project which provides for a wide range of agendas that can be tailored to the specific needs of almost any large city. There is the allure of being an 'Olympic city'; a member of a prestigious club whose members have received the accolade from the IOC that infers confidence in the quality, competence and creativity of their cities. Increasingly, too, the Games are seen as offering an unparalleled opportunity to develop and expedite projects that might otherwise have taken decades to initiate. The nature of the benefits are now embraced within the holistic concept of 'legacy', which incorporates the short- and long-term outcomes of the many tangible and intangible factors encompassed by Olympic event planning and implementation. These might include strengthening the urban economy, promoting regeneration of rundown districts, revamping transport and service infrastructures, encouraging the construction of landmark buildings for culture and sport, inculcating an enhanced skills base, permanently repositioning the city more favourably in the global tourist market, creating vibrant cultural quarters, and establishing a network of high-grade facilities to serve as the basis for future bids.

Yet perhaps the most eagerly sought and most elusive benefits stem less from establishing new facilities on the ground than from opportunities for place promotion – the conscious use of publicity and marketing to communicate selective images of towns and regions to a target audience (Gold and Ward, 1994: 2) – or its more focused incarnations as 'city marketing' (Ashworth and Voogd, 1990) or 're-branding' (Kavaratzis, 2004). In a world where large cities actively compete for recognition and status, the prestige of the Olympic Games and the sustained attention that they attract provides unparalleled opportunities to make a statement on the world stage. While even constructing a serious bid shows that a city is ambitious for global attention (Ward, 2011), capturing the Games allows municipal authorities to undertake long-term activities designed to boost or alter the image of their cities. Nevertheless, changing a city's image in the outside world is far more difficult than, say, the rebranding of a commercial product and the perceived excellence of the Olympic 'brand' as the summit of sporting achievement often fails to rub off on the city that stages the Games. History reveals numerous occasions on which inadequate planning, poor stadium design, the withdrawal of sponsors, political boycotts, heavy cost overruns on facilities, the forced eviction of residents living in areas wanted for Olympic facilities, and subsequent unwanted stadia leave a legacy that tarnishes rather than enhances the reputation of the Host City (Gold and Gold, 2008).

Seen against this background, this chapter explores the way in which processes of negotiation and contestation have shaped the plans of the last three cities to have emerged victorious in the battle to become Summer Olympic cities. In doing so, we seek to complement the more specific analyses of London's bid found in Part 1 of this volume by placing the 2012 Games in the context of a ceaseless, but not unchanging, process that continues to throw up Host Cities every four years. As such, we consider the shaping of the plans for Beijing, London and Rio de Janeiro (see Tables 21.1 and 21.2 for chronologies and brief analyses of the major aspects of strategy).

These bids operate on two levels: the first is tackling the very real but quite different social, economic and planning challenges in the three cities; the other is addressing their global positioning in the media, business and political arenas. We begin by considering Beijing 2008, the growing capital of the world's most populous state and an emerging economic superpower, where candidacy for the Games supplied the city and state with an opportunity to proclaim their place in the world, but at the same time provided the opportunity to address longstanding planning challenges for the city itself. In the process, the Beijing organisers crafted a festival that may well represent the high-water mark for lavish spectacle for many Olympiads to come. The second section offers brief observations on London 2012, highlighting sources of continuity and divergence that link London back to Beijing and forward to Rio de Janeiro, the subject of the third section of this chapter. Here, we consider the aspirations of Rio's promoters and the way that they sought to promote a coherent image of their city to the international community, while tackling the social, economic and infrastructural problems that have bedevilled the city for decades.

Beijing 2008

Each successive Olympic Games creates a point of reference for the events that follow and, in the case of Beijing 2008, it was always likely to be 'a hard act to follow' (Robb, 2008). It was, of course, an event of considerable political significance. The People's Republic of China (PRC) did not participate in the Olympic Movement between 1952 and 1979 due to the inclusion of Taiwanese teams that competed as the 'Republic of China'. Its re-engagement with the Olympic Movement had only begun with the 1980 Winter Games at Lake Placid, but quickly developed in light of policies designed to treat sports as an extension of foreign policy. Interest in staging a Summer Games quickly followed. After undertaking an element of preparatory work through hosting the 1990 Asian Games, which they were awarded in 1986, Beijing sought the nomination for the 2000 Summer Games in 1991. Its acceptance as a Candidate City alongside Berlin, Manchester, Istanbul and Sydney followed the next year. The bid was more a national than city bid, as symptomised by its slogan, 'A more open China awaits the 2000 Olympic Games'. However, lingering international disquiet over the suppression of the protests in Tiananmen Square in 1989, plus the misgivings of the IOC's Evaluation Commission about the environment, transport and communications, foreign-language skills, city management and venue plans (Broudehoux, 2004: 159) worked against the bid. Eventual loss to Sydney by two votes in the final round of voting at the IOC's meeting in Monte Carlo (September 1993) led to a period of critical reappraisal before Beijing re-entered the fray for the 2008 Games. It was accepted as a Candidate City in August 2000, with a shortlist that also included Toronto, Istanbul, Paris and Osaka.

Beijing's bid document (BOBICO, 2001) can be interpreted at several different levels. At one level, it clearly identifies three themes for the Beijing Games – green, high-tech and people's Olympic Games – and offers action plans for each theme. At another level, it expresses an intertwining of national and city agendas on a scale that is unusual in recent Olympic practice. A typical example of this fusion is conveyed by the bid team's assertion that 'a fast-growing and

Table 21.1 Chronology of bidding for Summer Olympic Games, 2008–2016

Bid process	*2008*	*2012*	*2016*
NOC submit name of applicant city	1 February 2000	15 July 2003	13 September 2007
Applicant file deadline	20 June 2000	15 January 2004	14 January 2008
Candidate Cities named	28 August 2000	18 May 2004	4 June 2008
Candidate File deadline	17 January 2001	15 November 2004	12 February 2009
Evaluation commission report	15 May 2001	6 June 2005	2 September 2009
Election	13 July 2001, Moscow	6 July 2005, Singapore	2 October 2009, Copenhagen
Applicant Cities; Candidate Cities*	Bangkok	Paris*	Baku
	Beijing*	Leipzig	Chicago*
	Cairo	New York*	Doha
	Havana	Moscow*	Madrid*
	Istanbul*	Istanbul	Prague
	Kuala Lumpur	Havana	Tokyo*
	Osaka	London*	Rio de Janeiro*
	Paris*	Madrid*	
	Seville	Rio de Janeiro	
	Toronto*		

Table 21.2 Key aspects of the successful bids, Summer Olympic Games, 2008–2016

City and bid slogan	*Vision and themes outlined in the bid document*	*Key points*
Beijing 2008 *New Beijing, Great Olympics*	Green Olympics High-tech Olympics People's Olympics	'Dispersion supplemented with centralisation' Olympic Green: 13 venues, Olympic Village, press and media centres Environmental strategy Infrastructure improvement Urban modernisation and redevelopment Social strategy for education, training, volunteering, sport participation
London 2012 *Make Britain Proud*	Putting the needs of athletes first Harnessing London's passion for sport Creating a legacy to transform sport in the UK Regenerating East London communities and their environments	Centralised Olympic Park with additional world-famous venues (e.g. Wimbledon) Economic and environmental transformation of a large and deprived multi-ethnic area of East London Inclusivity, especially with regard to the status of the Paralympics Promotion of sport participation International inspiration
Rio de Janeiro 2016 *Live Your Passion*	Uniting the power of sport with the spirit of Brazil Games of celebration and transformation Engaging and inspiring the youth of the world Games delivery aligned with legacy plans Promoting the Olympic and Paralympic values globally	Four interlinked Olympic zones Transformation of the city – upgrading and integrating favelas; regeneration of the port Crime reduction Social inclusion (homes, training, jobs, sport) Environmental improvements to the urban forest and coastal areas

vigorous Beijing is now poised to speed up its modernisation and integration into the international community, to make new friends, and to expand the scope of its cooperation with other countries' (ibid.: vol. 1, 3). The bid sought to blend local tradition and 'a city with an ancient civilization' (ibid.: vol. 3, 131) with a sense of national modernity (for example, with reference to China's high rate of economic growth and attempts to develop leading-edge technologies). Beijing emphasised its ability to bring the Olympic message to the world's largest 'developing country', as well as being able to bring 'harmony between peoples' and promote awareness of the environment (ibid.: vol. 1, 3, 5). The environmental agenda was particularly interesting in this respect. Recognising that anxieties about environmental matters had been an issue with the first bid, the subsequent version stressed not just that Beijing had made great strides in ensuring there would be a safe environment for Olympic competition, but also claimed that, by 2008, China would be promoting environmentalism nationally and achieving internationally accepted standards for water and air quality.

Broader agendas also underpinned the plans for the spatial organisation of the event. The plans revolved around a strategy of 'dispersion supplemented with centralisation' (BOCOG, 2010: vol. 1, 71). Venues were concentrated in three principal areas of the city, with the most important being the Olympic Green – a 1215 ha site in the north of the city which is where the main stadium would be located. Yet from the outset there was a sense that the Olympic developments would serve a developing country's quest for urban and national modernisation. Beijing had already embarked on large-scale urban renewal, with the elimination of slum housing, development of shopping malls, cultural facilities, business plazas, and new central business and financial districts. The government were resolved to make Beijing look international and contemporary in a manner that reflected not just on the city but also on China as a whole (Li *et al.*, 2007: 257–258). The attachment of the Olympic schemes to this style of thinking was made to seem effortless by the bid document and gave a strong sense of the positive legacy likely to result from these developments. However, as frequently occurs, its authors skated over potential social costs. Renewal policies of this type here, as in densely packed cities elsewhere in the world, can often only be achieved by application of swingeing clearance-based programmes that lead to the destruction of swathes of traditional housing. These, when located in places that inconvenienced the Olympic projects, had a habit of being designated slums and cleared accordingly (COHRE, 2007).

Such reservations, however, did not temper the view offered by the IOC's Evaluation Commission. They noted that the Beijing bid was 'a government-driven bid' in contrast to the other Candidate Cities, which were 'city-driven' (Osaka), city- and sport-driven in the case of Paris, and National Olympic Committee (NOC)-driven (and so sport-driven) in the cases of Toronto and Istanbul (IOC, 2001: 95–96). As such, they essentially accepted the assurances offered by the Beijing team as to the linkage of city and state objectives for development and modernisation. Although concerns were expressed over air-pollution levels, standards of water and sewage, environmental protection and road congestion, they felt that the Games would provide 'an impetus and a catalyst' that would ensure that the plans put in place for improvements would be achieved by 2008 (ibid.: 62). The voting at the IOC's meeting in Moscow in July 2001 certainly had no qualms, awarding Beijing the 2008 Summer Games on the second round of voting, with 56 votes against 22 for Toronto, 18 for Paris and 9 for Istanbul.

The process of realising the 2008 Games essentially consolidated the approaches developed in the bid documents with the hegemony of the national agenda. During the preparation stages, China's hopes to change international perceptions of the country had only been partly achieved. The Beijing organisers, for example, later complained in their Official Report that the international community, and particularly the West, had only 'vague' ideas about China with regard to political stability, economic growth and social development. Indeed, they argued that 'some Western media' had failed to report the reforms and China's 'opening up endeavours' (BOCOG, 2010: vol. 1, 16). The PRC had conceived of Beijing 2008 in the same vein as Tokyo 1964 – emerging economically and politically after the Second World War and wanting to increase awareness of its ancient culture and traditions – and Seoul 1988, which used the Games to showcase South Korea's economic transformation and to develop diplomatic links with countries that had refused to recognise it. Instead, Beijing found the foreign media consistently comparing the Beijing Games not with Tokyo or Seoul, but with Berlin 1936 and Moscow 1980 (Macartney, 2008). For its part, however, the IOC saw China as an important exemplar of its desire to take the Games to the world and was even prepared to deflect mounting criticism over human rights and China's policy towards Tibet. For example, Philippe Furrer, the Head of the IOC's Games Management and Special Projects, defended China by saying that the IOC could not compromise universality: 'The moment you start setting boundaries about human rights or any other aspects', he announced, 'you limit the number of countries that will be able to host the event and we don't want that to happen' (WUOC, 2008: 13).

In the event, it was the reality of the Games that did most to ameliorate the adverse press. Beijing was able to mobilise resources on a scale that is unlikely to be repeated in the near future. Outlay of around US$40 billion brought the spectacle of the 'Bird's Nest' and 'Water Cube' before the world's television audiences, as well as the most lavish Opening and Closing Ceremonies ever seen. The Games' organisation and implementation were widely praised. The IOC (2010: 42) contentedly commented that choosing Beijing had favoured 'universality' and 'cultural openness', leaving the Olympic Movement with a less Western-oriented approach to sport and representative of a 'shifting of international sport's centre of gravity towards the east'. At the same time, it recognised the danger that Beijing 2008 could become a benchmark for future hosts and work against the goal of more inclusive and cost-effective games. They therefore counselled caution against attempts to emulate:

> Organisers of the London 2012 and Rio 2016 Olympic Games should not seek to replicate Beijing's magnificence and grandeur. The 2008 Games were a reflection of the host country and the vast population that supported this effort. Other hosts should be focusing on making their Games unique and inspirational, and contributing in their own distinctive ways to the Olympic vision. If that means many aspects of the Beijing Games remain unmatched, then so be it!
>
> *Ibid.: 21*

The Chinese leadership could scarcely have sought a more resounding endorsement of the value of staging the Games.

London 2012

Neither projection of nationhood or lavish spectacle had ever been essential parts of London's core proposals for the Games. Long before the scale and lavishness of Beijing 2008 had become apparent, London's team had concurred with a public mood which supported slaying the 'bloated beast' of the modern Olympic Games (Tomlinson, 2004: 158) and favoured a more cost-effective approach to the event. As noted above, its project was driven by city- rather than nation-based objectives; indeed, the British Government initially only gave reluctant support. The goals were less to build up a tourism industry, develop a cultural sector or prove its credentials as a world city than, first, to rebrand London as a contemporary rather than historical city and, second, to expedite an extensive regeneration scheme in the deprived east of the city along with related transport and infrastructural improvements. The theme of the world coming to London to meet the world was carefully fostered in marketing the notion of London 2012 and, indeed, was tellingly picked up in the presentation made at the IOC's final selection meeting in Singapore in July 2005.

There were, of course, traditional attributes that could be mobilised in support of candidacy – most notably the long-established British enthusiasm for sport, with the prospects of full stadia and the likelihood of a festive atmosphere. After all, the city had successfully staged the Games twice previously: stepping into the breach after Rome withdrew from hosting the 1908 Games; and staging the 1948 Olympic Games under conditions of severe war-time austerity. Moreover, besides being popular with spectators, both Games had important consequences. The former stabilised the Olympic Movement after its disastrous liaisons with World's Fairs at Paris 1900 and St. Louis 1904 and supplied the first instance of a stadium purpose-built to house the Games (the White City). The latter re-established the Games after the Second World War, saw the first links between Olympic and Paralympic sport, and established the first volunteer programme. These were positive credentials to have when dealing with a body as self-aware of its own history as the IOC.

The three-volume Candidate File, which was submitted to the IOC in November 2004, placed 'greatest emphasis … on the legacy and after-effects of the Olympic leverage opportunity, rather than the event, its content and purpose' (Evans, 2007: 299). The contents are described in Part 1 and therefore require only the briefest description here. The bid strove hard to offer a rebranding of London away from being identified by its historic heritage to that of a 'diverse, creative and vibrant city' (London 2012, 2004: vol. 1, 11) with a dynamism stemming from its multiculturalism. The bid contained explicit plans for the Cultural Olympiad, with the outline of a four-year programme designed to fit alongside the city's regular cultural sector. It made considerable strides towards integrating the Paralympics into the Games' planning (Gold and Gold, 2007). It aimed to increase sport participation more widely and raise health and fitness levels locally and nationally. Its core proposals for the sporting competitions foresaw a small number of events being held at internationally recognisable venues scattered across the capital, such as Lord's, Wimbledon, Horse Guards' Parade and Greenwich Park. Most activities, however, would be centred on a 246 ha nucleated Olympic Park at Stratford, with another smaller river cluster in the near vicinity. The Park would house events in a mixture of permanent buildings, designed to add substantively to London's sporting infrastructure, or demountable temporary structures capable of removal to other locations after the Games. Much of the genuinely animated excitement behind the Park proposals lay in its legacy opportunities. Despite its remarkable centrality – less than 5 km from London's financial heart – this project would, first, act as a vehicle for decontaminating and regenerating a considerable expanse of brownfield land and, second, the regeneration would revitalise an economically and socially deprived zone of the city. After the Games, the Lower Lea Valley would undergo environmental transformation, helping to rectify the area's deficiency in open space, with injection of investment and social capital providing new housing and employment. It was a bold and ambitious scheme that could capture the imagination and supply a powerful message to set before a body anxious to see that its sporting and cultural festival could truly make a difference.

In this respect the Beijing and London Games both expressed the aim of reshaping their cities, with the Olympic Park contributing new neighbourhoods and amenities to the north of the ancient centre in the case of Beijing, and to the east in the case of London, redressing decades of imbalance of investment between east and west London. The pattern of governance by which this was achieved is very different in the two cities, with contrasting traditions of disclosure, consultation and critical evaluation of implementation. Beijing was creating a modern city to meet the requirements of the twenty-first century and wished to communicate this fact to the wider world. For London, already on the map, and one of the world's major tourist destinations, it is about maintaining its position in a more competitive world.

Rio de Janeiro 2016

If London was an unexpected victor in its bidding competition, then Rio de Janeiro's success in gaining the 2016 Summer Games was even more surprising. South America had never staged either Winter or Summer Olympic Games. Rio annually hosts the world's largest street carnival, but during the twentieth century Brazil had only previously staged two major sporting festivals: the 1950 FIFA World Cup Finals, shared between six cities, and the Fourth Pan-American Games (São Paulo, 1963). Brasília was shortlisted for the 2000 Olympic Games, but withdrew its candidacy after a damning report on its facilities by the IOC's inspection team. In 1996, Rio bid for the 2004 Summer Games, with a plan commissioned by the mayor that proposed constructing an Olympic Park and Village in the southwestern suburb of Barra da Tijuca. Its proposal failed to make the shortlist, due partly to insufficient planning for associated urban infrastructure and, more generally, to concerns about the aspiring host's lack of experience in staging sports mega-events. Eight years later, Rio experienced the same result, being one of four cities deemed not to have 'the requisite level of capability at this time to host the 2012 Olympic Games' (IOC, 2004: 90). Its success in gaining the nomination for the 2016 Games, therefore, indicates the extent of efforts to overcome Rio's initial credibility gap (Gold, 2011: 392).

Much of the reason for the city's persistence lay in the municipality's determination to use the Olympic Games to halt the city's perceived decline. Rio has suffered from soaring crime (fuelled by the Latin American drug trade), severe problems of deprivation and poverty of the favelas (informal housing areas) and poor infrastructure. Surveying the scene in 1996, for example, Rio's Mayor Cesar Maia (Del Rio, 2009: 226) despairingly described it as being in

> a process of accelerating deterioration, generated by the impoverishment of its population, by the disorganized occupation of private and public spaces, by the deterioration of public services, and by the flight of financial and human capital. A city without defined vocations, with a distorted image in a growing process of disintegration.

Any sporting mega-event-led strategy to improve matters, therefore, would be closer to Beijing's strategy for transforming the whole city rather than London's site-specific approach. Externally, too, it was felt that action was needed to rectify loss of status. Although a city of more than six million, Rio's status within the nation had declined in the face of São Paulo's emergence as an economic powerhouse of 20 million people and the decision to move the national capital to Brasília in 1960. In this sense, seeking to turn Rio into an Olympic City was synonymous with efforts to rebrand it as a modern world city (Cidade Olímpica, 2011).

Rio's attempts to gain the right to stage international sporting events quickly bore fruit, being nominated to stage the 2007 Pan-American Games and Paralympic Pan-American Games (Parapan) in August 2002, as well as the Fifth Military World Games in May 2007. Both events followed the Olympic template, requiring that the host supply venues for a variety of sports, a main stadium capable of accommodating Opening and Closing Ceremonies and 'village' accommodation for participants. In October 2007, Brazil received the nomination to stage the 2014 FIFA World Cup – in which Rio would again play a major role. However, it was the winning and staging of the Pan-American and Parapan Games in particular that lent gravitas to Rio's subsequent efforts and supplied facilities for future mega-event bidding. While infrastructural, construction and budgetary problems did arise, the fact that the festival passed off without 'logistical failures or public violence' allowed any future Olympic bid to make capital out of the success of the Pan-American and Parapan Games (Curi *et al.*, 2011: 152). For another application, therefore, real progress could be demonstrated for what previously was regarded as an area of crucial weakness.

That application would be for the 2016 Summer Games. Once again, when the responses of the Applicant Cities to the 11-criteria first-phase questionnaire had been analysed, Rio was in danger of elimination. The IOC's controversial decision to allow Rio to proceed to the candidate stage alongside Chicago, Tokyo and Madrid rather than admit the higher-scoring Doha led the Rio team to redouble efforts to improve the technical quality of the city's candidature before the submission of the Candidature Files on 12 February 2009 and the visit of the ten members of the IOC's Evaluation Commission on 29 April–2 May 2009. The effectiveness of the campaign team's subsequent actions can be discerned by the fact that Rio had moved to the top of the list by the time the Evaluation Commission's report was published on 2 September 2009.

The bid document, with the slogan 'Live your passion', had an agenda for the nation and the city. For the nation, it was about placing Brazil in the global spotlight and reinforcing its status as a 'major and growing economy and unique visitor destination', a place to live, do business and visit (ROCOG, 2009: vol. 1, 19, 21). Interestingly, apart from a change in the order of the wording, this is identical to the fifth legacy promise for the United Kingdom contained in DCMS documentation from 2007, namely to 'demonstrate the UK is a creative, inclusive and welcoming place to live in, visit and for business' (DCMS, 2007: n.p.). For the British, the emphasis was on maximising the business opportunities for UK firms while attracting inward investment and export capacity and bringing tourists to Britain in the aftermath of the Games

Somewhat reminiscent of Barcelona 1992, with which Rio's Olympic plans have been latterly compared, there are four Olympic zones at, respectively, Barra da Tijuca, Copacabana (to the south of the city centre), Deodoro (northwest) and Maracanã (north). The Olympic Park itself will be at Barra, which will host 19 Olympic and 13 Paralympic sports. These will partly be housed in facilities that were introduced for the Pan-American Games, such as the Maria Lenk Aquatic Park and the Velodrome, but there will also be new construction, including the Olympic Village and Training Centre. The clusters will be tied together by improved communications, particularly by developing dedicated express bus lanes and extending the rail and metro networks. These will be designed to have long-term importance in encouraging use of public transport. Unusually, the Opening and Closing Ceremonies will be at the Maracanã stadium and not at the main athletics venue, the João Havelange Stadium. The only events that will go outside the city boundaries are the soccer tournaments, which will also use stadia in Brasília, Belo Horizonte, São Paulo and Salvador. In another development reminiscent of Barcelona, the bid document also included the Porto Maravilha waterfront regeneration project, designed to 'reintegrate' the declining port districts into the city. The cultural agenda was advanced by the prospect of two landmark facilities: the Museu do Amanhã (science museum) and a Museu de Art. Environmental problems would receive attention, such as upgrading the urban forest parks and improving the state of the Jacarepagua Lakes (coastal lagoons). More generally, the bid document looked to provide a positive environment in which to help reduce violent crime, promote social inclusion and integrate the marginal favelas into the built and social fabric of the city.

As with London, the Rio organisers had sensitively interpreted the IOC's known predilections in terms of both the arrangements for the sports events and the broader social, economic and environmental legacy for the city. Their message struck a balance between natural advantages and potential sources of weakness. Notably, for example, the writers delicately addressed lingering doubts about Brazil's ability to deliver the Olympic festivals by reference to recent experience of running large-scale events – the Pan-American Games received no less than 91 mentions in the Candidature File. Above all, it combined this message with the plea for the IOC to trust a young and dynamic nation on a continent that had never staged the Games. Appealing to the unwritten law of continental equity in his speech to the IOC's decision-making meeting in Copenhagen in October 2009, the Brazilian President Lula Da Silva argued: 'I honestly think it is Brazil's turn.... It is South America's bid' (Gardner, 2010). It proved to be a winning hand. In the voting that followed Chicago, the long-term favourite, was eliminated in the first round, with Rio proceeding through to the final round where it defeated Madrid by 66 votes to 32. However interpreted, it was an enormous vote of confidence in a city that, had the IOC adhered to its own conventions, would have been eliminated in the previous year at the short-listing stage.

Conclusion

This chapter has explored the campaigns waged by Beijing, London and Rio de Janeiro in successful pursuit of the Summer Games of 2008, 2012 and 2016. It notes that while the cycle of competition to stage the Olympic Games may continuously roll onwards, with a new Host City emerging from the selection procedures every four years, the new issues that continually arise show that the process is far from unchanging. Yet at its core remains a Host City using the Games to address its unique set of social, economic, infrastructure and planning challenges, often going beyond what is strictly necessary for the staging of the Games in the process. For Beijing, the goal was to promote urban modernisation as part of a process of national modernisation and to use the Olympic Games to communicate that image to the wider world. For London, it was selective urban regeneration in the context of a reinvigorated and multicultural city. For Rio de Janeiro, the agenda had again shifted, with plans for city-wide transformation from housing improvements to crime reduction, social inclusion, regeneration and communications infrastructure combined with an attempt to revive the city's national and international image. For all three cities the aim was to create a legacy that would be the basis from which they could compete for business, investment and tourists while providing regenerated neighbourhoods for their citizens.

These additional agendas would have once seemed inappropriate, but are now, of course, actively encouraged through the applicant and candidature procedures. The IOC has warmed to the concept of the Olympic city as a genre and happily endorses the idea of 'Once an Olympic City, always an Olympic City' (IOC, 2010: 3). There is pride within the Olympic Movement at the record of achievement of the select group that have striven to meet the exacting standards required to stage the Games. For the cities concerned, these are achievements that remain as legacies and form the basis for place promotion and destination marketing in following years. Yet as shown by each of the successful candidates from the Games of 2008–2016, there is a real hunger for proposals that are out of the ordinary and that capture the imagination by offering, for example, to enhance universality, provide a significant positive legacy and, above all, show that the Olympic Games can make a difference. Innovative, exciting but inevitably higher-risk projects, however, need nurturing by learning from good practice, recognising the predilections of the international movement, building support and exercising effective persuasion. In such circumstances it is inevitable that the army of professional fundraisers and specialist consultants who advise cities about their Olympic nomination campaigns will continue to make a comfortable living.

References

Ashworth, G.J. and Voogd, H. (1990) *Selling the City: Marketing Approaches in Public Sector Urban Planning*, London: Belhaven Press.

BOBICO (Beijing 2008 Olympic Bid Committee) (2001) *Beijing Candidature File*, 3 vols. Available: http://en.beijing2008.cn/spirit/beijing2008/candidacy/files (accessed 28 October 2011).

BOCOG (Beijing Organising Committee for the Games of the XXXIX Olympiad) (2010) *Official Report of the 2008 Olympic Games*, 3 vols., Beijing: BOCOG.

Booth, D. (2005) 'Lobbying orgies: Olympic city bids in the post-Los Angeles era', in Young, K. and Wamsley, K.B. (eds) *Global Olympics: Historical and Sociological Studies of the Modern Games*, Oxford: Elsevier, pp. 210–225.

Broudehoux, A.-M. (2004) *The Making and Selling of Post-Mao Beijing*, London: Routledge.

Cidade Olímpica (2011) 'Today, tomorrow and forever: the challenge'. Available: www.cidadeolimpica.com/en/today-tomorrow-and-forever (accessed 28 October 2011).

COHRE (2007) *Fair Play for Housing Rights: Mega-Events, Olympic Games and Housing Rights*, Geneva: Centre on Housing Rights and Evictions.

Curi, M., Knijnik, J. and Mascarenhas, G. (2011) 'The Pan American Games in Rio de Janeiro: consequences of a sport mega-event on a BRIC country', *International Review for the Sociology of Sport*, 46: 140–156.

DCMS (2007) *Our Promise for 2012: How the UK will Benefit from the Olympic and Paralympic Games*, London: DCMS

Del Rio, V. (2009) 'Reclaiming city image and street liveability: Projeto Rio Cidade, Rio de Janeiro', in Del Rio, V. and Siembieda, W. (eds) *Contemporary Urbanism in Brazil beyond Brasília*, Gainesville, FL: University of Florida Press, pp. 224–245.

Evans, G. (2007) 'London 2012', in Gold, J.R. and Gold, M.M. (eds) *Olympic Cities: City Agendas, Planning and the World's Games, 1896–2012*, London: Routledge, pp. 298–317.

Gardner, D. (2010) 'Slap in the face for Obama as his personal plea to back Chicago backfires for the U.S. and the 2016 Olympics goes to Rio', *Mail Online*,. Available: www.dailymail.co.uk/news/worldnews/article-1217595/Rio-Janeiro-awarded-2016-Olympics.html#ixzz0k25O56t6 (accessed 28 October 2011).

Gold, J.R. (2011) 'Rio de Janeiro 2016', in Gold, J.R. and Gold, M.M. (eds) *Olympic Cities: City Agendas, Planning, and the World's Games, 1896–2016* (2nd edn), London: Routledge, pp. 392–402.

Gold, J.R. and Gold, M.M. (2007) 'Access for all: the rise of the Paralympics within the Olympic movement', *Journal of the Royal Society for the Promotion of Health*, 127: 133–141.

Gold, J.R. and Gold, M.M. (2008) 'Olympic cities: regeneration, city rebranding and changing urban agendas', *Geography Compass*, 2: 300–318.

Gold, J.R. and Ward, S.V. (eds) (1994) *Place Promotion: The Use of Publicity and Marketing to Sell Towns and Regions*, Chichester: John Wiley.

IOC (1957) *Information for Cities which Desire to Stage the Olympic Games*, Lausanne: IOC.

IOC (2001) *Report of the IOC Evaluation Commission for the Games of the XXIX Olympiad in 2008*, Lausanne: IOC

IOC (2004) *2012 Candidature Procedure and Questionnaire: Games of the XXX Olympiad in 2012*, Lausanne: IOC.

IOC (2010) *Final Report of the IOC Coordination Commission*, Lausanne: IOC. Available: www.olympic.org/Documents/Reports/EN/Br-Beijing-ENG-web.pdf (accessed 28 October 2011).

Kavaratzis, M. (2004) 'From city marketing to city branding: towards a theoretical framework for developing city brands', *Place Branding*, 1: 58–73.

Li, L.M, Dray-Novey, A.J. and Kong, H. (2007) *Beijing: From Imperial Capital to Olympic City*, Basingstoke: Palgrave Macmillan

London 2012 (2004) 'Introduction', in *Candidate File*, vol. 1. Available: www.london2012.com/documents/candidate-files/introduction.pdf (last accessed 8 December 2011)

Macartney, J. (2008) 'Reporting the Olympic year'. Available: www.chinainstitute.anu.edu.au/morrison/morrison69.pdf (accessed 10 December 2011).

Robb, S. (2008) 'Beijing 2008: a hard act to follow?' Available: http://news.bbc.co.uk/1/hi/uk/7579381.stm (accessed 28 October 2011).

ROCOG (Rio di Janeiro Organising Committee for the Olympic Games) (2009) *Candidature File for Rio de Janeiro to Host the 2016 Olympic and Paralympic Games*, 3 vols., Rio di Janeiro: ROCOG.

Rogers, P. (2010) '2016's costs revealed'. Available: www.nbcchicago.com/news/local/Final-Olympics-2016-Tally-93958864.html (accessed 28 October 2011).

Theodoraki, E. (2007) *Olympic Event Organisation*, Oxford: Butterworth Heinemann.

Tomlinson, A. (2004) 'The Disneyfication of the Olympics: theme parks and freak-shows of the body', in Bale, J. and Christensen, M.K. (eds) *Post-Olympism? Questioning Sport in the Twenty-first Century*, Oxford: Berg, pp. 147–163

Ward, S.V. (2011) 'Promoting the Olympic city', in Gold, J.R. and Gold, M.M. (eds) *Olympic Cities: City Agendas, Planning, and the World's Games, 1896–2016* (2nd edn), London: Routledge, pp. 148–166.

WUOC (2008) *The Lausanne Summit 2008: Post-Event Report*, Lausanne: World Union of Olympic Cities.

PART 6

Conclusions

22

MAKING THE 2012 LONDON GAMES

Taking stock and looking forward to celebrating the Games

Vassil Girginov

The first volume of the *Handbook of the London 2012 Olympic and Paralympic Games* has endeavoured to capture the key players and processes involved in making the 2012 London Olympic and Paralympic Games from inception to its staging. To that end, 21 contributions have analysed various aspects of London 2012 under three broad headings, including bidding, delivering and engaging with the Games. This concluding chapter provides a summary of the main lessons learned so far and outlines the issues to be addressed in the second volume of the collection.

The London Games has been won and organised in testing political, economic and social times. For the first time in history UK debt soared through the trillion barrier, reaching £1,003.9 billion or 64.2 per cent of GDP, coupled with an unemployment rate of 8.3 per cent, the highest for 17 years (the introductory chapter written only a few weeks ago reported a figure of £966.8 billion, or 62.6 per cent of GDP). As a result, the UK government has implemented a programme of drastic budgetary cuts, which have been impacting adversely on the ability of the main sport and leisure providers – local authorities and sport organisations – to deliver on the main promise of the Games to leave a lasting sporting legacy. Many groups and individuals are set to miss out on the unique Olympic opportunity as well. According to many commentators, including British Prime Minister David Cameron, we have been living through a deep material and moral crisis of capitalism. Against this background, the government has tried to frame the Games as a counterpoint to the 'gloom and doom' of daily life, but it would be naive to assume that even the world's greatest sporting festival could rectify the deeply rooted social divisions and economic inequalities of British society.

The idea of an Olympic Games in London has appealed equally strongly to the three main political ideologies in the UK. When it was first articulated in 1995, the bid had the support of the then Conservative government, led by John Major, with its belief in minimal state and more market. The bid was won in 2005 by the Labour government of Tony Blair, which subscribed to the philosophy of the 'third way' or social development between the state and the market. A strong commitment was made to tackling social inequalities and to expanding democratic governance. The Games will be delivered by the Conservative–Liberal Democrat coalition government, led by David Cameron, with its visions for 'big society' and moral capitalism. Hoberman (1984, p. 17) has this to say about the link between political ideology and the Olympic Games:

'German Nazis, Italian Fascists, Soviet and Cuban Communists, Chinese Maoists, western capitalist democrats, Latin American juntas – all have played this game and believed in it'.

It is this broad political appeal of the Olympic Games that gives it the power to affect social change, and that simultaneously makes it vulnerable to criticism. As an educational ideology, Olympism seeks to address a range of social, political and cultural needs, such as equality, education, respect and excellence. It is a reformist ideology (i.e. favouring gradual change), advocating change by advancing a system for restructuring society through sport and education. In particular, Olympism incites young people around the world to join the Olympic Movement in order to realise this ideology. The British government has played its part in promoting Olympic ideology, first by making a commitment that 'we will transform the lives of young people through sport' (DCMS, 2008: 3), and second, by inviting them to embrace the Olympic values and to participate in the Games. The former Olympic Minister Tessa Jowell stated in the foreword of the government action plan for the implementation of the five promises made for the Games: 'This plan is an invitation to get involved and a challenge to everyone to show just how much can be achieved through the Games' (DCMS, 2008, p. 2). Thus, similar to political ideology, which Macridis (1989, p. 3) observed 'involves action and collective effort', Olympic ideology has also been used to bring visions, actions and collective efforts together.

Therefore, an examination of the bidding, delivery and engagement with the London Games represents, amongst other things, a practical test of the educational and intercultural meanings of Olympism. It should be remembered that the ideas of Olympism, as politically appealing they may seem, have hardly ever been comprehensively tried out in any country, and definite claims about the role of Olympism in modern society have inevitably been limited to suppositions. London is striving to achieve exactly that – to put the aspirations of Olympism in Britain to the test. The Games have also provided a rare opportunity for collective reflection about the kind of society we live in and our sense of direction; and in the case of London the two previous occasions for hosting the Olympic Games in 1908 and 1948 allow for an examination of the changing relationship between the Games and society.

The London Olympic bid has been in the making for some 20 years, which is a long period for any project. During that time, significant changes have taken place, both in the domestic and international environments within which the Games are planned and delivered. There has also been a long and controversial learning curve, which has seen changing political visions about the role of potential Games and the involvement of different institutional and individual actors. For example, the word 'legacy', which largely defines what the London Games stand for, does not appear in any of the earlier unsuccessful bids (Girginov and Hills, 2008). Changes in visions and personnel make long-term strategies difficult and uncertain. This is why the London bid is to be best seen as an evolving and socially constructed process.

What has made the London bid both appealing and successful has been a combination of a strong national and city-level political support and strategy for the regeneration of East London, and a clear vision about how the Games were to enhance the Olympic ideals. It was clear to Games proponents that no city regeneration agenda alone, no matter how ambitions and important, was going to win over the International Olympic Committee's (IOC) vote. It had to be accompanied by an equally strong commitment for sports development and contribution to the Olympic Movement. London was able to capitalise on the IOC's growing concerns about the disengagement of the younger audience with the Games. This was reflected in the core messages of the bid designed to engage young people with the Games, nationally and internationally. To that end, a group of young people from East London were flown in to Singapore to help present the bid to the IOC session.

Another important lesson from the bid process concerns the need for meticulous preparation and a skilful presentation. Knowledge and appreciation of Olympic heritage have also been indispensible parts of the Olympic bid. In contrast to Beijing 2008, which involved more abstract notions of a 'Green, High-Tech and Humanistic Olympics', London has established a very direct and tangible focus on youth, with which anybody can easily get involved. The Games imagery has reinforced the words. The official emblem of the Games – 'Join in London' – is a dynamic image designed to inspire youth and reflect the multicultural nature of British society. LOCOG's Chairman Seb Coe echoes this agenda: 'the vision of the London 2012 Olympics is to stage inspirational Games that capture the imagination of young people around the world and leave a lasting legacy'. To illustrate this vision, the jagged 2012 logo, according to its designers Wolff Olins, projects ahead into the future: 'The audience you're addressing are kids between the ages of, say, eight and 16, and in a few years' time they're going to be 12 to 20. Those kids look at the web all the time, and what they look at is things that move' (Girginov, 2008, p. 903).

Getting the inspirational message of the Games across has not been that straightforward though. Join in London's design cost £400,000 and was met with some public disapproval, triggering early-day motions from MP Philip Davies and an online petition with nearly 50,000 signatures to force LOCOG to remove the logo,[1] and there was hasty withdrawal of a promotional video that caused seizures among epilepsy sufferers. The National Olympic Committee of Iran went even further and sent a letter to the International Olympic Committee (IOC) objecting to the 2012 London Olympics logo for resembling the word 'Zion' and promoting the Jewish state. 'Selling' the bid and the Games to society has always been a major task for London organisers (see chapter 2).

The delivery of the Games required putting in place an unprecedented public contract. This was a major first for London, despite the fact that the original 2008 80-page action plan document drawn up by the Labour government (DCMS, 2008) was replaced in 2010 by a much slimmer and less glamorous 14-page plan by the coalition (DCMS, 2010). The UK government pledged to use the Games to transform British society in exchange for trust and a mandate for action. Thus, together with the Games imagery, London has largely served to reinforce in the public consciousness what Hobsbawm (1992) called 'invented traditions' in relation to the Olympic Games and other cultural manifestations. Both the UK government and LOCOG have assumed trusteeship in developing aspects of society in return for massive public and private investments and the authority to act on the public's behalf. The true public costs of the Games will probably never be established as it goes well beyond the much publicised £9.3 billion funding package. The support offered by various governmental departments as well as governing bodies of sport, in terms of staff time, logistical arrangements and opportunity cost, has been both indispensable and hard to quantify. For example, for some five years the Higher Education Council of England has fully funded Podium, a new organisation created in 2007 to act as a conduit between the tertiary and higher education sector and the Games. The big question remaining is to what extent the invented traditions of London 2012 have helped to enhance the fundamental values of Olympism.

The Games has created a new policy space for interaction between the state, civil society and the market and has helped to expand governability (the capacity for effective guidance). Games delivery was also contingent on complex governance arrangements designed to ensure consensus amongst stakeholders about the main objectives of the Olympic Games and to steer collective actions towards achieving them. Although LOCOG has established new sustainability standards for mega event management (BS 8901, Sustainability Management Systems for Events), the limitations of governance have been exposed, in particular in relation to human capacity to predict the future. This has been a major issue as it underpins the notion of sustainability on which the delivery of the Games has been premised.

Public participation is a crucial element of governance and the London organisers have gone to unprecedented lengths to ensure as wide an engagement as possible. Six chapters in this volume specifically examine the public engagement with the Games – from the bid consultation process through the planning and implementation of legacies. Analyses have revealed a range of engagement mechanisms used to mobilise different segments of society. For example, schools' involvement has been promoted mainly through an exchange mechanism that invited schools to join 'Get Set', the educational programme of London 2012, in return for Games tickets. Another main instrument ensuring the engagement of non-government bodies in particular has been through framework regulations. This instrument is based on binding laws but allows actors some leeway in implementing various agreements (Girginov, 2011). The relationships between the main actors responsible for the Games – the government, city of London, LOCOG, ODA and the British Olympic Association – have also been fixed through a framework regulatory mechanism. Coercive instruments were also applied, but mainly in the form of bespoke Olympic legislation to ensure that public and commercial engagement is within certain legal boundaries and that there is no illegal appropriation of Olympic properties (see chapter 6). However, the combination of different mechanisms of engagement has created tensions and has impacted variously on the lives of various communities.

While engagement with the Games has taken a multitude of forms at individual, group and corporate levels, these have yielded two main returns. For society, this related to the 'inspiration' to do something better, whereas Olympic commercial partners were given 'exclusive rights' to associate their products with the five Olympic rings, and to profit from that. Individuals, communities and organisations have benefited from the Games through enhanced personal skills, self-confidence, facilities, equipment and infrastructure. A further layer of engagement with very different returns concerns the 205 participating countries. For many of those countries a success in London will provide a much-needed boost for national identities and sport systems. London's cultural diversity and the high level of deprivation in the five host Olympic boroughs have presented a major challenge to engagement. Planned and forced administrative and structural changes have made public involvement more uncertain.

This volume has provided some answers to the main conceptual and practical question posed in the opening chapter: 'what has been done in the name of the Games, for whom at what cost and to what effect?' The full answer to this question will perhaps not transpire even years after the second volume has been completed. However, two main lessons have become clearly apparent. The first concerns the framing of the Games. The UK government has used the London Games to stimulate public energy and creativity in various domains, thus cutting across the interests of an array of stakeholders and raising their expectations in the process. But steering expectations and consensus in challenging social and economic environments can easily produce disillusionment.

The second lesson concerns a wider point about the contribution of London 2012 to the future of the Olympic Movement. The approach to the Games by the British government and LOCOG will provide the International Olympic Committee (IOC) with good reasons for optimism, partly because of the explicit link that was made between the Games and social development, the construction of a more robust evaluation programme to demonstrate those links, and sound management practices. But it is precisely at this juncture that the contentions arise. At the heart of Olympic enterprise is an expressed concern with education and intercultural understanding aimed to educate the younger generation. London's educational programme, as good as it is, has been entrusted to LOCOG who, with all the good will in the world and the work of an enthusiastic and dedicated team, cannot achieve what other host countries have been able to do. Both Greece in 2004 and China in 2008 put in place structures, resources and an army of specifically trained physical education teachers to carry on the Olympic message when the OCOGs were dismantled at the end of the Games. The recognition of cultural diversity within LOCOG as an organisation has not been met in the other Olympic initiatives. Setting, enhancing and maintaining a performance culture in elite sport Britain, particularly in the run-up and during the Games, has been designed to 'insulate athletes from the rest of the world' so they can concentrate on their performances (see chapter 9). This runs counter to the role of Olympic competition as an ambassador of international understanding.

Two points deserve particular attention here. First, if at the heart of the Olympic message is the idea of a new moral education that is to be achieved by the means of sport participation, the agencies involved have yet to show that this has been happening. As demonstrated, young people overwhelmingly consider playing sport as a critical condition for getting involved with the Games. Given the low levels of physical activity amongst 16–24-year-olds in particular, this automatically precludes many from associating themselves with London 2012. Thus, there is a danger that the absence of politically endorsed success indicators for legacy outcomes of the Games may result in concentrating efforts on demonstrating that legacies have been achieved rather than actually delivered. The institutionalisation of the Olympic legacy scene and the emergence of a myriad of legacy enforcers serve to substantiate such concerns.

Second, the IOC acceptance of the concept of the Olympic city as a genre and the endorsement of the idea, 'once an Olympic city, always an Olympic city' (IOC, 2010, 3; see also chapter 20) further reinforces the need for bridging the gap between elitism, as a tool promoted by the Games, and wider social and sport development. London 2012 has further reinforced the tensions between Olympism as an ideology for social change and sport as its main tool for achieving this aim. While the UK public has been generally supportive of the Games as a sporting spectacle, it has been equally concerned about the accompanying environmental, economic and social costs, thus challenging the main premise of the Olympics. So far, London has been able to make a convincing case neither about the positive impact of Olympic athletes as role models to the young nor about the trickle-down effect of investment in elite-level facilities and support services, and it is doubtful whether the government is interested in gathering such evidence. There is still a great deal of work to be done to address this issue.

It is expected that, as result of various Games evaluations, a great deal of rational scientific knowledge will be produced. This is because the prevailing current intellectual climate in the UK favours measurable targets and performance. However, it is not entirely clear how the inspirational effect of London 2012 is going to be captured and if it will be afforded the same status as the more tangible deliverables such as participation numbers, jobs created and national and global viewing figures. This is an issue of ontology, and one that concerns the tensions between what MacAloon has called the Olympic sport industry (OSI) and the Olympic Movement. The OSI, according to MacAloon,

> can be thought of as Olympic sport without Olympism, or stated more precisely, the OSI, as an ideal type, reverses the means/ends relationship between sport and the intercultural, diplomatic and educational meanings characteristic of the Olympic Movement. For the OSI, Olympic symbols, values, social projects and histories are mere instrumentalities available for the expansion of Olympic-style competitions, for the 'growth of the brand' as many of its paid professionals like to put it.
>
> *(MacAloon, 2011, p. 293)*

The second volume of the *Handbook of the London 2012 Olympic and Paralympic Games* will concentrate on the celebration of the Games by examining what has actually happened during the Olympic and Parlympic festival from a range of perspectives, and what this means for the Olympic Movement. Topics to be addressed include: how Britain has welcomed the world; the experiences of various stakeholders, from athletes to shoppers and the local communities of East London; the use of the Olympic platform for the communication of messages; the rise and fall of Olympic stars; and the legacies of the Games. In summary, the second volume will scrutinise LOCOG's Chair, Seb Coe, and the six 'Ss' of success: (1) Sport must be vibrant and compelling, to inspire young people; (2) Streets must be festive and buzzing, with a party atmosphere; (3) Screens: large screens at Live Sites must be places where people can celebrate together; (4) Stadia must be full of excited and passionate fans; (5) Service must be helpful with polite, friendly and well-informed volunteers; (6) Sustainability must produce long-lasting social, economic, environmental and sporting benefits (LOCOG, 2011, p. 8). The second volume will also examine the wider issue concerning the sustainability of the current Olympic Games model and how the London experience is likely to influence the future organisation of the world's greatest sporting festival and what it stands for.

Between 27 July and 12 August and 29 August and 9 September, spectators, staff, sport enthusiasts and students of Olympism worldwide will engage with the experience of the 2012 London Olympic and Paralympic Games respectively. Volume two of this collection will report on their experiences.

Note

1 To see the petition, visit www.gopetition.co.uk/petitions/change-the-london-2012-logo.html.

References

DCMS. (2010). *Plans for the legacy from the 2012 Olympic and Paralympic Games*. London: DCMS.

DCMS. (2008). *Before, during and after: Making the most of the London 2012 Games*. London: DCMS.

Girginov, V. (2011). Governance of London 2012 Olympic Sport Legacy, *International Review for the Sociology of Sport*, 1–16.

Girginov, V. (2008). Creative Tensions: 'Join in London' meets 'Dancing Beijing – the cultural power of the Olympics, *The International Journal of the History of Sport*, 25 (7), 893–914.

Girginov, V. and Hills, L. (2008). A Sustainable Sports Legacy: Creating a Link between the London Olympics and Sports Participation, *The International Journal of the History of Sport*, 25 (14), 2091–2117.

Hoberman, J. (1984). *Sport and political ideology*. Austin: The University of Texas Press.

Hobsbawm, E. (1992). Mass-Producing Traditions: Europe, 1870–1914, in E. Hobsbawm and J. Ranger (eds)., *The Invention of Tradition*. Cambridge: Canto/Cambridge University Press.

IOC. (2010). *Final Report of the IOC Coordination Commission*. Lausanne: International Olympic Committee. Online: www.olympic.org/Documents/Reports/EN/Br-Beijing-ENG-web.pdf (accessed 28 October 2011).

LOCOG. (2011). *One Year to Go. Annual Report 2010–2011*. London: LOCOG.

MacAloon, J. (2011). Scandal and Governance: Inside and Outside the IOC 2000 Commission, *Sport in Society*, (14) 3, 292–30.

Macridis, R. (1989). *Contemporary political ideologies: Movements and regimes*, fourth edn. London: Scott, Foresman and Company.

INDEX